ENGLISH TRANSLATIONS OF
ALAIN CHARTIER'S

Le Traité de l'Esperance

AND

Le Quadrilogue Invectif

VOLUME II. INTRODUCTION
NOTES AND GLOSSARY

EARLY ENGLISH TEXT SOCIETY
No. 281
1980

FIFTEENTH-CENTURY ENGLISH TRANSLATIONS OF ALAIN CHARTIER'S

Le Traité de l'Esperance

AND

Le Quadrilogue Invectif

EDITED BY

MARGARET S. BLAYNEY

Published for

THE EARLY ENGLISH TEXT SOCIETY

by the

OXFORD UNIVERSITY PRESS

1980

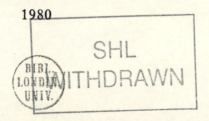

Oxford University Press, Walton Street, Oxford OX2 6DP

OXFORD LONDON GLASGOW
NEW YORK TORONTO MELBOURNE WELLINGTON
KUALA LUMPUR SINGAPORE HONG KONG TOKYO
DELHI BOMBAY CALCUTTA MADRAS KARACHI
NAIROBI DAR ES SALAAM CAPE TOWN

© *Early English Text Society, 1980*

British Library Cataloguing in Publication Data
Chartier, Alain
    Fifteenth-Century English translations
    of Alain Chartier's 'Le traité de l'esperance'
    and 'Le quadrilogue invectif'
    Vol. II: Introduction, notes and glossary –
    (Early English Text Society. Publications,
    no. 281)
    I. Title   II. Blayney, Margaret Statler
    III. Chartier, Alain. Le traité de l'esperance
    IV. Chartier, Alain. Le quadrilogue invectif
    V. Series
    848'.2'08 PQ1557.E5 78–40092
ISBN 0–19–722283–8

*Printed in Great Britain
at the University Press, Oxford
by Eric Buckley
Printer to the University*

CONTENTS

ERRATA IN VOLUME I

p. xv. l. 17   *For* Thirty Years' War *read* Wars of the Roses
p. 171 n.   *For* 27 *read* 26
p. 194 n. 26 *Delete 'see n.'*

INTRODUCTION

I. ALAIN CHARTIER AND ENGLISH INTEREST IN HIS WORKS

ALAIN CHARTIER (*c.* 1385–1433)[1] wrote his French and Latin poetry and prose between 1414 and 1429, during the Hundred Years War, when the histories of England and France were inextricably bound together. Chartier was a prominent participant in the struggles which overwhelmed his country, not as a soldier, but as secretary to the Dauphin, later Charles VII, as ambassador and orator for France, and as propagandist and political writer in support of the Dauphin against opposing factions in France and against the English invaders. It is significant that France says to the author in *Le Quadrilogue Invectif,* 'Et puis que Dieu ne t'a donné force de corps ne usaige d'armes, sers a la chose publique de ce que tu pués, car autant exaulça la gloire des Rommains et renforça leurs couraiges a vertu la plume et la langue des orateurs comme les glaives des combatans.'[2]

The story of France's deplorable condition during the first third of the fifteenth century, because of both division within and English attack from without, has been often told. This was the period of the Burgundian occupation of Paris and the great victories of Henry V. Chartier used his pen and voice to rally support for the weak Dauphin, to urge reunion between the warring French factions, to point out the shortcomings of the three estates in France, and to offer spiritual consolation to the suffering people. His constant concern with his country's social and political problems is revealed by his many works forming a background for this period in French history. Among these are *Le Quadrilogue Invectif* (1422), *Dialogus familiaris amici et sodalis super deploratione gallicae calamitatis* (*c.* 1425), *De vita curiali,* or *Le Curial,* and *Le Traité de l'Esperance, ou Consolation des Trois Vertus* (1428).

But Chartier was not only a political propagandist; he was also a man of the Dauphin's court, a social group which, led by the

---

[1] For the best accounts of Chartier's life and works, see E. J. Hoffman, *Alain Chartier, His Work and Reputation* (New York, 1942), and P. Champion, *Histoire poétique du xve siècle* (Paris, 1923).   [2] Ed. E. Droz (Paris, 1950), p. 65.

B

irresponsible Charles, was, alternately and paradoxically, serious, melancholy, hard-pressed by the state of war in France and by exile from Paris, and, on the other hand, extravagant, profligate, light-hearted in revels. Many of Chartier's poetical works were written especially for the court audience. Two of his poems, although not propagandistic in reflecting political events in France of the time, nevertheless grew partly out of the war: both of these poems, however, treat their subjects in accordance with patterns that had long been familiar to court audiences. The longest poem by Chartier, *Le Livre des Quatre Dames* (1415), has the form of the traditional *débat amoureux*, but lacks the usual erotic interest of the form and instead treats the reaction of four ladies to the fates of their lovers at Agincourt. The other poem is *Le Bréviaire des Nobles*, thirteen *ballades* presenting the knightly code of honour and virtue. Chartier's other poetical works, such as *La Belle Dame sans Mercy* (1424), *Le Débat des Deux Fortunés d'Amours* (1425), and a considerable body of *rondeaux* and *ballades*, are concerned not with such realities of French life of the period, but with the always popular court subject—love.

It is not surprising to find that the works of Chartier, who was acclaimed as the greatest writer of his day by his contemporaries and honoured with the title 'father of French eloquence' by the rhetoricians, aroused interest in England and Scotland. Seven fifteenth-century translations of various works by Chartier are now known, while one sixteenth-century Scottish work is a partial translation of two of his French prose works. Sir Richard Ros's translation of *La Belle Dame sans Mercy*, made toward the middle of the fifteenth century and extant today in six manuscripts, is probably the best known of the translations because until the time of Tyrwhitt's edition in 1775 it was attributed to Chaucer.[1] A prose work by A. Cadiou, which was printed in 1508 by the early Edinburgh printers W. Chepman and A. Myllar and which also appears in Asloan's Manuscript, has recently been recognized as a translation of Chartier's *Bréviaire des Nobles*.[2]

[1] Ros's translation has been edited in F. J. Furnivall's *Political, Religious, and Love Poems*, EETS, o.s. 15 (1866), p. 52; and in W. W. Skeat's *Chaucerian and Other Pieces* (Oxford, 1897), p. 299.

[2] Only the last three leaves of the printed volume have been preserved in the National Library of Scotland. A facsimile was first published by D. Laing in *The Knightly Tale of Golagrus and Gawane, and other Ancient Poems* in 1827. The work in this edition is perfected from the Asloan MS. Another facsimile was

The other translations of Chartier are of the political and propagandist prose works. Five of these were made in the second half of the fifteenth century, while the other was written nearly a century later in 1549. Caxton's translation of *Le Curial*, printed in 1484, is well known.[1] In 1549 this translation was reprinted from Caxton's edition with the claim that it had been 'newly augmented, amplified, & inrytched' by Francis Segar.[2] There is little augmentation, amplification, or enrichment evident in the two leaves preserved in the only extant copy in the Bodleian Library. Besides Caxton's translation of *Le Curial*, translations of *Le Quadrilogue Invectif*, *Le Traité de l'Esperance*, and *Dialogus familiaris amici et sodalis super deploratione gallicae calamitatis* by one author and a translation of *Le Quadrilogue* by a different writer also were made in the second half of the fifteenth century. Then in 1549 both *Le Quadrilogue* and *L'Esperance* were partly translated and adapted for propagandistic purposes by a Scottish writer in *The Complaynt of Scotlande*.[3]

Thus, it is against this background of English and Scottish interest in the works of Alain Chartier for over a century after his death that we must view the two translations of *Le Quadrilogue Invectif* and the translation of *Le Traité de l'Esperance* mentioned above and edited here.[4]

published by W. Beattie, *The Chepman and Myllar Prints* (Edinburgh Bibl. Soc., 1950). The Asloan version, probably copied from the printed 1508 text, was edited by Sir W. Craigie in *The Asloan Manuscript*, i, STS, N.S. 14 (1923), pp. 171–84.

[1] This translation, along with a translation by Caxton of one of the *ballades* attributed to Chartier, was edited by F. J. Furnivall, EETS, E.S. 54 (1888).

[2] A Brefe de-/claration of the great and / innumerable myseries & / wretchednesses vsed in courtes ry-/all, made by a lettre, whych may-/ster Alayn Charatre wrote to / hys brother, which desyred / to come dwel in the court, / for to aduyse, & counsell / hym not to enter into / it, lest he after re-/pent, newly aug-/mented, ampli-/fied, & inryt/ched, By / Francis Segar. / 1549 (Bodleian Library, Douce fragments f. 46).

[3] Ed. J. A. H. Murray, EETS, E.S. 17, 18 (1872, 1873). See also W. A. Neilson, 'The Original of *The Complaynt of Scotlande*', *JEGP*, i (1897), 411–30; and M. S. and G. H. Blayney, 'Alain Chartier and *The Complaynt of Scotlande*', *RES*, N.S. ix (1958), 8–17. Other sources of *The Complaynt* are discussed by J.M. Smith, *The French Background of Middle Scots Literature* (Edinburgh, 1934).

[4] The present editor is now engaged in editing the translation of *Dialogus familiaris amici et sodalis super deploratione gallicae calamitatis*.

II. THE R TRANSLATIONS: *THE TREATISE OF HOPE* AND *THE QUADRILOGUE INVECTIVE*

A. *The Manuscripts*

1. Oxford, Bodleian Library: Rawlinson MS. A. 338, the Copy Text (R)

a. *Description*

Vellum, 112 numbered leaves plus flyleaves at beginning and end, the end one numbered 113, 13¾ × 11 in. (350 × 280 mm.), 2 columns usually with 30 lines each, lined in red and brown[1]

Collation: 1–14⁸

Contents: *The Quadrilogue Invective*, without title, ff. 1–33ᵛ (to 8 lines from bottom of col. 1)
The Treatise of Hope, without title, ff. 33ᵛ–111

The manuscript is copied in a large late fifteenth-century hand. The script of the first nine folios is unsettled, and there may be two scribes at work.[2] Beginning with f. 9ᵛ, however, the script is regular, and the rest of R is certainly the work of one copyist, who identifies himself on ff. 111–111ᵛ in Latin verses:

> Qui scripsit monumen sit benedictus Amen.
> Nomen scriptoris dei gracia plenus amoris,
> Careat meroris deus det sibi omnibus horis.
> A tetras grece Tetralogus sit tibi dictus;
> Est tetras quatuor grece, logos est quoque sermo.
> A quibus dictis opus hoc trahit sibi nomen,
> Quod patet in capite horum versuum tibi certe.

Here the scribe not only gives the explanation of the name of Chartier's work, *Tetralogus*, or 'Quadrilogus', but also calls himself *plenus amoris*. His first name may have been John, latinized as *dei gracia*.

The scribe of R has usually indicated the breaking of a word at the end of a line by two oblique lines lighter than the text. He has also ticked *is*, although not always accurately. His punctuation and capitalization are erratic, often misleading.

[1] Sometimes, because of the end of a section, a line or two at the bottom of a column are not filled, and at times illuminated capitals beginning sections cause a column to have fewer than 30 lines.
[2] I am indebted to Mr. Neil Ker for his opinion in this matter.

At the bottoms of the pages he has added more catchwords than usual for manuscripts of this period.[1] These catchwords present an interesting bibliographical problem which remains unsolved. At the bottom of f. 9^v, the first leaf of the second gathering, the usual scribe, in place of the normal catchword or words, has written b1̈ (b1^v), the correct signature for the page. Again at the bottom of f. 10^v, however, he has written c1̈ (c1^v), obviously not the correct signature. The interesting thing is that, immediately after the latter signature, ff. 11–12 are out of place in the text and should follow f. 14^v. Folio 13 follows f. 10^v in the proper continuation of the text of *The Quadrilogue*. This error in the order of folios has occurred during folding. Was the signature c1^v an attempt of the scribe to indicate a following error in order? If so, why has he put c1^v on b2^v? Also, it should be noted that the colour of ink and the general hand indicate that the signature was probably written when the text was, and any error in folding and binding would have occurred after the page was written. Is there any possibility that the scribe was copying from a printed book and that this signature, completely wrong in terms of R, was a signature that crept into R from the printed source?[2]

R is not elaborately illuminated, although there are usually illuminated capitals at the beginnings of sections. On f. 1 the margins are decorated with leaf and flower designs, and the initial capital is illuminated with the arms of the Heydon family (quarterly, argent and gules, a cross engrailed counterchanged). The scribe has added decoration of his own in the form of amusing men's and dogs' faces as extensions of certain letters, especially *A*s (see Frontispiece, Vol. I). The men's faces sometimes are caricatures with features like long, multiple-notched noses, large ears, bulging eyes, or thick lips; and at times they seem to have been fitted to the context: for example, when the work speaks of *thes good fadirs* on f. 34, the head of a long-bearded, sage old man appears in the margin. The dogs are sometimes equally interesting and amusing: one suspects the scribe of putting some of his dogs in monks' hoods; and sometimes, as on ff. 27 and 103, a dog has a bone

---

[1] Dr. R. W. Hunt confirmed this judgement.
[2] There is no evidence of a printed text of this work, but copying a manuscript from a printed text was certainly done in the fifteenth century. Dr. Curt Bühler has shown, for example, that Earl Rivers's *Dictes and Sayings of the Philosophers* in the Newberry MS. was probably copied from the Caxton printed text. See *Anglia*, lxxiv (1957), 281 ff.

in its mouth, while on f. 68 it carries either a leaf or a bit of lace.

R is generally in good condition, with, however, occasional rubbings, sometimes caused by erasures, and, especially towards the end, frequent blurrings, probably caused by wet ink. Despite these, R is always legible.

In addition to the corrections in the text and the insertions which relate directly to the text, there are scribbles and notes in R, both in the margins and on the fly- and binder's leaves, some of them important in R's history, some of them undecipherable or historically and textually probably unimportant. In the top right margin of f. 16 is the word *Wigna*, and on f. 111 in the top margin is *Bindon*,[1] probably written by the same hand that wrote what looks like *Amy* in the right margin. The most extensive scribbling in R occurs at the top of ff. 111ᵛ–112. Here two couplets of verse in a hand of the late fifteenth or early sixteenth century appear:

> He that to women hys credens gyffe
> Ordeynith snares hymselfe to myscheffe.
> Better yt is for loue good seruise to do
> Than thankeles to be compelled therto.

The first of these evidently proverbial sayings is essentially the same as no. W 505 in B. J. Whiting's *Proverbs, Sentences, and Proverbial Phrases* (Cambridge, Mass., 1968). The second does not seem to appear there.

b. *Owners*

The other instances of writings in R unrelated to the text must be discussed in relation to the owners of the manuscript. First, a note of price with *Sir John for ye great and intollerable wrong, which you have basely and vngentlemanly*[?] on the front binder's leaf should be mentioned. The hand is probably of the seventeenth century, in any case much too late to be relevant to the attribution of the work to Sir John Fortescue. Secondly, certain marginal scribblings support the conclusion, originally suggested by the Heydon arms used as the illumination of the first capital, that R was copied for the Heydon family, probably in the last quarter of the fifteenth century. On f. 41, *elysabe* is scribbled; on f. 42, *elysabe* and three *e*s; on f. 47, *elysabeth* with what looks like the beginning of *Heydon*

---

[1] Neil Ker conjectures that this may be *Heydon* again. See below.

crossed out; on f. 111, *Amy*; on f. 102ᵛ, *Anne Heydon*; on f. 112, *Anne* six times and *Anne Heydon* again, almost worn away; and at the bottom of f. 111ᵛ, the initials *AH*. The names indicate that R was probably made for Sir Henry Heydon and his family, who had their seat in Norfolk, the county with which much of the history of R is associated. Sir Henry, who died in 1503, was the son of John Heydon of Baconsthorpe, a notorious lawyer of the period of Henry VI and Edward IV. Henry, steward of Cecilia, widow of Richard Duke of York and mother of Edward IV, married Elizabeth or Anne, daughter of Sir Geoffrey Boleyn.¹ By her he had five daughters—Anne, Elizabeth, Amy, Dorothy and Bridget. Hence, it is probably the names of Henry Heydon's daughters that appear in the margins of R.²

Besides the Heydons, the names of several other owners have come down to us in R. The first of these is Robert Dudley, Earl of Leicester (1532?–88). His badge of the bear and ragged staff and his motto *Droit et loyal* appear on the front and back bindings of R,³ and on the end flyleaf is his shield with a lion rampant, and his name *Robertus* printed in large letters with a very small *Dudley* added beneath. The second later owner of whom there is evidence in R is Henry Spelman (1564?–1641), the famous antiquary and historian. In the bottom margin of f. 1 his name is written.

This list of owners is interesting and significant. It will be shown that the connection of R with the Heydons is important because of their relationship with the Fortescue family, since Sir John Fortescue may be the author of the translations in R.⁴ The Heydon ownership is important also as an additional instance of the interest in literary activity in East Anglia during the fifteenth century, especially among the landed gentry.⁵ This group of patrons (Sir

---

¹ Sources differ about the name of Henry Heydon's wife: R. Clutterbuck, *History and Antiquities . . . of Hertford* (London, 1827), iii. 94, lists her as Elizabeth in the Boleyn pedigree, but says that Harleian MS. 6161 calls her Anne. F. Blomefield, *Topographical History of . . . Norfolk* (London, 1807), vi. 505, gives Elizabeth, but in parentheses adds 'some say Ann'. E. Hasted, *History . . . of Kent* (Canterbury, 1778), i. 108, calls her Anne, but D. Gurney, *Record of the House of Gournay* (London, 1848), pp. 411–12, gives Elizabeth.

² Neil Ker confirmed this judgement, as well as the date of R.

³ This binding is not mentioned by W. Moss, *Bindings from the Library of Robert Dudley, Earl of Leicester* (Sonning-on-Thames, 1934). The arms which appear on R are like those in plate 13, no. 51, in Moss, but the binding is otherwise plain.   ⁴ See below, pp. 26 ff.

⁵ See S. Moore, 'Patrons of Letters in Norfolk and Suffolk, c. 1450', *PMLA*, xxvii (1912), 188–207, and xxviii (1913), 79–105.

John Fastolf, Sir John Paston, and others) was noticeably interested in translations, a fact witnessed by those done for Fastolf by
Stephen Scrope and William Worcester. Perhaps significantly,
William Worcester copied French passages from both *Le Quadrilogue Invectif* and *Le Traité de l'Esperance* in his notebooks in
November and December 1453.[1] He mainly copied historical
examples used in the French works to illustrate Chartier's general
commentary. In Royal MS. 13 C. 1, ff. 136–8ᵛ in the British Library,
the extracts are from *Le Quadrilogue*, and on ff. 138ᵛ–41 from
L'Esperance.[2] Worcester's extracts show clearly then that there
was interest in Chartier among the Norfolk translators and that
Worcester had access to a French manuscript of Chartier's works at
the time when the translations edited here were made. It is interesting also that Sir John Fortescue and Worcester were well
acquainted. Fastolf Paper 42, m. 4, notes that Fastolf sent a bribe
to Fortescue through Worcester.[3]

The Earl of Leicester's ownership likewise is interesting. He
was active in Norfolk local affairs early in his career, just following
his marriage in 1550,[4] and it may have been at this time that he
acquired R. If so, the manuscript was probably in the hands of the
Earl during the period when Edmund Spenser was in his service,
and was thus no doubt part of the library used by the poet. In
fact, there is evidence that Spenser was acquainted with the
translation of *Le Traité de l'Esperance*.[5]

The connection of the third known owner, Henry Spelman, with
the Heydons is also suggestive: a direct ancestor of the famous
seventeenth-century Henry was a certain Henry Spilman, tutor
of Henry Heydon, and later Recorder of Norwich.[6] Later the
families were connected when Dorothy, Henry Spelman's aunt,
married Thomas Heydon of Baconsthorpe, a direct descendant of

[1] K. B. McFarlane, 'William Worcester: A Preliminary Survey', *Studies Presented to Sir Hilary Jenkinson*, ed. J. Conway Davies (Oxford, 1957), p. 212, noted
that Worcester made extracts from *Le Quadrilogue*, but did not mention that
some of the passages are from *Le Traité de l'Esperance*.

[2] Occasionally Worcester's French reading is different from the French
manuscripts I have examined and supports the English reading in R or U. Such
instances are recorded in the Explanatory Notes to the texts.

[3] McFarlane, p. 214.

[4] *DNB*, 'Robert Dudley'.

[5] See M. S. and G. H. Blayney, '*The Faerie Queene* and an English Version of
Chartier's *Traité de l'Esperance*', *SP*, iv (1958), 154–63.

[6] *Paston Letters and Papers of the Fifteenth Century*, ed. N. Davis, Part I
(Oxford, 1971), p. 285.

Henry Heydon's branch of the Heydon family.[1] Spelman's owner-ship may be significant also because of his known interest in Sir John Fortescue; he had in his library at least one early printed edition of Fortescue's *De Laudibus Legum*[2] and was certainly interested in and influenced in his own works by Fortescue's legal writings.

2. Chicago, Newberry Library: MS. f. 36, Ry 20 (N)

a. *Description*

Vellum, 242 leaves (misnumbered with 2 folios marked 201), $12\frac{1}{16} \times 9$ in. (306 × 226 mm.), 33–40 lines to usual page in the Chartier translations

Collation: 1^{10} wants leaf 1, 2–5^{10}, 6^{12}, 7^{10}, 8^{8}, 9–16^{12}, 17^{14}, 18^{12}, 19–23^{8}+1 full leaf and 6 cropped leaves

Contents: *The Quadrilogue Invective*, without title, ff. 1–23
    A Famylyer Dialoge of the Frende and þe Felawe vppon the Lamentacyon of the Miserable Calamyte of Fraunce, ff. 23ᵛ– 32ᵛ
    The Treatise of Hope, without title, ff. 33–78
    John Walton's translation of Boethius' *Consolation of Philo-sophy*, without title, ff. 78–207ᵛ
    Earl Rivers's *Dictes and Sayings of the Philosophers*, ff. 208–41

N is written somewhat roughly in several late fifteenth-century hands. All the Chartier translations are copied in a single rather cramped hand, with many scribal cancellations and many corrup-tions. Of all the manuscripts N is most corrupt. A different scribe (possibly two scribes) copied Walton's Boethius, and still another scribe copied Rivers's *Dictes and Sayings*. Catchwords occur frequently, and there are some brush-work initials at the begin-nings of sections. There are numerous marginal comments on the texts of the translations, both in English and in Latin.

When Dr. Pierce Butler and Professor J. M. Manly examined N, according to the Newberry Library folder about the manuscript, they noted that it was valuable 'as a specimen of the ordinary book used by scholars at the end of the middle ages in contrast with the finely made volumes for special uses'.

---

[1] Blomefield, vi. 132, and a pedigree in *The English Works of Henry Spelman*, ed. E. Gibson (London, 1732), show this relationship.

[2] This book is listed in *Bibliotheca Selectissima being the Library of . . . Sir Edmund King . . . also the Library of Sir H. S[pelman]* (London, 1709), p. 54. There seems little doubt that the Fortescue book was Spelman's.

b. *Owners*

The names of several owners appear in N. The earliest is *Christopherus: Lincolne monachus* in a fifteenth-century hand on the front binder's leaf. On f. 207ᵛ following a summary of Boethius is this rubric: *J. Clynton prorē scrpt. 148–.* Thus, N may have been copied in a Lincoln monastery.

In the sixteenth century N was owned by Thomas Sowthen. On f. 241ᵛ a poem by Isaac Frise is prefaced by the comment *Mr Thomas Sowthen dyed the last day of Aprill 1579.* The folder about N at Newberry Library and earlier comments about ownership read the date as 1519. But the verses by Frise unmistakably refer to Sowthen's owning the book in 1577, and a marginal scribbling of an indenture drawn up between *Thomas Southen* and *Iohn Craven* on f. 98 is dated 1574. The verses read:

> Mr Thomas Sowthen did owe this boke
> God give him grace theron to loke
> and when he hath lokte to tak good hede
> and marke the thinge that he doth rede
> and I Isaac Frise will bere record
> that it was Thomas Sowthens in the yere of our lord
> 1 thousand fyve hundred seventie and seven
> and so god send vs all the blis of heaven
>   Amen qoth Isaac Frise.

The indenture on f. 98 reads:

This indentur mayd the xvth day of march[?] in the xvj yere of the raynge of our sufrayne lady Elysabeth [1574] by the grac of god of England Franc and Ireland and defender of the Feyth and so forth betwene Thomas Southen of the 1 partie[?] and Iohn Craven on the other partie next[?].

The date of Thomas Sowthen's death then must have been 1579. Probably after Sowthen died, N came into the hands of Isaac Frise, who also has acrostic verses on the unnumbered leaf after f. 241ᵛ:

I   Instructt well thy familie
S   Sucor the pore
A   Ask counsell at the wise
A   And thou shalt hav store
C   Content thy self with thyn estate
E   Emput no shame to ficle fate

> F Fear god always nyght and day
> R Reioyce not to se thy nyghbors decay
> I In all the nede call to god for grace
> S So will he sone help from his holy place
> E Evell will stereth strife.

On this last full leaf in N, Frise has also written the names *Roger Bush* and *Robt*, as well as a list of years 1571 to 1581 with notes by each. A similar list also occurs on f. 127, perhaps in a different hand and with some changes in the notes.

A later owner seems to have been *R. Alsen*, whose name in an Elizabethan hand appears on the last leaf and on the front binder's leaf. N was bought by the Newberry Library in 1937 from William Robinson, Ltd., London, who obtained it from the library of Lord Clifford of Ugbrooke Park, Chudleigh, Devonshire.

3. London, Sion College: MS. L. 40.2/E 43 (S)[1]

a. *Description*

Vellum, flyleaf+90 numbered leaves, $10\frac{1}{16} \times 7\frac{7}{8}$ in. (254×198 mm.), 25–30 lines to a page

Collation: $1-4^{12}$, 5^{12} wants 11, 12 (probably blank after f. 58), $6^{10}+1$ leaf after 9 (f. 68), $7^{12}+1$ leaf after 8 (f. 78), 8^{10} wants 9, 10

Contents: *The Quadrilogue Invective*, without title, ff. 1–39
           A Famylyer Dyaloge of the Freende and the Felaw vppon the Lamentacion of the Myserable Calamyte of Fraunce, ff. 39–58ᵛ
           The Treatise of Hope, without title, ff. 59–90ᵛ

The Treatise of Hope breaks off about one-third of the way through, at 47/3. S may have been complete originally, or at least the scribe intended to copy the entire treatise, since on the back of the flyleaf he has written:

The last Chapitre of this booke begynneth as folowith after / Esperaunce / Les premiers hommes qui habiterent la terre cercherent premier leur necessite and the last clause of the same seyth this wyse Que les seigneuries anciennes furent tousiours establas tant comme ilz seruirent et sacrifierent deuement a diuinite.

It is interesting that the scribe refers here to the last speech of Chartier's original work rather than to the English text.

S is copied in a fairly current hand of the second half of the

---

[1] Much of the descriptive information about S was obtained from Neil Ker, who has catalogued the Sion College Library.

fifteenth century. Occasionally as on f. 88 (43/28–9), the manuscript is illegible because of rubbing. The initials are not filled in,
and there is no decoration. There are, however, Latin comments
in the margins of *A Famylyer Dyaloge*.

b. *Owners*

The early ownership of S is not known. On the flyleaf is the note
Explicit Petre Idyll. The other name that occurs in S is *Ihon
Smythe of Sussex*[?], which is on f. 53ᵛ with the scribbled comment
*peple and whel belouyd Brother rychard my dewtye concyderyd I
haue in*, followed by several illegible words. The first certain
knowledge of ownership is that S was at one time in the library
of Sir Robert Coke, son of Edward, the well-known Chief Justice.
Since the Cokes were an old Norfolk family and neighbours of
Sir Henry Spelman, a later owner of R, the Coke connection with
S is interesting. Sir Robert Coke was the husband of Theophila,
the aunt of George Berkeley (1629–98), 1st Earl of Berkeley and
Viscount Dursley, who presented S to Sion College in 1682.[1]

4. Cambridge: St. John's College MS. 76. D 1 (J)

a. *Description*

Vellum, 91 unnumbered leaves, 11⅜ × 8 in. (263 × 203 mm.), 27–43 lines
    to a page
Collation: 1–4⁸, 5¹⁰, 6⁸, 7⁶, 8–10⁸, 11⁸ wants leaf 7, 12⁷ (four)
Contents: *The Quadrilogue Invective*, without title and Prologue, ff. 1–27
          *A Famylyer Dyaloge of the Frende and the Felowe vppon the
          Lamentacion of the Myserable Calamyte of Fraunce*, ff. 27ᵛ–41ᵛ
          The Treatise of Hope, without title, ff. 43–91ᵛ

There are gaps in J following f. 53ᵛ (*T.H.*, 23/12–27/30);
following f. 56ᵛ, after quire 7 (*T.H.*, 33/18–50/7); and following
f. 86ᵛ (*T.H.*, 120/6–122/9). As pointed out by J. C. Laidlaw,[2] an
entire gathering has probably been lost after quire 7, where there
is a change of hand. Quire 7 may also have had eight leaves, the
middle two probably lost, accounting for the gap after f. 53ᵛ.
Leaf 7, omitted in quire 11, accounts for the gap after f. 86ᵛ.

    J is written in two late fifteenth-century hands. Scribe 1 copied
all of *The Quadrilogue Invective* and *A Famylyer Dyaloge*. After

---

[1] William Reading, *Bibliothecae cleri Londinensis in collegio Sionensi catalogus*
(London, 1724), sign. Ppppp.
[2] 'English Translations of Alain Chartier', *MLR*, lvi (1961), 223.

f. 42, which is blank except for scribbles, scribe 2 took over at the beginning of *The Treatise of Hope* and copied ff. 43–56ᵛ. Scribe 1 then finished the treatise, ff. 57–91ᵛ.[1] The upper right corner of f. 1 is torn away. Here a different hand has added the first words in the space allowed for an illuminated capital.

There is no illumination in J, and the capital letters at the beginnings of sections are not even filled in. The character headings at the beginnings of speeches are in red. The margins contain many comments in both English and Latin relating to the text, as well as many pen trials.

b. *Owners*

No clear evidence of the early ownership of J exists. There are some marginal scribbles and some notes on f. 42, but they are not always legible. The earliest near the bottom of f. 42 is in a late fifteenth- or early sixteenth-century hand and seems to read *be et knone to aull men that I Robert Aulbrow*[?] *as*[?] *boute*[?] *of thomas* [illegible word] *off* [two words illegible] *xxᵗⁱ*[?] *bag*[?]. The name *Aulbrow* probably came from one of the villages called Alburgh, Aldborough, or Aldbrough in Norfolk and Yorkshire. Among East Anglia and Yorkshire pedigrees the names 'Alborowe' and 'Alburgh' occur, and in 1479 William Paston III wrote of a Mrs. Alborow and her daughter Margaret of London.[2] However, the name in J is too unclear to be conclusive. The same hand may have written *In nomine patris & filij & speritus sancti amen qd robert* on f. 75ᵛ. Just above this *In nomyne patrys et fylyy et speritus sãnty amen sayd robt stotterd* is scribbled.

One Thomas Allott was probably an owner of J since on f. 21ᵛ *This is Thomas Allottes book*[?] is written upside down in the bottom margin in a Renaissance hand, and again on f. 42 this name is scribbled several times. Also on f. 42, the name *Thomas Taylur* appears, and on f. 16, *Thomas Smyth*. Finally in the margin of f. 1 at the beginning of what looks like a personal letter *Dame Jane* is written.

Later ownership of J is more certain. The manuscript was in the library of William Crashawe (1572–1626)[3] and in 1636 was

---

[1] Laidlaw, p. 223, believed that ff. 57–91ᵛ are in a third hand.

[2] *Paston Letters and Papers of the Fifteenth Century*, ed. N. Davis, Part I (Oxford, 1971), p. 651.

[3] See P. J. Wallis, 'The Library of William Crashawe', *Trans. Camb. Bibl. Soc.*, ii, pt. 3 (1956), 213–28.

given to St. John's College by Thomas, Earl of Southampton. William Crashawe was a Puritan divine of Yorkshire, and one wonders whether Thomas Taylur might not be the Puritan divine of the same period (1576–1633) in Yorkshire.[1]

5. British Library: Cotton Vitellius MS. E. x (C)

Cotton Vitellius E. x, written on paper in a hand of the late fifteenth century, contains on ff. 176–81 a fragment of *The Treatise of Hope* (33/23–44/10). In Thomas Smith's catalogue of the Cotton Library made before the fire, the fragmentary work was attributed to Sir John Fortescue, Chief Justice of the King's Bench during the reign of Henry VI. The 1869 two-volume edition of Fortescue's works by Thomas Fortescue, Lord Clermont, prints the fragment very inaccurately. C is misbound and is printed by Lord Clermont in the incorrect manuscript order. F. 177 should follow f. 181. C is badly burned and charred around the margins, especially at the bottoms and tops of the leaves; such burning frequently cuts out words or phrases from the C text.[2]

It is interesting that the C fragment corresponds somewhat in extent with the missing gathering in J: the J lacuna begins at *T.H.* 33/18, but goes on further than C, to *T.H.* 50/7. C, however, is not part of the missing gathering in J, since C is on paper and is different in hand, decoration, and written area. J. C. Laidlaw suggests that C might be a copy of a gathering that was detached early from J, 'although it is difficult to see any good reason why this should have been done'. He concludes, 'At the same time, the similarity of content between the missing St. John's quire and the extant Cotton fragment is remarkable, and may be due to more concrete causes than mere coincidence'.[3]

B. *Relationships of the Manuscripts*[4]

The evidence of the variants in RNSJ leads to the conclusion that all four manuscripts have come down to us ultimately from

[1] *DNB*, 'Thomas Taylor'.

[2] These omissions have not been noted in the critical apparatus or Explanatory Notes except where there is some question about the R text or a variant in the other manuscripts.   [3] Laidlaw, *MLR*, lvi (1961), 223.

[4] In this discussion of the manuscripts, as in the texts, the errors emended by a corrector of R will be placed in round brackets and those emended by the editor or by a reading from NSJC in square brackets. Moreover, words and phrases from the English manuscripts are italicized and those from the French are placed in quotation marks.

a manuscript which itself was not copied directly from the author's draft. The most important misplacement of an element in RNJ at 64/8 suggests that RNJ are at least three times removed from the author's copy.[1] Here following *withowt herte* in RNJ there is more than a line which should have been placed at 64/17 following *counseile*. This misplacement clearly shows that RNJ have behind them a manuscript in which this copying error occurred. Since the passage is not repeated in its proper place (cf. 44/6), we cannot assume that the scribe of a manuscript simply looked back to his copy text and picked up the wrong sentence, which occurred in approximately the same position in another column or on another page as the sentence for which he was looking. This misplacement may, therefore, represent an error made when an ancestor manuscript of RNJ was copied from a version which omitted the passage in its proper place (an error easily made—note the *le* and *te* endings), but, the error being realized, had it written in a margin. It would seem then, if this is true, that a scribe simply inserted the passage at the wrong place during some later copying and the corruption thus was carried down to RNJ. A similar explanation may also apply to the misplacement of *Allas yet nat* at 46/19; here RS[2] both misplace the words and do not repeat them in the proper place at 46/20, while N omits them entirely.

There are many other corruptions in all four manuscripts or in RN and S or J that support the theory of an exemplar which was not the author's original. In several places there are omissions in all the manuscripts that seem to have come from corruption in an earlier manuscript. One homoeoteleuton occurs at 33/1, where part of a sentence has been omitted because of the similarity between *perfeccion of the creature* and *perfeccion of the Creatour*. This omission, which explains the unclear English passage in RNSJ, is obvious when the reading is compared with the French.[3] At 144/18, there is another omission in all four manuscripts. RNSJ read:

and on hir heede she ware a crowne of fyne golde which by diuerse punchingis [pusshinges NSJ] was so soore brwsid that hit hynge ryght

---

[1] Since S breaks off after about one-third of *The Treatise of Hope*, at 47/3, we have no S reading here, but it will be shown below that S and J are very closely related manuscripts.

[2] This passage occurs in one of J's lacunae. See note above.

[3] See Explanatory Note to this passage.

soor on the one syde; and specialy of the mantell that couerid hir body, of which the mervelous werkmanship ought to be remembrid.

The French has:

et une couronne d'or fin sur son chief portoit, qui par divers hurs si fort estoit esbranlee qui ja penchoit de coste, enclinee moult durement. De sa vesture ne me puis je pas passer ne taire, et mesmement du mantel ou paille qui son corps couvroit, dont le merveilleux artifice fait a ramentevoir.

The English sentence is so poorly constructed in a place where the author is translating accurately elsewhere that there must certainly be a scribal omission.[1]

Similarly, all the manuscripts sometimes show evidence of misreading at an early stage which makes nonsense of a passage, but which can be emended by comparison with the French. Note the following confusions in common or graphically similar words:

	Corruption	Emendation	French
55/33	polytyke by RNJ	polytykely	politiquement
58/14	A vice thanne RNJ	Avicenne	Auicenne
61/34	favoure RNJ	furoure	fureur
79/29	rebellion RNJ	relation	relation
80/22	hope RNJ	height	comble
83/13	reuocacion RNJ	renovacion	renouation
87/18	interdiccion RNJ	introduccion	introduction
128/29	by R, by thei NJ	but they had	mais ils eurent
150/21	to do RNSJ	yow	vous
168/17	vnnethe RNSJ	rennethe	encourt
244/22	of RNSJ	if	se
246/6	yow RNSJ	veyn	vain.

Several other distinctly corrupt passages in RNSJ seem to have arisen from an early scribe's difficulty in reading the author's draft. At 21/29–31, RNSJ read:

let fall the [þi] perdurable sowle into perille, which is moche the losse where is gretter thanne of the mortall body.

The French after *perille* reads: 'dont la perte est trop plus grande'. It seems possible that the corrupt reading of the English manu-

---

[1] See also notes for 48/28, 79/21, 166/21, and 182/31, where there may be other omissions in all the manuscripts. Other shorter omissions in them all occur at 19/14, where RNSJ omit *moved* after *musculles*; 53/36, where in *the name only* N omits *the name* and RJ omit *name*; 89/5, where RNJ omit *voide* after *made*; and 210/27, where RNSJ omit *yoke* after *yevin*.

scripts represents two attempts of the translator to render the French, a combination of which was carried over into the first copy from the author's draft. The translator may have tried *of which the losse is moche gretter thanne of the mortall body*, and perhaps not liking this, changed it to *the losse whereof is moche gretter thanne of the mortall body*. With such an alteration in the author's manuscript, the reading of the passage may well not have been clear to the first copyist.

Something of the same kind appears in RNJ in this unclear passage at 100/20–4, which reads:

and comfort the evile folkis bi pacience, which may cause them of amendment, and [þan *add.* NJ] the good men woll turne the to helpe and socour and the evill men by pacience of amendment. Thanne shall the good helpe of seurte turne vnto the and the evill of prouision.

This translates the French

& conforte les mauuaises par patience aduisee d'amendement. Si te tournera la bonne Esperance [*om.* BClRo, as probably in the translator's exemplar] en aide de seurté, & la mauuaise en prouision d'auis.

Two distinct attempts to render the French seem to be reflected here.

Other passages also show the probability of a sometimes illegible copy lying behind the extant manuscripts. At 134/23, for example, for *atemprate* N has *atempray*, S *atemprar*, and R a blank space. Again, at 114/33, where the French has 'estre prié d'omme', J perhaps comes nearest to the original in *to the preyde*, with *the* a corruption of *be*; N has the further corrupted *the pride*; and R has changed the reading to *the to praye*. Illegibility in an earlier copy also seems to be reflected at 224/12, where, for the correct *prosperite*, N has *prosperite propyrte*; S has *psperite* [cancelled] *prosperyte* [perhaps cancelled] *properte*; and RJ have *properte*.

Thus, it seems likely that RNSJ have all ultimately descended from a copy that was at least once, probably twice (if we consider the readings at 64/8 and 46/19 discussed on page 15) removed from the author's draft.

The variants also show that RNJ could not have served as copy texts for each other or for S. N is the most corrupt extant manuscript, with frequent omissions of complete sentences or parts of sentences[1] and with frequent corruptions of the sense of passages,[2] corruptions that do not occur in the other manuscripts. R also has some longer omissions, among them an entire short section at 25/28–34, assigned to the Author in the other manuscripts.[3] R also omits the speakers' names in both treatises. A substantial number of shorter omissions of a word or phrase and more instances of dittography than in the other manuscripts[4] also show that R did not serve as copy text for NSJ. The evidence that RNS were not copied from J is not as plentiful, but three short passages omitted in J (5/4–5, 118/15–16, and 228/26–8) seem conclusive.

S and J are very closely related manuscripts revealing so many of the same peculiarities that it is possible that J was copied from S (if S was once complete, as suggested on page 11); but J's correct readings in a few places where the other manuscripts are corrupt make this relationship somewhat doubtful. In these places where J is superior, however, it seems likely that the J scribe merely deciphered an unclearly written copy text or grasped the context of a corrupt passage more successfully than the other scribes. It is interesting, but possibly only coincidental, that the most notable instances of J's superiority occur in *The Treatise of Hope* on pages 73–8 (ff. 67–8 of J) and in *The Quadrilogue Invective* on page 156 (ff. 4ᵛ–5). At 73/26, for example, where R has *a voice here* and N *her a voyce*, J follows the French with *alweys here*. (In line 25 the phrase *here the voice* occurs to account for the corruption in RN). Similarly, at 75/9, J's *yn Hys bote* follows the French, while N has *is his bote* and R further corrupts the phrase to *is but*.[5] J's seemingly better readings at 156/5 and 156/20 might easily have resulted from the scribe's closer attention to the context of the passages.

Even if J was not copied directly from S, it seems almost certain that at least both were written from the same exemplar. They agree with each other not only in substantive variants, but in minor corruptions and variations of spelling. In a few places the

---

[1] See 10/18–23, 10/31–2, 34/11–12, 67/31, 79/8–9, 85/13–14, 91/22–3, 104/22–3, 112/26–7, 115/27–33, 119/27–8, 124/10–11, 126/31–2, 131/3–6, 132/24–33, 156/8–9, 180/9–12, 180/21–2, 182/2–3, 184/10–12, 186/17–18, 234/13–14, 234/27, for the longest omissions in N.

[2] See 24/8–9, 24/12–13, 115/6, 127/2, 178/25–6, 182/28–9, and 234/21.

[3] See also 8/29, 14/10–12, 46/31–3, 58/16–18, 67/12–13, 85/7–8, 119/8–9, 123/2–3, 128/1–2, 129/6–7, 162/20–1, 212/10–11.

[4] See especially the long passage repeated at 44/6, and see also 146/2, 206/24, 224/3.

[5] See also 77/29–30, 78/6, and 78/11.

SJ reading is superior to that in RN. At 18/5, for instance, *lakketh* (SJ) is superior to *laweth* (RN). *reentre* (SJ) at 238/21 follows the French more closely than N's *entre* and R's *and entre*; and *me semyth* (SJ), omitted in RN, at 186/9 translates the French 'm'est advis'. Even more important are the corruptions common to S and J. At 210/17, where RN have *Isai*, SJ both repeat *Isay*; and at 180/26, where R has *iuberte* and N *ieoperte*, SJ both have *iuberte iuperte* with *iuberte* cancelled in J. The following spelling corruptions also show the very close relationship between S and J:

	RN	SJ
9/14	folish	folyseth
19/7	malencolye	merencolye
19/20	dremyng	drenynge
180/4	movyngis	moyevynges
200/20	darist	draryst
212/20	purveye (-vaye)	purvoye
216/30	bityng	bydyng
242/3	practicke	praetyk.

In addition, the variants show that R is probably at least once removed from the exemplar that lies behind RNSJ. Two passages omitted in R, but present in the other extant manuscripts, seem to date back to corruptions in the manuscript from which R was copied; in each case the R scribe, faced with a poor reading, seems to have added a few words of his own in an attempt to make sense of a sentence. At 109/25–30, NJ have the following reading which follows the French:

herken hough paciently and in the drede of god Saynt Lyeu meyntened hymself ayenst Athila the kyng of huns in the tyme of hys persecucions and thu shalt fynde humble doctrynes [*sing.* J] and profytable obeissaunce his legend reciteth how the holy man made opyn the gates of the [his J] cite to the tiraunte Athila which was a myscreaunte.

The manuscript from which the R scribe copied probably omitted *the kyng . . . how the*; the R scribe, recognizing the absurdity of *Athila holy man*, supplied *ayeinst whom a* to gain a semblance of sense. Again at 164/34–166/2, NSJ have:

I may well be lykned to þe asse þat berith the importable [ynpotable S] charges and am betyn and prykkyd to do and suffre suche þinges as is not in my power. I am allso the Butt ayenst whom euery man shetyth the arrowys of tribulacyon.

Here R's *and anempst me* for *I . . . whom* may be the scribe's attempt to emend a faulty manuscript.

The position of N in the textual history of the manuscripts is rather enigmatic. Although N is not related as closely to SJ as the two are to each other, it shows a closer relation to SJ than to R in many variants and even in its verb endings. Corruptions sometimes appear in NSJ where R is correct. For example, at 228/4, where the French has 'Nature admonneste d'estre', R's *nature gaue to be* seems a closer translation than NSJ's *to haue bene.*[1] R's *grette sleuthe* at 180/7 is corrupted to *grete slouther* in SJ, and further corrupted to *slaughter grete* in N. Similarly, R's *affliccions* at 182/11 has the peculiar spelling *affleccions* in SJ, and becomes the meaningless *affeccions* in N, while at 244/17, R's *offences* is spelled *affences* in SJ and becomes *affeccions* in N.[2] In verb endings NSJ show a greater preference for *n* in the present plural than does R, and all three tend to have the ending on the same verbs where R does not.[3] While R has an occasional *s* in the present third singular, NSJ all have *s* in eight places where R does not. Thus, since N does not share all of the striking peculiarities of SJ, but does reveal some of the same corruptions and verb endings, it seems possible that N and SJ's exemplar are both descended from a common version.

The line of descent of RNSJ[4] may be conjectured then to look something like this, *a*, *β* etc., being hyparchetypes that have not come down to us:

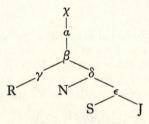

[1] A corrector of S has tried to gain sense here by adding *by* before *nature* and *owght* before *to haue ben.*

[2] Cf. also 80/28, 124/28, 128/30.

[3] NSJ have *ben* for *be* about eighty times, and have the *n* ending thirty-eight times in other verbs where R does not.

[4] C is so fragmentary that it is impossible to establish clearly its relation to RNS (J, of course, omits the part that appears in C; see above, p. 14.) The evidence that RNS were not copied from C, however, seems conclusive. At 34/20–2, R reads: *O ye erthely kyngis, which sitte in youre trembling chayers and haue*

C. *Analysis of Scribal Error and Correction in R*[1]

The R scribe has most of the usual types of scribal errors. Frequently he omits sentences, clauses, and phrases because his eye has picked up a similar word later in the line or column. Nearly all of his longer omissions are caused by *sauts du même au même*, as with the words *hir* at 8/29; *and* at 14/10–12; *him* at 34/12–13; *closed* at 85/7–8; *same* at 107/32–3; *ayeinste him* and *that* at 119/8–9; *ordeigned* at 123/2–3; *man* at 128/1–2; *sacrifices* at 129/6–7; *life* at 162/20–1; and *bondage* at 212/10–11. At 58/16–18, the scribe has jumped from *in* to *Iulius*. The scribe of R also omits many syllables, letters, or entire words supplied in the text from NSJC or by a corrector of R. Often these omissions are of linking verbs or auxiliary verbs, pronouns, linking or emphatic adverbs, articles, and connective words. Many of the omissions cause difficult or stylistically poor readings because of lack of parallelism or of transition, or because of abruptness or roughness in the flow of language, qualities seldom found in Chartier's French. It is good then that we have NSJC to give authority to readings that follow the French more closely than R.

commaundingis by auctorite disseyveable ly vpon the people peruertible, lothe to lerne your [leccons] of the Kyng of hevene. For *and . . . to,* S has: *and haue commawdyn by auctoryte dysseyvable ly vppon the peple pevertybloth*; N has: *and haue commawnden by auctoryte deceyvable ly vppon the peple and þer fore.* RNS are all corrupt in the addition of *ly* after *disseyveable,* and R's *lothe to* (omitted in the French and changed in NS) may be corrupt. C, however, omits *and . . . to.* This omission must be viewed with some caution since the omitted passage would have occurred in C exactly at the bottom of a page. Because of the burning around the edges, it is just possible that the passage in question, which would fill about one line in C, may have been burned off. But this is not supported by the present condition of C, since the page in question seems to agree with the other folios in number of lines and with the opposite side in the positions of the first and last lines. It seems significant also that at no other place in the six folios are any complete lines burned off the tops or bottoms. Hence, unless this passage was omitted by the scribe of C and added in a portion of the margin that was burned off, this omission in C seems admissible as evidence that RNS were not copied from C. The next omission in C of a passage present in RNS is more conclusive. At 35/11–13, RNS read: *For the feer that his people and subiectis haue of hym for his grette power makith him to forgette the dreede which he shulde by reason owe to Almighty God.* C omits *for . . . him* because of the repetition of *him.* Of course, we have also no evidence to show whether C was ever part of a complete text of *The Treatise of Hope.*

[1] The section above on relationship of the manuscripts has already discussed some of the scribal errors that can be shown to go back to earlier copies of the treatises. The present section will deal only with the scribal errors peculiar to R, the copy text.

An even more significant contribution of NSJC, however, is in supplying words in R that not only improve the sense and style but give Chartier's original ideas more sharply. We may note, for example, the restoring of Chartier's original tone and meaning in these additions in R from NSJC: *euyl* (Fr. 'mauuais') at 45/34; *dreme* (Fr. 'desuerie') at 80/26; *Kyng* (Fr. 'roy') at 134/5; and *easy* (Fr. 'aisié') at 170/25. There are also abundant examples of important words essential to the sense that are omitted in R but supplied by the other manuscripts: *preysed* (Fr. 'prisent') at 46/24; *shewede* (Fr. 'monstra') at 65/29; *grace* (Fr. 'Grace') at 66/19; *fell* (Fr. 'vint') at 142/8; *hold* (Fr. 'accueillez') at 156/14; and *defendid* (Fr. 'defend') at 166/18. Special note should also be made of the addition from NSJ of a word that confirms the fact that the translator misunderstood the French original at some places, as at 242/30, where *disconfidence* (NSJ), a mistranslation of 'de confidence', is omitted by the R scribe.[1]

In addition to omitting parts of the text, the R scribe sometimes writes the wrong word either because two words are graphically similar or because an incorrect word has been picked up from another place nearby on the page. A combination of graphic similarity and sentence context accounts for some word errors. At 14/7, for instance, in *thou wer bowne to begynne a newe prentishode*, R's *bowne* is perhaps more suitable to the context than *borne* (NSJ), which translates the French 'ne', and it is easy to see why the R scribe was misled. Likewise, R's *remainnith* at 57/1, in the clause *for at this day their remainnith a folische langage in courte*, fits the context as well as *renneth* (NJ), which translates the French 'court'.[2]

Other word errors in R occur merely because of graphic similarity, i.e., *dissolue* for *disseiue* (Fr. 'deceuoir') at 57/32; *finite* for *feynte* (Fr. 'fainte') at 100/33; *wake* for *werke* (Fr. 'besongnent') at 101/19; *followed* for *fowled* (Fr. 'souilles') at 131/14; *declined* for *delyueryd* (Fr. 'delivres') at 152/21; *hath* for *helth* (Fr. 'salut') at 154/15; and *prignaunte* for *poignaunte* (Fr. 'poignant') at 200/22.

A few word substitutions in R result from the appearance of the

---

[1] At 242/31, 'de sceurté' has similarly been mistranslated as *disseurte*. See Explanatory Note.

[2] Other interesting word errors of this type in R are *thinges* for *signes* (Fr. 'signacles') at 63/23; *pleacid* for *peesed* (Fr. 'r'apaise') at 66/10; *he nethir* for *here beneth* (Fr. 'ça ius') at 121/19; *distruccions* for *distraccion* (Fr. 'distraction') at 132/26; and *litill* for *light* (Fr. 'legier') at 144/5.

incorrect word nearby on a page. For example, at 79/33, *fever*, picked up from earlier in the line, appears for *comforte* (Fr. 'conforte'). At 99/1, R has *body* from earlier in the line in place of *soule* (Fr. 'esperit'). Again at 168/26–7, R reads: (*it*) *is a more pituous thing to susteyne my desolacion*; but where R has *pituous* NSJ have *grevous* (Fr. 'griefve'). The R scribe's eye has evidently jumped ahead and picked up *pituous* too soon, and then, finding the word again later, has replaced it with *my*.

Another common type of scribal error in R is dittography, especially at the end of one line and the beginning of the next and on the first or last line of a column. The scribe also occasionally adds words not necessary to the text, sometimes for completion of a common phrase, sometimes by repetition from a position nearby. At 12/28, the scribe has written the phrase *the powr comon people* before realizing that *the powr comon wele* was in the manuscript before him. Again at 146/2, the reading in R, *so riche a werke as was so displesaunt made,* is nonsensical and can be accounted for by the scribe's picking up of *so displesaunt*, omitted in NSJ, from the phrase *so excellent a werke so moch was displesaunt* in line 6.

In addition to these, which have been emended fron NSJ, R has many other additions of words or phrases that are not in NSJ nor in the French. They do not change the meaning, even though they are sometimes redundant, and they may be scribal flourishes in R. But since the translator himself, like many other authors of the period, was so prone to add such flourishes to his French original, I have not omitted these additions in the texts. Some of them probably represent the R scribe's copying into the text glosses that appeared in the manuscript he was using. At 23/14–16, for example, R reads:

the oon is callid Demonstratyue or serteyne, the othir Dialetique, dowtfull, and the thryd Sophistique, dissaiveable.

dowtfull and *dissaiveable*, omitted in the French, are added as glosses in NS, as is *or serteyne* (omitted in N) in S.[1]

Among the less important scribal errors in R are certain letter confusions. In common with many other copyists, the scribe has confused *c* and *t*. He also commonly has not crossed the letter *f*,

---

[1] See also 95/18, where a gloss may account for the addition in R.

thus making a long *s*. Such scribal carelessness occurs almost always before another crossed letter, either *t* or *f*.[1] The scribe has also occasionally crossed an *s*, hence making an *f*. R shares with other manuscripts many other common letter errors: too many or too few minims in a word, as well as confusion of *e* and *o*, final *e* and *s*, *e* and *a*, *r* and *i*, *r* and *e*, and *r* and *o*.

Several errors of transposition also occur, as at 5/27, where the R scribe has written *man of parte* instead of *parte of man* (NSJ). Three errors of illumination appear as well: at 4/17, the *n* in *In* has originally been a capital *A*; at 41/19, the illuminated *F* in *Fayier* has been made from an *I*; and at 85/25, the *Y* in *Yet* has been illuminated as *L*.

The scribe of R has often noticed and corrected his own errors. Sometimes he seems also to have changed letters which are not incorrect in medieval spelling: he has changed *o* to *v* in *cvrse* at 45/28, in *stvdye* at 65/15, and in *tvnges* at 67/2; and he has changed *strenght* to *strenghe* at 194/6.

But there are also corrections in R by other hands. Both *The Quadrilogue Invective* and *The Treatise of Hope* lack identification of characters as they speak.[2] In *The Quadrilogue* a corrector has attempted to remedy this deficiency by adding sporadically, especially toward the beginning, in a secretary hand, a description of who is about to speak and the gist of the speech that follows. For example, the first of these additions on f. 5 reads: *the wordes of the mother to here iij sons*. These descriptions are not always accurate: for instance, on f. 21, *the iij sonne speaketh whiche ys regalyte or gouernans* is inserted before the Clergy speaks. Parts of such additions have been cut off by the cropping of R.

In addition to these insertions, R has been corrected by various hands, which are sometimes noticeably different from the scribal hand. But, especially on ff. 1–9ᵛ, where the scribal hand is unsettled, the corrector's hand is sometimes hard to distinguish from that of the scribe. After f. 100ᵛ no corrections have been made. Some of the corrections seem to be in the hand of whoever wrote

---

[1] I have not burdened the critical apparatus with these errors where *f* is obviously required. I have, however, noted instances where the correct word is not obvious or where the intended word might be mistaken for another. SJ contain even more such carelessness than R.

[2] These identifications have been added in the texts from N. They also occur in SJ.

Henricj Spelmanni on f. 1, numbered the folios and occasionally added marginal comments, such as *8 Hen. 5.* to identify the date and English king mentioned on f. 2^v.

The corrections in R are neither comprehensive (many corruptions have been overlooked) nor always entirely necessary; indeed, in some places the obvious sense intended by the translator is perverted by a corrector's additions. Yet in some of the additions, a corrector, probably not the scribe correcting his own work, may possibly have been following some authoritative source. Most such corrections occur when omitted words which agree with the other manuscripts and translate the French exactly are added. In one place at 204/10, where the French has 'toy', the R corrector's *the* is even superior to NSJ's *them.* Elsewhere the additions in R agree with NSJ. For example, *hynge* and *bagges* are added at 6/22, *þei persyd* at 24/8, *inhabitable* at 36/30, *distincions* at 58/16, *his sciens but* at 95/23, *tresours* at 112/25, and *contagyous* at 208/27. It is possible, of course, if perhaps doubtful, that at these points the corrector, sometimes merely by chance, sometimes by careful attention to the translator's vocabulary in surrounding passages (e.g., *þei persyd*), sometimes by common sense, struck the exact reading without the aid of any authoritative text.

This conjecture, indeed, seems to be corroborated by the following examples where the corrections seem unnecessary or decidedly inferior. At 75/1, the correction is inferior. The scribe of R has written: *Awake and forgete nour powr and feble impotencie. nour* is a scribal error for *not our* (NJ). The corrector, however, although he has added *not,* has incorrectly changed *nour* to *your.* Again at 44/24–6, a corrector has made one necessary correction, but has not seized upon the full scribal error. The uncorrected R reads: *For some lyue in grette synne in dissimelynge hath yeuen preuy consentement to the euile.* As the corrector has noted in his addition of *and* after *synne,* there is an obvious omission here, but, as shown by NS, *and some* has been omitted.[1] Besides these notably inferior changes, some unnecessary corrections, sometimes in an attempt to standardize or modernize, have been made in R in both spelling[2]

---

[1] For other examples of inferior corrections, see the Explanatory Notes for 13/33, 44/30, 51/29, 136/5, 194/11, and 234/9.

[2] For example, one corrector seemingly active only on ff. 36–36^v has changed the second *e* in *repreve,* the usual scribal spelling, to *o* (7/20, 7/23, 7/28) and has made the scribe's *Vndistondist* read *Vnderstondist* (8/17). See also 27/16, 28/25, 47/12, 50/30, 84/5, 96/15, and 98/3 for other unnecessary corrections in spelling.

and verb endings.[1] In addition, it was probably a corrector, not the scribe, who cancelled *and* at 38/18, in the phrase *nyce and owte of mesure* used as a modifier of *subiectis*. Since *and* appears in NSC and since *owte of mesure* as an adjective meaning 'boundless' or 'excessive' is an especially Scottish use (among various Scottish and northerly characteristics in the treatises), it seems probable that *and* was cancelled by a corrector to whose ear *owte of mesure* sounded adverbial.

The other corrections in R seem quite usual, and many could easily have been made through the corrector's common sense.

D. *The Author of the R Translations*[2]

RNSJ contain no indication of authorship for either *The Quadrilogue Invective* or *The Treatise of Hope*. Nor is there now any indication of authorship in Cotton Vitellius E. x for the fragment of *The Treatise of Hope*. In Thomas Smith's catalogue of the Cotton Library made before the fire, however, the fragment was attributed to Sir John Fortescue.[3] It is impossible to conjecture what kind of evidence Smith, usually considered a reliable authority, had for his attribution, since the manuscript was badly burned around the edges and the table of contents where this work should have appeared is almost completely gone. It seems likely that later cataloguers of the Cotton collection, as well as editors of Fortescue's works, have taken without question Smith's ascription. The *Dialogue*, printed with Fortescue's works in 1869 by Thomas Fortescue, Lord Clermont, is called by Charles Plummer, in the introduction to his edition of *The Governance of England* (Oxford, 1885), the most important miscellaneous tract by Fortescue. Plummer adds: 'It is moreover the only one the authenticity of which is tolerably certain' (p. 79).

---

[1] Final *t* is changed to *d* in *compassid* at 29/27, in *moeuid* at 47/13, and in *mouid* at 75/23. Because of the difficulty of distinguishing the corrector's hand from the scribal hand, I have accepted the corrections in the text, but it should be noted that the *t* ending appears elsewhere in R in the past tense and past participle.

[2] For a fuller discussion of the attribution to Fortescue, see M. S. Blayney, 'Sir John Fortescue and Alain Chartier's "Traité de l'Esperance"', *MLR*, xlviii (1953), 385–90.

[3] Smith in *Catalogus Librorum Manuscriptorum Bibliothecae Cottonianae* (1696), p. 98, x. 25, lists 'Dialogue between the understanding and faith, in quo ostendit: Quibus modis & rationibus Deus saepe castigat, & punit Reges per eos, qui magis contra illum deliquerunt'.

In spite of these repeated attributions to Fortescue, his authorship cannot be taken for granted. The evidence that he may have
been the translator, however, is strong, if not sufficient for positive
conclusion.

Although nothing is known of the history of the Cotton fragment before it came into the Cotton collection, it is noteworthy
that Robert Cotton was a good friend of the well-known Sir John
Fortescue of Queen Elizabeth's time, a direct descendant of the
Chief Justice; and it is known that Fortescue gave Cotton at least
one famous manuscript. It is just feasible then that Cotton may
have obtained the fragment in question from Fortescue.

More is known, as we have seen, about the history of R. The
fact that Henry Heydon, for whom R was made,[1] was connected
with the Fortescue family by marriage is significant. While Anne
or Elizabeth, the second daughter of Geoffrey Boleyn, married
Heydon, her younger sister Alice married Sir John Fortescue of
Ponsbourne, son of Sir Richard, younger brother of the Chief
Justice.[2] Hence, at about the time that the manuscript was made
for Henry Heydon, his wife's sister was married to the nephew of
the conjectured translator, a nephew who is noted by Clermont to
have taken an interest in his uncle's activities. Moreover, it is
probable that John Heydon, father of Henry, was associated at
least politically to some extent with Sir John Fortescue, since both
were well-known lawyers and strong supporters of the Lancastrian
cause. They are twice mentioned in the same context, together
with other names, in letters by Friar Brackley in 1460 in the Paston
Letters.[3]

The later history of R reveals little more of importance in
regard to the authorship of the translation. But the ownership of
S by the son of Sir Edward Coke of Norfolk may be suggestive.[4]
Sir Edward took great interest in the works of Fortescue, as might
be expected, and stated that he owned at least two books by
Fortescue.[5]

The case for Fortescue's authorship may be somewhat strengthened by consideration of the opportunity which he had to translate Chartier's works, and of the circumstances of Fortescue's life

[1] See above, pp. 6–7. [2] *DNB*, vii. 476; Clutterbuck, iii. 94.
[3] See *Paston Letters and Papers of the Fifteenth Century*, ed. N. Davis, Part
II (1976), pp. 210, 221.
[4] See above, p. 12. [5] Clermont, i. 49.

which might have led him to an interest in the French works—
works only slightly similar in content to Fortescue's other writings.
Fortescue's father was himself at the Battle of Agincourt, the
severe losses at which Chartier refers to directly and indirectly
in both treatises, and was also resident in France for a time when
he was appointed governor of the fortress of Meaux in the Province
of La Brie. Thus the Chief Justice Sir John had an early intimate
connection with French–English relations during the period when
Chartier was writing.

The circumstances of Fortescue's later life are strikingly similar
to those of Chartier's. Chartier was exiled from Paris in 1418 when
the Burgundians took over the city and was with the Dauphin as
secretary during the period of greatest stress in France, stress
created, from Chartier's point of view, as much by the struggle
between differing factions within France as by the attacks of the
English from without. These feelings he reflected in both *Le
Quadrilogue Invectif* and *Le Traité de l'Esperance*. There are clear
parallels between Fortescue's life, especially in the second half of
the fifteenth century when the translations were written, and
Chartier's life. As a prominent Lancastrian personally associated
with Henry VI and Queen Margaret, Fortescue may well have
accompanied Queen Margaret to France for several months in
1462 to secure help from Louis XI. After the Lancastrian defeat
in 1464, Fortescue was in the party of Queen Margaret and her
son when they returned to France and were given St. Mighel to
settle in by the Duke of Anjou, her father. During the next several
years Fortescue was occupied in journeying to the court in Paris to
secure aid for the Lancastrian cause. Thus, the fact that the situation of Fortescue, exiled with a monarch whom he supported, his
cause defeated, was like the plight of Chartier in France earlier in
the century might well have led to Fortescue's interest in Chartier's
works.

Fortescue would also have had ample opportunity to know the
works of Chartier, which almost certainly were available in the
French court of Louis. Moreover, even before Fortescue's journeys
to France, there is evidence that the court of Henry VI and Margaret
had access to at least some of Chartier's works, for, probably in
1445, a copy of his *Bréviaire des Nobles* (Royal MS. 15 E. VI in the
British Library) was presented to Margaret by John Talbot, first
Earl of Shrewsbury. It will also be remembered that William

Worcester, whom Fortescue knew, was copying extracts from Chartier's works into his notebooks in 1453.

In further consideration of whether Fortescue was the translator, the style of the translations themselves must be taken into account. The quality of the prose is uneven: the translator gains control of the language of the French original and interprets it more vividly as he progresses. The translations are at times quite powerful in their style, so effective indeed that, in many of the passages where the translator has fully understood the French, the style surpasses that of Fortescue's well-known *Governance of England*.

In two passages, however, the translator's rendering of the French creates doubt about whether Fortescue could have been the author. In a passage early in *The Treatise of Hope*, 21/16–19, Faith addresses Understanding:

Now thou arte ioynned to man for to governe [the] Party Vegetatyve by dwe ordir and the apetite sensitif by royall lordeship. And the poletike Nature, that God hath yevin the to helpe, is nat ydill in his commission . . .

The French reads:

Or es conioint à corps humain, pour gouuerner la partie vegetatiue despotiquement, & l'appetit sensitif par seigneurie royale, & politique. Nature, que Dieu t'a baillée en ayde, n'est pas oiseuse en sa commission.

In this construction the French 'politique' might easily have been read by many English translators as a modifier of 'Nature', rather than of 'seigneurie', through use of a French manuscript like E. D. Clarke 34 (Cl) without any sign of punctuation after 'politique'. *by dwe ordir* for 'despotiquement' is more difficult to justify. Either misunderstanding is certainly out of character for Fortescue, since it seems to show a lack of understanding of the medieval concept of the opposition between despotic and politic government, an opposition which Chartier intends and which Fortescue expounds at length in his other works. If Fortescue translated this treatise then, we must assume either that he was using an extremely corrupt French manuscript here or that *the* before *poletike* in RNSJ is a scribal error; for neither of these assumptions has evidence been found. To be considered with the preceding passage is a later section on types of governments in *The Treatise of Hope*, 55/20–56/10, which is at best a confused exposition of the Aristotelian ideas about governments. Although an examination of French manuscripts demonstrates clearly that in many of the confusions the translator had before him corrupt French readings, it seems likely that, had Fortescue translated the passage, he would have realized and corrected the slight corruptions in his French text, since he showed clear knowledge of Aristotle's ideas in his other works.[1]

In summary then, there is some evidence in the history of the manuscripts and in the life of Fortescue to suggest that he may have translated Chartier's works, although certain unclear translations of French passages, although possibly explained by scribal error or by a bad French manuscript, suggest an author less versed than Fortescue in concepts of government.

Although we may not be sure that Fortescue was the translator, we may at least be certain that *The Quadrilogue Invective* and *The Treatise of Hope* were translated by the same person. The similarity between these works in both style and manner of translation is clear. Many of these characteristics of style and peculiarities of translation—for instance, the notable tendency to simplify the often complicated sentence structure of the French, the use of more transitional elements for clarity, and the freedom and vigour of certain passages—will be revealed in the discussion comparing methods of translation in these two works and the other translation of *Le Quadrilogue*.[2] A few of the most obvious characteristics of the R translator may, however, be mentioned here.

The author has a distinct habit of rendering certain French words by the same words or phrases, which would probably not be used as translations by another author. For example, the French word 'industrie' is repeatedly rendered by some word or phrase connoting wisdom: *witty excercyse(s)* in *T.H.*, 10/32, 64/3, 103/19, 113/10, and in *Q.I.*, 134/4; *witty policie* in *Q.I.*, 142/24; and *wisedome* in *Q.I.*, 146/9. Similarly, 'buissons' is translated *bushes and breres* both in *T.H.*, 107/34, and in *Q.I.*, 138/4–5. Likewise, the French 'abisme' evokes in the translator's mind the phrase *deep darkness*. In *T.H.*, 29/15, 'parfont d'abisme' becomes *the deepe derkenesse of helle*; in *T.H.*, 30/33–4, 'abisme' becomes *the deepe derknesse*; in *Q.I.*, 138/35, 'abisme parfonde' becomes *diepe*

---

[1] See Explanatory Note to this passage, as well as Plummer, notes to chap. 1.
[2] See below, pp. 46 ff.

derkenes; and in *Q.I.*, 224/32, 'abisme' becomes *depe pitte full of derkenesse*. Again 'intestines', perhaps a word unfamiliar to the translator, is rendered *grette* both in *T.H.*, 63/15, and in *Q.I.*, 176/ 20 (*grette discordis*).

Another characteristic method of translation of the R author may be cited from *Q.I.*, 226/21–2, where the French 'Et qu'est discipline de chevalerie si non' becomes in the English *Now I aske a question: what is knyghtly discipline? Nothing ellis but . . .*[1] (This is in contrast to the U translation which renders the French word for word: *And what is disciplyne of knyghthode sauf oonly.*) The more direct and emphatic rendering of Chartier's question here in R may be compared with many similar translations, as in *T.H.*, 16/ 18–21, 55/14–16, 68/10–12, 81/29–31, 94/21–3, 104/12–14; and in *Q.I.*, 186/15–18.

The R translator also characteristically dramatizes and emphasizes points by adding words or phrases which do not have French equivalents, such as *Lorde God* in *T.H.*, 95/15; *O Lorde God* in *Q.I.*, 166/12; *O good God* in *T.H.*, 130/6; *Parde* in *Q.I.*, 162/36; and *anon(e)* in *T.H.*, 64/11, 131/16, and in *Q.I.*, 156/20, 174/20, 178/21. Other such words and phrases added include *O poete, O lady, lette se nough, I wote wele, bewar also, And loke thou, Remembir that, But her, reason wolde that, me semith (that), I suppose, me thinkith, Yes certeyn, certeynly, alas, Lo, O,* and so forth.

These tendencies are only a few among many similar characteristics of style and translation which show that the same writer translated both *The Treatise of Hope* and *The Quadrilogue Invective* in RNSJ.[2]

E. *The Language of the R Manuscripts*

The spelling of the R manuscripts is for the most part fairly consistent within each, and is broadly that of large numbers of late Middle English texts. Deviations are generally isolated, and some are probably simply errors, perhaps sometimes caused by palaeographic problems. For instance, 'said' is normally *saide/*

---

[1] Cf. *T.H.*, 131/3: *the woll aske a question*, also not in the French.
[2] The Glossary reveals many vocabulary similarities between the two translations in RNSJ: see *shewe*, for example, and compare its use as a utility word in the R translations with its much less frequent use in U. Note also various forms of *grugge* (even the word *engruggement* unrecorded elsewhere).

sayde, seide/seyde, but *side* RSJ 146/8 (*saide* N), *syde, side* N 150/
17, 164/19 (*seide* RSJ); and 'rain' is *ryne* N 180/24.

Occasional spellings, especially those that affect the meaning,
might be noted.

Before *mb, nd, ng* ME *a* is written as both *a* and *o* in all manuscripts, as in *lambe, lombes, stande, stonde,* but the normal *stronge,
strongly* becomes *strangly* S, *strangely* J, corrupted to *straungely* R,
straungly N at 11/31.[1]

'Together' is usually *togedir* (the *e* normal in East Midland),
but *toguyder* N 120/29, and this form is shown to have occurred in
the copy text also at 120/26 and 120/31, where N has *to guyde*
and *the guyder*.

ME *i* is occasionally written *e* in all manuscripts, sometimes
affecting the meaning: *wedowis* RNSJ 168/33, RNJ 63/30; *leve*
('live') RJ 188/11, *leved* S 178/22; *smetyn* R 50/30; *whedir* ('whither')
R 202/22; *wretyn* RJ 57/20, RS 33/20, 160/14; *begennyth* J 18/10;
reght J 116/20; *forweldyd* (from 'wild') J 168/32; *heder, thedyr* N
154/2, etc. So also in French words: *preuy* RNS 44/25; *prevelage*
RJ 54/23; *mesery* SJ 168/9; *affleccions* SJ, corrupted to *affeccions*
N 182/11; *accomplesseth* N 85/12; *accompleschyd* J 150/28; *destenyes*
R 30/35; *depreveth* S 45/2; *seruece* J 10/29; *contenuynge* NS 222/29;
inequytees (for 'iniquities') J 200/7; *Dealetyque* N 23/15.

OE *u* is usually written *v* initially, and *u, o, ou* medially, but
raungis (*rungys* S) appears in R at 24/13.

ME *c* (*k*) is occasionally written *g*: *degre* (OF *decré, decret*)
RNSJ 24/5; *Aristogracye* RNJ 55/26, 56/8; *regoinessaunce* R
(*reconnessaunce* J) 123/1; *drongen* C 35/9. Similarly, *g* is twice
represented by *c*: *chalence* R 29/5; *discrecion* (for 'digression') RNJ
127/3, and once by *k*: *kepynke* J 228/8.[2]

Voiceless *s* (*c*) appears twice as *k*: *sykyng, sekyng* (for 'ceasing')
RJ 93/4, 126/25.

An inorganic *gh* appears in some words, especially R's *perfight,
profight,* where the other manuscripts prefer *perfite, profite*; but
gh also occurs in *slewgh* R (*slow* NJ) 78/26; *sloughe* R 73/3; *sloughth*
R (pr. pl. *slowth* NSJ) 204/36; *tough* R, *towgh(e)* NS (*towe* C) 40/12;
ought N (*owte* RSJ) 90/10, 154/1; *abought* N (*abowte* RJ) 123/31;
faught N (*fawte* R, *faute* SJ) 202/6.

---

[1] Cf. R's *straunge* at 148/21, and U's *straunge places* at 237/18.

[2] *g* for *c* may be a palaeographic problem, however, since at 39/28 RNSC have
grace where the French has 'trace'.

t is sometimes written *d*, and in some words affects meaning: *conuersaund* R 98/4; *condidith* R 40/3; *condideth* N 40/5; *wyked* J (*wiket* RNS) 20/21; *appetyde* J 92/25; *bydyng* SJ (*bityng* RN) 216/30.

The N scribe's tendency to add *h* before an initial vowel might also be noted: *hangyr* ('anger') 11/23; *harme* ('arm') 7/17, 23/29; *hasse* ('ass') 57/12; *heerys* ('ears') 73/25; *hought* ('ought') 172/32; *howe* ('owe') 55/4. The *h* is cancelled in other such words.

Like the spellings, the grammatical forms of the R manuscripts are generally typical of late Middle English texts.

The uninflected genitive singular of a noun occurs only once: *Alysaunder* N 242/4. Uninflected noun plurals occur in the words *yere, folke, vois, richesse, largesse, vnkyndenesse*, but not always. The weak plural ending *-n* is found very seldom in nouns: *peesen* RJ 91/1; *brodern* R, *bredren* J, *brothren* N 99/12; *yghen* RNSJ 5/4; *yen* RN, *yyn* S 234/21.

The inflected adjective ending *-s* occurs occasionally by French influence: *transitories* RNS 34/28, RJ 73/32; *prophetikis* RNJ 84/3; *myscreauntes* RNJ 99/12; *corporellis* RNJ 120/28; *temporalles* RJ 131/15. The demonstrative adjective plural is usually written *thes(e), thees* in all manuscripts, but *theis* NSJ 172/27, N 138/24, 184/8, 186/12; *thise, thyse* RSJ 188/30, SJ 178/33, S 178/21, 186/12; *þais* N 28/8, 108/6, 122/23, 152/27, 178/21, 178/33, 246/22; *this, thys* RNS 12/1, RSJ 184/11, R 186/12.

For the second person singular pronoun NJ often and S less frequently use *thu*, but R always has *thou, þou, thow*. N once has *thaw* 70/6. Although *ye* is preferred, *you* sometimes occurs in all the manuscripts for the second person plural subjective pronoun. The usual feminine third person singular pronoun is *she* in R, *sche* in NSJ, but SJ once have *scho* 158/24. *it* is the usual neuter third person singular, but *hit, hyt* sometimes occur. *Is* once appears at 68/13 as the masculine third person singular genitive, but here perhaps the scribe misunderstood the possessive ending of *God* as the pronoun. The usual form of the third person plural subjective pronoun is *thei, they*, but all the manuscripts occasionally have *the*, and NSJ sometimes have *thai, thay*. In the genitive and objective cases, R prefers *their, them*, but sometimes has *thair, thaim*, which are found much more frequently in NSJ. NSJC often use *her, hem*, and J once has *ham* 53/30. *hym, him* occur twenty-six times in the manuscripts as variants of *hem*, perhaps indicating a late occurrence of this form, rather than scribal error.

In the present third singular of verbs, all the manuscripts prefer the *-th* ending, although *-s* occurs sometimes. RN in some places have only *-t*, and N sometimes omits an ending entirely. N also has *hafe* (*haþ* R) 130/14 and *lyftyfe* 68/2. Present plural verbs are usually written without inflection, but both *-n* and *-th* endings occur frequently, especially in NSJ. *-s* also occurs as the ending three times: *hase* N 9/5; *makes* NS 35/26; *folowes* N 12/4. *a* as the auxiliary 'have' occurs only seven times, always in N. *mowe* as the plural auxiliary 'may' occurs twice in NSJ (5/27, 13/18) and once in J alone (59/12). It is interesting that this form occurs much more frequently in *A Famylyer Dialoge*, a translation of a Latin work by Chartier which appears only in NSJ. In the past plural the *-en* ending occasionally appears in R and a little more often in NSJ.

In the verb 'to be', all the manuscripts prefer *be* or *ben* in the present plural, but NSJ have *ben* much more frequently than R. *ar(e)* and *arn* occur occasionally, *arn* more frequently in R; and *is* also is used occasionally, especially in NJ. *beth* (*bith*, *byth*) occurs once as the present plural in NSJ 5/25. Both *war(re)* and *wer(e)* occur as the normal past plural indicative and as the past subjunctive in all the manuscripts, with R having *war(re)* much more frequently than NSJ. *weren* appears once in all the manuscripts as the past plural at 33/23, and *waere* occurs once as the past singular subjunctive in J at 14/7. *was* as the past plural indicative is used occasionally in NSJ. *wast* occurs once in SJ as the past second singular indicative at 9/27.

The manuscripts have a slightly northern flavour, with northern and Scottish words, meanings, spellings and verb forms scattered through them:

1. Words

    penetrife N (*penetratif* RJ) 125/34
    satify RJ (*satisfy* N) 125/10, 126/31
    trastyng J (*trustyng* RN) 86/7
    trestith J (*trustith* RN) 68/24

2. Meanings

    aftir whatkyns, suche whatkyns (wherever) RNJ 120/25, 121/7
    retourne into (change into something else) RNSJ 105/18, 115/29

3. Spellings

approwith (approves) RN 170/9
cowarte, cowert (covert) R 202/29, 206/25
dowe (dove) R 91/1, 91/3
gyffe (if) NSJ 240/29
lawe (low) R 121/8
lowynge (loving) J 10/19
mayte (pp. from OF *mater*) RNSJ 148/29
mowe (move) J 172/24
purweyed (purveyed) R 95/22
þais (these) N frequently—see Glossary
warke, warkes (work, works) R 104/15; J 5/28, 19/10, 202/26, etc.
wesche (wash) SJ 198/13
weschynge J 24/5

4. Verb forms

bracke (pa. t. pl. of ME *breken*) R 106/1
kepit (pp. of ME *kepen*) J 194/30
ȝalde (pa. t. sing. or pp. of ME *yelden*) NS 27/21

The vocabulary of the R translations is of great interest. A tabular analysis seemed the clearest way to present as concisely as possible the most significant elements in the vocabulary.[1]

1. Words and phrases not recorded in *MED* (A–M) and *OED*

(*a*) Borrowings of French words: *esperable* 67/33; *regnault* 111/16; *suppositif* 21/22; *vendengith* 85/17

(*b*) Words created by addition of prefix or suffix: *disseurte* 242/31; *engruggement* 43/10; *forwildid* 168/32; *iniquityf* 172/27; *tyteleris* 196/30; *vnmeryte* 112/30; *wele-countenaun-cid* 20/24

(*c*) Words made from another part of speech: *disknowlegyng* (vbl. n. from v.) 196/17; *enbrowdour* (n. from v.) 144/21; *humanite* (adj. from n.) 112/33; *mysknowlechinge* (vbl. n. from v.) 37/3

[1] Most material in this analysis is based on the records in *MED* (A–M) and *OED*. Occasionally, however, I have found unrecorded examples of usage similar to that in the R translations. See Explanatory Notes and Glossary for further comments on some of the words and phrases listed here.

(*d*) Word formed by combination of two related words: *compacite* ('capacity' and 'compass') 210/22

(*e*) Phrases: *grette chepe* (as quasi-adv.) 190/13; *for no displesaunce* 236/17–18; *dryed vp in þe brest* 174/1; *at longe goyng* 106/34; *vnto his necke* 62/24; *were the occasion of* 105/8; *what (which) party that euir* 14/18, 114/9; *put in preefe of* 30/30; *by long processe* 174/31; *in shorte processe* 146/28; *sette at the poynte* 204/23; *now on this syde, now on that syde* 64/29; *thrown vndir* 86/4–5; *thrown at large* 222/3; *vndir title of* 51/9

2. Rare words and phrases

(*a*) Borrowings of French words: *comunycant* (adj.) 71/26; *confiaunce* 67/29, 198/31; *frustratyve* 85/26, 89/5; *langustes* 13/22; *prodiciouse* 74/26; *vsurpacions* 56/7

(*b*) Words not borrowed from French: *doctrinable* 33/6; *enlonge* 103/25; *ouirpride* 31/17, 41/33; *tyrauntly* 162/5

(*c*) Words made from another part of speech: *excellentes* (n. pl. from adj.) 64/3; *ouirmoche* (n. from adj.) 220/26

3. Words and phrases used in unrecorded meanings

(*a*) Borrowings of meanings of French words: *commyxtions* (parts, substances mixed) 71/28; *distraccion* (misappropriation) 132/26; *hoste* (vassal) 188/32; *iniquitees* (sinners) 42/26 (cf. *repreues* under 4)

(*b*) Words in meanings not borrowed from French: *abandoneth* (discards) 85/17; *clennesse* (clean uses) 30/12; *coment* (commentator) 58/17; *comynges* (coming events) 13/14; *compassion* (passion) 79/14; *dispose* (refl., expose) 150/25; *fleing* (fickle) 160/9; *poynte* (kind) 85/25; *retournable* (reciprocal, mutual) 10/11; *roylith* (totters, reels) 142/11; *seducyous* (tending to lead astray) 19/3; *towaile* (shroud) 7/17; *traversable* (moving back and forth, complicated) 119/7; *vanischid* (in a swoon) 5/9

(*c*) Special uses of various parts of speech: *Assimylatyve* (adj. used as n.) 21/23; *Formatyve* (adj. used as n.) 21/23; *Vnitive* (adj. used as n.) 21/23;[1] *dowbte* (refl., conjecture, suspect)

[1] See Explanatory Notes.

220/22; *egrith* (abs., sours) 95/26; *enforceth, enforced* (refl., strengthens oneself, grows stronger) 16/16, 102/14; *enhaunce* (abs., elevate spiritually) 115/1; *mystoke* (refl., wrongly viewed themselves as) 77/8; *obserued* (ppl. adj., ? observant) 228/5

(*d*) Phrases: *berith witnesse* (is evident) 61/19; *bete down* (? build, in sense of write) 95/27; *close from you* (exclude you) 50/11–12; *come in* (grasp by) 103/16 (*MED* 'by'); *for (to) thoccasion of* (on account of) 37/27, 39/1 (*OED* 'by'); *parteable to* (able to partake of) 68/22 (*OED* 'in', 'of'); *aftir the reason of* (because of) 100/17; (according to) 220/22 (*OED* 'by'); *gaue receipt to* (received, harboured—especially criminals) 102/6; *reste at*, ~ *in*, ~ *vpon* (stop over, fix the attention on) 62/13, 65/33, 107/8; *stryve with* (stick obstinately to) 80/33; *tary vpon* (put trust or confidence in) 100/1–2

4. Words and phrases used in rare meanings: *apparence* (sign to sight or understanding) 70/27; *compacte* (are suitable or applicable) 117/26; *discomfiture* (physical injury) 18/25; *endeinith* (with n. cl. as obj., desire) 222/18 (*MED* with inf.; *OED* only in refl.); *patron* (likeness) 26/2; *repreues* (reprobates) 61/20; *residwacions* (relapses, error for 'recidivations') 208/24; *restore* (repair, amend) 110/18; *suffre* (admit of) 127/11; *vaylid* (lowered) 154/3

5. Words and phrases used in transferred, figurative or somewhat different meanings from those recorded

(*a*) Transferred: *busshement* (things concealed) 85/6 (*MED*, *OED* examples refer only to ambushment of troops); *flesshely* (given up to carnal lusts—referring to people) 94/33; *penetratif* (piercing) 125/34 (*OED* examples refer only to the senses until 1819)

(*b*) Figurative: *entermedlid* (mixed up, confused) 204/31, 208/25; *miscownted* (refl., made a wrong calculation) 116/1; *sideling* (situated to the side of, hence not directly concerned with) 127/2

(*c*) Other somewhat different meanings: *cheef* (masterpiece, important thing) 27/19; *clere* (free from any trouble) 188/35 (*MED* only in phr. 'quit and ~'); *faade* (that has lost the sense of taste) 6/8; *norisshith* (intr., is encouraged and strengthened) 105/9; *retourne* (tr., reverse) 119/14; *shewith, shewed* (foretells) 61/1, 73/21, 85/10; *troublouse* (unclear) 84/31; *voyde* (unfilled—with sustenance) 99/1

6. Words and phrases presenting clear-cut instances of meanings questioned and recorded as rare: *clene armyd* (fully armed) 224/31; *diffence* (offence) 34/6, 35/6; *embrace* (grasp with the mind) 30/36 (*MED* questioned; *OED* 1831); *emprise* (spoil, prize) 124/28; *inpaciente* (intolerable, not to be borne) 18/13; *party* (plight, condition) 111/23, 204/4; (matter) 123/25, 184/1

7. Words or meanings not recorded in *MED* and first recorded in *OED* after 1560 (i.e. approximately 100 years after these treatises were written)[1]

adhesion 1624
alerion 1605
apparence 1587
appostomed 1626
argument 1570
as (to introduce contracted question) 1579
atcheue 1607
attribucions 1596
bodeneth 1566
bostingis 1600
botoume 1577
clere 1635
condicioned 1619
constreyned 1588
consumpcion 1677
content (n.) 1579
countenauncid (wele-∼) 1594
disconfidence 1621
disknowlegyng (as v.) 1576
doctrinable 1581
enbracementis 1630
enrichid 1601
faade 1715
feere (n.) 1601

florishyng youthe 1562
forge 1601
foundid (evell ∼) 1605
frustratyve 1730
hardnesse 1579
indignite 1584, 1589
introduccion 1603
invariable 1607
invariablely 1646
invariablenesse 1654
mysknowlage (n.) 1579
mystoke 1589
moderacions 1598
norissh 1560
Oligracie 1577
opyn (adj.) 1597
ouirlargely 1576
perfeccion 1594
peryode 1613
peruertible 1611
piete 1579
pite 1579
possessid 1595
premission 1609
presentes (n.) 1578

---

[1] The words starred occur also in U. Consult the Glossary and Explanatory Notes for more information about the uses and meanings of some of the words listed here.

preuaricacion 1615

prodiciouse 1635

prophetikis (adj.) 1604

pursute 1650

rebateth 1570

rebukyng (adj.) 1611

receueable 1581

reconsilenge (adj.) 1594

relatif 1704

releef 1691

restith 1577

restore 1567

satify 1596

semblaunce 1599

serymonyously 1596

*softe 1593

sophistyk 1591

*sparyngis 1628

sprynges c. 1616

stablischid 1591

subaltare 1581

subdewed 1605

substantyve 1561

superexcellence 1652

supposid 1582

swollowe (n.) 1607

Thymotracye 1586

tonnefullis 1562

trinall 1590

tvnnith 1589

vnkempte 1742

vnkyndly OED 1590, but also in
    Malory

vnreyned 1609

vsurpacions 1654

vaylid 1591

vertuously 1588

violent 1560, 1593

volucion 1610

*waste (n.) 1560

webbe 1576

III. THE U TRANSLATION: *THE QUADRILOGUE INVECTIVE*

A. *The Manuscript*: Oxford, Bodleian Library, University College MS. 85 (U)

1. *Description*

Vellum, 90 leaves paginated on the rectos and p. 180, bound in quires of eight, $13\frac{3}{4} \times 9\frac{3}{4}$ in. (350×247 mm.), 28 lines to a full page, lined in red with titles and names of speakers in red

Contents: *The Quadrilogue Invective*, ff. 1–35
    The Secret of Secrets, ff. 35^{v}–68
    These *.iij. consideracions beth right necessarye to the good gouernaunce of a prince*, ff. 68^{v}–90

U is written in a legible and regular hand, certainly later than 1450 and probably as late as 1475; it appears to have been written somewhat earlier than R.[1]

Preceding the treatise on f. 1 (see Frontispiece) is an interesting miniature illustrating the characters of *The Quadrilogue Invective*. The lady symbolic of France (called only *The Land* in U) is shown

[1] Dr. R. W. Hunt confirmed this dating.

much as she is described in the work. Her mantle, with its repre-
sentation of the three estates, is especially interesting. Her three
sons—the Knight, leaning on his axe; the Clergy, carrying a
scroll; and the People, holding a shovel—are pictured around her.
In the background of the miniature is the motto *Oublier ne doy*,
the same motto that is in the coat of arms which appears at the top
and bottom of f. 1, and again on f. 35ᵛ at the beginning of *The
Secret of Secrets*. The motto occurs twice also in the decorated
edges of f. 1. The coat of arms is a man's arms embowed, clothed,
azure, supporting between the hands a wheatsheaf, proper, above
a green mound. Besides this miniature and one preceding *The
Secret of Secrets*, there are also frequent illuminated capitals in U.

The scribe has written the direction *Nota bene* in the margins
beside passages at 163/33–165/1 and 173/2, and *Nota bene proces-
sum* as an interruption in the text itself at 159/28. In addition, the
scribe has added various flourishes as extensions of letters in the
upper margins: on f. 9ᵛ, for example, between upward lines ex-
tending from a *k* appear the words *viue la belle*; and on f. 14ᵛ and
f. 33, between the same type of extended lines occur the syllables
Pre, nes, en, gre in that order from bottom to top.

2. *Owners*

The history of U remains sketchy. The manuscript must have
been copied for the unidentified family whose coat of arms has
been described above. The very similar device of the Wheatley
family of Echingfield, Sussex (two arms embowed, clothed, azure
cuffs, holding between the hands, proper, a wheatsheaf) lacks,
however, the green mound at the bottom of the U coat.[1] The added
mound perhaps suggests one of two possibilities: (1) the device
was adopted with this change by a branch of the Wheatley family,
perhaps a married daughter; or (2) the mound might suggest use
of the coat by the Wheathills, although it is not recorded under the
Wheathill families in the heraldry lists.

Only in the mid-sixteenth century can we definitely establish
an owner for U. Then it was in the possession of Michael Otthew,
whose French and Latin verses appear on f. 90ᵛ. Otthew describes
himself there as 'Maximiliani secundi, Caesaris semper Augusti,
Medicus et Chirurgus ordinarius, Artium et physice Medicine

---

[1] Dr. W. O. Hassall pointed out the Wheatley coat of arms to me.

Doctor'. On f. 1ᵛ his French verses dedicate the manuscript 'A la tresillustre Dame, Madame Anna duchesse de Somerset', the wife of the Lord Protector of England. This dedication is dated 4 April 1565. The date 'M.D.LXV. Martij Vltima' appears with the verses on f. 90ᵛ. Hence, we may be certain that U belonged to Michael Otthew in 1565, when he probably presented it to the Duchess of Somerset, whose 'treshumble et obeisant seruiteur' he styled himself. But there are no other indications in U of either ownership or authorship.

3. *Analysis of Scribal Error and Correction in U*

The scribal errors in U are not so interesting as those in R. The errors reveal very little about the manuscript from which U was copied, except perhaps for a few palaeographic difficulties in the copy text. Most of the errors in U are those observed in most manuscripts and may be dealt with summarily.

The only important example of dittography in U occurs at 211/ 8, where *for to doo redily actuell deedys* is added in error after *obeissaunce* because of its appearance after *obeisaunce* in line 11. The double occurrence of *where is now* at 139/16 is interesting: the scribe has remembered a final *w* to indicate his place in copying, but has picked up an initial *w* instead. The process is reversed in *yit yit they* at 191/10, where he has remembered an initial *t* and picked up his place at a final *t* in error. The other examples of dittography occur at the end of one line and the beginning of the next or because of similar beginnings or endings of words.

Superfluous words or letters sometimes appear in U. Because of the scribe's addition of a superfluous letter, peculiar spellings occur: *borldenesse* 179/11; *constented* 187/4; and *retrayned* 227/19. This type of error does not occur in R.

Readings in U, when compared with the French, point to six possible omissions of more than one word because of *sauts du même au même*.[1] Omissions of single words (always monosyllables) are also frequent in U. In one place, 149/36, where a blank space occurs after *and*, the scribe seems to have omitted a word because he could not read his copy.

The confusion of two graphically similar words accounts for the most interesting class of scribal errors in U. The scribe tends to

---

[1] See Explanatory Notes for 139/26, 161/6, 171/27, 191/2, 201/33, and 243/ 32.

confuse the same two words more than once in his copying. For example, at both 165/13 and 219/4, he has written *desire* for *deserue*; and at both 189/28 and 215/21, he has written *redouteth* for *redondeth*. More interesting from the point of view of the palaeographic peculiarities of U's exemplar, the scribe has confused *reames* with the correct *reuenues* at both 189/8 and 219/26. At 187/16 *deprime* appears for the correct *depriue*, while at 193/23 *depriued* is written for *deprimed*. At 139/8 *seth* occurs for *sed*, and at 199/12 *deeth* for *deed*. *and* appears in error for *of* at 203/25; *as* for *of* at 205/19; and *of* for *and* at 219/10.

The U scribe has also sometimes misinterpreted the context in which a word occurs and accordingly written an incorrect word. For instance, at 185/13, in the series *parill of bod[y]*, *trauaile of thought nor expense of richesse*, he has interpreted *body* as a modifier of *trauaile* and written *bodily*. Errors at 189/22 and 231/20 might almost be aural errors. But it is more likely that at 189/22 *outrageous be doon* is corrupt either because of omission of a word after *outrageous*, or, in the light of the French, because of the scribe's confusion of the adjective with the noun *outrages*. At 231/20, the infinitive *to can* is written *two can*.

Graphic similarity seems to have been responsible for the substitution of *bright* for *birth* at 143/23; *smert* for *suerte* at 157/31; *wordes* for *woodes* at 159/1; *callith* for *coolith* at 163/32; *touchynge* for *techynge* at 235/29; and *werres* for *weyes* at 243/21. Graphic similarity may account also for the reading *I seid* for *of Ysaie* at 141/20. At 163/25, however, *to defende* has been written for *to defoule* because *to defende* appears in line 24.

The scribe, or possibly some would-be corrector of U, has made some unnecessary changes: at 153/11 and 161/32, the *o* in *most* has been altered to *v*, despite the fact that the verb form *most* occurs frequently elsewhere in U; and at 159/12 *han*, a form which also appears elsewhere in U, has been altered to *haue*.

Correction in U, however, is much less extensive than in R. Only five cases of certain correction by someone other than the scribe himself, all in the same hand, are found. One is the addition of the speaker's name *The Knight* at 241/17.[1] The method used shows clearly that the other four corrections are the work of only

---

[1] The name of the speaker was probably omitted in U not through scribal error but because of its omission in U's French exemplar. See Explanatory Note to this line.

one corrector. At 149/1 in the scribe's *repararacion, racion* is cancelled and *cion* placed in the margin. In the same way *the* is corrected to *to* at 151/24, *tkink* to *thinke* at 173/22, and *diease* to *disease* at 175/9.

B. *The Language of the U Translation*

U is even more regular and consistent in both spelling and grammar than are RNSJ. At 169/16, *laid*, past participle of OE *lǣdan*, may be a late spelling arising from monophthongization of the diphthong *ai* to slack *e*.[1] An inorganic *s* is introduced in *catell* producing *castell* 169/31, 185/27, 187/18, 191/10, and *castelles* 181/23.

The weak plural noun ending is used only in *brethren* 217/6 and *yien* 141/21, etc. The inflected adjective ending occurs occasionally by French influence: *delicatiues* 157/6; *femynyns* 159/10; *femenyns* 149/29; *particulers* 211/24. The third singular masculine genitive pronoun is usually *his*, but occasionally *is*: 141/13, 151/21, 173/26. The usual third plural subjective is *they*, occasionally *thay*, and twice *the* 183/22, 207/20. The third plural genitive is usually *their(e)*, *thair(e)*, less often *her(e)*, *hir(e)*. The objective, however, is often *hem*.

In verbs the infinitive has the *-n* ending five times. The present plural usually has no ending, but *-n*, *-en*, *-ith*, *-eth* sometimes appear. Although *haue* is the usual form, *han* appears six times, and *hauen* once at 203/7. The past participle, weak and strong respectively, nearly always ends in *-ed*, *-en*, with only fourteen omissions of an ending: in verbs ending in *t* like *empreent* and *inhabite*, for example, and occasionally in verbs like *establisshe* as at 135/13. The past participle *spared* occurs as a substantive once at 203/20.

In the verb 'to be', U has both *be* and *ben* in the present plural, *ben* somewhat more frequently. *is* occurs occasionally, but nearly always in constructions like *othir ther is* or *there is* with plural complement. *arn* occurs only twice at 155/19 and 155/30. *were* is always used in the past plural indicative and past subjunctive. *ben* is the past participle in all but three places.

U, like RNSJ, has scattered northern and Scottish words and forms. At 165/19, *affrayingly*, related to Sc. *affrayitly* (with alarm) appears; at 243/4, *practiked*; and at 169/6, *soc*. The spelling *lawe*

---

[1] Similarly, U has *rayne, rayneth* at 169/19, probably for ME *renne*.

(low) occurs at 203/2, and *wayn* (vain) at 195/24 and 201/24. *seet* is written as the present plural of 'set' at 165/13.

The most significant elements of the vocabulary of U are tabulated below.[1]

1. Words and phrases not recorded in *MED* (A–M) and *OED*

   (*a*) Borrowings of French words: *deprimed* 165/7, 193/23, 235/7; *entowned* 203/18; *estayinges* 149/4; *indeuiable* 165/1; *opprimed* 213/19; *publiquers* 205/10; *recelled* 187/1

   (*b*) Words created, sometimes by addition of prefix or suffix: *affrayingly* 165/19; *beggernesse* 167/8; *distiped* 241/4; *enlowed* 139/23, 155/26; *ennake* 153/28; *grefauntes* 221/12; *litle feith* 215/10; *vntestable* 205/3

   (*c*) Words made from another part of speech: *excercinge* (vbl. n. from v.) 227/23; *flaielinge* (vbl. n. from v.) 209/10; *spared* (n. from pp.) 203/20

   (*d*) Phrases: *grete cheepe* (as quasi-adv.) 191/13 (also in R); *in questions* 207/31; *that than* 145/10; *at the longe wey* 225/3

2. Rare words and phrases

   (*a*) Borrowings of French words: *diminuacion* 161/2; *disconisaunce* 143/31, 207/10; *naturiens* 137/14; *regle* 143/25, 171/16, 197/6, 223/4; *replike* 241/15, 245/13; *secretaire* 135/8

   (*b*) Words not borrowed from French: *conquestioned* 141/17; *ennoyouse* 169/28; *skaundre* 179/29; *tirauntlye* 163/5 (also in R); *triumphous* 161/24; *worldy* 137/17, 227/7

   (*c*) Word made from another part of speech: *ouermiche* (n. from adj.) 221/23 (also in R)

   (*d*) By-forms blending two words: *agraued* ('aggrieve' and 'aggravate') 177/30; *skonche* ('squench' influenced by 'sconce') 165/10

3. Words and phrases used in unrecorded meanings

   (*a*) Borrowings of meanings of French words: *desercion* (destruction) 149/34; *disconisaunce* (ignorance, lack of knowledge) 143/31, 207/10; *hostes* (vassals) 189/31 (also in

---

[1] See Explanatory Notes and Glossary for further comments.

R); *saluable, soluable* (saving, that protects from anything undesirable) 239/27, 225/3

   (*b*) Words in meanings not borrowed from French: *abandouned* (given away without restraint) 223/4; *beggyng* (causing begging, accompanied with begging) 169/12; *chargeable* (accusing) 205/27; *disknowen* (scorned, unrecognized) 165/21; *dispoose* (tr., refl., expose) 151/31, 193/24 (also in R); *raunsoms* (soldiers' pay) 169/31; *vnthankfully* (disagreeably, uncomfortably) 189/30; *wherfore* (where) 137/32

   (*c*) Special use: *doute* (refl., conjecture, suspect) 221/20 (also in R)

   (*d*) Phrase: *voluntary will* (self-will) 157/1–2, 171/6

4. Words used in rare meanings: *pollisch* (smooth or gloss over) 203/28; *purveye* (make adequate provision) 173/11, 213/20; *refeccion* (repair, restoration) 149/4; *reherce* (intr., give an account) 145/18; *troubled* (intr. for pass., was disturbed or agitated) 141/16

5. Words and phrases used in transferred, figurative, or slightly different meanings from those recorded

   (*a*) Transferred: *delicatiue(s)* (luxurious, indolent) 157/6, 177/18; *quyntyne* (object set up as a mark) 167/1

   (*b*) Figurative: *anoynted* (glutted) 197/16; *destressid* (? exhausted, hence dead) 243/12; *entermedled* (mixed up, confused) 205/31 (also in R); *releeuid* (lifted higher) 207/9

   (*c*) Other somewhat different meanings: *bref* (quick to come) 141/23; *disposicions* (uses) 241/19; *repent* (impers. inf., cause to regret) 235/20; *sparynge* (something saved— recorded only in pl.) 171/20

6. Words or meanings not recorded in *MED* and first recorded in *OED* after 1560 (i.e. approximately 100 years after this treatise was written)[1]

*adhesion 1624	*braunle* 1581
anaged 1593	*capitally* 1619
aruspices 1584	*chefe (in ~)* 1607–12

---

[1] The words starred occur also in R. See further the Glossary and Explanatory Notes.

conquestioned 1656   *peryode 1613
*consumpcion 1677   *pite 1579
cordage 1598   profoundenesse 1642
disknoweth 1605   redondeth vpon 1589
dispoosinge 1638   refeccion 1656
enposteme 1565   reioysinges (in pl.) 1707
*enriched 1601   rome (n.) 1577
enroote 1595   scandalouse 1611
enswe 1581   seruaunt (attrib. n.) 1832
fauted 1608   *softe 1593
forced 1576   somme (in a ~) 1562
ignore 1611, 1801   *sparynge 1628
iniuried (one ex. MED) 1592   surmountable 1611
miche (so ~) 1560   vnroted 1570
*open (adj.) 1597   *waste (n.) 1560
peeplid (best ~) 1588   weye (in this ~) 1598

IV. COMPARISON OF METHODS OF TRANSLATION OF R AND U

The translator of *The Treatise of Hope* and *The Quadrilogue Invective* in RNSJC and the translator of *The Quadrilogue Invective* in U[1] were unlike in approach, method, and style of translation. Neither accomplished in English what Chartier, whose contribution to the development of French prose is universally recognized, had achieved in French. Neither produced in translation the periodic Senecan style of the original.[2] U, not perhaps because of any conscious attempt, but because of a more literal bent and a more exact knowledge of French, reproduced more nearly a prose style like that of Chartier; in his literal renderings, however, he frequently did violence to English idiom and sometimes, because of only a momentary slip from the original's rigid pattern in a sentence, created great awkwardness. R, on the other hand, seems to have been interested in turning Chartier's works into an English prose that is straightforward, clear, and vivid, inso-

---

[1] Here for the sake of convenience, R and U will refer to either the respective translators or their translations, not to the manuscripts.

[2] An adequate study of Chartier's prose style would be helpful as a point of departure for a study of the translators' methods. Unfortunately, however, the older studies of Chartier's style are based on Duchesne's edition of his works, many of which are not by Chartier. Hence, these studies are not completely trustworthy. See H. Eder, *Syntaktische Studien zu Alain-Chartiers Prosa* (Würzburg, 1889), and E. Höpfner, *Die Wortstellung bei Alain Chartier und Gerson* (Grimma, 1883).

far as his somewhat less adequate command of French would allow.

A knowledge of the purposes with which these fifteenth-century translators set out would be invaluable, but all that may be said must be based on the manner of translation itself. There are no prologues or epilogues, like Caxton's, about the aims of Chartier's translators. Fortunately, however, one interesting observation about these aims may be made. Despite U's general faithfulness to the French text, he omitted almost every reference to France, the French situation, and the French people, where Chartier commented directly about the people and conditions of his country. The character of France is called only *The Land* in U. At 155/22–3, where Chartier wrote, 'Qu'est devenue la constance et loyauté du peuple françois', U has *Where is bycome the constaunt trouth of the peeple*. Again at 171/9–10, the French 'la nostre police françoise' was rendered *the polecye of this land*. Later in the same paragraph at line 16, where Chartier apostrophized, 'Haa, hommes françois', U has *Ellas men out of regle*. At 191/30, a specific reference to the Battle of Agincourt has become the general *vnhappy bataill*.[1] R, in contrast, retained all these references to France, and indeed at 140/8 made the indefinite 'ceste seigneurie' the more specific *lordship and howse of Fraunce*.

It is possible to conjecture then that U turned Chartier's work into English during the Wars of the Roses, when many of the conditions prevalent in France earlier in the century existed in England; Chartier's observations and criticisms about his own country could thus be cogently applied to the state of affairs in England. If this is true, U was not quite as thorough as he might have been in making the work applicable to the English situation: England remains the *auncien aduersarie* at 141/7, and *floure-de-lyses* at 145/22 are left as a main part of the decoration on the mantle of the figure of the land. Perhaps the writer meant to revise further at a later time.

Similar use of parts of both of Chartier's prose works in *The Complaynt of Scotlande* in 1549 shows that it is not unlikely that U translated with the purpose of edifying the English. The Scottish writer of *The Complaynt*, in translating passages from Chartier's *Quadrilogue* and *L'Esperance*, changed specific references to

[1] For similar changes, see the Explanatory Notes at 135/7, 145/24, 157/4, 173/9, 179/30, 185/5–6, 195/5.

France to references to Scotland. For instance, after translating, with only a few minor omissions, an early passage from *Le Quadrilogue* on the mutations of realms (corresponding to 134/10–140/5 and 135/13–141/5 in the English translations), he replaced Chartier's mention of 1422 and the French calamities of that year with his own account of 'the grite afflictione quhilk occurrit on oure realme in september m.v.xlvii. 3eris on the feildis besyde mussilburgh'. Later the Lady Scotland and her three children, modelled on the Lady France and her sons, appear to the author in a dream. Some of the matter of their speeches of complaint was translated from *Le Quadrilogue*, but this was woven into *The Complaynt* along with detailed accounts of Scottish problems and grievances against England.[1] Hence, the writer of *The Complaynt of Scotlande* did freely what U in *The Quadrilogue* intended but accomplished less comprehensively. R, on the other hand, had no such definite purpose, although the interest of Chartier's works for him was doubtless similar since his translations also were probably made during the Wars of the Roses.

Although U frequently mistranslated passages, his command of French on the whole was better than R's. Only occasionally did U completely misunderstand a French passage and substitute his own interpretation: at 209/14–15, where the French reads,

Entreprengne [En gre prengne ABH, like U's exemplar] Cellui qui en a le povoir [de *add.* BH] l'adversité que nous souffrons et plus en gré que nous ne la recevons ou congnoissons,

U has,

He that hath the power to take this aduersitee in gree that we suffre he is happy.[2]

Likewise at 227/5, U rendered the French 'ou ilz tenoient leurs grans conviz' as *wherynne they kept thaire counsaile*.

Although there are a few other similar mistranslations in U, many more occur in R. R's tendency to substitute his own sense when he did not understand the French might be illustrated from almost every page of both translations. A typical example is his rendering of a French passage which reads:

---

[1] See M. S. and G. H. Blayney, 'Alain Chartier and *The Complaynt of Scotlande*', *RES*, N.S. ix (1958), 8–17.

[2] R also has a mistranslation of this difficult French passage. See Explanatory Note to 208/13–14.

et consentirent leur plus chier et naturel adournement estre converti
en rude mistere et traitié par les dures mains d'ouvriers mecaniques ce
que depuis l'eure de leur naissance avoient espargné sur leurs chiefs et
de leurs mains soigneusement cultivé.

R at 186/5–8 has:

and co[n]sentid also to yeve away their best kerchewis and their best
array and take themself to boistous garmentis and labored with their
hondis as thei had be powr people for the comon profyght of their cite.

Again, at 222/17–19, for the French 'monstre par sa privee affection que son couraige est indigne de service publique', R has,
*shewith that his prive affeccion and his corage endeinith nat that the
comon wele shuld prospere.* Even the changed NSJ readings do not
follow the French (see critical apparatus). Another mistranslation
in R occurs at 224/4–6, where the French

Car le proufit et la proye mainent les affections legieres et variables des
convoiteux a soy mettre en aventure

becomes in the English:

For the prosperite of the goodis that thei gette makith their affeccions
light and variable insomoche thei dar nat put themself in aventure of
the warre.

These mistranslations from *The Quadrilogue Invective* in R
might be strengthened by many similar examples from *The
Treatise of Hope*. For instance, at 14/21–6, Chartier's image is
lost because of mistranslation and omission. The French reads:

Ou il fault toutes les euures du temps present renuerser au contraire: ou
qu'elles vous mainent briefuement à ce que vous auez, à tel meschief
fouy, puisque ie voy que en souffrant nonchalamment regner la tirannie
de vos ennemis, vous cheez par vne recruë souffrance en leur seruitute,
comme les perdris qui en fuiant à despourueuë negligence le perdriour
que les cheuale, cheent en sa tonnelle.

The English has:

Wherin must be reuercid all the werkis of this present tyme to þe
contrarye, which hath brought you shortly to the myschief that causith
you to flee, wherethrough ye fall as a man that sette not by hymself or
recrayed in the seruage of your enemyes like as þe partriche which in
fleing from the horse necligently fallith into the tonelle.

E

Chartier's meaning in the phrase 'premier leur necessité que leur perfection' has also been completely perverted in R's *furst what was most necessary to their perfeccion* at 127/8–9.

Although U was frequently awkward in his rendering of the French, he was seldom awkward because he did not understand the grammar of the original. When a grammatical confusion does occur in U (as at 221/29, where 'des' is translated *of the* instead of 'some' in its second occurrence in the sentence), it has probably occurred not because of the translator's misunderstanding, but because of his carelessness. In R, on the contrary, it is not unusual to find grammatical oversights such as the translation of 'que' as *which* in contexts that demand 'that', e.g., at 34/30, 166/4, 180/13, and 202/29. Verb forms also have sometimes not been understood by R. An extremely awkward sentence at 29/18–27, has resulted from R's mistaking of the imperative 'Ferme' for the past participle and of the present third singular verb 'a' for the preposition 'à'. Likewise, at 77/10, the awkward verb phrase *can bryng of thoes discordis* on the end of an already complete sentence represents a complete misunderstanding of the imperative 'Infere de ce discours', which begins a new sentence in the French. At 142/28, translation of the infinitive phrase 'a mettre' as *hath putt* has caused a change in Chartier's meaning. Again, a verb is lacking in the subordinate clause at 115/5–8, because the translator rendered the verb 'faulz' as the adjective *false* so that the sentence reads:

Thanne if thou by thi disceiveable ignoraunce or by thi false, frowarde affeccion to do thi askyng, His invariable rightwisenesse and His infallible science shall not faile to do His disposicion.

Similarly at 101/18, the French noun 'conseil' mistranslated as the verb *counseilith* has caused the reference to *thre thynges* (science, experience, counsel) in the next sentence to be meaningless. Both R and U occasionally mishandled French idiomatic expressions: at 174/1 and 175/1, for example, R's *am dryed vp in þe brest* and U's literal *drye standing* are attempts to render the idiom 'seiche sur le pié' (wilt, pine away).

One more comparison illustrates U's better command of the French. R, many more times than U, confused two French words which look alike or used an English word which looks as if it is associated with the French word (sometimes even as its opposite), but which has a different meaning. U has only a few such confusions:

	French	U
135/7, 147/9	industrie	instruccion
137/8	instrument	instruccion[1]
135/24	crainte	constrainte
141/15	discours	discordes
149/32	musardie	musinge
171/4	impetuosité	impediment.

R has many more such confusions, as shown in the following selected list taken from both *The Quadrilogue Invective* and *The Treatise of Hope*:

	French	R
4/28	blesme	blemeshid
7/18	cheuestre	here
14/25	cheuale ('chase')	horse
20/15	esuanoy	noyed
30/1	habitudes	habitacions
37/17	desroguer	shulde be as a rygoure
46/6	commis	comowon
124/11	commis	comon
74/31–2	soulagemens	only alightyngys
77/10	discours	discordis (cf. U)
77/19, 77/24	mort	liffe
82/30	mourir	to lyve
78/27	oraison	Reason
81/20	filé	mayde
89/28	zizanie	cenefye
90/8	robustes (adj.)	a people callid Robusces
94/32	boucqs	Bacus
116/2	trespassant	myghty man
123/30	druëment	dewly
124/17	prieres	stones
134/29	loiale DAH, louable B	lawfull
142/25	naissance	norischyng
178/5	naissance	natur
146/21	paleteaux	hepis
166/14	transiz	evyn as I go on the erthe
210/6	maine	maynteynith
222/3	cures	hertis.

[1] Some of these errors, especially when the scribe may have misread the same word more than once, as here, may be scribal in the English manuscript or in the French manuscripts from which the translations were made. Sometimes such confusions can definitely be shown to have occurred in the translators' French exemplars. These have not been listed here, but have been noted in the Explanatory Notes.

Since poetry occurs only in *The Treatise of Hope*, thus only in R, the two translators cannot be compared in their rendering of it. It should be noted, however, that R usually was especially inadequate in conveying Chartier's poetic meaning and construction in English prose. He omitted many lines, although never an entire section of poetry. These omissions probably often occur because of difficulty of understanding, but sometimes perhaps as a commendable means of reducing Chartier's poetic redundancy of expression and idea into concise prose.

U was not only linguistically more capable as a translator, but also more literally minded than R. For the modern reader, the R translations gain because of the freedom of translation, but the judgement of a fifteenth-century reader might have been different. Certainly a style of the kind achieved by R in his better moments of understanding and vigour belongs more in the tradition of what is regarded as good modern English prose than does the usual style of U, so frequently intent upon reproducing the original word for word, construction for construction.

The general freedom of rendering in R may be noticed best perhaps in the passages where historical illustrations are translated. R and U may be compared, for instance, in their handling at 216/23–35 and 217/17–26 of this French passage about Scipio Africanus:

il, qui le peril commun de lui et des autres cognoissoit, le vouloir aussi du Senat qui se vouloit departir, vainqui les doubtes de son cuer par l'affection publique, si tira son espee emmy le conseil et jura haultement que qui parleroit plus de habandonner la cité sentiroit au trenchant de son espee que doit estre le guerredon de ceulx qui la chose publique delaissent pour leur singulier salut. Et en tele voulenté fut suivy par ceulx qui avoient bon vouloir, et depuis demourerent a Rome et se releverent en leur haulte autorité.

R is free here not only in structure, but in expressions like *by his gretre wisedam* (om. Fr.), *the tendir love that he had to the comon wele* ('l'affection publique'), *sodeinly* (om. Fr.), *all the conseylours* ('le conseil'), *with a sterne countenaunce* (om. Fr.), *and abandone it [to] their enemyes* (om. Fr.), *sharpe bityng* ('trenchant'), *and grauntid to do theire powere in the same* (om. Fr.). It is interesting to compare also R's *the comon wele for their singular wele* with U's *the publique well for thair singuler saluacion*, or R's *Thanne all suche as were of goode wille and corage acceptid grettely his wisedam* with U's *And to his volunte folowed all suche as were well-wylled*.

Other passages which show the literalness of U sharply contrasted with the freedom of R are plentiful:

French	R 164/3–4	U 165/3–5
leur eur ne sera pas Fortune leur estre tousjours propice, qui de sa nature est envers tous muable.	Their vre shall nat alweyes be fortun- able in their dedis forasmoch as fortune is alweye variable.	Thaire happe shall nat be fortune all- weyes to be to thaim propice, whiche of hir nature is euer chaunge- able to alle maner of peeple.

French	R 210/19–24	U 211/21–6
L'autre obstacle si est que, quelque grace de bon enten- dement ou discretion de bien jugier que Dieu ait mis en testes et [discrecions ou *add*. B] compre- hencions des jounes hommes, leur capa- cité ne pourroit les regards particuliers et cauteles ingenieuses qui affierent a si hault oeuvre bien conduire ne comprendre.	Anothir obstacle is this, that whatsoeuyr grace God hath sette in the hedis of yong men, othir of good vndirstondyng or of discrecion in iugeyng, yette their compacite may nat welle condyt ne comprehende the particulare considera- cions ne the witty and subtile cawteles that belongith to so high a werke.	The othir obstacle is this, that who that euer hath grace of good vndirstandinge or discrecion well for to iuge that God hath put in the heedys and comprehencions of the yonge men, thaire capacite might neuer the regardes particulers and cau- teles ingeniouse whiche longeth to soo high a werke well to guyde nor to comprehende.

The Explanatory Notes reveal many comparable passages. The U
translation is also frequently more awkward and less idiomatic
in expression than R, as for example:

French	R 224/1–4	U 223/31–225/3
Et ceulx qui le bien de vertu et le salut publique, mesmement aux entreprinses de guerre, ne veulent plus que le gaing n'y feront ja au paraller oeuvre salvable.	And thei that leve the goodnesse of vertu and the welthe publike and woll nat take vpon them the enterpryses of warre for the same, but entende on nothing but to gette goode, may nat be callid the wele-willars of the comon wele.	And they that the well of vertu and the publique saluacion, namelye in thenter- prises of werre, desire nothinge ellys sauf the gettinge of goddes, they shall neuer doo at the longe wey no soluable ne actuell deede.

Sometimes also R eliminated awkward French constructions which U allowed to stand, as in the following passage:

French	R 208/24–9	U 209/23–8
aussi ne povons nous gecter de ceste tribulacion tumultueuse et entremeslee sans souffrir mains doubteux assaulx et mortelx perilz et [que *add*. ABH] la contagieuse infection qui entre nous court ait prins son cours, si que par aprés les choses retournent a leur nature.	likewise we may nat be cast owte of this grette entermedlid tribulacion withowte sufferyng many dowbtefull assawtis and mortall perilles vnto þe tyme that the (contagyous) infeccion which reynith amongist vs haue accomplischid and fulfillid his course and vnto the tyme [þat the thyng hyt]self may retourne to his own nature.	also we may nat bringe us out of this sorowfull tribulacion withoute suffring many doutefull assautes and mortall parilles and that the contagious infeccion that reigneth amonge us haue finallye ended his cours so that aftirwarde all thinge may retourne to thaire naturall kynde.

Although the word order in some of Chartier's sentences confused both translators, and perhaps misled R more often, U was much more inclined to follow the French order despite the awkwardness thus created in his English rendering. Occasionally neither translator grasped the inverted order of a French sentence:

French	R 138/23–6	U 139/21–4
Par ceste maniere, chascune en son tour et en son ordre, si changent, rabbaissent ou subvertissent, les eureuses fortunes et le bruit des royaumes.	And so by thes meanys euery man in his turne and aftir his ordir chaungith, rebateth or subuertith from the happy fortunes and grete brute of realmys.	And by this meene all erthly lordshippes and citees, ichone in thaire cours and ordre, ben chaunged, enlowed and subuertid by the operacions of fortune and the brute of the reaumes.

Although neither reproduced Chartier's inverted structure here, U at least, by the addition of the subject *all erthly lordshippes and citees*, made better sense of the idea. In the following passage again, U, although awkward, came nearer to Chartier's meaning than R, who was misled by the inverted verb-subject structure of the French:

French	R 200/10-11	U 201/10-12
te rendent tes pechiez et l'orreur des cruaultez de ta compaignie indigne . . .	thi companye shewe þi synnes in horrour and cruelte, which be nat wourthi . . .	they yeelde the—thy synne and the horrible crueltes of thy felawship—vnworthy . . .

The inverted order of the long prepositional phrase beginning with 'pour' in the following French sentence may well have confused U; R, on the other hand, managed a straightforward, sensible rendering here:

French	R 226/2-5	U 227/2-5
Sanson le fort, pour les Philistiens ennemis du peuple d'Israël acravanter et confondre, abbati sur soy et sur eulx par sa grant force la maison ou ilz tenoient leurs grans conviz.	Sampson forte also for to distroye the Philistiens, which wer enemyes to the childern of Israel, through his grette myght kest downe the paleys whanne the Philistiens war most in their royalte.	Sampson the mighty, for the Philistiens confounde and destrue thaim, that were enmyes to the peeple of Israel, he brought down [by] his grete might the hous vpon thaim and him bothe wherynne they kept thaire counsaile.

Many additional passages show U's tendency to follow the French word order, in contrast to R's adoption of English order.[1]

These two translators also show distinctly different tendencies in changing French constructions. R habitually expanded French sentence elements into less subordinate constructions. Subordinate clauses were translated as main clauses:

French	R
qui aprés lui se recloy pour le sauvement de la cité	and as soone as he was in the pitte it closid [agayn], through which the cite was savid (224/32-3)
car, comme il lui fut noncié que son filz s'en retournoit villainement d'une bataille et venoit devers lui, il respondy	for it was on a tyme shewed him hough his sone came shamefully from a bataile home towarde his fader. But whanne the fadir vndirstode the meene of his comynge, said these wourdis (238/8-11).

[1] See, for example, 204/12-14, 205/13-14, and 214/29-30, 215/23-4.

Appositives, adjectives, participles, prepositional phrases, and infinitives were made clauses:

French	R
en hommes parfaiz	till thei come vnto the perfect age of man (136/26–7)
fontaine de sapience	which was the veray founteyne of sapience (138/13)
en sommeillant	as I laye thus half sleping (144/7)
reprouchier ses faultes	that he was so repreued of his fawtis (194/17–18)
prennent l'argent des gaiges de leurs souldoiers sans le leur departir, en les faisant vivre sur le peuple	take away the wages of the souldiours and yeve them but litill or nought, which causith them of necessite to live vpon the poore people (222/25–7).[1]

In contrast to this tendency in R toward 'open translation', U, when he did not follow the French construction for construction, seems to have worked in almost the opposite direction; that is, he often translated main clauses or main verbs as subordinate clauses or phrases, and rendered subordinate clauses as phrases:

French	U
et ne comptes a rien	setting at nought (181/13)
et de fait y meurent	and so in deed so to dye (181/24)
qui estrivoient ensemble	strivinge togedir (207/18).

Related to this characteristic process of subordination in U is his common practice of rendering two French nouns in conjunction, or a noun followed by a prepositional phrase, as an adjective-noun construction:

French	U
corruption de leurs meurs	coruptible condicions (157/33)
d'aguet et de sens	awaytinge wysdome (193/8)
droit par la force	forced right (195/20)
appaisement de conscience	peasible conscience (211/1)
les fuitiz et les desolez	the woofull fliers (217/4).

In contrast, this pattern appears only occasionally in R.

---

[1] The same type of expansion of elements is found in *The Treatise of Hope* in R:

French	R
organicques	which stret[c]hen to euery [parte of man] (5/26–7)
impunité de mal faire	inasmuche as thei war not punysshed for their evile dedis (90/12–13)
& à approuchier à celuy	For thei wolde fayne haue ben nygh Him (127/26–7).

In addition to the above differences between the two translators' methods, the works of both have characteristics common in fifteenth-century prose, which are generally considered flaws by a modern reader. One such characteristic is particularly prevalent in R, where certain sentences, which consist of loosely strung together clauses and phrases, have endings which do not structurally remember the beginnings. This sentence from R well exemplifies this defect:

O thou infortunat man, which hast passid the daungerous wayes and the anoyeng watchis, and othir also which haue borne vpon their shuldirs the hevynes of theire exile and travailed in pouerte for the wele publike, which your troughe ought full litill to preyse forasmoche as ye be for the same diffowlit, sette at nought and nough in captyuyte. (11/12-17)

R becomes particularly confusing in the clause *which your troughe ought full litill to preyse*, which in the French reads 'deuez vous pou priser vostre loyauté', as the main clause of the sentence. The highly rhetorical style of Chartier, with his use of the long direct address phrase, seems to have caused the R translator difficulty in the above passage and elsewhere, as at 26/2-11. The following sentence in R also has clauses and phrases aimlessly sprawling together:

French	R 142/4-7
Environ l'aube du jour, lors que la premiere clarté du soleil et nature contente du repos de la nuit nous rappellent aux mondains labours, n'a gaires me trouvay soudainement esveillié . . .	Aboute the sprynge of the day whanne the sune shewyth his furst light and nature content through kyndly rest of the nyght, which callith vs vp to wordly labour, and nat long aftir I fonde myself sodanly awaked.

Other examples occur at 156/21-6, 216/15-22, and elsewhere.

U much less frequently constructed these loose sentences which do not follow the pattern of the French. Only occasionally do we find sentences like this one:

French	U 137/7-16
Encore, selon les drois de Nature qui ont leur commencement en la divine providence et l'instrument de leur ouvraige ou mouvement, en la lumiere et en l'influence des corps celestielz, [comme *add.* BH]	And ferthermore aftir the right-wisnesse of nature, whiche hath begynnynge of the dyvyne prouidence and instruccion of the corages and meevinges in brightnesse, the influence of bodyes celestiall

French	U 137/7–16
nous demonstrent les maistres de tresinestimable science d'astrologie que [*om.* BH] ou livre des cieulx, qui en si large volume est escript de tant diverses empraintes et ymaiges, se peult cognoistre le cours et la duree des seigneuries et des citez, que les naturiens appellent periode, et que elles ont leurs maladies et leur mort comme les hommes en leur endroit.	ben shewde vnto us by the maisters of the moost inestimable science of astronomye, that in the celestiall book of the firmament, whiche is writen in so large volume of so many empreentid ymages, by the whiche may be knowen the cours and lastinge of the lordshipps and citees, the whiche the naturiens callen the periode, and that they haue sekenesse and deth as mankynde in thaire nature.[1]

Another characteristic common in fifteenth-century translation and shared by R and U is the addition of unnecessary links, such as conjunctions, relative pronouns, and prepositions, which confuse the sentence pattern. This practice will have been noticed already in the loosely put together sentences quoted above: at 142/4–7, for instance, both *which* and *and* are superfluously added in the English structure. An unnecessary *and* appears frequently in both R and U, to the detriment of the sentence pattern.[2] A superfluous *but* also occurs occasionally in both translations. In the awkward sentence at 45/7–12, the first *but* has no French equivalent. *but* also is superfluous at 244/13 in R and at 173/24 in U.

The relative pronoun *which* is inserted unnecessarily in R at 21/31–22/2:

And knowest nat thou that the high Maister of werkis, whose prouidence makith nothing in vayne, which hath putte the in mannys body to excercise the . . .[3]

Similarly, *the whiche* added without reason in U at 191/1–5 makes the structure at the end of the sentence awkward:

this avauntage hath the comon peeple that is as the cisterne that receyueth the watirs and droppinges the whiche of all the richesses of this

---

[1] Here part of the difficulty may have been caused by the French manuscript used by the translator. See Explanatory Notes.

[2] See R 232/23, and U 139/24, 203/19, 219/6. Some of these superfluous words may be scribal errors, especially in U, where we have no other English manuscripts with which to compare readings.

[3] See also R 86/14.

reame, that were in the cofirs of the nobles and clergye, ben spairboilled
and lessed by the longe continuaunce of the werre.

Unlike U, R sometimes added superfluous subordinating conjunctions and prepositions which confuse the sentence structure.
An unnecessary *hough*, for example, occurs in this sentence at
212/12–16:

Now is to be iugid aftir the forsaid writingis hough the state and infelicite of princes, whiche, for the geting of lordeshippis and for abydyng
of the same as to them belonge, be now made subgettis and bonde to
men of diuerse affeccions and contrary wille.

At 214/30, *as whanne* is added as an extra link, and at 178/13, the
preposition *through*. In such passages R perhaps began to translate
the French according to one pattern, changed his mind about the
structure somewhere in the middle, and forgot to reword the
beginning to make it consistent with his alteration. Such anacolu-
tha are frequent in fifteenth-century style and indeed are sometimes believed to have been conscious sins of writers of the period.[1]
A. T. Byles, however, in commenting about *The Book of Fayttes
of Armes and of Chyualrye*, notes that Caxton is awkward in deal-
ing with conjunctions and prepositions, and adds, 'The mastery
of conjunctions and prepositions seems to be the last achievement
in the development of literary prose'.[2]

Again in accordance with the practice of other fifteenth-century
authors, R and U omitted sentence elements which modern
structure demands for coherence: subjects, relative pronouns,
and conjunctions. U, however, omitted such elements less often
than R. (Perhaps the scribe of U was merely more careful, since
some omissions of this type may represent scribal errors.[3]) Omission of the subject is especially frequent in R, sometimes because
no subject is expressed in the French, where verbal inflections
make it unnecessary. In some sentences when the subject is the
same in two clauses, the second subject is omitted, as at 186/30–3:

thei shuld fynde the comon prosperite and the welthe of their estate
and of their lyvis, wheras nough by their parciall desyirs lette their
lordeship fall into pardicion.

---

[1] See *Caxton's Blanchardyn and Eglantine*, ed. L. Kellner, EETS, e.s. 58
(1890), p. cxii.

[2] EETS, 189 (1932, rev. 1937), p. liv.

[3] When scribal error has seemed particularly probable in the texts, omitted
elements have been supplied.

Such omission is particularly striking when another clause, sometimes even a main one, is placed between two coordinate clauses,
as in R at 108/10–14:

Remembir thiself hough Chelderych, the thirde Kyng of Fraunce, was
chased in(to) Loreyne and depryved of his royall crowne, and yet
aftirward the Frenchmen restored him ageyne to his grette honour and
glorye; and had a sone named Clouis . . .[1]

In other passages when the subject is the same in a main and a
subordinate clause, the pronoun is omitted in one of them, as in
R at 238/10–11: *But whanne the fadir vndirstode the meene of his
comynge, said these wourdis.*[2] Elsewhere the subject must be inferred
from the context of the rest of the sentence, where it is usually
mentioned, as in R at 86/16–20:

And thus came vp in vsage the ydoles of the paynemys, and, by the
commemoracion of the ydoll Belus, made name their ymages . . .[3]

Subordinating conjunctions seem sometimes to have been
omitted by both translators, as in U at 185/30. Once in R, unless
there is scribal error, both a subordinating conjunction and a
subject have been omitted:

French	R 172/8–12
Trop bien pourveurent a telz incon- veniens les anciens Rommains quant, pour garder les parties de leur communité chascune en sa dignité et en son ordre, ilz establi- rent les tribuns [tribus D *before emendation*, H] du pueuple . . .	Wherfor the auncient Romayns purueid them wele ayeinst suche grette inconueniences; for kepyng the parties of their commynte, euery man in his dignite and in his ordre, stablisch[ed] the tribus of the people . . .

It is clear then that, although the U translator (or scribe)
occasionally omitted unifying sentence elements, such omission is
much more common in R. In addition, R, in accordance with his
freer method of translation, often omitted phrases, clauses and
even entire sentences or paragraphs of the French.[4]

Another characteristic of fifteenth-century prose writers was
their love of repetition and tautology. Leon Kellner writes:

---

[1] Cf. 87/13–18.   [2] Cf. 69/14, 92/12, 113/29.   [3] Cf. 73/18, 140/9.
[4] Some, but by no means all, of these omissions have been shown to have
resulted from a corrupt French exemplar. See the Explanatory Notes for such
omissions both caused and not caused by a French manuscript.

With regard to Caxton's style, its main feature is the *tiresome tautology*, which is apparently produced by the translator's desire to make as much as he could of his work, to render it as showy as possible; his whole age was affected by this fashion of intolerable verbosity: to convey an idea through the medium of as many words as possible was considered as a beauty of style.[1]

Chartier himself was often tautological; hence, some of the repetitions in the translations are those of the original. U, however, not only seldom omitted any of Chartier's pleonasms, but, like Caxton, regularly added repetitive words and phrases of his own. R, on the other hand, did not always retain the tautologies of the French and added redundancies of his own only about half as frequently as U. The contrast may be observed in the translators' practices in the use of two synonyms together in *The Quadrilogue Invective*. U used two synonyms (sometimes even three, as at 199/31) to express one French word in approximately 140 places, and eliminated one of Chartier's pair of synonyms only about ten times. R, in contrast, used only about seventy pairs of synonyms in place of single French words and in at least twenty-five places cut out one of Chartier's superfluous synonyms. Both R and U sometimes translated a French word by two English words which have slightly or totally different connotations, each of which helps to render Chartier's idea. The following phrases from R and U illustrate the practice:

French	R
crevee de toutes pars	brokyn all abovte and disparpulid (202/24–5)
repentance	sorow and repentaunce (206/17)
maulx	myscheves and foliship (234/20–1)[2]

French	U
debatu	troubled and conquestioned (141/16–17)
refection	refeccion nor help (149/4)[3]

[1] *Caxton's Blanchardyn and Eglantine*, p. cxii.
[2] The same type of doubling occurs in R's *Treatise of Hope*:

destourne	breke and putte owte of ordir (29/26–7)
dissolus	nyce and owte of mesure (38/18)
misericorde	grace and mercy (60/13).

[3] The U translator may not have known the meaning of the French word here, since it is not used again until much later in English.

French	U
volupté	uolupte and self will (157/22)
sens	wysdome and conduit (191/20)
hault sens	hygh wysdome and naturall wytt (211/17–18)
adhesion	adhesion and presence (215/11)
salvable	soluable ne actuell (225/3)
arrogance	arrogaunce and lettinge (233/30)
fructueuse	vertuous and frutefull (247/10–11).

The list from U reveals yet another fifteenth-century pattern in doubling a French word in translation: both translators, but again especially U, sometimes borrowed the French word and then attempted to explain it by adding a synonym, a common practice with Caxton and others, sometimes as a means of enriching the language. The following doublets, especially those from U, demonstrate the practice:

French	R
reputé	reputid and takyn (190/22)
lacheté	latches and slowe (192/35)
despence	dispenses and paymentis (218/28)

French	U
desertion	desercion and destruccion (149/34)
deprime	deprimed and vnderlaied (165/7)
bien heureux	right eureuse and right happy (185/7)
forclorre	forecloose and stoppe (187/14–15)
souldees	saude and wages (201/9)
englouty	englouted and swellid (203/16–17).

Certain doublets which are common in Middle English prose occur in both R and U (e.g., *travale and labour, kepe and diffende*), but some recurring patterns of doubling and special doublets seem to have been characteristic of these translators. R, for instance, used the following types of doublets:

> answere and say (84/7)
> compleyne and axe (188/16)
> brayde owte and saide (200/16–17)
> made his othe and said (216/28)
> sought and founde owte (212/24)
> wente and gadird (216/6)
> take and write (246/16)

daunger and hurte (152/23)
evils and hurtis (174/23)
more greuous vice or more hurte (200/29).

U repeated the following types of doublets:

good and first (137/1)
good and sad (193/2–3)
good and nygh (201/15)
trauth and dutee (159/5, 221/15–16)
trauthe and conscience (245/3–4)
contencion and debate (207/17–18)
contencion and stryf (207/29)
contencion or strif (241/8).

On the whole then, the R translations gain, from the modern reader's point of view, because of moderate use of the rhetorical device of duplication found in Old and Early Middle English prose and especially common in fifteenth-century and Renaissance translations.[1]

While R did not add coordinate synonyms so frequently as U, he added much more freely than U other small elements for explanation or clarification, emphasis or highlighting, and greater coherence. Neither writer added at any time more than a sentence. The portions italicized in the following passages have no French equivalents and have been added by R to explain or clarify the structure or idea:

Policitatus . . . trusted so moche *in fortune* ['y' Cl, om. other MSS.] (86/5–6)

Whethir *did this holy man opyn the ʒatis of his cite* ['Le fist' Fr.] more for favour of any man or for drede of any man? (109/33–110/1)

thanne thought (I) ageinward vpon the greete largenes *of the realme* and on the grette distaunce of parties being in the same, *wheras I sawe clerely that* ['dont' Fr.] the enemyes myght nat suffice to kepe, *to maynetene nor to enhabite* the fourth parte *of the seide realme. Also their fell vnto my mynde* the merueylous noumbre of nobles and defensable people that myght be founde therin . . . (142/17–22)[2]

---

[1] See Inna Koskenniemi, *Repetitive Word Pairs in Old and Early Middle English Prose* (Turku, 1968), and F. O. Matthiessen, *Translation: an Elizabethan Art* (Cambridge, Mass., 1931).
[2] This passage illustrates also R's characteristic division of Chartier's long sentence units into smaller units for clarity. It shows also R's desire to strengthen transitions and his frequent additions to the personal tone.

The ampte purueith and sparith *his store* in the *season of* somer . . .
(170/15–16)[1]

Thow . . . makest noyse and clamour vpon thi present losses and affliccions withowte remembring thyn owne fawtis of tyme passid, which is the cause *of thyne owne myschef and of many othir* ['en' Fr.] (174/22–8)

Yet the wilfull mysknowlege of estates woll nat suffre the entre *of the said trouthe* ['en' Fr.] ne list to knowe the fruytfull ende and isswe *of the same.* The contrarye therof, *that is to say vice,* takith anothir way . . . (206/12–15)[2]

With these examples from R the following examples of additions in U for explanation or clarification may be compared:

the potter . . . makith diuers pottes of different bignesse and facions, *bothe more and lesse* . . . (137/20–2)

Enquere we most yf we haue *theise .iij. thinges* ['les' Fr.]. But yit *and we haue theim* it suffiseth nat oonly to haue thaim . . . (211/13–15)

Well aught they to haue regarde to that is said, they that *in court* ['y' Fr.] purchase for thaimself *more than for suffisaunce* ['trop' Fr.]. Mich more synne and charge is vpon thaim than on the prince *for his liberaltee* . . . (223/11–13)

From these passages, like many others, we may observe that the additions in R generally add more to the meaning than do those, often superfluous, in U. Only occasionally in U is there an addition which clarifies Chartier's structure or idea (223/11–13). R, however, much more frequently than U, made clear the French 'y' or 'en' or other indefinite pronoun references by an explanatory translation. In other passages R similarly often increased emphasis by adding references to the time of an action or state of affairs: he added *at all tymes* at 53/2, *at this howr* at 196/20, *now at this tyme* at 218/3, *to this day* at 242/11, and so on.

Frequently in R, and much less often in U, connectives have also been added or altered in order to introduce better transitions between sentences or ideas. At 152/27–8 in R, for instance, after making a series of bitter charges against her children, the three estates, the character of France says:

---

[1] The translator may have been working for extensive alliteration in his additions here.

[2] The translator is probably incorrect in his explanation of *the contrarye* here; see Explanatory Notes.

Now me semith or thinckith that thes wourdis shuld seme to yow bothe boistous and full of rigour . . .

The italicized introductory part added by R not only provides more emphatic, if somewhat wordy, transition, but also introduces the more personal tone of discourse typical of R. Compare also 156/12–15 in R, where France complains about the devotion to pleasures common to the three estates and adds,

Wherfor I see wele that it is an hard thing to leve an olde custome.

In other places R strengthened, by changing, the French connectives. In *for the profight hath nat be myne, wherfor the represe ought nat to be leyd vpon me* at 202/15–16, *wherfor* replaces the French 'ne'. Similarly, at 23/1, the weaker French link '&' has been changed to *through which*. U sometimes added or changed a connective, as at 205/29, where he added an emphatic *in the contrarie*. R, however, was much more consistent in making such changes.

Even more important, R also elaborated his text with words, phrases, and clauses intended to emphasize, highlight, or embroider an idea. Such elaboration occurs only one-third as often in U, and when it does is less effective. When the following passages are compared with the French, they reveal clearly R's heightening of idea by the italicized additions:

French	R
Leurs noms sont Indignation, Deffiance, & Desesperance.	*For and þou take good heede thou maist clerely vndirstonde that* the names *of those ladies* be *of wondirfu[l] condicion, for the furst of them is callid* Indignacion, *the second is callid* Diffidence, *and the thredde is callid* Dispeyre *of thingis for to come.* (20/4–8)
Or se sentit puissant par rapine, & doubté par fureur.	Thanne he felte himself mighty through rapyne and *vndirstode wele that* for his furour *the people* feryd him *soore, and thought that* [h]e s[e]tte on a grette hight. (90/19–22)
ses contraires des peines d'enfer	*all suche that louet not the worlde that thei shulde haue* the peynes of hell *for their rewarde* (92/13–15)

French	R
changez et matiz de leur premiere vertu	chaungid from their furst vertu *of manhod into ydelnes, into plesaunt desyrs and lust of their bodyes* (156/ 25–6)
Et telz y a qui jour et nuit sont par les bois et par les champs a chacer les bestes et au gibier des oiseaulx	Yet suche ther ben that gon nyght and day to the feldys and woodis *an huntyng [and] an hawkyng* to chase the bestis and bryddis, *which tak litill hede of their grete distruccion* (156/34–158/3).

Effective additions like these abound in R,[1] but are much less frequent in U.[2]

Only once in each translation were entire short sentences added by the authors: at 232/33–4, R inserted, *Wherfor our infortune is the more*, while at 167/18–19, U commented, *I see all that is taken with riall power is well taken.* In context R's addition typically serves to heighten the point made by Chartier, whereas U's comment unnecessarily interrupts the course of Chartier's thought.

Especially in R again, even shorter elements were added for dramatic effect and emphatic expression. Exclamations of direct address to God are sometimes particularly effective in heightening the mood of a passage. A long section in *The Treatise of Hope* about the evils of Mohammed, for example, reaches its emotional climax in this sentence at 95/15–16:

Lorde God, what laughtir and iape war this and the losse of so many sowles had not fallen therupon!

Another point in *The Treatise of Hope* is made forceful by the same technique at 130/6–8:

O good God, what thei be grettely disceved which in their olde age make theire offeryng of suche goodis as wer vntruely gotyn in their yong age.

At 166/12–14 in *The Quadrilogue Invective* in R, a similar addition is found:

O Lorde God, hough myght eny man in this werke haue perfight pacience whanne to my persecucion may nothing be ioyned but deth?

---

[1] See 15/31–2, 17/10–12, 46/11–12, 88/31, 116/17, 180/17–18, 198/19–20, 224/19, 224/24–6, and so on.
[2] For a few examples from U, see 151/1–3, 157/5–6, 157/15–16.

Again at 162/36, the R translator added *Parde* in the same way for emphasis.

R was also especially fond of adding interjections to emphasize an idea. For instance, at 29/31-2, he put in *Nay forsothe*, and at 138/15, *Yes certeyn*. In *The Quadrilogue Invective* alone he added *O* nine times, as compared with U's addition of *A* three times. R added *Alas* twice; U, *elas* once. R also put in *Lo* four times. Likewise, R often added such elements as *I wote wele, I see wele, I counsell the, I cannat see but we must, I cowde wele say, I woll that*, and *me thinkith*, not in the French. U, on the other hand, almost never introduced such personal constructions. Unlike U again, R sometimes added imperatives like *bewar also, bewarre and follow not, loke thou*, and *Remembir yow wele*.

Both R and U frequently added ordinary modifiers like *grette, high, noble, powr, mighty, olde*, and *good*. But in addition to these, R added *hasty, false* (twice), *small, vnstaunchable, manly, sorowfull, mereveillous, glorious, swet, wilfull, evile*, and *wourshipfull*, while U added only *actuell, cowarde, worldy, playn*, and *gracious*. Moreover, R was prone to add adverbial modifiers also for emphasis: *owt of all reason, of reason, right well, of right, right so, of very necessite*, and *certainly*. He also put in adverbs like *gladly, royally, anone*, and *sodanly*. U added some such emphatic adverbs: *truly, at neede, actuelly, sharply, ouermiche, fast, finallye, diligently, cleerly*, and *tendrely*. In R, additions of noun constructions like *the noble (royall) cite of* and *the noble man callid* are frequently found. Likewise, in contrast with U, R often substituted specific nouns for a pronoun in the French, for example, *a grette lawde, his greef, foles, multitude of*, and *wepyngis*. R then, it is clear, pointed up, dramatized, or embroidered passages much more frequently than U, and usually more effectively.

The R translation surpasses U in effectiveness not only because of these vivid additions, but also because of a more apt selection of word or phrase to translate the French. Indeed R is often more vivid than the original passages in Chartier. Two illustrations may be cited from *The Treatise of Hope*:

French	R
queuurechief sale, encendré	[suyled] kerchif like as it had ben through suotte and asches (4/33-5/1)

French	R
& donner sec passage entre les vndes au peuple d'Israel	suche wise þat all the people of Israell passed through withowt weting their feete (125/21–2).

The strength of R's phrasing may be still more forcefully brought out by a comparison of passages like the following from R and U with each other and with the French:

French	R	U
de matiere artifi-cieuse pour plus durer aux hommes	by crafte of mas-onrye so stronge that the makers supposed neuir to haue failed (136/31–3)	of artificiall matere for longe lastinge (137/33–4)
chaude colle	hasty buffettis (192/9)	hoote corage (193/9)
Les maulx, ce qu'il en y a, sont mis en compte	And all þe evill dedis that be doon thou tellist them forth (204/17–18)	The yll deedes, as miche as there [is], is well remembred (205/17–18).

R is also conspicuously in contrast with U in choice of vocabulary. From the discussion of translation in Caxton's Prologues and Epilogues, we know that the question of vocabulary was being seriously considered by both translators and readers at about the time when these translations of Chartier's works were written. R seems to have followed Caxton's policy, as stated in the Prologue to *Eneydos*, of selecting words. Like Caxton, he translated Chartier's works 'in to our englysshe not ouer rude ne curyous but in suche termes as shall be vnderstanden by goddys grace accord-ynge to my copye'.[1] He thus had a strong tendency to select, when possible, a familiar vocabulary, whereas U might at times have been justly accused, as was Caxton, of using 'ouer curyous termes'. The following list has been compiled almost at random from R and U to illustrate the marked contrast between the vocabularies of the two translators.

R	U
thral(l)dom 134/18	seruitute 135/21
sought owt 140/14	encerched 141/15
vttirmest vndoynge 140/18	determinacion 141/19

---

[1] *The Prologues and Epilogues of William Caxton*, ed. W. J. B. Crotch, EETS, 176 (1928), p. 109.

R

rule, rewle 142/28, 222/4
vnknowyng 142/34
wilfull mysknowlege 206/12
a werke 146/2
witt and wisedome 146/32
wittis 160/9
slewthe, sleuthe 148/21, 180/7
cowardnes 238/19
signis 158/31
scarcete 160/2
fleing 160/9
rewardis 160/15
fredom(e) 166/32, 172/12
power 172/13, 210/7
but sodanly goost from the wey 174/22
fulfillid 174/32
shamefull 176/7
rebukyng 202/32
vnkynde 176/18
causes 180/4
wille(s) 182/27, 212/16, etc.
worthi, wourthy 184/3, 224/30
hidd 184/33
welthe 186/22, 186/31
wele 216/32, 244/23
welefar 244/8
maners 186/25
is lorde 188/25
makit the lasse 190/6
that he occupied the office of dictatour 192/11
contrary in a maner to 195/25–6
deepe 198/23
money 202/19
cursid 204/3
them that publisch 204/10
wages 220/12
yefftis 222/10
closyng 228/17
put vndir 234/7
repreuable 238/19
wisedam (-dom) 238/31, 240/2
subtilte 238/32
gret riches 238/34

U

regle 143/25, 223/4
disconisaunce 143/31
disconysaunce 207/10
ourage 147/2
engynes 147/29
engynes 161/8
lach(e)nesse 149/25, 181/7
lachenesse 239/18
demonstraunce 159/24
diminuacion 161/2
volage 161/7
guerdon 161/14
fraunchise 167/29, 173/14
puissaunce 173/15, 211/7
withoute foruoyeng 175/21

replenysht 175/31
opprobriouse 177/6
obprobriouse 203/31
ingrate 177/18
encheson 181/4
volunte(e)s 183/27, 213/13, etc.
digne 185/2, 225/23
recelled 187/1
saluacion 187/21, 187/28
saluacion 217/24, 245/23
saluacion 245/9
disposicions 187/24
hath dominacion 189/23
hath diminued 191/6
of his dictature 193/10

in deregacion of 193/26
obscure 199/19
pecunie 203/17
vntestable ('detestable' Fr.) 205/3
publiquers 205/10
saudes 221/9
donacion 223/9
closture 229/17
deprimed 235/7
vituperable 239/18
sapience 239/30, 241/2
cautele 239/31
havure 239/32[1]

---

[1] This is not to say that R never used such words: *fraunchise, puissaunce,*

Many conclusions may now be drawn about the differences in skill and method between the two fifteenth-century translators of Chartier. U must, as a mere translator of the French, be considered superior to R; however, although U, to begin with, had greater skill in the French language, he was generally content to follow his original as literally as possible, a practice which led him to frequent awkwardnesses, but which also enabled him at times to imitate in his English work the spirit of Chartier's prose style. R, on the other hand, frequently misunderstood the French; however, when he did understand, he expressed himself freely in English idiom and with English sentence order, many times only by paraphrase of Chartier's ideas. Although the work of U must then be considered better as a mere translation, R's rendering, on the whole, is more effective as a work of English prose. U's greater faithfulness to the original is offset by R's more direct and vivid style in both *The Treatise of Hope* and *The Quadrilogue Invective*. The R translations are prose works which, despite all their faults, merit attention as works of art in their own right, not just as translations. Of the short portion of *The Treatise of Hope* which R. W. Chambers knew, he wrote:

Fortescue's beautiful and touching *Dialogue between Understanding and Faith* shows his style at its best; it is the prose which for centuries had been used for such works of edification.[1]

Had he seen the entire work of this translator (possibly Fortescue), he would perhaps not have been disappointed.

V. THE FRENCH MANUSCRIPTS

The English translations of *Le Traité de l'Esperance* and *Le Quadrilogue Invectif* have been compared with four French versions which for each work seem to give at least two distinct families of readings. By such comparison several types of problems may be dealt with: (1) partial determination of which type of manuscript the English translators used; (2) explanation of various corrupt

---

encheson, and other such words occur occasionally in R. See the Glossary. R's preference was, however, for the more familiar words.

[1] 'On the Continuity of English Prose from Alfred to More and his School', Introduction to *The Life and Death of S*r *Thomas More*, ed. E. V. Hitchcock, EETS, 186 (1932), p. cxxxvii.

readings which resulted from corruption in the French text; and (3) support for emendations of corrupt English readings.

The four French versions used for comparison with R's translation of *Le Traité de l'Esperance* are as follows: (1) *Les Œuvres de maistre Alain Chartier*, edited by André Duchesne (Paris, 1617), referred to as D; (2) Bodleian Library, Oxford: MS. E. D. Clarke 34, referred to as Cl; (3) Bodley MS. 421, referred to as B; (4) British Library: MS. Royal 19 A. xii, referred to as Ro. A word must be said about each of these texts. Duchesne's 1617 edition, although the text is uncritical, inaccurate, and sometimes tampered with, has been selected as the basis for comparison because it is the most recent edition of the work, badly in need of a modern editor, and hence is the most easily accessible. Duchesne seems to have taken his text from an earlier printed text (only a careful collation of the many fifteenth- and sixteenth-century printings of Chartier's works would reveal which) and to have compared this printed text with one of the many French manuscripts, the variant readings of which are sporadically recorded in the margins of the edition. These marginal readings are referred to as D_1 in the critical apparatus and Explanatory Notes of my editions.

Of the four (or five, including D_1) French texts compared with *The Treatise of Hope*, MS. E. D. Clarke 34 (Cl) is without doubt the one most nearly like the English translation. It omits fairly long passages also omitted in the English; it has more variant readings that support the English readings than any of the other French versions have; and in many passages even in minor details, such as spelling of proper names, it is similar to the English work.[1] There are, however, enough similarities to the other French texts (where Cl is different) to make it certain that the translation was not made directly from Cl, but from a manuscript which belonged to the same family as Cl, but which had some readings from another type of manuscript. B and Ro, in contrast to Cl, are probably both members of another family of manuscripts, and D possibly of even another (if its changes do not merely represent a printed version). B, although not quite complete and somewhat corrupt, is a much more accurate manuscript than Ro, which in numerous passages is corrupt. A close comparison of Ro with the other French manuscripts

---

[1] The selected examples given in the Explanatory Notes will clearly reveal these similarities.

suggests that it may have been copied from a manuscript like B by an English scribe who was not completely at home with the French language; but this should not be taken as proved without much further investigation.

The four French versions selected for comparison with the two translations of *Le Quadrilogue Invectif* are as follows: (1) the revised edition by E. Droz (1950), referred to as D;[1] (2) Bodley MS. 421, referred to as B (also containing *Le Traité de l'Esperance*); (3) British Library: Harleian MS. 4402, referred to as H; (4) British Library: Add. MS. 15300, referred to as A. Droz reproduces in her edition the text in B. N. fr. 126, corrected in fourteen places from B. N. fr. 1124. The text is not a critical one and has serious shortcomings in readings which are passed by without comment by the editor. The Explanatory Notes to the English translations note some of the most serious inferior readings in Droz's edition.

D and A are members of the same family of manuscripts, while B and H seem to represent a somewhat different family. On the whole, the English translations are more nearly like the French family of B and H than they are like that of D and A, but the evidence is too slight to form any firm conclusion.

VI. A SELECTED BIBLIOGRAPHY

A. *English Manuscripts*

Oxford, Bodleian Library:	Rawlinson A 338.
	University College 85.
London, British Library:	Cotton Vitellius E. x.
	Royal 13 C. i, ff. 136–41 (William Worcester's Notebooks).
Cambridge:	St. John's College 76. D. i.
Chicago, Newberry Library:	MS. f. 36, Ry 20.
London, Sion College Library:	MS. L. 40. 2/E. 43.

B. *French Manuscripts*

Bodleian Library:	Bodley 421.
	E. D. Clarke 34.
British Library:	Add. 15300.
	Harleian 4402.
	Royal 19 A. xii.

---

[1] D has been chosen as a symbol for both French texts used as the basis for comparison—Duchesne's edition of *Le Traité de l'Esperance* and Droz's edition of *Le Quadrilogue*—in order to keep constantly before the reader the French text used as a norm.

C. *References Related to Alain Chartier's Works and Their Translations*

The Asloan Manuscript, ed. Sir W. Craigie, STS, N.S. 14 (1923).

Blayney, M. S., 'Alain Chartier and Joachism?', *MLN*, lxx (1955), 506–9.

Blayney, M. S., 'Sir John Fortescue and Alain Chartier's "Traité de l'Esperance" ', *MLR*, xlviii (1953), 385–90.

Blayney, M. S. and G. H., 'Alain Chartier and *The Complaynt of Scotlande*', *RES*, N.S. ix (1958), 8–17.

Blayney, M. S. and G. H., '*The Faerie Queene* and an English Version of Chartier's *Traité de l'Esperance*', *SP*, lv (1958), 154–63.

Brière-Valigny, 'Le quadrilogue invectif d'Alain Chartier', *Séances et travaux de l'Académie de Reims*, xi (1849–50), 403–12.

[Caxton, W.], *The Curial made by Maystere Alain Charretier*, ed. F. J. Furnivall, EETS, E.S. 54 (1888).

Chartier, Alain, *Le curial, texte français du xve siècle, avec l'original latin*, ed. F. Heuckenkamp (Halle, 1899).

Chartier, Alain, *Dialogus familiaris Amici et Sodalis super deploratione Gallicę calamitatis*, ed. G. Rosenthal (Halle, 1901).

Chartier, Alain, *Les Œuvres de maistre Alain Chartier*, ed. A. Duchesne (Paris, 1617).

Chartier, Alain, *Le Quadrilogue Invectif*, ed. E. Droz, 2nd ed. rev. (Paris, 1950).

Chaucerian and Other Pieces, ed. W. W. Skeat (Oxford, 1897).

The Chepman and Myllar Prints, ed. W. Beattie (Edinburgh Bibliographical Society, 1950).

The Complaynt of Scotlande, ed. J. A. H. Murray, EETS, E.S. 17, 18 (1872–3).

Delaunay, D., *Etude sur Alain Chartier* (Rennes, 1876).

Denifle, H., and A. Chatelain, *Chartularium universitatis Parisiensis* (Paris, 1897), iv. 381–2.

Eder, H., *Syntaktische Studien zu Alain-Chartiers Prosa* (Würzburg, 1889).

Hoffman, E. J., *Alain Chartier, His Work and Reputation* (New York, 1942).

Höpfner, E., *Die Wortstellung bei Alain Chartier und Gerson* (Grimma, 1883).

Laidlaw, J. C., 'English Translations of Alain Chartier', *MLR*, lvi (1961), 223.

Lami, G., *Deliciae eruditorum* (Florent., 1737), iii. 38.

Lemm, S., 'Aus einer Chartier-Handschrift des kgl. Kupferstichkabinetts zu Berlin', *Archiv für das Studium der neueren Sprachen und Literaturen*, cxxxii (1914), 131–8.

Mancel, G., *Alain Chartier, étude bibliographique et littéraire* (Bayeux, 1849).

McFarlane, K. B., 'William Worcester: a Preliminary Survey', *Studies Presented to Sir Hilary Jenkinson*, ed. J. Conway Davies (Oxford, 1957).

Neilson, W. A., 'The Original of *The Complaynt of Scotlande*', *JEGP*, i (1897), 411–30.

Pagès, A., 'La belle dame sans merci d'Alain Chartier, texte français et traduction catalane', *Romania*, lxii (1936), 481–531.

Paris, G., 'Un poème inédit de Martin le Franc', *Romania*, xvi (1887), 383–437.

Perret, P.-M., 'L'ambassade de l'Abbé de Saint-Antoine de Vienne et d'Alain Chartier à Venise', *Revue historique*, xlv (1891), 298–307.

Piaget, A., *La belle dame sans mercy et les poésies lyriques*, 2nd ed. (Paris, 1949).

Piaget, A., '*La belle dame sans merci* et ses imitations', *Romania*, xxx (1901), 22–48, 317–51; xxxi (1902), 315–49; xxxiii (1904), 179–208; xxxiv (1905), 375–428, 559–602.

Piaget, A., 'L'épitaphe d'Alain Chartier', *Romania*, xxiii (1894), 152–6.

Piaget, A., 'Notice sur le manuscrit 1727 du fonds français de la Bibliothèque Nationale', *Romania*, xxiii (1894), 192–208.

Piaget, A., 'Un prétendu manuscrit autographe d'Alain Chartier', *Romania*, xxv (1896), 312–15.

Political, Religious, and Love Poems, ed. F. J. Furnivall, EETS, o.s. 15 (1866).

Quicherat, J., *Procès de condamnation et de réhabilitation de Jeanne d'Arc* (Paris, 1849), v. 131–6.

Segar, F., *A brefe declaration of the great and innumerable myseries & wretchednesses vsed in courtes ryall, made by a lettre, whych mayster Alayn Charatre wrote to hys brother, which desyred to come dwel in the court, for to aduyse, & counsell hym not to enter into it, lest he after repent, newly augmented, amplified, & inrytched* (London, 1549) [Bodleian copy: Douce fragments f. 46].

Thomas, A., 'Alain Chartier chanoine de Paris', *Romania*, xxxiii (1904), 387–402.

Thomas, A., 'Encore Alain Chartier', *Romania*, xxxvi (1907), 306–7.

Thomas, A., 'Un document peu connu sur Alain Chartier', *Romania*, xxxv (1906), 603–4.

Thomas, A., 'Une œuvre patriotique inconnue d'Alain Chartier', *Journal des savants*, N.S. i (1914), 442–9.

Thuasne, L., 'Le curial d'Alain Chartier et la traduction de Robert Gaguin', *Revue des bibliothèques*, xi (1901), 13–19.

Vandier, M., 'Alain Chartier et son époque', *Annales de la société académique de Nantes*, xxii (1851), 127–45.

D. *Other References*

Beaucourt, G. du Fresne de, *Histoire de Charles VII*, 6 vols. (Paris, 1881–91).

Bibliotheca selectissima being the library of . . . Sir Edmund King . . . also the library of Sir H. S[pelman] (London, 1709).

Calmette, J., *Le moyen âge* (Paris, 1953).

Caxton, W., *Caxton's Blanchardyn and Eglantine*, ed. L. Kellner, EETS, E.S. 58 (1890).

Caxton, W., *The Book of Fayttes of Armes and of Chyualrye*, ed. A. T. Byles, EETS, 189 (1932, rev. 1937).

Caxton, W., *The Prologues and Epilogues of William Caxton*, ed. W. J. B. Crotch, EETS, 176 (1928).

Chambers, R. W., 'On the Continuity of English Prose from Alfred to More and his School', Introduction to *The Life and Death of S*ʳ *Thomas More*, ed. E. V. Hitchcock, EETS, 186 (1932).

Champion, P., *Histoire poétique du 15ᵉ siècle*, 2 vols. (Paris, 1923).

Fortescue, Sir J., *De laudibus legum Angliae*, ed. S. B. Chrimes (Cambridge, 1942).

Fortescue, Sir J., *The Governance of England*, ed. C. Plummer (Oxford, 1885).

Fortescue, Sir J., *The Works*, ed. T. Fortescue, Lord Clermont, 2 vols. (London, 1869).

Huizinga, J., *The Waning of the Middle Ages* (London, 1924).

Kaminsky, H., *A History of the Hussite Revolution* (Berkeley, 1967).

Koskenniemi, I., *Repetitive Word Pairs in Old and Early Middle English Prose* (Turku, 1968).

Matthiessen, F. O., *Translation: an Elizabethan Art* (Cambridge, Mass., 1931).

Moore, S., 'Patrons of Letters in Norfolk and Suffolk, c. 1450', *PMLA*, xxvii (1912), 188–207; xxviii (1913), 79–105.

Moss, W., *Bindings from the Library of Robert Dudley, Earl of Leicester, K.G.* (Sonning-on-Thames, 1934).

Paris, G., *Esquisse historique de la littérature française au moyen âge* (Paris, 1907).

Paris, G., *Mélanges de la littérature française du moyen âge* (Paris, 1912).

Paston Letters and Papers of the Fifteenth Century, ed. N. Davis, Parts I and II (Oxford, 1971, 1976).

The Paston Letters, ed. J. Gairdner, 6 vols. (London, 1904).

Perroy, E., *The Hundred Years War*, trans. W. B. Wells (London, 1951).

Reeves, M., *The Influence of Prophecy in the Later Middle Ages: a Study in Joachimism* (Oxford, 1969).

Smith, T., *Catalogus librorum manuscriptorum bibliothecae Cottonianae* (London, 1696).

Spelman, H., *The English Works*, ed. E. Gibson (London, 1723).

THE EXPLANATORY NOTES

THE Explanatory Notes to the English translations have been designed to perform a number of functions. First, they attempt to explain complicated textual problems which cannot be dealt with in the necessarily brief critical apparatus. Next, they compare the English texts with the French texts discussed in the Introduction (pp. 70–2). The French reading has not been given when the translations follow Duchesne's edition of *Le Traité de l'Esperance* or Droz's edition of *Le Quadrilogue Invectif*. Important variations in the translations from the French of the D versions are noted, however—both variations supported and unsupported by one or more of the other French versions compared with the English. The Notes also contain selected examples to indicate that the translators followed one type of French manuscript or another or that there is support in any of the French versions for a reading in the English, although often it is impossible to say certainly that such changes have not been made independently by the translators. The Notes also record significant variations from the French in the English translations in order to support with additional evidence the discussion of methods of translation in the Introduction. In general, readings given in this section of the Introduction are not repeated in the Explanatory Notes. The Notes likewise discuss briefly historical, religious, or political events which help to explain the meaning of some of the references in the French and English texts. They also make a limited attempt to indicate possible sources for Chartier's information if his use of such sources is especially interesting, although the Notes are certainly not a study of his sources, a very complicated matter far beyond the scope of the present editions.

In the Notes R refers to the English texts in RNSJ or to the translator of these texts, unless variant readings from NSJ are given, in which case R refers only to the Rawlinson reading. U refers to the University College MS. text of *The Quadrilogue Invective* or to the translator of that text. To avoid duplication in the Notes to *The Quadrilogue* the two parallel texts are treated together when there are comments on both translations. If the reference words are the same in both translations, the Rawlinson spelling only is used.

THE TREATISE OF HOPE

3/1. *The Auctour*: These character-headings appear in NSJ, not in R. In these editions they are taken from N, as are the spellings of emendations and variants.

3/2. *the . . . exile*: Chartier refers here to 1428, ten years after the Burgundians took Paris and he accompanied the Dauphin into exile in Bourges.

3/4. *thankid . . . God*: 'Dont i'ay souffert graces à Dieu assez'.

3/8. *the same*: i.e. France.

3/14. *and feers*: 'and they were fierce'.

3/32. *mystaken*: Fr. has 'despiz'. It is unclear whether R means 'scorned, despised' (not in *OED*) or the weaker 'misunderstood' or even 'erring'.

4/3. *but . . . hope*: The Fr. manuscripts read, 'Fors que petit desperance y auons'; the 1617 edited D correctly interprets the phrase as 'petit d'Esperance', but R interprets it as 'little despair'.

4/13. *and . . . natur*: R misunderstood 'malgré nature' DCl ('contre nature' BRo), confusing 'maigre' with 'malgré'.

4/20–1. *and . . . vndirstonding*: Misunderstanding of '& ma vie ennuyeuse; ay long temps trauaillé & foullé mon petit Entendement'.

4/27. *power*: 'paour'.

4/28. *blemeshid*: 'blesme' (livid, pale).

4/32. *swollen*: 'ternie' (dull, leaden, lifeless).

4/33. *suyled*: Since *suyvelid* (R) is not recorded in *OED*, it is probably a scribal error for *suyled* (NSJ), translating 'sale'.

5/1–2. *lyke . . . mantille*: 'mantel de tenné [chentue B]'.

5/9. *vanischid*: Fr. has 'euanouï'. R seems to be using *vanischid* in the Fr. sense 'in a swoon', a meaning not in *OED*. Note *or in a swowne* that follows.

5/11–17. *Yet . . . litargie*: Fr. has 'Mesmes Entendement ce ieune & aduisé bachelier, qui m'auoit suiuy vne foiz de loing, l'autre de prés, selon ce que Dieu m'en donna l'acointance, abuura elle de si estranges & merueilleux buurages confis en forcenerie & en descognoissance; que le bon & saige, qui ad ce besoin m'auoit conduit iusques au lict, demoura de couste moy estourdy, estonny, & comme en litargie'. *mysknowlage* here translates 'descognoissance', and as at 21/3 the word seems to mean 'lack of understanding' (*OED* 1579). Elsewhere the word in R means 'failure to know, recognize or acknowledge (sometimes implying scorn)' and 'refusal to know, lack of knowledge', to translate not only 'descognoissance' but also 'mescongnoissance' and 'mespris'. See 89/32 n. and 206/12–13 n.

Cf. in the Glossary *mysknowe, mysknowlechinge, disknoweth, disknowlege,* and *disknowlegyng.*

5/20. *spirite sencetif*: This conception of the sensitive soul extends back to Aristotle's *De Anima* and has its most notable medieval exposition in Thomas Aquinas' *Summa Theologica.*

5/21. *Aftir hir doctrine*: 'Par elle, selon la doctrine de Aristote'.

5/22. *persones*: 'parfons' DCl; 'parfais' BRo.

5/24–6. *fowir . . . vertues*: The reference is to the faculties of the sensitive soul listed by Aquinas: *sensus communis*, memory, imagination, and *vis aestimativa* (in animals) or *cogitativa* (in man). See *Summa Theologica*, i. 78. 4.

5/27–9. *by . . . acheve*: 'par trop souuent, ou en trop fort euure les exploicter'.

5/31–2. *vpon . . . fygurys*: R used a manuscript like D: 'sur choses menuës, & deliees, ou de differente figure', in which he confused 'deliees' (sometimes 'delise') = 'fine, delicate', with the noun 'delice'. BClRo have 'sur choses menues ou [*om.* ClRo] de delie ou different figure'.

6/1. *put . . . vertu*: 'te deuertuë'.

6/2–4. *it . . . helth*: The reading of R is supported by NJ and was originally in S; although another hand has written the present S reading over the original, the last two words *in helthe* can still be made out. In places the corrector's reading in S is nearer to Fr. than are RNJ:

> Et à non sçauoir te maine.
> Tant es de pouure venuë,
> Se des cieux n'es soustenuë,
> Que tu ne peuz viure saine.

Note the omission in RNJ of a translation of the second line, whereas in S we find *Being of so pore strenght and vertu*. On the other hand, the last line is translated in RNJ, not in S. Some time in the early history of S then, a corrector, perhaps not able to read the manuscript because of blurring, seems to have retranslated Fr. Perhaps whoever did this also eliminated *both* at 5/34 and changed *by* to *thy* at 6/1 in S.

6/8. *faade mouth*: This is an exact translation of 'fade bouche'. *faade* to mean 'that has lost the sense of taste' is thus used here in English long before the first *OED* record from 1715.

6/25. *asyde*: *side* and *said* are confused several times as they are here in N's *a saide*. Cf. 146/8, 150/17, 164/19.

6/27. *hir*: R has *her* and *hem* for *their* and *them* only occasionally, but NSJ frequently have these forms. The R scribe here and at 6/29 incorrectly changed *her* of his copy text to *their.*

6/28. *constaunce*: R followed an inferior manuscript like Ro, which has 'constance'. DBCl have 'contenance'.

6/31. *Indignacion*: It appears odd that R named Indignation before the description, and not Defiance and Desesperance. Since even Indignation is named, however, he may have worked from a manuscript like Cl, in which a correcting hand has added marginal notes about the persons mentioned. Here, for example, 'nomee Indignacion' has been inserted after 'seconde'.

7/12. *attendaunce*: 'vent'.

7/17. *towaile*: 'suaire' (shroud).

7/18. *here*: Fr. has 'cheuestre' (halter of a beast of burden), which R confused with 'cheueux'.

7/22-3. *and . . . tonge*: '& faisoit sa langue bauboyer'.

7/32. *side or parte*: Fr. has only 'pars', and NSJ omit *side or*. The R scribe seems here and elsewhere to have added redundant words to the text. Cf. 9/8, 13/9, 42/28, 42/31, 68/6, 125/2, etc.

8/20-1. *to . . . wele*: This phrase is an unclear translation of 'se fait ouyr dehors par publicques euures' in conjunction with 'a hurté'. *schewe* seems to mean 'instruct'.

8/21-3. *Lucan . . . werr*: *Pharsalia, M. Annaei Lucani Belli Civilis Libri Decem*, ed. A. E. Housman (Oxford, 1927), i. 92–3.

8/23. *betwene*: J is unclear, and such a manuscript might easily have been misread as *be veyne*, thus producing R's *biveyne*.

8/27-30. *But . . . returned*: R's exemplar may have been like B, which has 'Et se tu veulx congnoistre fortune & a sa variable· de tout temps a court le trouueras La sesbat elle de ses tours bestournez'. DClRo have '& te soubzmettre à sa variableté' for '& a sa variable'.

8/31-9/4. *For . . . lyves*: Free rendering of 'Ores prant son deduit à faire d'vn cheitif mescogneu vn puissant orgueilleux, qui tout descongnoist, & d'vn hault Satrape esleué en vaine gloire, & en pompe, vn meschant, foullé, & deffait, qui depuis vit en vergoingne du dechiet de son estat, & en deffiance de sa vie'.

9/6-7. *to . . . treasour* (1): Fr. has 'pour adiouster au grant monceau'. N's addition *godys and* does not have Fr. support.

9/8. *a bare . . . voyde*: Fr. has only 'la place vuide', followed by NSJ. The R scribe again may have added the redundancy.

9/9. *grette ryalte*: 'bruit'.

9/14-15. *to* (3) *. . . prees*: This phrase translates 'toy . . . ingerer' (to take upon yourself, to presume, to push your way). *OED* questions this meaning, but here is a clear instance of its use. 'to go' is understood after the phrase.

9/21-2. *the . . . anothir*: This awkwardness was probably caused by a bad Fr. reading, something like that in B: 'et le delit que lomme appete dauoir pouoir sur autruy'. DClRo have '& le delit [delict Cl] que l'erreur humaine [mondaine Ro] prant d'auoir pouoir sur autruy'; and a Cl corrector has added 'auctorite'.

9/30. *content . . . litill*: Misunderstanding of 'content appetit [apetit B̄j̄]̄.

9/31-2. *so . . . ambicion*: Mistranslation of 'de contente parcité en ambition souffreteuse'.

9/32. *thy . . . cast*: Mistranslation of 't'a fortune gectée'.

10/11. *retournable*: Fr. has 'reciproque'. R seems to mean 'reciprocal'. The nearest meaning in *OED* is 'that is to be returned' (1658).

10/15. *of thy mayntenaunce*: Misrendering of 'de maintenant', caused by confusion of the similar Fr. words.

10/18-23. *but . . . werkis*: The first of a large number of omissions in N, giving evidence that RSJ were not copied from N.

10/21-2. *or . . . lawde*: 'Tu languiras en celle loüange'.

10/29. *Senecke*: This is the first of many examples used also in Boethius' *Consolation* (Lib. iii, Prosa 5). *Le Traité de l'Esperance* was, of course, partially modelled on Boethius.

10/35. *ought . . . Athenyences*: 'should not be forgotten as far as the Athenians are concerned' (*Athenyences* is the spelling in all the manuscripts).

11/6-7. *so . . . seruices*: Perhaps the use of the singular form *vnkyndnesse* occurs because of translation from a manuscript like Cl: 'tant de Ingratitude et de seruices'. DBRo have the plural. At 7/6, however, R seems to have *vnkyndenesse* as the plural.

11/7-9. *Thy . . . peyne*: In the first part of the sentence R follows a manuscript like Cl: 'Ton couraige se doit apaisier de souffrir'. DBRo have a question: 'Ton courage se doit il appaiser'. In the last part, however, R follows an inferior manuscript like DB, which lose the parallelism of the construction by omitting the first 'en' in the ClRo reading: 'seruice en pourete et traueil en peril'. Perhaps *passed* in RNSJ is a scribal error for *paised*, rendering 'apaisier'.

11/12-16: Here Chartier refers to his life with the exiled Dauphin's court. *hast passid the daungerous wayes* probably refers to his 1428 mission to Scotland.

11/17. *ye . . . captyuyte*: Fr. has 'pour la garder vous estes desheritez de vostre pays; & pour la soustenir & seruir, vous estes foulez, auilez, & chetifz'. R's exemplar possibly omitted 'desheritez . . . estes' because of the repetition of 'vous estes'.

11/18. *Tholome*: R is like BClRo. D has 'Diogenes'. Chartier probably intended Ptolemy since medieval writers attributed these words to him, as in Chaucer's *Wife of Bath's Tale*, D 323-7, Walter Burley's *De vita et moribus philosophorum*, and the introduction to the translation of Ptolemy by Gerard of Cremona.

11/22-3. *what . . . myschief*: R mistranslated a manuscript like Ro:

> Tout ce qui desire
> Et a meschief tire
> Nostre humanite.

For 'desire' DCl have 'descire', and B has 'deschire'.

11/23–5. *For . . . trouthe*: R's exemplar probably interchanged lines 2 and 3 of the following passage:

> Courroux nous martyre,
> Faueur, hayne, ou ire,
> Nuisent à eslire,
> Penser, faire, ou dire [*line om.* Ro]
> Ce qu'est verité.

Whether my punctuation of this awkward passage creates the sense intended by R is uncertain, although it does help to retain Chartier's idea.

11/31. *straungely*: Fr. has 'fort'. *straungely* seems to be an error in RNJ for *strangly* (S), the northern form of 'strongly'.

12/19–20. *what . . . seuirly*: R is like BClRo: 'En quoy peus tu auoir maintenant ta seurte· Ne ou fiches tu lattente de ta fiance'. D has only 'en quoy pues tu auoir ta fiance'. R's vivid image may be only mistranslation.

13/8–10. *seeng . . . indigence*: 'since your estate is greatly diminished, it would be very painful for you to suffer harmful poverty among the rich citizens'. This is a free translation of 'sans auoir quelque regrait au rabais de ton estat, & amere poincture de souffrir entre les riches citoiens dangereuse indigence'. The R scribe probably added *abatid or*.

13/16–17. *no . . . life*: Free translation of 'homme n'y a la maistrise sur sa cheuance, ne seurté de sa vie'.

13/21. *ravinours straungiers*: *ravenous* (NSJ) may be the original reading. However, R's reading may have arisen through translation from a manuscript like Ro, which has 'estrangiers rauisseurs', instead of 'estranges rauisseurs' (DBCl).

13/22. *langustes*: The only *MED* (other than this) and *OED* example of this rare word is from *Trin. Coll. Hom.*, 127 (*c.* 1200).

13/24–6. *seenge . . . owte*: R is like Cl: 'les champs Inhabitez feront les citez familleuses & laguillon de fam· Et contraincte de viure fait saillir le loup'. D has 'contraincte necessité de querir à viure' for Cl's 'contraincte de viure', and B has 'Et laguillon de viure· contraint par fam' for Cl's '& laguillon . . . fait'. Ro omits 'les champs . . . familleuses' and has 'laguillonde viure en constrainte de fam fait saillir le lou'.

13/33. *mystye tyme*: 'brouillas de temps'.

13/33–4. *duelle . . . nacion*: The Dauphin himself is said to have contemplated flight to Scotland at about this time.

14/1–3. *Remembir . . . banischid*: Omission of part of Fr. greatly alters the meaning. D has 'Recorde toy de Virgile, qui en sa tres-delicieuse poesie racompte les destourbiers, & desesperez meschiefs, où ledit Enee fut par sept ans deietté en sa fuite ennuyeuse'.

14/7. *borne*: See Introduction, p. 22.

14/15. *esclaue*: Although I have emended R's *estlauene* to *esclaue* (NSJ), it is interesting that *sclauene* (slavery) occurs in Scrope's *Dicts and*

Sayings (EETS, 211, 262/11): 'And a-nother called Sigonee was prisoner in sclauene'.

14/21–6: See Introduction, p. 49.

14/31–2. *Acuron . . . Cesar*: R is like Worcester's notebook, which has 'Acurion'. Cl has 'Curion', while D has 'Caton', B 'Turion', and Ro 'tirion'. R is like BClRo (and Worcester) in their reading: 'qui delaissa la liberte de sa Cite espouentee pour fouyr la fortune et la force de cesar'. D has 'qui delaissa sa liberté, & saillit hors de sa cité', etc. Chartier might have intended either 'Curio' or 'Cato' here. C. Scribonius Curio's relationship to Caesar and his enemies was more nearly like Calchas' relationship to the Greeks and Trojans than was Cato's relationship to Caesar. Curio, pretending to be on Pompey's side to restore full power to the Senate, was secretly paid by Caesar to serve him. The last phrase of the sentence supports the reading 'Caton', however, unless in transmission of the text, 'suivre' has become 'fouyr'. Cato with Scipio led the Republicans against Caesar and in 46 BC, when Scipio was defeated, fled to Utica, where he committed suicide. This suicide was considered in the best tradition of the Republic, however, and Chartier's references to Cato's death later (17/1, 76/18) indicate that he probably meant this example of a traitor to refer to Curio.

14/33. *inconstaunce*: 'inconstance' Cl, Worcester; 'constance' D (BRo omit clause).

15/11. *Trinite*: DBRo have 'eternité'. Cl had 'trinite', but it was corrected to 'eternite'.

15/19. *and . . . othir*: Mistranslation of 'Et vouls que l'vn l'autre engendre'.

15/31–2. *and . . . pleasur*: om. Fr.

16/4–5. *supprised . . . ordir*: Free rendering of 'tout suspens, & surpris, & mes pensees vagues & esgarees, sans ordre, & sans certaine fin ne vraye election'.

16/17. *Thyn . . . declyne*: 'you are growing old'. Since NSJ have *falleth* here, R seems to have picked up *waxith* in error from earlier in the line.

17/1. *seruage*: Fr. adds 'ou preuenir mort plus vergoingneuse'.

17/1. *hymself*: Like B, which omits 'à Vtice', added in DClRo.

17/7. *Pharnates*: Both 'Pharnastes' (B) and 'Phanartes' (Cl) support R's spelling with *t* rather than *c*.

17/10–12. *that . . . wallis*: 'que leur pouoir, qui le monde seigneurissoit, fut restraint & serré dedans leurs seulles murailles'.

17/12. *But*: This has no Fr. equivalent. *Haniball* in l. 9 is the subject of 'porta' (*bar*) in l. 13.

17/14–15. *and . . . venyme*: Fr. has 'comme remede final de ses doubtes au besoin, & au destroit du peril de sa vie donna au venin le nom de sa mort'.

He bar on honde he was slayne seems to mean 'he made known that he was slain'.

17/23–4. *for . . . depe*: 'pour mort abregier' BRo; 'par mort abregee' DCl.

17/26–7. *Dido . . . plesaunce*: R is like BClRo: 'Et dido contraincte du dolant regret de perdre sa plaisance'. D has 'Et Dido contrainte du doulant regret de perdre sa plaisance, soy mesmes se ietta en vn feu où fut arse, & bruslee'.

17/27–8: This passage refers to Sophonisba (whose name is in B), wife of King Syphax of the Massaesyli, a Numidian tribe. In the Second Punic War she was captured by Laelius, a Roman, and Masinissa, King of the Massyli. According to Livy (xxx. 12–15), she pleaded with Masinissa not to let her fall into Roman hands, whereupon he married her. When Laelius demanded her as a prisoner, she took poison.

17/29. *watche*: R either followed a manuscript like Ro, which has 'veiller', or misunderstood the better reading 'vieillir' (DBCl).

17/30. *Euery day*: RNSJ follow the punctuation of BClRo; D places this modifier with the preceding sentence.

17/32. *as . . . voyde*: 'vague' (vagabond, forsaken).

18/4. *Lordship*: Like Cl, which omits 'iuste', a modifier of 'seigneurie' in DB (Ro has 'iustice').

18/10. *angre . . . thoughtis*: Fr. has 'chagrin, & soucy de pensee'. R seems to have confused 'soucy' with some form of 'soupir'.

18/13. *inpaciente*: Fr. has 'impatient'. R uses the word in the rare meaning 'intolerable', the first *OED* record of which is from Spenser, *F.Q.*, II. i. 44.

18/27–8. *the* (1) *. . . Trinite*: 'la trinel exemplaire' D₁; 'l'Eternel exemplaire' DBClRo.

18/33. *forgette*: Either *forgette* (RN) or *foryuge* (SJ) could be translations of Fr. 'foriurer'.

18/34–5. *and* (1) *. . . bapteme*: R omits part of Fr. here:

> C'est contre soy coniurer,
> C'est raison desmesurer,
> C'est du tout auenturer,
> Pour le moins le necessaire:
> Loy [Le Ro] forfaire,
> Et estre au cresme pariure.

19/2. *haynous . . . sharpe*: 'espouuentables, & tresperçans le cœur, & la pensee'.

19/3. *seducyous*: 'tending to lead astray' (related to v. 'seduce' rather than to adj. 'seditious').

19/6–18. *Natur . . . followith*: The translator or the scribe of a manuscript behind RNSJ had difficulty with pronoun gender here. *Natur* is feminine in ll. 8, 13–14, but masculine in ll. 9–10. Perhaps the confusion arose through the introduction of *fortune* (feminine) in l. 11 and *Vndirstondinge* (masculine) in l. 15. Cf. 21/19. R may have *lamentable* from a manuscript like BRo and uncorrected Cl, which have 'lamentaire'; D has 'l'elementaire'. *put vpon hym* here may mean 'assail him' or 'incite, impel, urge him'. Cf. *Cloud of Unknowing*, ed. P. Hodgson (EETS, 218, 1944), 15/20–1: 'if þou be willy to do þis, þee þar bot meekly put apon him wiþ preier, & sone wil he help þee'. Hodgson glosses the phrase as 'assail him', a meaning not in *OED*. R may mean literally 'beat him', however; then *shaking and betinge* in l. 14 may mean Nature's shaking and beating of Understanding rather than her own body's trembling.

19/21–2. of the, man,: Punctuation follows Fr.: 'de toy homme'.

19/24: Cf. Understanding's berating of Indignation, Defiance, and Desesperance and Faith's driving them out later with Philosophy's driving out of the Muses from the sick body in Boethius, Lib. i, Prosa 1.

20/12–15. *Thes . . . loste*: 'Par telles parolles me amonestoit en gros, & en trouble, encores tout pesant de trop dormir, & degousté par l'amertume des poisons de melencholie. Et ie qui estoie apres tant d'ahan'.

21/8. *Trinall*: 'trine' Ro; 'eternelle' DBCl.

21/9. *shyning*: By this misunderstanding of 'ruisselet', R has spoiled the effect of Chartier's image. An unclear word beginning *bro* (? *browgh*) inserted here in S may represent a corruption of 'brook'.

21/15–16. *turnith . . . erthe*: Mistranslation of 'tournent, influent, & esclairent sans cesser enuiron la terre'. R was probably thinking of the astronomical phrase *turnith the influence*, meaning 'influences the character and destiny of man'.

21/16–19: See Introduction, p. 29.

21/18–22. *Nature . . . suppositif*: Awkward, inaccurate, and partially meaningless translation of 'Nature, que t'a baillée en ayde, n'est pas oiseuse en sa commission, ainçois par ses belles vertus, qui luy ministrent chascune en son ordre, s'estudie à continuer l'espece humaine, & conseruer le indiuiduel suppost'. Ro has a different reading: '. . . Aincois par sa belle vertu lui administre chacun iour en son ordre ses estudes . . .' The emendation in R from NSJ somewhat improves the sense of the English, but the passage is still awkward and unclear. *suppositif*, not recorded in *OED*, seems to be an adjective created from Fr. *suppost* (derived from L. *suppositus*, pp. of *supponere*), and seems to mean 'particular' or 'subordinate'.

21/19. *his*: Perhaps a scribal error for *hir*, since R's references to Nature are usually feminine. Cf. 19/6 ff., where there is a similar confusion in gender. Or *his* may have been written here in an attempt to distinguish between *the Power Vegetatif* (feminine, l. 22) and Nature.

21/22–7: This passage refers to Aristotle's discussion in *De Anima* and *Nicomachean Ethics* of the relationship between Understanding (or Reason) and the vegetative (or nutritive) part of the soul and the sensitive (or perceptive) part (see above, 5/20 ff.), and to Aristotle's division of the vegetative power into the nutritive, formative, assimilative, and unitive functions. The reference to the bellows blown by the spiritual members of life, moving, and knowledge is to Aristotle's discussion of the necessity of movement and perception in the animal to enable him to secure and recognize his food. The *radicall humour* refers to the medieval philosophical concept of the presence in all plants and animals of a humour or moisture as a necessary condition of vitality.

21/30. *which . . . gretter*: Fr. suggests the emendation here. See Introduction, pp. 16–17.

21/32. *which*: *which* is superfluous in an otherwise good sentence which follows DBCl exactly: 'Ne scés tu que le hault Maistre des euures . . . t'a mis en corps d'omme', etc. Ro, however, adds 'il' before 't'a'; it is perhaps this which R attempted to render by *which*.

22/1. *dompte*: Since *doubte*, the reading of RNSJ, does not make sense in this context; since *doubte* and *dompte* might easily have been confused by a scribe; and since Caxton used *dompte* several times, showing that the word was known, I have emended here. It is possible, however, that the confusion occurred in R's French exemplar; such confusion does occur in the French manuscripts of *Le Quadrilogue* at 138/17, where D has 'avoit dompte'; H 'domptoit'; A 'donctoit'; and B 'ne doubtoit'.

22/2. *it*: 'te'.

22/16–20. *He . . . anguysche*: In DRo the participial phrase 'vainquant [exaulce Ro] le monde charnel par l'espirituelle puissance' is added to the preceding sentence; in BCl it is omitted. R added the phrase to the next sentence, which in Fr. reads: 'La porte, par qui on entre à vie bien heureuse, est bien petite, estroite, & penible: & se faut baissier, humilier, & courber ses membres en mes-aise & angoisse'. R somewhat improved the structure by his change in the last clause.

22/27. *loke vpe, arise*: Fr. has 'le . . . enluminer et ressourdre'. N's *and ryse* may be the original reading since *a* is used elsewhere for *and* in RNSJ.

22/29. *infelicite . . . synne*: 'infecte par lorgueil de pechie' Ro; '& infecte par l'originel pechié' DBCl. *infelicite* may be a scribal error for *infecte* in RNSJ.

22/33–23/1. *wake ageyne*: There is confusion here of Fr. 'se recueillent' (are gathered) and 'se reveillent' (waken), an error made either by the translator or by the scribe of R's French exemplar.

23/9. *point*: Fr. has 'empreinte'. Although *point* may be a scribal error in RNSJ for *print*, it may mean 'distinguishing feature or characteristic', which fits the context.

23/10. *Than . . . hymself*: 'Si se vergoingna de sa faute, confuz, & humble'.

23/12. *mighty officers*: 'officiaulx puissances'.

23/13. *troublid with*: Fr. has 'esgarees és destours des'. *troublid* (RS) seems a better rendering than *tremblid* (N).

23/14–16. *of* (2) . . . *dissaiveable*: R is like Cl, where 'qui d'apparence verballe pouoient troubler, & empescher sa raison', which describes the three sisters in DBRo, is omitted. Aristotle (*Topics*) distinguishes between the demonstrative method, in which the premises are true and primary, or *serteyne*, and the dialectic method of probable reasoning, in which the conclusions are *dowtfull*. These two, in turn, are distinguished from sophistic, or *dissaiveable*, reasoning in the *Sophistic Elenchi*. In this passage Understanding is suspending for the moment the activities of the reason in order to understand the truths which only Faith will enable him to reach.

23/17. *fredom*: 'franche seruitute'.

23/18–19. *Thanne . . . wourdis*: 'Adonc celle Dame congneut sa contrition, & le vid humilié & docile'.

23/28. *ceryously*: 'cerimonieusement'.

23/28. *close*: The phrase *bar close* suggests that *close* here is an adverb, but the doublet *close and folden* (Fr. 'clos, & ploié') must be adjectival describing the book Faith is carrying.

23/29. *arme*: Like Cl, which omits 'senestre', added in DBRo.

24/1. *of yren*: 'de fer' (in corrector's hand) Cl; 'defermez' DBRo.

24/4. *alliauneces*: 'alliances' BRo; 'raliances' DCl.

24/5. *degre*: 'decret'.

24/11–14. *avision . . . bothe*: Like DCl; *om.* BRo.

24/12–15. *of . . . feithe*: N is corrupt here; RS follow Fr. exactly.

24/21. *and to*: *to* has no Fr. equivalent. *the lif of grace* is thus in conjunction with *mortifieng* in Fr.

24/26. *in . . . merytes*: 'en la puissance & merites [*sing.* BRo]' BClRo; 'en la puissance & par les merites' D.

24/30. *iurisdiccion*: Like Cl, which omits 'espirituelle', added in DBRo.

24/30–2. *as . . . hevine*: DCl read 'par Vicariat diuin exercé en terre, & approuué és cieulx'; BRo have 'par diuin excercite en terre et aprouue es cieulx'. *bothe* is probably an adjective rendering Fr. 'et' and meaning 'also, at the same time'. It is possible, however, that R intended *approued bothe in hevine* as an elliptical clause meaning 'both are approved in Heaven', *bothe* referring to the double function of Peter.

25/2. *clere tokyns*: 'cleres enseignes' Cl; 'douloureux enseignes' D; 'clers ensengnemens' BRo.

25/2–4. *þat . . . meditacions*: 'celle que tant souuent en l'estude de saincte [*om.* Ro] Theologie & en ses secrettes meditations [ou *add.* Cl] il auoit [lauoit ClRo] suyuie [seruie B, like R] & honoree'.

25/7–9. *Thanne . . . merite*: R mistranslated 'Si se print à reuerer Foy en coniouyssement d'esperit par ce nouueau metre'. The understood Fr.

subject is 'Entendement'. Note the confusion between 'metre' and 'merite'.

25/12–14. *O . . . helpe*: R used an inferior manuscript like ClRo:

> O [*om.* Ro] clarite qui [tout *add.* Ro] enlumine
> Quant Raison fault & decline
> Et oppinion Indigne
> Pour donner soulaigement.

B improves the sense of l. 3: 'En oppinion Indigne'. D does not correct l. 3, but adds between 3 and 4 the line 'Tu vins du haut firmament'.

25/29. *or song*: *om.* Fr.

26/2–7. *O . . . face* (2): R did not understand the Fr. construction here: 'O Tu Entendement figuré au patron de la Trinité, & par ces trois puissances, Cognoissance, Volenté, & Memoire, vnies en la substance diuine [dune BClRo] seule ame qui par les creatures faictes en ce visible monde congnois par reflection comme en vn mirouer obscur enluminé de Foy, les inuisibles euures de Dieu, que apres ta glorification verras face à face'. *or* in l. 2 shows an easy confusion between 'ou' and 'au'. R had an exemplar like BClRo, which have 'dune' for 'diuine'.

26/10. *oonly*: *oonly* may mean 'specially', rendering 'du tout', or it may merely be misplaced in its usual meaning.

26/20. *Ye, I beleve*: Even though Fr. has no support, I have added this positive *Ye*, omitted in RN, from S, because such an added exclamation is typical of the translator. See Introduction, p. 67.

26/29. *piete*: Since *piete* (RN) and *pyte* (S) are used interchangeably and their meanings must be determined by context, R may mean either 'pity' in the modern sense or 'affectionate loyalty and respect between parents and children'.

27/5. *So . . . perill*: R may have used a manuscript like Cl, which has 'Ainsi en soy congneut le peril', rather than like DB, which have 'foy' for 'soy'. Because of the position of *through his trewe feithe*, however, it is difficult to tell. 'par Foy' is part of the Fr. main clause, as shown by my punctuation.

27/36. *And in erthe*: Fr. 'en terre' completes the parallel construction of the preceding sentence.

28/4. *the vniuersall worlde*: 'luniuersel monde' B; 'luniuers monde' Cl; 'tout le monde' D; 'le monde' Ro.

28/5. *vndir foote*: 'à mes piez'.

28/13–15. *O . . . workingis*: R increased the vigour of this passage and somewhat altered Chartier's meaning: 'Beaux [haulx BClRoD₁, like R] enseignemens, miraculeux exemples, & artificieulx ouurages m'as à present declarez & ouuerts (mere tres-charitable, & maistresse excellente) & qui surmontent [surmonte Ro] la comprehension naturelle de ma pensee'. In Ro with 'surmonte' and without Duchesne's parentheses, the 'qui' clause might have gone with 'maistresse', as R placed it.

28/21–3. *in . . . divine*: 'se par vertu supernaturelle participant [a *add*. Ro] celle haulte infinité, il [*om*. Ro] n'est esleué en grace sus nature'.

28/23. *lady*: 'mere' BClRo; *om*. D.

28/23. *and pite*: *om*. Fr.

28/26. *O lady*: *om*. Fr.

28/31. *hasty anguschis*: Fr. has 'angoisses tantost surmontées'. *hasty* evidently translates 'tantost'.

29/2. *question*: Fr. adds 'fondée'. Perhaps there is a scribal omission in RNSJ.

29/4–5. *but . . . seurte*: 'ainçois veulx l'vsage du corps chalenger par droit, pour demeure seure & permanente'.

29/14. *of* (1) *. . . affliccions*: These phrases are in conjunction in Fr., as in R, rather than as in NSJ.

29/16. *prikkyng*: 'agileté' (confused with 'aguillon').

29/20–7. *fermed . . . ordir*: Fr. has 'Ferme en ta memoire par deuotes considerations, que cil qui tout fit sans besoing d'aide, & sans requeste d'autruy conseil, mais pour espandre la largesse de sa bonté, a la cure, & le gouuernement vniuersel des Royaumes, & des personnes, & que sa prouidence adresse toutes choses aux fins pourquoy il les crea, se leur desordonnance ne les en destourne'. In this awkward translation R rendered 'Ferme' as a past participle rather than in the imperative, and 'a' as *to* rather than *has* in l. 23. *helpe* for 'cure' may be a scribal error for *helthe*.

29/29–30. *that . . . therof*: 'qu'il n'y a que redire [quil y ait que reprendre Ro], en establissant soubs luy les terriennes puissances'.

29/31–2. *Nay . . . do*: 'Certainement sa charité n'est point oiseuse sur nous'.

30/3–6. *lymited . . . glorye*: Here R becomes almost meaningless because of use of an inferior exemplar like D or perhaps because of similar misinterpretation. D reads 'limite de sa permanence, maintient leurs mutations, & diuersitez, & leurs mouuement, & diuers estat, monstrent la magnificence de sa gloire'. Cl has 'Lunite de sa permanence maintient souuerain bien· Leurs mutacions et diuersitez et leurs mouuemens et diuers estas monstrent . . .'; BRo have yet another, even better reading: 'Lunite de sa permanence [permanente prouidence Ro] maintient leurs mutacions et aduersitez· et leurs mouuemens et [en Ro] diuers estas monstrent . . .' The main confusion in R and D is the mistaking of 'lunite' for 'limite'.

30/18. *mak reasons*: *mak reasons* (Fr. 'raisonner') means 'give reasons', hence 'argue', with a play on the idea of arguing by the use of reason, indicated in *Hym that made reason*.

30/20–1. *where . . . be*: 'qui remple [supplie Ro] les autruis deffaux' DClRo; 'qui congnoist les deffaulx dautruy' B.

30/23. *suppose*: Like Cl, which omits 'sans doubter', added in DB.

30/24. *inevitable*: 'ineuitable' BCl; 'irreuocable' D.

30/24-6. *Thanne . . . power*: 'Then your poor capacity could not understand enough to appreciate his infinite power'.

31/1. *to the conclusions*: '& la dependance [*pl.* BRo]'.

31/27. *dedis*: Fr. adds '& limitees par sa iustice'.

31/27-8. *the . . . Cristendome*: Fr. has 'nostre Chrestienne France'. R confused 'France' and 'franc'.

31/29. *in . . . areyse*: R probably used a manuscript like D_1, which has 'en vertu de qui est le merite, de estre preseruée & ressourse'. Ro omits 'en vertu' and DBCl have 'elle' for 'est le'.

32/27. *hir declaracion*: Fr. 'La declaration' refers to the preceding statement of Faith.

33/1. *creature*: Following this in RNSJ, there is an omission crucial to the understanding of the sentence. Fr. reads 'Mais par la perfection des choses creées, doit on entrer à congnoistre la perfection du Createur, qui leur foiblesse soustient, & leurs erreurs corrige'. 'doit . . . Createur' is omitted in the English. The sense of the passage should be 'but only by the perfection of the creature may one come to know the perfection of the Creator'. The omission in an English manuscript behind RNSJ probably occurred because of the similarity of *creature* and *creator*. J regularly has *creatour* for *creature*. RS are usually, however, more careful in distinguishing the two words; and it is thus significant here that S has *creatour*, while R has *creature*.

33/6. *doctrinable*: This rare word is not listed in *MED*, and the only example in *OED* is from Sidney, *Apol. Poetrie* (1581).

33/10. *course*: 'discours'.

33/18. *affeccion*: For a discussion of this lacuna in J, roughly corresponding to the C fragment, see Introduction, pp. 12, 14.

33/26-34/1. *But . . . begynnynge*: Free rendering of 'Et qui diroit que seigneurie fut [comprinse ne *add.* Ro] entreprise par la violence des plus fors sur les mendres, peu de merueilles seroit de veoir [*om.* Ro] subuertir [subiuguer Ro], ou muer chose fondée sur si petit & inique commencement [fondement BRo]'.

34/6. *diffences*: The meaning here and at 35/6 is certainly 'offences', listed in *MED*. OED questions this meaning, and Vinaver, in his edition of Malory, considered the noun and verb forms in this meaning scribal errors in the Winchester MS. and emended from Caxton. The Malory passage, before emendation, reads: 'And sytthyn I deffended never as to her owne persone, and as for the offence that I haue done, hyt was ayenste youre owne persone, and for that deffence ye have gyvyn me thys day many sad strokys' (844/27-30). The evidence suggests that these are not scribal errors, but examples of the substitution, more common than realized, of *defence* for *offence* and *defend* for *offend*.

34/6–7. *our . . . heyris*: Cl has 'osta il le Royaume a ses hoirs'; Worcester omits 'il' in this reading. D has 'luy osta il par mort en bataille, & à ses hoirs le Royaume'. BRo have 'lui osta par mort le Royaulme et a ses hoirs'.

34/20–2. *and . . . lothe to*: See Introduction, p. 20, n. 4. C's omission of this passage and the variant readings in RNS suggest that it may have been marginally inserted in an earlier manuscript. *and haue commawnden* in NS may better render Fr. 'commandez' than R's *and haue commaundingis*. *lothe to* has no Fr. equivalent, but note S's *pevertybloth*, which may have occurred through a scribal jump from *l* in *pe[r]vertyble* to *l* in *lothe*. A copy text that was difficult to read is further indicated here by N's *and per fore* for *peruertible, lothe to*.

34/26. *deth*: Like Cl, which omits 'de tous, & de toutes choses', added in DBRo.

34/30. *which*: Here R translated Fr. 'que' as *which*, but the context demands *that*.

35/4–5. *the . . . Himself*: Mistranslation of 'le delit de l'onneur ne feist mescongnoistre la charge'.

35/8. *that . . . heuy*: This is a meaningless rendering caused by misinterpretation of an unpunctuated Fr. manuscript. Fr. has 'Maleureuse, & trop pesante est la Couronne'. R took 'Maleureuse' as the modifier of 'roys' in the preceding sentence.

35/11–12. *For . . . dreede*: The pronouns here are singular in contrast with those in the preceding and following sentences. R is free in construction also. Fr. reads: 'Et pour la cremeur qu'ils tiennent par force sur leurs suiects, oublient la crainte'.

35/19–20. *be . . . office*: 'est pis soustenu'.

36/17–22: See Hebrews 12. Chartier used the idea, but changed the image.

36/24. *whanne he trespassith*: This clause, omitted in NSC, was probably picked up in error by the R scribe from l. 23, where it also occurs.

37/3. *mysknowlechinge*: Fr. has 'descognoissance'. The verbal noun is not in *OED*, which records the verb *misknowledge* as 'Sc. obs.', with a single example from 1600. The verb occurs in NSC at 35/10 as a variant for R's *mysknowe*.

37/13. *many . . . people*: 'de son peuple grant nombre' Cl; 'LX. mille [lxx^m BRo] hommes de son peuple' DBRo.

37/17–18. *shulde . . . true*: 'desroguer à la diuine Iustice, & dementir le texte'.

38/2–5: Cf. Fortescue, *The Governance of England*, ed. C. Plummer (Oxford, 1885), chap. 1.

38/12–13. *for . . . renowm*: 'pour lonneur de sa renommee' Cl; 'par [pour BRo] l'honneur de ses iustes faits, & renommée' DBRo.

38/18. *looke wher*: This construction here and at 96/12 (a passage cited in *MED*) is noteworthy because *OED* says, 'The absence of examples between the 12th and the 16th c. is remarkable' (*look* v. 4b.).

38/27. *Likewise the vices*: 'Par semblable le vices' BClRo; 'Le vice' D.

38/27. *that*: D has 'qui', omitted in BClRo, and Fr. adds 'du Prince'. R's omission of this phrase causes *his* in l. 29 to be meaningless.

38/34–39/5. *Now . . . vengeaunce*: Free translation of 'Or en droit s'ensuit il, se les Roys furent establis à occasion du pechié du peuple, & à sa requeste, & les pechiez des Roys redondent és suiects, que sur ceulx dont vient l'achoison, & où se multiplie la coulpe, doit tourner la vengence'.

39/9. *charges and affliccions*: Both nouns are singular in Fr. NSC have *charge*, but like R the plural *affliccions*.

39/9. *kynges*: Fr. adds 'Pourtant est puny vn peuple pour son Roy'. Because of the repetition of 'Roy', the clause may have been omitted in R's exemplar.

39/10. *his*: 'sa' Cl; 'la' DBRo.

39/11. *dissolucion . . . them*: 'dissolution leur est ouuerture [ouuerte BRo, like R] de vices'.

39/11–13. *through . . . dissordinaunce*: 'sa negligence d'exaulcer les vertus, & reprimer [approuuer Ro] les meffais, est commencement de leurs desordonnances [*sing.* Ro]'.

39/14–15. *Wherfor . . . vertue*: 'Grant mouuement de discipline & de meurs doit exciter les Princes à vertu'.

39/19. *schewith*: 'se iugent'.

39/25–7. *But . . . certainly*: R here more nearly follows Fr. than do NSC: 'amez vertu pour laquelle seruir les auez, & sans laquelle garder ne les pouez'. R was originally corrupt and was given sense only by the corrector's addition of *owt* and the erasure probably of *t* before *hom* (the only instance of this spelling of 'whom'). The original translation probably had *that ye shulde serue hym with hem withowt hom ye cannat kepe them*. An intermediate copy between the original and RNSC may have had *that ye shulde serue hym with [t]hom ye cannat kepe them*, with a scribal jump from *hem* to *hom*. The scribe of a manuscript behind NSC seems to have added what he considered enough to gain a sensible reading, while the R corrector was more fortunate in his change.

39/28. *grace*: 'trace'.

39/29. *goodnesse*: 'lieu' (confusion with 'bien').

39/31. *who*: Fr. has 'vice'. This may be a scribal error repeated in RNSC from an earlier manuscript.

40/3. *by lyne*: 'au ligneau' BCl; 'au lieu' Ro; 'au liueau' D; 'au niueau' D₁.

40/7–8. *woll . . . ruyne*: 'se encline et tend a son premier estre et dechiet a Ruyne' B; 's'encline, & tend [sent Ro] de son premier estre à [et Ro] dechiet & [vient *add.* Ro] à ruine' DClRo.

40/11–12. *of their digniteis*: 'des indignes'.

40/25. *from their enheritaunce*: *into disherytesone* (NSC) perhaps translates more exactly Fr. 'en desertion'.

40/29. *roote ne braunchis*: 'branche ne racine' B, Worcester; 'branche, tige, ne racine' DClRo.

41/1. *desertes*: Like Cl, which omits 'Et pource faut il par force que', added in DBRo.

41/4–5. *causith . . . othir*: Mistranslation of 'attrayent aussi telle generalité de paine sur tous'.

41/9–11. *Wherfor . . . people*: Free translation of

> Que vault à tort amasser,
> Et poure peuple lasser.

41/14–16. *in . . . acompte*: *in . . . vnbindith* is part of the next thought in Fr.:

> Se vostre cueur ne s'afferme
> En Dieu, qui ferme & defferme,
> Compter fault au rapasser.

41/22–42/3: In his Introduction to *The Governance of England* (p. 80), Plummer, in discussing the C fragment, attributed to Fortescue, says of this passage: 'The thoughts and even the expressions are strikingly like those of Shakespeare's Sonnet lxvi'.

41/28–9. *chastite . . . constreyned*: *MED* omits this meaning of *constreyned* (violated, forced). *OED*'s only example is from Shakespeare, *Tit. Andron.*, v. ii. 178: 'Her spotlesse Chastity,/Inhumaine Traytors, you constrain'd and for'st'.

41/30. *So . . . owtrage*: Fr. has 'par necessité & par outrage' with the preceding sentence.

42/5–6. *your . . . life*: Fr. has 'vostre arrest s'y fichoit sans autre vie attendre, ou plus hault bien esperer'. 'vostre arrest s'y fichoit'='your judgement were determined'. R's *your beyng fyxid* seems to mean 'your existence securely established or determined'.

42/8. *the . . . damned*: DCl have 'la droicturiere & finable punition des damnez'. BRo omit '& finable'. The confusion in R may have been caused by a corrupt French exemplar which had 'est' for 'et', or the English manuscripts may be corrupt (perhaps *is* should be *of*).

42/9. *is . . . worlde*: 'nest pas aquerir en ce monde' Cl; 'n'est pas à acquerir les biens & honneurs transitoires [*om.* Ro] de ce monde' DBRo.

42/12. *anothir thing*: Originally Cl had 'autre', perhaps the reading in R's exemplar. 'vie' has been added by a corrector, making the reading like that in DBRo.

42/17. *suche . . . me*: Like BClRo, which omit 'a ordonné' in 'ce que le Createur en a ordonné, & voulu par moy annoncier' (D).

42/26. *iniquitees*: Fr. has 'iniques' (evil ones). R seems to mean 'sinners' in light of *good and rightwise men* (Fr. 'iustes') in l. 28.

42/28. *good and*: Omitted in NSC and Fr., this is another of the additions probably made by the R scribe. Cf. l. 31.

42/29: Cf. Feythe's speech here with Boethius, Lib. iv, Prosa 6.

42/31. *euile or*: om. NSC and Fr.

42/32–43/1. *For . . . vengeaunce*: R used a manuscript like Cl, which reads: 'Les punicions des hommes ne sont pas tousiours selon le present meffait· Mais prent souuent dieu en faisant bonnes oeuures la vengeance'. DBRo have the following longer reading after 'meffait': 'ne pas ne leur en est besoin. Car se à tous propos qu'ils commettent pechié estoient punis, on les cognoistroit par spectacle [grant obstacle Ro]. Mais Dieu premuni de toute misericorde punist souuent les pecheurs quant il les trouue faisant bonnes euures presentes, pour la vengeance'.

43/2–3. *Man . . . penaunce*: 'Ou temps du meffait n'est pas homme capable de la grace de correction & de penitence'.

43/4–9. *His . . . merite*: Fr. has 'Tant est longue sa sapience, & sa iustice si enlacee à sa pitié & grace, qu'il attent longuement à flageller les mauuais, en espoir de leur amendement, & remunerer les bons pour esprouuer leur souffrance, & accroistre la perfection de leur merite'. The addition of *but He abydyth* (inserted in S) makes sense of the corrupt reading in RNC. Here we have more evidence of a corrupt original lying behind RNSC.

43/10. *engruggement*: Fr. has 'agrauement'. *engruggement*, not in *MED* or *OED*, seems to be related to the verbs *engreg(g)e* and *aggreg(g)e*, both of which can mean 'aggravate'. It may be an error for *engreggement*, influenced by *grugge* in l. 13.

43/14–15. *sweting . . . heete*: Like Cl, which has 'esseuer' for 'esleuer' in 'en telle chaleur esleuer' (DBRo).

43/17–18. *right scharpely*: Strange translation of 'mon greffier'.

43/19. *stryving . . . desyers*: Fr. has 'escriuant en la personne des hastifs desirs'. 'estrivant' and 'escriuant' have been confused either by R or in his Fr. exemplar.

43/20–1. *formed . . . helthe*: Part of Fr. is omitted, probably because of a scribal error in R's Fr. exemplar. Fr. reads 'forma la demande/pareille à la tienne: & là en trouueras tu la responce plus amplement, & entendras comme l'ignorance humaine demande/souuent à Dieu contre son salut'. Omission of Fr. between the lines I have inserted, caused by repetition of 'demande', produces the exact equivalent of the English reading.

43/24. *eleccion*: 'election' ClD₁; 'affection' DBRo.

43/31. *Salomon*: Fr. adds 'qui fu aprentif à ton escole'.

44/5–6. *blandisch . . . synne*: Because of mistranslation the meaning of *blandisch* is unclear. Fr. has 'blandissent à la fortune des pecheurs [*om.* Ro]'.

44/11–13. *by . . . pride*: Free translation of '& quelz hommes ont honoré la vaine gloire des mauuais esleuez, & quis l'ombre & le port sous l'orgueil des authorisez par iniquité'.

44/14–15. *And . . . vp*: Like BClRo, which omit 'qui' in 'Et vous tous François, qui auez rendu' (D).

44/20–1. *seeng . . . ydolatrie*: D has 'd'auoir en cest endroit commis ainsi que vne publique Idolatrie'. D₁ has 'comme vne priuee' for 'ainsi . . . publique', and BClRo have 'ainsi comme vne pollitique'.

44/28–33. *Othir . . . rewle*: D has 'Autres par encliner & tenir en reuerence & chierté les puissans dissolus, leur ont donné cueur & entreprise de soy estudier à vice: & leur ont esté la vergoingne de leur eshontee dissolution, laquelle par volenté les fauorisans ont ensuie, & desirée'. R is like ClRo, which change 'ont esté' to 'oster' (B has 'oste'). In mistranslation of 'tenir . . . dissolus', 'chierté' has become *cherisch* with no object, although it seems to carry the meaning 'encourage', with the intended object *myghty men*.

45/1. *contagiousenes*: Cf. the only example of this figurative meaning in *MED*, from Rolle, *Mend. L.*, 40: 'The steppes of god [to] folowe . . . of al contagiousnes of mynde and body hym to purge'.

45/2. *deprivith*: 'priue' BRo; 'preuient' D; 'reprime' Cl.

45/10. *but*: *om.* Fr.

45/19. *dedeifyed*: This is either an eccentric spelling of *dedify* or a blending of *dedify* and *deify*. Fr. has 'desdiez'.

45/20. *people*: Fr. adds '& enuahiz les premiers'.

45/27 ff.: This passage, which treats the evils of the clergy, a common theme in this period of church strife, should be compared with the nearly contemporary condemnation by Nicolas de Clémanges, in 'De Corrupto Ecclesiae Statu' and 'De Ruina Ecclesiae', *Opera*, ed. Lydius (1613).

45/32. *sharpe*: 'Ange' (confusion with 'aigre').

46/5–6. *thes . . . comown*: 'sont les cas commis'.

46/7. *vnstable*: 'insatiable' DCl; 'vicieuse' B; 'viceable' Ro.

46/9–10. *hauyng . . . benefices*: A new sentence begins here in Fr.: 'Tant en est huy qui quierent la praye des reuenues, les fruicts des benefices'.

46/12. *that . . . substanciall*: *om.* Fr.

46/13–14. *in . . . worlde*: 'par les delictz mondains' Cl; 'par les desirs mondains' DBRo.

46/20–2. *Allas . . . sacrifice*: 'Las! non pas le deuoir & le sacrifice seulement ont ils en mespris'. See Introduction, p. 15.

46/26. *of benefice*: This phrase has no Fr. equivalent and is omitted in NS. It may be a scribal error in R picked up in recall from *dignite of benefice* in ll. 19–20.

47/5–13: See Dante, *La Divina Commedia, Inferno*, xix. 115–17.

47/13. *lawde*: Like BClRo, which omit '& en merite' (D).

47/19–21. *And . . . synne*: This is little more than a paraphrase with much omission. D reads: 'Ie ne t'accorde pas que pour l'abus des receuans soit frustree la charité du donneur. Et se les Clers ne peuent abuser des possessions sans damnation, il ne s'ensuit pas que Constantin ne fist chose de bonne entente à les donner sans son pechié'. The last clause in ClD₁ is 'constantin ne les peust bien donner sans pechie', and in BRo 'constantin qui fist chose a bonne entente a les donner y eust pechie'.

47/23–6. *seynge . . . power*: D reads '& affin que necessité de viure ne induisist & menast à pechié les ministres de saincte Eglise, ou que la simple poureté de l'Eglise ne fut foulée trop de legier par temporelle puissance, ou desdaigneuse disette'. R is like BClRo in the omission of '& menast' and 'les ministres . . . Eglise', and further like Cl in the omission of 'ou desdaigneuse disette'.

47/27. *God*: Like Cl, which omits a long passage added in DBRo: 'pource qu'il veoit que l'Eglise, & mesmes l'ordre Catholique estoit comme en voye d'estre delaissee, pource que peu de gens se ingeroient au lieu sainct Pierre recueillir, pour le petit prouffit ou reuenu qui y estoit. Et lors Constantin meu au bien & releuement de l'Eglise, luy donna les possessions terriennes qu'elle tient, qui depuis s'est augmentée des dismes & oblations courans, auecques les censiues & offertes Ecclesiastiques'.

47/29. *oonly*: This modifier is in the next Fr. sentence.

47/30. *the . . . ministracion*: Fr. has 'sont les Prestres dispensateurs, & ministres'. N is corrupt here.

48/3–4. *Thou . . . to*: 'tu les condamnas à estre comme'.

48/7. *the* (1) . . . *oppressions*: R is like BCl, which have 'la moleste et loppression'. D omits 'et l[e]', and Ro has 'noblesse' for 'moleste'.

48/8. *preestes*: DBCl add 'de Bahaingne', but Ro has the meaningless 'messages'. R's failure to include here these references to the revolts against the clergy in Bohemia results in the loss of much of the significance of Chartier's passage. The reference is to the movement which stemmed from the influence that Wyclif's writings had on John Hus, Jerome of Prague, and other leaders. When Hus was burned at the stake, Bohemia rose in arms: priests were driven from their parishes, and monasteries were robbed and burned. When Sigismund was to have succeeded to the throne in 1419, force seemed necessary, and a series of crusades against Bohemia, led by Sigismund and the Pope, began. During Chartier's lifetime there was continual strife, during which the crusaders were defeated. For another reference in *The Treatise of Hope*, see 131/16 ff.

Chartier's third Latin discourse before the Emperor Sigismund in 1425 was an attempt to influence the Hussites to return to the orthodox faith. This Latin discourse should be considered with the discussions here. See also Howard Kaminsky, *A History of the Hussite Revolution* (Berkeley, 1967).

48/14. *which*: R is like Cl, which has 'que celle secte perilleuse'. DRo have 'Car' for 'que'. B has 'Car telle sequelle perilleuse'.

48/16. *bareyne*: 'en Bahaingne' (see 48/8 n.).

48/18. *The . . . nycete*: 'La dissolution'.

48/19. *into the chirche*: 'en Bahaingne' (see 48/8 n.).

48/26. *His body . . . Fadir*: R is like BCl, which have 'son corps et sa vie a dieu son pere'. D omits 'a dieu son pere'.

48/28. *thing*: Fr. adds: 'les subiects se veulent maintenant tous exempter de leurs Prelats. Mais plus dure chose y a'. The omission is probably scribal, occurring either in R's French exemplar or in an English manuscript lying behind RN. Such an omission might easily have occurred because of the repetition of 'dure chose' (*hevy thing*).

48/28. *lyven*: Like Cl, which omits '& contiennent', added in DB.

48/34. *Ysaye*: R is like BClRo. D has 'Ezechiel', probably the intended reading as suggested by 49/20: *Nowgh woll I sende the ageyne to Ezechiell*. The passage probably refers to Ezekiel 34: 2, although there is also an injunction against bad shepherds in Isaiah 56.

49/6. *wourthi*: Fr. adds 'dont l'Eglise gemit, & ie m'en plain'.

49/9–10. *lak . . . ignoraunce*: It is difficult to know how R interpreted Fr., which has 'ont faute de conseil, disette de doctrine, exemple d'iniquité, & spectacle d'ignorance'. Cl places a stop after 'doctrine'. Perhaps the first *spectacle* in the English is a scribal error in anticipation of the second, and *as* may also be a scribal error for *is*.

49/12–13. *the* (2) *. . . dignite*: The correct Fr. reading is 'la dignité de l'estat'. It is interesting, however, that again R is like uncorrected Cl, which has 'de lestat de la dignite'; 'de lestat de' is cancelled, and 'de lestat' inserted in the proper place.

49/13. *thoffence*: Like Cl, which omits 'Car à ce mesmes propos, te dy au contraire de la crainte de Dieu, qui a deffendu de toucher à ses ministres. Certes qui abuse de son priuilege il le pert, & qui se transporte en aucune apostasie, ou irregularité, il est hors d'administration Ecclesiastique, & priué de tout son priuilege' (DBRo).

49/17–18. *causith . . . diffoulyng*: 'n'encoulpe en rien l'immunité [lumilite Ro]'.

49/25. *punycion*: 'punicion' BClRo; 'permission' D.

49/33. *dedes*: Fr. adds 'ou pour qui pechié Dieu le souffre faire. L'euure [iniure Ro] est de soy vile'.

50/1. *Cristen men*: The R scribe has dropped *men* out here because of the *en* endings. It is clear from *parteners* later that the reference is intended to be plural. Cf. *O ye Cristen men*, 75/18.

50/9. *a . . . counseill*: 'attrait de larrecin. C'est le lieu de reconciliation, & vous y exploictez par force les conseils de iniquité [& . . . iniquité *om.* Ro]'.

50/11–12. *close . . . grace*: *close from you* here with the following negative clause seems to mean 'exclude you from being sharers in His grace'.

50/13. *sacrid*: DBCl have 'sacrileges'. Note that J has *sacry*, perhaps indicating that the meaningless *sacrid* is corrupt.

50/19. *disknowlege*: This noun is not listed in *MED* and *OED*. The verb *disknowledge* to mean 'put out of knowledge, make unrecognizable' and the verb *disknow* to mean 'fail to know or acknowledge' are labelled noncewords in *OED*. The noun here, which renders Fr. 'descongnoissance', means 'failure to acknowledge'. Again at 62/26, *disknowlage* occurs in the meaning 'lack of knowledge, lack of recognition', translating Fr. 'nonchalence'. At 196/17, the verbal noun *disknowlegyng* means 'lack of knowledge, failure to know', translating 'descognoissance'. Cf. also 5/11–17 n.

50/21. *and . . . mischief*: *om.* Fr.

50/24–5. *grace . . . wele*: 'toute grace de bien faire, & tout cueur de prouffiter en vertu'.

50/27. *good*: Fr. has 'fruict'. R is like Cl and Worcester, which omit 'à soy ne', added in DBRo.

50/27–9. *and . . . deth*: D has 'ains de toutes ses entreprinses ne luy aduint sinon desconfitures, fuittes, & villaine mort'. B has 'sur lui' for 'fuittes'; Ro 'faictes sur luy'; and Worcester just 'faictes'. Cl has 'fautes et villenies de mort' for 'fuittes . . . mort'.

50/30. *Goddis*: This may be a scribal anticipation of the word later in the line, since NJ have *the* agreeing with Fr.

51/9–10. *which* (1) . . . *God*: R omitted some of Fr. here: 'dedié par eux au titre de deité, pource que les mescreans ne deuoient sainnement villener ne mescraindre ce que par erreur ils adouroient comme Dieu toutpuissant'.

51/10–14: See Valerius Maximus, i. 5. ext. 9.

51/27. *hevene*: Fr. adds 'Le foulé [foible Ro] se soustendra'.

51/30. *turne into*: 'tour[n]a en' Cl; 'tendra' BRo; 'cherra en' D.

51/36. *feer in concience*: 'craintiue conscience' BCl; 'craintiue obedience' D; 'certaine conscience' Ro.

52/18. *life*: Fr. adds 'grauité [crainte Cl] de meurs'.

52/20. *to*: Fr. adds 'debuoir de'.

52/28. *as sone . . . them*: 'si tost'.

52/28–30. *yet . . . abowte*: 'il a tant longuement enduré vos deffaulx? Mesure temps à temps, &'.

53/10–12. *Lette . . . confusion*: Indirect quotation in Fr. See Proverbs 1: 25–6.

53/15. *plente*: Fr. adds 'eureux de paix'.

53/21. *which . . . ligne*: Fr. has 'forlignez'. R apparently means 'degenerate' by the phrase. Cf. 148/25.

53/23. *suche*: 'Ceux Princes'.

53/26. *outereres*: 'aguillon [*pl*. Ro]'.

53/26. *make . . . subiectes*: 'se assubiectirent' ClD₁; 'se assentirent' D; 'se excerciterent' BRo.

53/33–4. *but . . . plesaunce*: 'Les nuits leur ont esté trop courtes pour leurs desuergondees plaisances, & les iours trop briefs pour dormir és liz sans exploit prouffitable'.

54/3. *iustice*: Like Cl, which omits 'qui sont les fais de leur principal charge & office', added in DBRo.

54/8–9. *What . . . werke*: 'Et que fera l'instrument sans l'ouurier, quant l'ostil, qui n'est pas propre à son ouurage'.

54/17. *and* (1) *. . . dust*: R follows Fr. more closely than do NJ: '& cil qui vous fait retourner en poudre'.

54/18. *all thes*: Chartier refers to 'seigneurie' by 'la', the object of the verb here. R then found it necessary to explain his object *all thes* as *rychesses and glories that ye mysvse in this worlde*, which has no Fr. equivalent.

54/24. *nakid*: Fr. adds '& plorans'.

54/25. *take*: Like Ro, which omits 'pour vous', added in DBCl.

54/25–6. *the . . . trespasse*: R misunderstood a manuscript like BClRo, which have 'trepas viatique'. D has 'repas viatique'.

54/31. *Noþing elles but*: I have accepted the reading from NJ since this construction in answer to a question is the translator's usual rendering of Fr. 'sinon'.

55/2–4. *Wene . . . peere*: RJ misplace *to* after *God*, whereas N has *to* both in its correct position before *holde* and in the incorrect place after *God*. Perhaps in a manuscript which lay behind RNJ the position of *to* was altered, a correction not noted by the scribes of the copy texts of RJ, while the scribe of N's exemplar noted the change but copied *to* again in the incorrect place as well. When *to* after *God* is omitted, N follows Fr. exactly: 'Cuidez-vous tenir de Dieu, par paraige, & parier auecques le nonpareil?' The R corrector, realizing that R was corrupt, inserted *þat* before *holde*. See *OED* under *parage* 4 for *holde by parag*, especially Cotgrave's definition.

55/5–6. *and as . . . ministour*: '& à son peuple iustice, garde [garder Ro] & droicture, comme administrateurs, & commis'.

55/13. *aftirwarde*: Fr. adds 'tournerent'.

55/18. *feere*: 'grauité'.

55/18–19. *is . . . generacion*: 'se espart, & communique à [auec Ro] leur generation'.

55/20–56/10: Books iii and iv of Aristotle's *Politics* discuss these types of government. Note especially the summary passage in Book iii, 1279a, in which the wording is strikingly like that of Chartier in the last sentence here. Chartier also probably knew the treatment of the subject in *De Regimine Principum* attributed to Aquinas, Book i, chaps. 1–5. See also the discussion of Fortescue's knowledge of Aristotle and Aquinas in Plummer's edition of *The Governance of England*, notes to chap. 1.

55/21. *heyers in reemes*: Like BRo, which have 'seignourie heredital en Royaume' (DCl have 'nommee' for 'en').

55/23. *where it beganne*: Fr. has 'lequel est commencement' and adds '& fin de toutes choses creées. Car là est perfection acheuee, où la fin & le commencement se reioingnent &'. Perhaps because of the repetition of 'commencement', the passage was omitted in R's exemplar.

55/24. *power*: At this point this passage on governments becomes confusing in R. It is quite possible that the translator had a bad exemplar, as is shown by the support he has for some of his corruptions in the Fr. manuscripts I have examined. (55/23 has already furnished one example.) Here, following *power*, R is like Cl in omission of 'qui est dicte ou appellee Monarchie', the D reading. (B has 'personne' for 'puissance' and adds the meaningless 'est ditte'. Ro has 'et est dicte indiuisa potestas'.) Hence, the name of the first kind of government mentioned by Chartier is omitted in R because of its omission in the Fr. exemplar.

55/24–6. *Othir . . . Aristogracye*: Cl omits 'ou principaulté' in this reading from D: 'Autres ont accepté les magistrats de homme choisy, & exaucé en seigneurie, ou principaulté pour sa vertu. Et ceste principauté s'appelle Aristocracie'. *principally* in R may be a mistranslation of 'ou principaulté'.

55/27–8. *senatours . . . Duke*: R is like Cl, which omits 'en vsent encore', added in DBRo after 'institucion'.

55/30–1. *which . . . degre*: 'pour garder le iour [terre Ro; tour BCl], & l'equalité [la qualite Ro] à [om. BRo] chacun de la communité en auctorité [haulteur Ro], & puissance [auctorite puissante Cl, like R] en son endroit, selon [soubz B; om. Cl] les estas & richesses'.

55/33. *Thymotracye*: R used a manuscript like Cl, which omits 'qui est en commun parler, election' (D). BRo have a different reading here: 'Et ceste puissance se appelle politiquement democracie et en comun parler ellection· Et la .iij.ᵈ maniere de seignourie est appellee timocracie'. Both ClD₁ have 'timocratie'. It should also be noted that the corrupt *by* before *Thymotracye* in RNJ reveals a corruption in an earlier English manuscript, the scribe of which evidently thought *Thymotracye* was a writer's name. Surely the translator himself is not responsible for this corruption.

56/7–10. *which . . . ordre*: R is like ClD₁: 'au royaume contraire tirannie A aristocracie· en laquelle peu de gens veullent maistriser par Iustice· Oligracie tymocracie· democracie qui est gouuernement populaire en confusion et sans ordre'. DBRo have 'Cest à sçauoir Tyrannie, confusion populaire, & pluralité seigneuriale'. The difficulty in this otherwise sensible reading from ClD₁ is the omission of 'a' before 'tymocracie', which has caused R's confusion in interpretation. We cannot perhaps blame the R translator too much for such misinterpretation since he is joined by Duchesne, Chartier's 1617 editor, who punctuates his marginal text (D₁) to support R's interpretation, placing a comma after 'contraire' and none after 'Tyrannie'. It seems unlikely, however, that such a translator as Fortescue would have so misinterpreted the passage, even with 'a' omitted. See Introduction, pp. 29–30. It will be noted that R's *Oligracie*, apparently in confusion with *-cracy* words, also has support in Cl.

56/18–20. *Chastite . . . certayne*: 'Tout est corrompu, chasteté qui souloit tenir ton estre certain, par son eslongnement la laisse souspeçonneux'.

56/21–2. *that . . . speke*: D places this clause with the first clause, but I have followed ClRo, which place it with the second.

56/24–7. *Who . . . werkes*: Mistranslation of 'Qui est celuy tant ignorant, qui ne sache bien que à l'entour d'eux se ingerent par presumption, ou entrent par faueur, hommes qui ne les seuffrent informer de science, ne vsager à quelque bon ouurage?' 'ingerent' has been confused with 'iugerent' in R. Like R, BCl omit 'tant ignorant', and BD₁ have 'sceuent' for 'seuffrent' (the Cl corrector has added 'sceuent &').

56/30–1. *And . . . pleasur*: om. Fr.

57/1. *the grette estates*: Fr. has 'noble homme'. The R scribe has incorrectly added *as* after *grette*. Since *as* occurs at the end of a line it may be the repetition of the first syllable of *estates*, sometimes spelled *astates* (for example, in C).

57/11–13: Duchesne's note on this quotation reads: 'L'Autheur des Gestes des premiers Comtes d'Anjou attribuë ce dit au Comte Foulques III, surnommé le Bon, & monstre que c'estoit vn prouerbe anciennement vsité parmy les François' (p. 853). E. Freeman, *The History of the Norman Conquest* (Oxford, 1877), ii. 277, also says that Numa, Fulk the Good, Count of Anjou in 942, was renowned as the author of the proverb. He refers the reader to 'Gesta Consulum', *Chroniques d'Anjou*, i. 245.

57/19–20. *for . . . Nature*: 'mais ils ont leur commencement en la faculté de dame Nature'.

57/20–1. *For . . . The Polesyes*: Fr. has 'Car ceux qui [les *add*. Ro] Politiques nous escrirent'. The awkward English clause means 'they that have before written *The Policies* (or *Politics* of Aristotle) for us'.

58/1–4. *Also . . . malice*: 'Car la discretion d'eslire & sens d'escheuer est seant à l'omme, que tous contendent à plus vouloir approuchier par auctorité, ou surprendre par malice'.

58/4–6. *And . . . perile*: This is little more than a paraphrase with much omission: 'Et plus doit cautement & sagement aller cil qui plus perilleusement doit trebuchier. Et par raison cil a besoing de sçauoir sur les autres qui ne puet errer sans dommaige des autres'.

58/8–10: See Plato, *Republic*, ed. Jowett and Campbell, i. 233; and Boethius, Lib. i, Prosa 4, where this statement is quoted from Plato in much the same phraseology as here.

58/14–18. *Avicenne . . . Grece*: *A vice thanne* (RNJ) for *Avicenne* gives further proof of a corrupt manuscript behind the English texts. In the passage added from NJ, *coment* may be a scribal error for *commentator* (Fr. reading). Worcester, like R, has 'baaly', where the French manuscripts have 'Aboaly'. The reference here is to Avicenna's well-known commentaries on Aristotle. The adjective *envyous* applied to Averroes refers to his rejection of Avicenna's ideas. See J. L. Teicher, 'Avicenna's Place in Arabic Philosophy' (chap. 2), and K. Foster, 'Avicenna and Western Thought in the 13th Century' (chap. 6), in *Avicenna: Scientist and Philosopher*, ed. G. M. Wickens (London, 1952).

58/21. *astrologie*: DBCl have 'Astrologie', Ro 'astronomie'. Because of the appearance of *Arystotle* in l. 18 and the possibility of scribal error as seen in J's *Arystole*, I have emended *Aristotle* to *astrologie*. Caesar is, of course, noted for his revision of the calendar, but not for 'amending' the works of Aristotle.

58/22. *Mageste*: This is a corruption of *Almagest*, the reading of D. Cl, however, also has 'Mageste'. Ro has 'tables la loy mageste'.

58/25–7: See Valerius Maximus, viii. 7. ext. 16.

58/29. *them*: Like Cl, which omits 'Et aussi par iceux sçauoir vient on à liberté, & par liberté à franchise, & seigneurie', added in DBRo.

58/31. *togedir*: Fr. adds 'Princes, &'.

59/4. *palsy*: R is like Cl, which omits a passage added in DB: 'Qui augmenta plus Rome à venir à seigneurie, que les artz liberaulx, que Numa Pompilius par grans amonitions de science annexa aux loix morales, & policiennes, & aux faicts triumphaux de Romulus son predecesseur; iugeant que euure de faict, supposé que executee soit, se elle n'est ratiffiee par la loy de prudence, n'est comme point durable?'

59/4–6: This passage (including the omitted portion quoted above) is very similar to Brunetto Latini, *Tresor*, ed. F. J. Carmody (Berkeley, 1948), i. 17. 31. Chartier mentions Brunetto Latini as a source at 103/23.

59/9–11. *But . . . lawes*: Fr. reads 'Mais le Prince est la loy viue, l'ame & [est BRo] l'esperit des loix'. R's mistranslation may have been caused by the confusion of 'est' and 'et' seen in the BRo variant.

59/16. *a* (1) . . . *vndirstonding*: 'non challant et non sachant' Ro; 'non sçachant' DBCl.

59/23. *ye . . . blaspheme*: 'vous auez par vne damnee & accoustumee blaspheme despité' D; 'vous auez par vne dampnee accoustumance blaphame [et despite *add.* BRo]' BClRo.

59/30. *vertu*: Like Cl, which omits '& mere de follie', added in DBRo.

59/33. *and leuith*: Fr. has 'Et qui laisse'. *And therfor* at 60/1 has no equivalent.

60/14. *misknowlage . . . vengeaunce*: Fr. has 'mespris & murmure aggraue [agrauent B; actraient Cl] vengeance'. See 89/32 n.

60/23-4. *namely . . . disobeysaunce*: 'De ceulx aussi qui furent chiefz de la Rumeur et achoison de desobeissance' Cl; 'Aussi as tu leu de ceulx qui furent', etc. DBRo.

61/6. *affliccion*: *afflicions* is spelled *affleccions* in SJ at 182/11. Such a spelling may account for the RJ error here in substituting *affeccion* for *affliccion*, the correct reading in N.

61/8. *God*: Fr. adds '& les violateurs de la loy [foy B], qui furent commencement & exemple d'inimitié [diniquite BClRo]'.

61/11. *recouerid*: Fr. adds 'comme innocens de peché'.

61/17-18. *thiniquitees . . . good dedes*: DCl have 'les iniques' and 'bons' ('the iniquitous ones' and 'the good ones'). But BRo, with 'les iniquitez', support R. Cf. 42/26.

61/19-20. *berith . . . repreues*: Fr. has 'se manifeste en extermination des reprouuez'. R means 'is manifested in the utter destruction of the reprobates'.

61/24. *infortune and discordis*: 'discors de l'infortune' DBCl; 'discort de fortune infortunee' Ro.

61/26-7. *þat . . . dethe*: 'que leurs coulpes selon le droit diuin ont semblablement tirez, & tirent chacun iour notoirement à despourueuë mort, ou publique male meschance'.

61/33. *of*: Like Cl, which omits 'son fils', added in DBRo.

61/34-62/1. *in . . . Sone*: 'en lumanite de son filz' ClD₁; 'qu'il appaire estre vray' DBRo.

62/1-2. *which . . . Testament*: 'que il retardoit aux enfans de lancien testament' Cl; 'qu'il n'a fait aux enfans de l'ancien testament, ausquels il retardoit sadicte clemence, & misericorde plus sans comparaison, qu'il n'a fait aux Chrestiens puis sadite Passion' DB.

62/5. *feer*: Fr. adds 'de Dieu'.

62/5. *shewith*: Like BCl, which omit 's'il te plaist', added in D.

62/9. *many . . . shewed*: 'manifestes' modifies 'choses' in Fr., thus supporting the addition of *openly* from NJ.

62/13-14. *I . . . thi discordes*: Fr. has 'ie ne m'arreste à tel discours'. Note the same confusion of *discordes* and *discours* at 61/24. Here *I woll not reste at thi discordes* is almost meaningless. *reste at*, like *rest vpon* at 65/33 and *reste in* at 107/8, all of which translate some form of the verb 'arrester', seems to mean 'decide on' or 'stop over, dwell upon'. R is like Cl, which has 'tes' as the modifier, not 'tel' (DBRo).

62/17. *furour*: The R corrector changed *fauour* to *furour* to agree with NJ. But at 61/34, all three manuscripts have *favoure* in error for *furoure*.

62/21–2. *put . . . worlde*: Fr. has 'deprimez en sens & en pouoir pour maleurté damnee. De ceste'. R's *of this worlde* seems to be intended to go with this sentence, but note that in Fr. 'De ceste' begins a new sentence.

62/22–5. *Dauid . . . armes*: Fr. has 'parla Dauid, qui disoit à Dieu: *Tu as feru la teste en la maison du mauuais, & desnué le fondement de sa force iusques au col. Tu as iecté ta malediction sur les Sceptres, & sur les cheuetains des gens-d'armes*'. Chartier attributes this saying to David, but it is almost certainly from Habakkuk 3: 13–14, a difficult Hebrew passage, which in the Vulgate reads, 'percussisti caput de domo impii, denudasti fundamentum eius usque ad collum; maledixisti sceptris eius, capiti bellatorum eius'. The Revised Standard version has, 'Thou didst crush the head of the wicked, laying him bare from thigh to neck. Thou didst pierce with thy shafts the head of his warriors'. 'the head of the wicked' is glossed 'Heb. head from the house of the wicked'; and the Hebrew for 'laying him bare from thigh to neck' is noted as obscure. In a translation of the Old Testament by Isaac Leeser this last phrase is rendered 'with the high-towering walls'. R's *vnknyt the foundament of his strenghe vnto his necke*, similar to the King James rendering, seems to mean 'destroyed the evil man completely'. *necke* figuratively here and elsewhere in the Bible often means 'the heart of man' or 'the whole man'.

63/3. *Abbot Ioachym*: This passage refers to the spurious *Scriptum super Esaiam prophetam*, written in the thirteenth century and attributed to Joachim (*c.* 1135–1202). See M. Reeves, *The Influence of Prophecy in the Later Middle Ages: a Study in Joachimism* (Oxford, 1969). For commentary on Chartier's possible connection with Joachism, see my 'Alain Chartier and Joachism?', *MLN*, lxx (1955), 506–9.

63/12–13. *which . . . resistence*: '& que la force de resister dehors est tournée sur soy mesme pour confondre sa propre [substance ou *add.* Ro] resistence' (B omits 'pour . . . resistence').

63/18–19. *by suche ensaumple*: This is not in Fr., which, however, adds 'si esleuéement, que nul autre mondain ne les peust humilier'.

63/21–2. *which . . . realmes*: R mistranslated 'que aux Royaumes diuisez mande desolation & ruine', confusing 'diuisez' with 'diuerse'.

63/25. *persones*: Fr. adds '& hommes esleuez de ton Royaume! Nombre par les ans les males auentures, & tu te esmerueilleras comme en si peu de temps'.

64/1. *lordshippe*: Fr. adds '& tant plus empeschans que exploicteurs'.

64/3. *the* (1) *. . . excercyses*: In Fr. 'les magnifiques en euure, les excellens en sçauance & en industrie' are subjects of 'sont fortraiz', as I have tried to show by my punctuation. If this is the structure intended in R, then the relative pronoun has been omitted after *men*. However, it looks as if R thought that 'euure' was a main clause verb. *excellence* (N) or *þe exceℓℓences* (J) may be the original reading rather than R's *thexcellentes*, a rare word with only one example (1502) recorded in *OED*.

64/11. *in . . . werres*: *om*. Fr.

64/17. *withowt . . . counseile*: 'sans mettre [sens ne *add*. Ro] nul arresté [de *add*. Cl] conseil en voz euures'.

64/25. *aftir your affeccions*: 'par affection'.

64/28. *like . . . foles*: Fr. has 'par telz termes'. *foles* then is an unusual form of *folowes* (NJ).

64/30–1. *men . . . feete*: 'serez marchiez sous les piez'.

65/4–5. *ye slepe in*: 'et vous endormez au' BClRoD$_1$; 'nonchalez' D.

65/22–4. *Why . . . self*: Because of the variants in RNJ here, it is difficult to tell what kind of Fr. exemplar the translator used. If J's reading, omitting *you*, is correct, then the translator had before him a manuscript like BClRo: 'Pour quoy gardera dieu des ennemis ce que vous perdez par vous meismes'. If, however, *you* (N, *ins*. R) is kept in the reading, then the English is more like D: 'Pourquoy vous gardera Dieu des ennemis, quand vous perdez vous mesmes'.

65/27. *to . . . kyssing*: 'à mordre & abbayer . . . en trauers, & en tapinage'.

65/28. *leve*: 'laissent' B; 'laissez' DClRo.

65/29–31: One old chronicle to which Chartier referred was probably the seventh-century *Chronicarum quae dicuntur Fredegarii Scholastici Libri IV*, ed. B. Krusch, in *MGH*: *Scriptores Rerum Merovingicarum*, vol. 2 of *Fredegarii et aliorum chronica, vitae sanctorum* (Hannoverae, 1888), iii. 12, 97. This story of Basina's dream is not in the two early chronicles, Gregory of Tours and *Liber Historiae Francorum*. R's *Quene of Saba* probably came from a manuscript like BClRoD$_1$, which have 'Sabine'; D has 'Basine'. *Achilperich* is an error for Childeric, which to some degree goes back to Fr.: DBRo have 'à Chilperic' but Cl has 'A cilperit' (showing why R attached the preposition to the proper name). Chartier himself seems to have thought the story related to Chilperic, who also had a son named Clovis.

65/33–4. *revoke . . . doubte*: This is probably a misunderstanding of the idiom 'reuoquez en doute' (call into question), but it is possible that R used an exemplar that had 'ne' for 'en'.

66/6–8. *loke . . . Lorde*: R used a manuscript like Ro, which substitutes 'te' for '&' in the first line of this passage:

> Ferme tousiours & presente
> Corps, cueur, sans [sens BClRo] fiance, attente,
> Conscience à Dieu patente,
> Force [Forte BRo], entente,
> Raison, voulenté, sçauoir.
>   En la bonté excellente . . .

66/9. *helthe*: Fr. adds 'Tu fuz né pour la deuoir'.

66/10–11. *the offences done*: om. Fr.

66/11. *Maker*: Fr. adds 'Là puet il confort auoir' in DBCl; 'La prent il consolacion' in Ro.

66/13. *but . . . substaunce*: 'force impotente'.

66/13–15. *For . . . iustice*: Cl has:

> Creinte ne la puet mouuoir
> N'affection desmouuoir
> De Iustice au droit du voir
> Pour mouuoir [Promouuoir DBRo].

66/18–20. *so . . . folkes*: RJ follow Fr. more closely than does N:

> Lors en faisant son deuoir
> Puet les sept dons receuoir,
> Que sainct Esperit fait plouuoir,
> Et r'auoir
> Grace prouchaine & presente'.

66/23. *aswryyd*: This strangely spelled word in R is a form of *assured*, the reading in N. Note that J has *answyryd*, reflecting a spelling like R's. ClRo have 'asseure'; D 'assoulagié'; BD_1 'assegrie'.

66/24. *murmours and grugynges*: 'scrupules'.

66/31. *barest*: Fr. has present tense. *barest* in R seems to be past tense, but N has *berest* and J *beryth*.

67/1. *to conforme*: Although NJ have *to conferme* and Fr. has 'confermer', I have not emended since these two words seem to have been used interchangeably by error in the fifteenth century. Cf. 116/23, 29, where *confirmed* is used for *conformed*.

67/2–3. *swerdis . . . sowle*: This passage is not coherent in R because of the omission of an equivalent for 'pour paruenir iusques à', perhaps scribally, after *swerdis*.

67/3–4. *that . . . God*: '& de l'esperit esleué à Dieu' (in conjunction with 'de l'ame').

67/9–11. *he . . . desert*: 'It is right that he who has deserved it should suffer the punishment'. *that hath* has no Fr. equivalent and may be added by scribal error in the English. The sentence may, however, reflect two attempts at translation.

67/11–13. *what . . . promyse*: 'quel soulagement donneras tu à nostre petite foeblesse? quel confort du temps auenir, ou quel espoir d'alegement nous promets-tu?'

67/29. *confiaunce*: *MED* does not list this word, but *OED* gives two examples from Caxton. Note that N has the more common *confydence*.

67/30. *drede*: 'crainte' Cl; 'creance' D.

67/34. *it*: i.e., 'faith'.

68/2. *by . . . cleving*: R's omission of Fr. 'les esles de' after *by* causes the comparison of faith to a bird to lose some of its effectiveness.

68/6. *alerion or*: The R scribe probably added this doublet since NJ omit it.

68/13. *Is*: Since this is the only occurrence in R of *is* as a form of *his* (although it occurs four times in the other manuscripts), it may have been intended as the possessive ending for *God*. Fr., however, has 'grace de Dieu, son aide'.

68/16–19. *Thanne . . . creat*: 'puis que és choses de ça ius ne s'arreste Esperance, se non en tant qu'elles sont les adresses & conduites de son chemin. Ainçois passe plus outre son appetit & sa fiance, & tire iusques au parfait & souuerain bien: outre lequel ne faut rien querir, & qui est la fin de toute tendence & inclination des choses creées' (BClRo omit '& conduites' and 'parfait &').

68/20. *hope*: Fr. adds 'par analogie, & par participation'.

68/24. *trustith . . . victorie*: 'espere en Dieu auoir santé ou victoire, ce doit estre pour appliquer celuy don de grace à gloire & à salut'.

68/28. *and . . . God*: 'et leur [le B] beneurete auec dieu' BCl; *om*. DRo.

68/29. *This . . . vertues*: Mistranslation of 'Cest ordre estably entre les vertus garda dame Foy'.

69/4. *puttith . . . restith*: '& mettent [en *add*. BClRo, like R] trouble & en dissention sur soy mesmes la pensee où ilz habitent'.

69/6. *hasty wrath*: *hasty* seems to be a rendering of 'meut', the verb of which Fr. 'Ire' is subject.

69/8. *We*: Before this Fr. adds 'Car comme la proprieté de sapience soit d'ordonner ses effects'.

69/9–11. *owt . . . disordinat*: 'tourne en desroy, en agitation confuse, & inuolution desordonnee'.

69/12–13. *Hope . . . ageyne*: 'mist Foy Esperance au deuant de la couche, & se retira vn petit'.

69/14. *dressid . . . lifte*: Fr. subject is 'Entendement'.

69/22–4. *a . . . hevenes*: Fr. has 'l'anel de la verge d'vn ancre d'or dont le bec estoit fiché dedans les cieulx'. *fycched* (NJ) or *fastened* (R) both are possible translations of 'fiché', but *fycched* may be the original reading since it is so like the Fr. verb. The translator's change of Chartier's image, which so clearly refers to the symbolic anchor of Hope, is interesting. It seems unlikely that the author merely did not understand Fr., which names the anchor, unless 'bec' misled him. If the change was deliberate, then R's language sounds like the description of a crest or coat of arms— *a turet of golde with a gossehawke theron*. Such a coat of arms does occur in English heraldry: a tower of gold with a hawk on it is listed for the Bridges family, and a tower with a bird on it is listed for the Felbrigg family. I have been unable to trace which branch of these families had these emblems, but the possible Felbrigg tie is interesting, since the Felbriggs of Norfolk (Sir Simon and Lady Felbrigg) were closely associated with Earl Rivers, whose later *Dicts and Sayings of the Philosophers* appears in the Newberry manuscript with the translations of Chartier, and of course the history of the Rawlinson manuscript is associated with Norfolk. It seems possible then that the translator, by his change of Chartier's image here, might indirectly have been paying a compliment to someone, perhaps a patron, with this coat of arms.

69/33. *with . . . oynement*: 'de loin de l'odeur'.

70/7. *hens*: Fr. adds 'pis qu'en sepulture'. Because of its omission in R, the next sentence loses some of its effectiveness.

70/14. *amonge . . . abidest*: R is like Cl, in which 'où' has been erased in the following reading from DBRo: 'entre lesquelles où tout autre conseil deffaut, tu demeures'.

70/17. *vnto . . . spirit*: The NJ reading maintains the sense of Fr. 'iusqu'à rendre lesperit'.

70/20–1. *it . . . violence*: Again the NJ reading keeps the sense of Fr. 'ne te puet force tollir, ne violence fortraire'.

70/27. *that*: Fr. adds 'tu t'es demuciée [mucee Cl; departee BRo] de moy au besoin'.

70/27. *comyng*: Fr. adds 'par grant temps; ainçois escoutoye & regardoie de toutes parts, se ie verroie ou orroye chose qui me donnast apparceuance de ton retour'. The omission in R probably occurred because of its omission in the Fr. exemplar. A Fr. scribe may have jumped from 'apparence de toy' to 'apparceuance de ton retour'. This supposition is supported by the English phrasing, since *of thy comyng* seems to be a rendering of 'de ton retour' rather than of 'de toy'.

70/32. *hir spirit*: 'l'esperit' in Fr. refers to the spirit of man.

70/33. *which*: In Fr. 'qui' comes after 'Foy' (*Feith*, l. 32), not here. Note that NJ have *whych* both here and after *Feith*.

71/9–11. *And . . . helpe*: 'A toy se reclament ceux qui par la tempeste de mer sont deiectez des vagues & des vents. En toy se asseurent ceux que les ceps & les manicles tiennent esliennez és tenebres des prisons'.

71/17. *in . . . necessite*: '& ne me vueilles en necessité esloigner'.

71/21. *vertues*: 'vertuz' Cl; 'varietez' DBRo.

71/22. Cf. the ideas in this speech with Boethius, Lib. v, Metrum 5.

71/24. *the . . . vndirstonding*: 'lordre entendement espirituel' Ro; 'ton ordre, Entendement espirituel' DBCl.

71/25. *made man*: 'baillé à l'homme'.

71/26–7. *his . . . stones*: Fr. has 'son estre communiquant auec les pierres'. *comunycant* means 'shared' or 'unified', a meaning omitted in *MED* and listed as rare for the adj. in *OED*.

71/31. *þat . . . elementis*: 'elementées' DBCl; 'elementaires' Ro.

71/32. *divided*: Mistranslation of 'duysible'.

72/12. *O alas*: *om.* Fr.

72/16–17. *at nede*: Fr. has 'd'aide' and adds 'se tu ne luy cuides auoir failly d'obeissance'.

72/28–9. *which . . . God*: Fr. begins a new sentence:

> De leger vers Dieu mesprennent,
> Et d'espoir tost se desprennent.

72/29–30. *toucheth . . . sharpely*: 'les surprennent'.

72/30. *erroure*: Fr. has 'ire'.

72/31. *repent them*: Fr. has 'se reprennent' (correct themselves) and adds 'Et sous Dieu tout entreprennent'.

72/34. *Like as*: R is like ClRo, which omit 'O' in 'O comme' (DB). Thus, the translator failed to see that 'comme' was the exclamatory *how*, not the comparative *Like as*. Note *hough many* in l. 35.

73/5. *promisses voyde*: Like Cl, which omits 'neant plus qu'il fut à Noë, lequel nous monstra permanableté de foy & d'euure sous feable esperance [et demoura soubz feal de son esperance Ro]', added in DBRo.

73/8. *of*: 'en' B; '&' DClRo; 'par' Worcester.

73/12–15. *And . . . peace*: '& de la seruitute de Babiloine reunidrent [remaindre B] par maintes tribulations, lxx. [lxxii BRoD₁] ans reuoluz dedans le pays de Syrie [desire ClRo], & en paix tres-souhaitee [tresdesiree retournerent B]'.

73/16–17. *the . . . abiding*: Fr. has 'ne la longanimité de bien attendre'. Worcester omits 'ne'.

73/17–18. *but . . . vertu*: Free translation of '& en perdant le cueur & en laschant la main & [*om.* Ro] la vertu'.

73/22. *by an angell*: *om.* Fr.

74/9–11. *of . . . counsaile*: Like BRo, which do not keep these virtues in pairs by using '&'; in DCl the first two, the second two, and the last three form groups.

74/20. *party*: The Glossary shows that *party* (less often *parte*), Fr. 'partie' or 'parti', was a utility word for both translators and Chartier. Here the word seems to mean 'way of life', a meaning not recorded in *OED*. The same meaning occurs in both versions of *The Quadrilogue* (194/32, 195/32, 204/4, 205/5), always in the same context: *party* or *parties* sustained or followed by one of the French estates.

74/23–4. *was . . . lif*: DCl refer to 'Saul' here: 'pourchassa Saul le peril de sa vie'. B, however, has the corrupt 'sans' for 'Saul', and Ro changes the thought: 'pourchessa le peril de sa vie & par quelle grace de Saul fut il preserue'.

74/26. *prodiciouse*: Fr. has 'prodicieuse'. *OED* has only one example of this rare word, from Heywood (1635).

74/30–75/8. *For . . . reste*: B adds 'par la bouche de Dauid'. This seems to be a reference to the appeal to the Beloved in Song of Solomon 2: 10, 13.

74/30. *people*: 'exemple'.

75/4–5. *syn . . . sufferaunce*: Mistranslation of 'depuis ce qu'il a permis son peuple tourmenter, & assez esprouué [esprouuer BRo] leur confiable & ferme souffrance [fiance Ro]'.

75/5. *in þis similitude*: Like BClRo, which place this phrase here; D places it before R's *The devoute*, 74/33.

75/9. *yn Hys bote*: See Introduction, p. 18.

75/10. *Apostulis*: Like BClRo, which omit 'qui perissoient, luy dormant, par tempeste de mer', added in D.

75/16. *God*: Fr. adds 'entre les perilz par exemple'.

75/22. *þingis*: The NJ reading *goodes* may be a closer translation of Fr. 'deliz'.

75/25–6. *He (2) . . . thiself*: 'He has humbled Himself (i.e., in becoming man) in order to elevate you above yourself (i.e., in arising to glory)'.

75/30. *to iuge*: 'mal iugier par deffiance'.

76/5–6. *for . . . liff*: D has 'pour laissier l'ennuy de vie temporelle'. R is like BCl in omitting 'temporelle', but Cl has an otherwise inferior reading. Ro has 'chemin' for 'ennuy'.

76/6. *maketh*: The subject is the same as in the main clause: *Dispeyre*.

76/17–18. *like . . . the (1)*: 'Et te viendra au deuant la mort'.

76/18. *wilfully*: This has no Fr. equivalent, but DBCl add 'à Vtice', omitted in Ro.

76/18–22. *Also . . . vnlawfully*: Fr. has 'Et le saut de Marcus Curtius [qui saillit *add.* Ro] en la fosse de Rome, ou l'occision que fit Lucrece de soy-mesmes, par vergongne de son cas'. *Tucius* has some support in B, which has 'tursus'. For the story of Marcus Curtius, Chartier probably used Valerius Maximus, v. 6. 2.

76/22–3. *Yet . . . dissceyving*: 'Les autruy fautes ne nous doiuent enseigner à faillir'.

76/36. *within theimself*: om. Fr.

76/36–77/2. *thei . . . woorship*: Mistranslation of 'ains arresterent leur desir, & assirent les bonnes [bournes Ro] de leur tendence au loz de vertu, & à l'onneur terrien'.

77/6. *othir lawes*: 'autres loix' BClRoD$_1$; 'Idoles' D.

77/8. *and (1) . . . aduersite*: Mistranslation of '& preschié humilité & mespris de soy mesmes, & constance en infortune'. There is confusion between 'preschié' and some form of 'perir'. There is also mistranslation of 'mespris de soy mesmes' (contempt or undervaluing of themselves) as *mystoke themself*, which in R's construction seems to mean 'wrongly viewed themselves as', a reflexive meaning not recorded in *OED*.

77/10. *can . . . discordis*: See Introduction, p. 50.

77/15–16. *thou . . . exaumple*: 'nas souuent [forme Ro] de aprendre a ouurer a leur exemple' BRo; 'n'as à prendre forme d'ouurer à leur exemple' DCl.

77/18. *nor*: D has '&', BClRo 'en'. By changing this word R has muddled the passage.

77/19. *liffe*: Fr. has 'mort'. The meaning of the sentence is lost because of this change. Here because of *thi liffe* in ll. 17 and 18, it may be a scribal error in RNJ. I have not emended it because of the occurrence of the same change in l. 24 and again at 82/30. Thus, it may be the translator's peculiarity, rather than a scribe's error, especially since there is no apparent reason for such a scribal error at 82/30.

77/24. *liffe*: Fr. has 'mort'. See preceding note. Here again a scribal error is plausible because of the appearance of *thi liffe* in l. 23.

77/25. *the* (1) *. . . termes*: Fr. has 'leurs termes'. *the houres and* may be a misinterpretation of the pronoun 'leurs'.

77/28–32. *soone . . . faile*: J follows Fr. more closely here:

> Est de legier obcuree [obscuree BClRo],
> Et eschiet
> Qu'en oubliance emmuree
> Enuie desmesuree,
> Detraction coniuree,
> L'omme enchiet
> Mais la bonté espuree
> A la vie mesuree
> De [A BClRo] tous par regle iuree,
> Qui ne chiet.

78/1. *ententis*: D adds 'sens, & esperances fainctes, & adulterines'; BClRo omit 'sens &'. Perhaps N's *thoughts and*, omitted in RJ, translates 'sens &'.

78/1–2. *taking . . . light*: BClRo have 'en retenant mon vmbre et [en *add.* Ro] laissant ma lumiere'. D has '& en retenant mon ombre, laissent ma lumiere'. Since RNJ all have *levin*, perhaps the translator's exemplar had 'et laissent'.

78/5–6. *that* (2) *. . . hir*: *om.* Fr.

78/10. *with lawghyng chere*: 'le bras au col, & en riant'.

78/11. *and . . . them*: R is like B, which has 'Et folle fiance mal fondee· les tire'. DCl have 'fiance' in conjunction with 'consolation' and 'tirent' with 'mainent'. Ro also seems to intend this reading although the conjunction linking the verbs is omitted.

78/13. *presumpcion*: 'Presumpcion' Cl; 'Presumptiue' DBRo.

78/23. *He . . . arte*: Fr. has 'il te laissera nonchaloir [non chalu BClRo]. Quoy que soit'. R's *And* has no equivalent. The stop in Cl before 'Quoy' has been added by a corrector.

78/27–9. *Reason . . . dedis*: Fr. has 'Et pour neant les requiert par oraison, qui n'aide sa requeste par faire deuoir. Mais en veillant, conseillant, & en bien faisant'. There is confusion between 'oraison' and 'raison' here.

78/30. *propirly*: Like uncorrected Cl, which has 'proprement', rather than 'prospérement' (DB, corrected Cl).

79/1. *I wote wele*: om. Fr.

79/2–3. *suche . . . honestly*: Fr. has 'pour preparer [passer Ro; pourpasser B] moissons en la vieillesse'. The image is lost because of R's change.

79/4–5. *and . . . fantasies*: 'ne legiers en souhaits fantastiques, & inutiles desirs; ainçois missiez l'engin à l'esgart, & la main à l'euure'.

79/6–8. *And . . . beleve*: 'Et soy frauder d'Esperance par crainte trop paoureuse, est [et Cl] pusillanimité deffiee [doffice BRo] de Dieu, & lascheté de courage recreu de bonne foy'.

79/10. *subiecte . . . howse*: Fr. has 'en vn mesme subiect'. *subiecte* in R seems to mean 'subordinate' or 'submissive'.

79/21. *suche*: Fr. adds 'la practiquent à leur dommage'. Its omission, which makes the English incoherent, may reflect scribal error in a manuscript lying behind RNJ.

79/31. *of* (2) . . . *age*: DBCl have 'd'autre part t'espaoura vieillesse'; Ro has 'ta des paoures vieillesse'. The addition of *he fereth* from NJ produces a better English reading, but still not a good translation. The scribal errors in RNJ at 79/21 and 29 seem to indicate that the scribe of an earlier English manuscript was copying more carelessly than usual throughout this passage.

79/32. *crepyng*: 'croulant' (ready to fall).

79/33–80/1. *If . . . awhile*: R used a manuscript like BClRo, which have 'se ta beaulte te delicte trop peu te durera la Ioye de lauoir et longuement la regretteras perdue'. D has a much longer passage, which includes this interesting image: 'Se ta beauté te delecte, c'est annuit herbe, demain foin. Telle fleur est plus tost passee que venue. Trop peu', etc.

80/5–6. *It . . . him*: 'It makes war upon and revolts against him'.

80/10–12. *Yet . . . hondis*: Fr. has 'Or regarde que tu ne preignes en lieu de la potence le baston pointu, & qu'en t'apuyant l'aguillon de ton appuy ne te entre dedans la main'. The metaphor seems to mean that one should depend on reliable friends who are like the *potence* (a crutch with a cross bar) rather than on friends who are like a pointed *staff*, which might cause pain.

80/24. *wene*: This verb is plural in Fr. also. The understood subject seems to be *ovirprowde men* in l. 18.

80/26. *cowarde*: 'cornart' (fool).

80/33. *to stryve with*: Fr. has 's'aheurter'. *stryve with* seems to mean 'stick obstinately to', a meaning not recorded in *OED*.

81/1–2. *for . . . alone*: This phrase, meaningless in English, is a complete clause in Fr.: 'L'auctorité de regenter reside à vn seul chief'. 'mais' follows, not 'car'.

81/3. *the wittes*: 'les dons'.

81/16. *of . . . secrete*: Chartier's image is lost because R misunderstood 'aux peres de famille en oeconomie'. Perhaps he had a bad exemplar: Ro, for example, has 'iherosme' for 'oeconomie'.

81/20. *mayde*: 'filé' (small thread).

81/20–1. *that . . . trust*: DBRo have a new sentence: 'Là se prennent ilz par cuider'. Cl, however, has no stop before 'la'. Following this, Fr. adds 'Et quant leur saige folie les a menez à non vouloir sobrement sçauoir, leur fol sens les tire à ignorer pereilleusement'.

81/30. *beleve*: 'mescreantise'.

82/9. *shewe*: 'forcer'.

82/15. *liiij*: 'cinquante quatre' ClRoD₁; 'soixante quatre' D; *blank space* B.

82/27–8. *for . . . mysbeleve*: Fr. has 'Et par ceste fantastique inuention les Docteurs de Iuifuerie les tiennent en infidelité'. NJ have *seyn* here for R's *sayne*. *seyne*, although an unusual spelling of 'see', may in the context mean 'see to it'. Cf. 92/28, where R has *saying that* for *seying that* (NJ), meaning 'since'.

82/30. *to lyve*: Fr. has 'mourir'. Cf. 77/19 and 77/24.

82/31. *seruage*: Like Cl, which omits 'à liberté', added in DBRo.

83/4–6. *and . . . worlde*: 'à la resurrection des hommes au monde, pour habiter la terre'.

83/6. *which*: Like Cl, which omits 'selon la lettre', added in DBRo.

83/8. *for þe sustinaunce*: This has no Fr. equivalent, but Fr. adds 'tous ensemble'.

83/9. *Iuda*: Like Cl, which omits a long passage added in DBRo: 'Mais par ceste parolle de Ezechiel est entenduë la continuation de l'espece humaine, qui par generation quotidienne ressuscite incessamment, & ressuscitera tant comme Dieu permettra que nature fructifie & croisse tout par sexe raisonnable. Car autrement le faudroit faillir & cesser, pource que sans faueur, mort la deprent & corrompt tousiours. Et plus feroit, se par continuation d'euure de nature n'estoit ressuscité & produit homme pour habiter la terre. Et Dieu qui l'a creée pour habitation des hommes, ne veut pas qu'elle demeure vacante. Et pource selon Ezechiel, la ressuscite d'hommes par generation contre l'opprimement de mort'.

83/12. *lost*: 'perdirent' BCl; 'Predirent' DRo.

83/25. *their . . . fawty*: 'leur attente est faillie'.

83/28–34: Josephus, *De Bello Judaico*, ed. H. St. J. Thackeray (London, 1928), says at vi. 386, that a great number of prisoners were sold, and at vi. 420, that 97,000 prisoners were taken and 1,100,000 perished during the siege of Jerusalem by Titus.

84/8–11. *as . . . tymes*: D reads 'comme gent abandonnee, pour vituperer la memoire de leur erreur, & en l'exemple de detestation de leur lignée à toutes generations, & en tous temps'. R agrees with B in placing '& en tous temps' with the following thought.

84/11. *rede and study*: 'lisent souuent et estudient' BCl; 'Lisent & relisent souuent, cherchent & estudient' D; 'lisent & relisent souuent estudient' Ro.

84/11–12. *callid Detharmich*: D has 'de Thalmut'; Cl 'de charmich'; B 'de carmich'; Ro 'de caruch'. R again attaches the Fr. preposition to the proper noun. Cf. 14/31 and 65/30.

84/18–21. *of* (1) *. . . shelle*: R enlarged upon and clarified this Fr. image: 'dont la loy Chrestienne en la plenitude du temps & meurté de fruict a gousté le noiau. Et se pour auoir le noiau, fault briser l'escaille'.

84/22–3. *and . . . figure*: '& couuertures, puis qu'ils ont attaint à la verité, qui dessouz estoit figurée & couuerte'.

84/32–85/2. *and . . . rewardis*: Fr. reads:

> Parolles prains & enceintes,
> Deffences tresfort restraintes,
> Ordonnances bien contraintes
> A grans promesses abstraintes
> Et par figures empraintes
> Auecques visions sainctes,
> Et Esperances non fainctes,
> D'auoir ioye apres les plainctes,
> Et attaindre à grans attainctes.

pregnaunte (NJ) may be the original reading instead of *pregnabull* (R) to translate 'prains & enceintes', but *pregnabull* occurs elsewhere erroneously for 'pregnant', according to *OED*.

85/3–4. *which . . . Testament*: Fr. has:

> Et descouuert tout à nu
> Ce que Dieu auoit tenu
> Clos, couuert, & contenu [court tenu Ro]
> Ou vieil testament chenu.

85/7–8. *that . . . budde*: NJ follow Fr.:

> Qui tenoit couuerte & close,
> En vert bouton rouge rose.

The R scribe picked up his place at the wrong *closed*.

85/13. *merkis*: 'bourne' B; 'bonne' DClRo.

85/17. *vendengith and tvnnith*: Fr. has 'vendenge & entonne'. Chartier intended an image of gathering grapes and making wine. *OED* does not give *vendengith*, but 'vendenger' in Fr. means 'to cut and gather grapes for wine, to make wine of grapes'. Cf. English *vendonginge* in *OED* (quoted only from *Ayenbite*).

85/27–8. *trusting . . . obteyne*: 'à esperer leur secours, & attendre leur bien, de chose qui ne puet prouffiter ne aidier'.

86/1. *Iulius*: Not in NJ nor Fr. and perhaps added by the R scribe.

86/3–4. *aftir . . . discomfite*: Fr. reads 'apres les glaiues de tout le monde surmontez'. Thus R's *all* or N's *all þe* translates Fr. more closely than J's *allso the*.

86/5–9: See Valerius Maximus, vi. 9. ext. 5, and Vincent of Beauvais, *Speculum Historiale*, iii. 22. For the name *Policitatus*, R used a manuscript somewhat like BRo, which have 'Pellicitatus'; Cl has 'Polliciatus', and D correctly has 'Policratus'.

86/6. *the tyraunte*: 'tirant' BClRo; *om.* D.

86/9–20: See Vincent of Beauvais, i. 102, and Lactantius, *Divinae Institutiones*, i. 8, both sources mentioned in *The Treatise of Hope*. Vincent lists the idols Bel, Beel, Baal, Baali, Beelfegor, and Belzebub. Note R's *Bell*, omitted in NJ and Fr.

86/14. *which*: This relative pronoun, which confuses the English structure, has no Fr. equivalent.

86/18. *made name*: The understood subject in both R and Fr. goes back to *men* in l. 13. Cf. 87/16.

86/19. *names*: Like BClRo, which omit 'leur ont esté imposez', added in D.

86/21–87/26: See Lactantius, i. 15.

86/21. *vnexpert*: 'Inexperte' ClRoD$_1$; 'inepte' D; 'experte' B.

86/22. *institucion*: 'instinct' DCl; 'instruit' BRo.

86/27–87/2: The origin of these false gods is discussed by Lactantius, i. 11, 18. In this account, however, it is Aesculapius, not Apollo, who was deified because of his medical skill.

86/29. *kyng*: Fr. adds 'de Crete'.

87/8. *and . . . of*: Fr. has 'en vertu de'. 'en' in Cl appears as a correction. Perhaps R used a Fr. manuscript which had 'et' for 'en'.

87/10–13. *it . . . myght*: N's reading is corrupt, as shown by Fr.: 'super- flue chose & inutile estoit que homme requerist par necessité celuy qu'il auoit fait Dieu, & eust besoin du pouoir dont luy mesmes donna la puissance'.

87/15. *themself . . . predecessours*: R is like BCl, which read 'eulx ou leurs predicesseurs'. D omits 'eulx ou', and Ro omits the entire phrase.

87/15-16. *to . . . drede*: Fr. has 'adorer par force ou par crainte'. A combination of N's *to wurship hem* and J's *be force* produces a reading which follows Fr. Perhaps again a marginal insertion in an earlier manuscript caused this confusion in RNJ.

87/16. *kept*: The understood subject in both R and Fr. goes back to *paynemes* in l. 14.

88/7-12: Augustine (*Retractationum Libri*) gives exactly these two reasons for writing *De Civitate Dei*: the first five books are to disprove the belief that man's prosperity is dependent upon a certain type of worship of the pagan gods and to refute the idea that the beginning of Christianity in Rome and the forbidding of pagan worship caused the city to fall in 410. In the second part of his work he directs his arguments against thinkers who, although they do not attribute the calamities of mankind to the anger of the pagan gods, do maintain that for the future life the worship of the gods is advantageous. Lactantius' *Divinae Institutiones* shows the falseness of the pagan religion and the vanity of heathen philosophy and defends the Christian religion against its adversaries.

88/8. *regarde*: 'regard' BClRoD₁; 'regret' D.

88/22-6. *For . . . power*: D reads: 'Car par similitude, & communication de mortelle nature le pouoient lors veoir, & oyr, & en vertu des euures diuines faictes en corps humain le croire, & adourer vn Dieu qui en sa simplesse est infiny à congnoistre, & homme en sa mortalité est impuissant en vertu'. Some of the English readings are like the other Fr. manuscripts. Like R, BRo have 'pourrez' for 'pouoient'. ClRo support R in the phrase 'en sa simple essence & infiny a congnoistre' (B has 'est' for '&' like D, but has 'simple essence' like ClRo). Ro, for 'en sa mortalité', has 'a mortalite', perhaps interpreted by R to mean *at His dethe*. The English sentence means: 'Because of his similarity to and communication with mortal nature (i.e., when Christ became man), you might have seen Him and heard of divine works done in man's form, so that you might believe in and worship God to be known in His single essence and infinity, and like man at His death without power'.

88/30. *gloriousely wourshippid*: 'triumphe en cest endroit glorieusement sur leur folle [erreur et *add*. Ro] creance'.

88/31. *that . . . beleve*: om. Fr.

88/32-89/2. *that . . . power*: 'que Dieu s'est peu faire homme, qui a l'eternelle vertu d'estre par luy mesmes'.

89/5. *power*: Fr. has 'erreur' and adds 'par contraire'. *power* in RNJ may be a scribal error for *errour* (note *power* in ll. 2 and 4 and elsewhere on this page). RNJ all are corrupt in omitting *voide* after *made*.

89/7-8. *to . . . the*: 'à le congnoistre . . . la sapience de Dieu t'a appellé'.

89/9. *which*: 'qui' ClRo; om. DB.

89/12-14. *And . . . worlde*: This passage is mistranslated. Fr. places '& illusion d'Esperance Opinatiue tournee en Esperance certaine' in conjunction with 'infusion'. A new subordinate clause begins 'quant le Deable pere de tenebres fist naistre sur terre, & esleuer au monde Machometh'. The material for this treatment of Mohammed and Mohammedanism probably came to a great extent from Vincent of Beauvais, xxiii. 39–57, much of which is an epitome of a disputation between a Saracen and a Christian of Arabia, translated into Latin by Peter de Toulette.

89/15–20: See Vincent of Beauvais, xxiii. 39.

89/22. *sedicion*: Although *OED* does not record any instance where *sedicion* occurs as a spelling of *seducion* and although Fr. has 'sedition' here, the context in this passage suggests the meaning 'action of seducing people to err in belief and conduct'.

89/22. *Solacye*: 'Salacie' BCl; 'Salarie' Ro; 'Galacie' D.

89/23. *Paphagonye*: 'Paphagonie' uncorrected Cl; 'Paphlagonie' D, corrected Cl; 'paphagoee' B.

89/23. *Nusye*: 'nusie' Cl; 'Misie' DRo; *om.* B.

89/23. *Carie*: 'Carie' ClRo; 'Catie' D; *om.* B.

89/25. *Ayse*: Fr. adds 'aux Eglises desquelles s'adressent les Epistres des Apostres, fut enuenimee. Toute Africque &'. Thus, there is no equivalent for *which* in l. 27.

89/28. *cenefye*: Evidently not understanding Fr. 'zizanie' (discord), the translator (or a scribe) substituted *cenefye* (mustard seed) in the familiar phrase 'the seed of senvy'.

89/32. *mysknowelage*: Here and at 60/14, *mysknow(e)lage* translates 'mespris'. Thus the meaning 'failure to recognize and acknowledge' takes on the added implication of 'scorn'. Cf. U's *disknowen* at 165/21, which also implies 'scorned' (Fr. 'mescogneue').

89/35–90/4: The story of Mohammed's first marriage to Khadīja from Khurasan is treated in Vincent of Beauvais, xxiii. 39, 41.

90/1. *was a*: Fr. adds 'marchant &'.

90/7–19: See Vincent of Beauvais, xxiii. 41, 42, 43.

90/8. *a people callid Robusces*: Fr. adj. 'robustes' (capitalized in BClRo) is in conjunction with 'malicieux'.

90/9–10. *whose . . . cunduyte*: 'ou que leurs vices auoient mis en mespris, ou leurs oultrages en depression, se adioingnirent à luy, & contrahirent soubz son conduit'.

90/17. *by . . . meanys*: Fr. has 'és [et Ro] entreprises de leur peruers cheuetaine, lequel moult de fois par trahison & aguet fist occire ceux qui luy contrestoient'. *fals meanys* (N) seems a better translation of 'aguet' than merely *meanys* (RJ).

90/21–2. *thought . . . birth*: 'Mais la vilté de son estat & de sa basse naissance'.

90/24. *office*: Fr. adds 'de simple [*om.* B] chamelier'.

90/26–7. *through . . . labored*: '& soubz ce nom gaingner adhesion & suite de peuple. Et pource se fit honorer & reputer'.

90/30–1. *som . . . him* (2): 'Les siens s'y assentirent, pour luy obeyr & flater'.

90/32–91/8: See Vincent of Beauvais, xxiii. 40.

91/4–5. *like . . . wounte*: om. Fr.

91/10. *O . . . Mahomet*: 'Et tu disciple de Mahomet' B; 'Et tu Macho-miste' DCIRo.

91/13–15. *the . . . folkis*: Fr. has only 'Le nom de Prophete'. As the subject of the next sentence, however, where R has *prophecie*, Cl has 'don de prophecie et du sainct esperit', and DBRo have 'Don de Prophetie'.

91/24–5. *he . . . cautele*: D reads 'se aida le malin esperit de ce deceueur du monde d'vne seconde cautelle'. R is more like BClRo, which omit 'de . . . monde'.

91/26. *requered*: Fr. has 'acquiert'. *requered*, which does not fit the context, may be a scribal error in RNJ.

91/33. *of . . . dedis*: 'sa forme de faire cauteleuse'.

92/10–12. *and . . . thereon*: This is an unclear translation of 'Auec ce pour non oster aux Chrestiens l'Esperance du ciel [siecle aduenir BClRo] où Dieu a reserué leur principale fiance'. Perhaps *and* is omitted scribally in RNJ after *comaunded*; then the English would mean 'and so that no man should put his trust thereon, i.e., on the Christian after-world'. Or *no* may be a scribal addition; dropping out *no* would make the English follow the Fr. thought more closely.

92/13–15. *all . . . rewarde*: Fr. has 'ses contraires des peines d'enfer', and adds at the beginning of the next sentence 'Mais il vsa du nom de Paradis pour non [mouuoir *add*. Ro] les estrangier [estranges Ro]'.

92/18–20. *delicate . . . ryvers*: BRo change the order of the items in the series, placing the *women* phrase before 'Et boire et mengier delicatiue-ment en [et Ro] riches vaisseaulx et auoir riuieres'. Although these two manuscripts are different in construction from R and the other Fr. versions, their reading 'riches vaisseaulx' is like the English, and Ro's 'et' for 'en' makes the similarity even greater. D has 'abondances de richesses, vaisseaux & riuieres', and Cl has 'habondance de richesses· Ruisseaulx et riuieres'.

92/22. *in thys worlde*: om. Fr.

92/25–6. *which . . . corrupcion*: 'pourrissable' (modifying Fr. 'corps').

92/28. *seying that*: NJ correct R's *saying that*. Cf. 82/28.

93/4. *sykyng*: Fr. has 'cesser'. I cannot account for this use of *k* for *c* or *s* in the English word, which obviously means 'ceasing' in RJ (N omits the phrase). The same peculiarity occurs again in *sekyng* in RJ at 126/25.

93/9–10. *nyght . . . meane*: R brought a phrase of the next Fr. sentence into this one: after 'nuit', Fr. reads '& de tant dissoluë charnalité. Des idolatres aussi & de leurs abusions voulut il retenir quelque chose'.

93/11. *the Bahach*: This is a good illustration of the western difficulty with Arabic names. D has 'Lalahah'; Cl 'la lahagh'; B 'le labach'; Ro 'le sabbat'. The pilgrimage referred to is that to the Ka'ba (i.e., Cube).

93/14. *pilgrimage*: Fr. adds '& [de Cl] la maistresse Mahommerie'.

93/19. *he . . . doctryne*: R is like BClRo, which have 'il monstra sa doctrine'. D has 'se monstra par' for 'monstra'. See Vincent of Beauvais, xxiii. 58, 60, 63.

93/29. *owt . . . reason*: om. Fr.

93/31. *all*: 'tout' Cl; 'ton' DBRo.

93/34–5. *But . . . refreyne*: 'But how may any man that no law may sufficiently restrain appropriately make the law less strict in any respect?'

93/36. *haue*: 'prendre' BClRo; 'perdre' D.

94/2–3. *the (2) . . . amysse*: 'la roide bride lui est excercite et la lasche· licence de mesprendre' BClRoD$_1$; 'la roide bride luy est cause de soy exerciter en vertu, & la lasche luy donne licence de mesprendre' D.

94/9–10. *promysed . . . worlde*: 'la [les Cl] prometz en l'autre siecle pour gloire'.

94/15. *for . . . mesure*: For Mohammed's lust, see Vincent of Beauvais, xxiii. 44.

94/16–17. *yn . . . mischieff*: 'loy a plus mestier de les en restraindre, que y contraindre'.

94/22. *a bandon*: Fr. has 'mettre à bandon'. R writes the phrase *a bandon* = 'at one's own free will'. But it may be intended as the infinitive *abandon* = 'surrender to natural impulses'.

94/27. *sowned*: Fr. has 'assouie' (appeased), but *sowned* here means 'declared, proclaimed'.

94/32. *Bacus*: 'boucqs'.

95/5–15: See Vincent of Beauvais, xxiii. 39.

95/11. *with . . . God*: Fr. has 'dont Dieu t'auoit feru'. Thus, NJ follow Fr. word order.

95/14. *which*: Refers back to *Gabryell*.

95/18. *devilrye or mokkerye*: Fr. has 'desuerie' (madness). *devilrye* seems to mean 'devilish behaviour'. The nearest meaning in *OED* is 'extreme wickedness', first recorded from 1637. In J *mokkerye* appears above *devilrye* as a gloss. In N *or* is omitted. Perhaps the scribe of a manuscript behind RN copied in a gloss here; or since the two words are not synonymous, the translator may have noted both in his copy as possible renderings of 'desuerie'.

95/18. *at Saignys*: Fr. has 'Sergius', the name of the monk. See Vincent of Beauvais, xxiii. 51.

95/23. *and þe sadnes*: Fr. has 'à l'agrauement'. Cf. the difficulties with forms of this Fr. word at 108/27–8 and in the U version of *The Quadrilogue* at 175/10 and 181/18.

95/27. *vessell*: Like Cl, which omits the following passage added in DB: 'Celuy Sergius ton pareil en ambition esleut ta proximité, pource qu'il auoit esté refusé en l'Eglise souueraine de Romme à y estre colloqué, & pourueu en auctorité de prelature Pontifical. Et pource indigné vers l'Eglise & cité Catholique, voulant s'en venger & soustraire les Chrestiens de leur sainct propos, se ioingnit à toy, & te informa de seditions erronees & controuuees'.

95/27. *bete down*: R seems to have confused 'battre' and 'bastir'.

96/1–4: See Vincent of Beauvais, xxiii. 62, 63.

96/7. *thin*: 'ton' B; *om.* DClRo.

96/28–9. *was . . . probacion*: Fr. has 'est attainte la reprobation [approbacion Ro]'. The English is not clear. *probacion* may be a scribal error in RNJ. If not, the English must mean either 'there the test of the false sects was achieved' or 'there the trial of the false sects was condemned'.

96/29–30. *fals (2) . . . doctrynes*: 'illegitimes, que loix, & preuarications, que doctrines'.

96/32. *renne*: 'courent' BRo; 'recourent' DCl; 'retournent' D₁.

96/33. *as . . . mankynde*: 'de l'outrage humain'.

97/2. *derkenesses*: Fr. adds 'enluminees'.

97/5. *wourthi*: 'digne' (after correction) Cl; 'diuine' DB.

97/9–10. *which . . . rehercid*: *om.* Fr.

97/15. *iniquite*: Fr. adds 'confors de pacience, d'obeissance, d'humilité, & de consolation'.

97/35. *beleuith therupon*: Fr. has 'ils croyent'. R used a manuscript like Cl, which omits the following passage added in DBRo: '& à l'honnesteté & prouffit des vrays croyans. Et finablement en tous & chacuns les points & ordonnances de la loy diuine tout tend & conclud à bien, à salut, & à honneur tant vniuersel que particulier. Et si respond aussi bien à l'eternel fait & louange qu'au mondain, & au mondain qu'à l'eternel: comme procedant & retournant à vn seul & vray Dieu, duquel toute saincte loy & toute vie humaine & perdurable par necessité & apparente raison depend'.

98/8. *opynion*: Fr. adds 'qui s'accorde à Chrestienne foy'.

98/9–11. *that . . . Mahomet*: Fr. reads 'que luy & sainct Denys/firent iadis autel au Dieu incongneu, mais en la fin le cogneut sainct Denys/par la predication de l'Apostre, & par la grace du baptesme. Dy moy que iugeroit Philosophie de la secte de Machometh'. R seems to have made the best sense possible of a Fr. exemplar which omitted 'firent . . . Denys' (caused by the repetition of 'Denys'). The reference is to St. Dionysius, Bishop of Paris, c.275. See Acts 17: 34, and Vincent of Beauvais, viii. 159.

98/13. *techeth*: 'aprendent' B; 'appreuuent' DClRo.

98/16. *diuinite*: Fr. adds '& pouruoit au [remede et *add*. Ro] regime de poure humanité'.

98/16. *a man*: Fr. has 'elle', referring to 'religion'.

98/20–1. *But . . . wisedome*: Fr. has 'Mais il est creu selon verité & l'enseignement de parfaicte sapience'. I have emended R's corrupt *prophete and* with J's *Hym ys perfyte*, making the second half of the sentence parallel to the first. N's *perfite*, however, follows Fr. somewhat more closely and may be the original reading.

98/33–4. *which . . . them*: 'qui selon la loy de Machomet luy sont plus chargeux que les ieusnes des Chrestiens, ne leur sont dommageables' D; 'macomet lui [leur BRo] est plus chargeux que les Ieusnes des Chrestiens ne leur sont domaigeables' BClRo.

98/34. *scarsete . . . helthe*: The meaning seems to be 'Scarcity is entrusted with the keeping of health'. This meaning of *tresoure* is not in *OED*; thus perhaps *tresoresse* (NJ), to translate 'tresoriere', is superior. However, *tresoure* may have the rare sense 'treasury', which occurs in U at 185/24 and possibly in R at 184/26.

99/3. *euery good conscience*: 'toute bonne conscience' Cl; 'toute Chrestienté' D; 'toute bonne Chrestiente' BRo.

99/4. *Godly*: 'duisable'.

99/5–6. *profitable . . . norisshinge*: Like Cl, which has 'vtile assoigneuse nourriture', unlike D's parallel 'vtile à soigneuse nourriture' and Ro's 'loyalle engendreure vtille'. (B is corrupt.)

99/13. *of the priorite*: Fr. has 'ou priorité'. *of* in RNJ may be a scribal error for *or*.

99/13. *moders*: Fr. has 'meres'. RNJ all have the corrupt *faders*, an error which must go back to an earlier manuscript.

99/14. *a viage*: Fr. has 'as voyagé'. Since NJ have *yn* here, *a* must mean 'in'.

99/16. *thaduersite*: 'la diuersité' (confusion with 'laduersite').

99/16. *sectes*: Fr. has 'sotes'. Cl, however, has been corrected, an *o* replacing letters which may be *ec*.

99/24. *hoope*: Like BCl, which omit 'en Dieu', added in D.

99/25. *may . . . assured*: 'ne puet estre asseuree' BClRo; 'ne puet estre ailleurs mieux ne si bien asseuree' D.

99/33. *consolatyve*: Fr. adds '& feable'. *OED* lists *consolatyve* as rare and gives an example from Caxton; *MED* omits the word.

99/34–100/1. *and . . . wourthi*: 'et te rendz digne' BCl; 'qui te rend indigne' D; 'et te rens indigne' Ro.

100/4. *Yet . . . them*: 'Ie tacorde que tu en vses' BClRo; 'Regarde que tu en vses' D.

100/6–7. *But . . . desperate*: Fr. has 'Mais ne fais pas ton Esperance serue à choses desesperees'. R seems to have confused 'serue' with 'ferme'.

100/7. *it*: Fr. 'les' refers to 'choses'.

100/8. *Also . . . willes*: 'Puis te conuient il laisser ahurtes volentez'.

100/14. *shal . . . frendis*: 'employera ses amis'.

100/20–4. *and . . . prouision*: See Introduction, p. 17. *prouision* has little meaning here because R omitted Fr. 'd'auis' in the phrase 'prouision d'auis'.

100/30–3. *thou* (1) *. . . fortune*: Fr. reads:

> De tes faits bien conuenir,
> Et au confort paruenir
> De bon espoir à venir [preuenir Ro; auenir BCl]
> Pour plus accroistre [congnoistre Ro] ton bien:
> De Dieu te faut souuenir,
> Paine & cure soustenir,
> A rien vain ne te tenir,
> Ton sens trop ne soustenir [si tenir Ro],
> Fortune ne maintenir'.

In l. 31, note NJ's *on*, which may be a form of R's *oone*; however, the original reading may have been *on God*, translating 'De Dieu'.

101/5. *frendis*: Fr. adds 'Sur ta garde te maintien'.

101/5–6. *Beete . . . lyon*: 'To punish a meane man in presence of, and for an example vnto, the mightie' (Cotgrave).

101/9. *presentes*: Although NJ have *presence*, I have not emended R since *presentes* for 'presence' occurs elsewhere. See *OED* under *present* sb.₁ 1b.

101/13. *knowe*: DBC1 add 'son faict'; Ro, 'son parfait'.

101/16–17. *for ... aventures*: Fr. reads 'pour la proportion & qualité [equalite BClRo] que noz singuliers cas ont auec les priuees aduentures des autres'. R is almost meaningless, especially because of confusion between 'priuees' and 'princes'.

101/18–19. *and . . . ensaumple*: '& conseil, qui besongnent par patron & par exemple'.

101/19–20. *thre thynges*: In Fr. the reference is to 'science', 'experience', and 'conseil', but because of mistranslation, 'conseil' is lost in the English. See preceding note and Introduction, p. 50.

101/22. *and that*: 'Et que' Cl; 'ce que' DBRo.

101/26. *amiable*: Cl has 'annables', and D 'annales'; BRo omit the word. *amiable* (RNJ) may be a scribal error for *annable*, but the translator may simply have misread the Fr. word, since *MED* and *OED* do not show *annable* as occurring elsewhere.

101/29–30. *and . . . othir*: R is like BRo and especially Cl, which have '& pour exemples aux [des BRo] autres'. D has 'Et pour exemple' at the beginning of the next sentence.

102/6. *gaue . . . them*: Fr. has 'donnoit attrait & recueil'. *gaue receipt* is related to the verb *receipt* (receive or harbour, especially a criminal), but *OED* does not give this precise meaning under the noun; the first example even in the meaning 'reception' is from 1557.

102/8–10. *that . . . and* (1): 'chassez, garniz de bonne Esperance, & [*om.* BClRo] entre les cas desesperez endurciz à tout [tant BRo] souffrir'.

102/11–12. *by . . . cuntre*: '& redarguerent par puissance & par iugement les reniez [irreguliers Ro; reginez Cl; renoyez B] de leur loy, & les traistres & turbateurs du pays commun [*om.* BCl]'.

102/12–13. *Hough . . . remedy*: R followed a manuscript which combined the reading of BCl with that of D. BCl have 'comment apparurent si vertueux ceulx qui nauoient esperance de remede'; D has 'Puis que tant apparurent vertueux ceux qui n'auoient apparence de remede'. That this kind of combination did exist is proved by Ro's reading: 'Comment apparurent si victorieux ceulx qui nauoient apparence de remede'.

102/16. *all their hertis*: 'tous leurs cuers' BRo; 'tous les cuers' Cl; 'leurs cueurs' D.

102/18–19. *and . . . maisters*: Fr. has '& de chassez assailleurs, & de humbles & deboutez les seigneurs & les maistres'. *of* (RNJ) seems to be a scribal error for *or*.

102/22. *Althinus*: R is like Cl. J, however, has *Alchinus*, like DRo. N gets nearer to the Biblical 'Alcimus' with *Alchimus*.

102/24–5. *made . . . cuntre*: 'finist miserablement'.

102/32. *renoveled*: Like Cl, which omits '& recouuree', added in DBRo.

102/33. *of*: D has 'comme', and BRo 'comment'. Cl omits both and precedes 'sesleua' (*rose*, 103/1) with 'qui'.

103/5. *of the enemyes*: 'des ennemis' B; 'des mains des ennemis' DClRo.

103/6. *a grette lawde*: *om.* Fr.

103/16. *come in*: 'comprendre' (see Glossary).

103/19. *more*: Fr. adds 'exemple de'.

103/23. *Ceste*: DRo have 'Celse', which is omitted in B and occurs in Cl after an erasure. The reference is to Celsus, but the translator may have confused him with Caesar because of *Iule*.

103/26. *dedis*: Fr. adds 'tout iugé'.

103/29-32: The usual story is, of course, that Hercules destroyed Troy in the time of Laomedon. It is not clear how Jason and Theseus become the agents here, although Theseus is in some accounts Hercules' friend and companion in some adventures, and in Brunetto Latini, *Tresor*, i. 32. 41, Jason is the companion of Hercules on this expedition.

104/6. *cites*: This is a strange translation of 'occis'. A scribal error seems likely. Note *cite* in l. 12.

104/17. *seche*: The J scribe interpreted the phrase as *such a seure restyng place*.

104/20-31: See Livy, xxvi. 11.

104/20. *take*: Fr. adds '& arse des Gaules iusques au Capitole? Ne fut elle aussi assiegee'.

104/21. *victoriouse*: Like BClRo, which omit 'de Carthage', added in D.

104/23. *in . . . Roome*: 'à la tierce pierre [prairie Cl; terre Ro] pres de Rome'.

104/24. *it*: In Fr. this refers to Hannibal.

104/32-105/6: See Boccaccio's *De Casibus Illustrium Virorum*, vii. 3.

104/35. *doubted*: Fr. has 'redouté', thus supporting the NJ reading. R's *doubty*, an erroneous form of *doughty*, also fits the context, however.

105/8. *were*: 'ont'.

105/9. *norisshith and enforcet*: These verbs are reflexive in Fr.

105/10. *helpe*: Since Fr. has 'salut', *helpe* may be a scribal error for *helthe*.

105/18. *retourne into*: *OED* (4d.) quotes this sense only from Dunbar and Douglas.

105/22-3. *that . . . empryses*: DCl have 'ont enuahy autruy, auoir eu louable fin ne honneste issuë de leurs entreprises'; B has 'ont enuay autruy orgueil soient paruenus en louable fin ne honneste de leur emprinse'; Ro has 'ont enuahy autrui orgueil en loable fin aient eu honneste fin de leurs entreprinses'. Since 'ont enuahy autruy' has no English equivalent, the *which* clause beginning in l. 21 has no verb.

105/24. *Aydes*: Fr. has 'Indes'. The translator may have changed the reading to *Aydes* (Hades), or this may be a scribal corruption in RNJ.

105/25. *Hercules . . . sonne*: R is like BCl, which have 'son propre filz hercules' and begin the next sentence with 'Il'. DRo have only 'son propre fils' with 'Hercules' as the subject of the next sentence. The latter is certainly Chartier's intended reading. In Brunetto Latini, *Tresor*, i. 122. 112, the conquests by Hercules and Semiramis are mentioned together.

105/34. *the . . . sepultur*: R is like B, which has 'a son corps souffit vne sepulture'. DClRo add 'au cueur &' at the beginning.

105/34-5. *for . . . in*: om. Fr.

105/35–106/1. *wheras . . . drye*: Fr. has 'par l'abeuruement de ses cheuaux s'asseichoient les fleuues'. The N reading may be somewhat nearer to the Fr. structure.

106/1. *ministirs*: 'maneuures'.

106/2. *to . . . way*: With the emendation from NJ the English follows Fr. 'faire trauerser'.

106/5. *by . . . ouir*: om. Fr.

106/9. *for . . . myschevousely*: 'par acheuer son meschief' Cl; 'pour escheuer son meschief' DBRo.

106/11–12. *The . . . manhode*: Fr. reads 'La Royne Thomiris [thamaris BClRo] nous fait sage de son issuë, qui le surmonta par vaillance'. *which* refers back to *Cyrus* in the preceding sentence.

106/27–8. *Seneck . . . men*: Fr. has 'Senecque és [*om.* B; en ses Ro] Tragedies, [*et add.* ClRo] Iehan Boccace en son Liure du cas des nobles'. The sentence in R is incomplete because part of the Fr. main clause is omitted: 'tu ne orras autre leçon que de la choiste [chance ClD₁; ruyne Ro] des haulx hommes'.

107/2–3. *in . . . them* (2): 'pour excerciter les assailliz et leur aprennent' Cl; '& par leurs violences les assaillis se exercitent aux armes, tant qu'ils apprennent de leurs ennemis' D (B omits 'de leurs ennemis').

107/14–19: See Boccaccio, *De Casibus Illustrium Virorum*, ix, and Brunetto Latini, *Tresor*, i. 96–7.

107/17. *Charles*: Fr. adds 'd'Anjou'.

107/19–27: For the English counterpart of Chartier's pro-French version, see Chaucer's *Monk's Tale*.

107/19. *thou . . . men*: 'pues auoir oy par le [grant *add.* Cl] rapport des vieulx' BClRo; 'pues auoir ouy parler' D.

107/31–3. *the . . . chased*: Fr. reads 'par ses aduersaires [les *add.* Ro] Anglois, & aucuns [de *add.* B] ses rebelles d'Escoce il fut persecuté en sa personne, & comme Prince desherité, guerroyé en son pays, & chassé'. The addition from N makes the English more like Fr. J corrupted *contryved* into *contre dyd*.

108/1. *aftir . . . batailes*: 'aprez certaines batailles de ses gens soubz son conduit desconfites' Cl; 'apres quinze tant rencontres que batailles de ses propres gents souz son conduit desconfites' D; 'aprez quinze que batailles que rencontres de ses propres gens soubz son conduit et soubz lui eulx desconfis' B (Ro is like B, but interchanges 'batailles' and 'rencontres').

108/3. *Yit*: Fr. adds 'Encore estoit il doubteux à si grant hoste sejourner en si forain heberge plus d'vne nuit'.

108/3. *he*: Fr. adds 'son Esperance ne l'heritage de'.

108/4. *victour*: Like Cl, which omits this passage added in DBRo: 'en la bataille de Benabourg, où luy accompaigné de trente & deux mille com-

batans ou enuiron, desconfit Henry Roy d'Angleterre, & sa compaignie &
aliez, qui estoient cent cinquante mille combatans, dont en la place & en
chasse moururent des Anglois plus de cinquante mille, & le remanant fut
chassé, & leur Roy aussi, bien cinquante lieuës dedans son pays d'Angleterre. Tant que apres celle grosse desconfiture & bataille ledit Roy
Robert porta', etc.

108/7. *serue*: 'seruir' Cl; 'querir' DBRo.

108/13. *and had*: Omission of the subject was probably caused by omission of the pronoun subject in Fr.

108/15. *all*: 'toute' BClRo; *om.* D.

108/16–109/6: This passage refers to the revolts against Louis the Pious
by Lothar, Pépin, and Louis, his sons.

108/19–21. *O . . . prince*: Fr. has 'O combien lamentable & perilleuse au
Royaume fut l'iniure & destitution honteuse de si grant Prince'. This
English sentence illustrates the translator's practice of shifting the con-
struction of a sentence in the middle.

108/23. *his*: Fr. construction is active, beginning 'nul ne pourroit . . .
penser'. *his*, the equivalent of which in Fr. is 'nul', is meaningless in the
changed structure of R.

108/23–4. *from . . . estate*: 'de l'honneur & de l'estat & enseignes de
cheualerie' ('& enseignes' *om.* Ro).

108/27–8. *was . . . that*: R misunderstood Fr. 'aggrauoit l'amertume de
sa [la BClRo] desplaisance. Entre lesquelz'. The reading from NJ added
in the text does not exactly follow Fr. either, but *byttyr* better renders the
idea of 'amertume' than does R's *displesaunt* alone.

108/31–2. *attempte . . . fadir*: 'attempter si honteusement sur son hon-
nouré filz & vostre pere'.

108/35–109/2. *he . . . offences*: 'il recogneut humainement vers vous, &
par humble pardon donna [pardonnance BClRoD₁] ce que grace diuine
auoit ouuré sur luy par pitié secourable'.

109/11. *Sarsines*: 'Sarsines' Cl; 'Sesnes' D; 'saxons' BRo.

109/21. *resyn vp*: 's'entrecoururent sus'.

109/23. *his bondis*: 'ces terreurs [eoreur Ro]'.

109/23. *Genouyeue*: Like Cl, which omits '& Xainctes en Xainctonge par
sainct Viuien Euesque d'icelle cité', added in DRo ('sainct . . . cite'
added in B).

109/24. *Toures*: Fr. adds 'ou lieu de sainct Martin le Bel'.

109/26–31. *Seint . . . olde*: For this apparent attempt of the R scribe to
correct a faulty exemplar, see Introduction, p. 19.

109/32–3. *of hundredis*: 'de centeines' BClD₁; 'de grant temps' D; 'mie
tant de cens' Ro.

110/1. *man* (2): May be a scribal error in RNJ for *manace*, to render Fr. 'menace'.

110/3. *sone of 3endebus*: Attila was the son of Mundiuch, or Mundzucus. For derivation of the name, see E. A. Thompson, *A History of Attila and the Huns* (Oxford, 1948), p. 162 n.

110/3. *in Gudy*: 'en Engady' DCl; 'et [*om.* B] en garde' BRo.

110/10–11. *and . . . mercye*: Like BClRo, which omit '& grace d'en eschapper' from this reading in D: '& en monstrant sa cité preste à la [*om.* BRo] correction, deseruit misericorde & grace d'en eschapper'.

110/16. *execucion*: 'execucion' Ro; 'executoire' DBCl.

110/20–7: Louis VII of France married three wives in order to get an heir. The last was Adela of Champagne, to whom Philip Augustus was born in 1165. This was a joyous event in France, partially because of the blow it gave to Henry II of England, who had his eye on the French throne in case of lack of heir. Thus, Philip was proclaimed 'God-given'.

110/23. *dispeyre*: 'desesperance' Cl; 'esperance' DBRo.

110/26. *and*: Fr. adds 'pour reünir [rauir Ro] en luy seul le couraige des François'.

110/27–111/13: This passage refers to the attacks on France by the Emperor Otto IV and King John of England in the early thirteenth century. While John was concentrating in Aquitaine, the Emperor, his nephew, fought in 1214 the Battle of Bouvines, where he was defeated by Philip Augustus. John's defeat in the south was as complete as that of his ally. In this period of confused allegiances, it is not strange that Chartier should not entirely agree with modern historical accounts of the allies of King John and Otto. The Count of Champagne, mentioned by Chartier, had been the leader of a strong faction against Philip, but seems to have taken no active part in this campaign against him. Hugh, Count of La Marche, head of the family of Lusignan, had become Duke by 1199, and passed from John's side to Philip's, and back, frequently during this period. At the time of this campaign, as Chartier indicates, John seems to have had his support. Arthur, Duke of Brittany, was supposedly murdered by John in 1203 before this battle, and his mother seems to have had no prominent part in this struggle. See *Cambridge Medieval History*, VI. ix.

110/34. *with ij hostis*: *om.* Fr.

111/13–15. *So . . . memorye*: 'Te ramenteuoir à present les exemples qui sont de fresche memoire, seroit plus narration superflue, que allegation necessaire'.

111/15–21: During Charles V's reign (1364–80) there was a period of revival for France, when the domination of the Plantagenets was not far from having disappeared from the country. As E. Perroy, *The Hundred Years War*, tr. W. B. Wells (London, 1951), so aptly puts it, 'Charles V has benefited from the popularity which, in times of misfortune, clings to the memory of a leader, who dies prematurely in what seems to be a vanished golden age' (p. 146). It is this sort of memory that Chartier expresses.

111/16. *ayel . . . Regnault*: 'qui ayeul fut de charles regnant' Ro; 'ayeul de Charles septiesme de ce nom à present regnant' DCl; *om.* B.

111/22. *derke*: Fr. adds 'ou moins appropriez à ton entente'.

111/23. *party*: The meaning of *party* here (plight, condition) is questioned and noted as rare in *OED*, but cf. Caxton, *Paris and V.*, 5 (1485): 'Ye see . . . in what party we be now'.

111/26. *writinges*: 'les histoires, Et poësies fictoires Narratoires'.

111/28–30. *through . . . dedis*: Much condensed translation of Fr.:

> Ainsi par verifier [versiffier Cl].
> Et temps en estudier
> Employer [Amplier Cl].
> Ont voulu certifier [rectiffier Ro]
> Les Clerz, & specifier
> Sans nier,
> Les cas qui aduindrent loires
> Et pour nous humilier,
> Et à vertu affier,
> Et lier,
> D'autruy faiz clarifier,
> Monstrer & [*om.* BClRo] exemplier,
> Et tirer [creer B; crier Ro]
> Noz presens cas peremptoires.

111/33. *hope*: Like B, which omits 'apres les autres', added in DClRo.

112/11. *the othir interrogacions*: *the tothirs* (NJ) may be superior here since Fr. has only 'les autres', and the R scribe may have recalled *interrogacions* from earlier in the speech.

112/20. *dispreyse them*: Fr. adds '& ne les demandent [congnoissent Ro]'.

112/26–7. *as* (2) . . . *them* (3): N's omission here occurs at the bottom of f. 71.

112/29. *devye*: Fr. has 'denier'. Although *n* has perhaps been misread as *u*, *devye* is a suitable translation.

113/1. *woll . . . iugement*: 'ne . . . iustifiera'.

113/4. *The makyng*: D seems to be wrong in placing 'faire' with the preceding sentence in Fr. There is clear evidence in Cl that it belongs where the R translator placed it and parallels in structure 'iustifier' in the main clause.

113/16. *to . . . for*: Fr. has 'aux fins où ils les [constraingnent et *add.* Ro] enclinent'. *dedis* may be a scribal error in RNJ for *endis*.

113/20. *haue sowle*: Like BClRo, which do not have D's negative.

113/22–3. *for . . . bestis*: 'selon droit de franchise et seigneurie sur les bestes' Ro; 'selon le droit de franche seigneurie' DBCl.

113/25. *determyned . . . dethe*: 'arrestez & desterminez' DBCl; 'arrestement determinez' Ro.

113/26. *and*: Fr. adds 'trauaille en l'election &'.

113/29. *secheth*: The pronoun subject omitted in R is also omitted in BClRo.

113/34–114/1. *cause and vndirstonding*: 'attente'.

114/1. *modir*: Fr. adds 'qui l'a appris à aller' (BClRo omit 'à aller').

114/10–12. *hath . . . spoken*: 'leur a denié la vocalle louange'.

114/13. *fadirs*: Fr. adds 'les descongnoissent, &'.

114/16. *mete*: Like BClRo, which omit 'iusques à tant que leursdits peres les ayent recongneus & pris en cure', added in D.

114/17–18. *entendith . . . himself*: 'ne s'attent à l'aide & secours de là hault'.

114/21. *defawte*: 'deffaulte' BRo; 'desdain' DCl.

114/30. *there enemyes*: R's reading fits the context of the English better than NJ's. Fr. has 'son ennemy', like NJ, because of the addition of 'chacune' after 'parties'.

114/33. *the to praye*: See Introduction, p. 17.

115/1. *enhaunce*: Like Cl, which omits the object 'le' which appears in DBRo.

115/3. *vndirstondist and felist*: 'sens'.

115/6. *false*: This mistranslates the Fr. verb 'faulz'. See Introduction, p. 50.

115/9. *thine . . . werkes*: R is like BRo, which have 'a tes oroisons ton appetit'. DCl have 'tes oraisons à [canc. Cl] ton appetit'. Note the mistranslation of 'oroisons'.

115/10–11. *him* (1) *. . . him*: The pronouns in Fr. are second person. Either the translator or a scribe switched person in the middle of the sentence in the English.

115/17–18. *that . . . vices*: 'qui es vaincu par les vices' BClRoD₁; 'qui as vaincu les vices' D.

115/19. *God . . . body*: Fr. has 'Dieu te laissera vaincre quant au corps'. R mistranslated 'te laissera vaincre' (to yield).

115/25. *through arrogaunce*: 'par l'aueuglement d'arrogance' is part of the next clause in Fr.

115/26. *it*: Fr. 'le' refers to the overcomer.

115/34. *mesure*: R, rendering Fr. 'mesure', means 'calculation, reckoning' in developing the image indicated by *cownte* and *miscownted*. OED does not record a use like this nor does it record the figurative use of the reflexive *miscownted* (made a wrong calculation).

116/2. *myghty man*: R confused 'tres puissant' with Fr. 'trespassant'.

116/5. *aske*: 'eslisent' BCl; 'eslisent pour les guider' D; 'les enseignent' Ro.

116/6. *the veray way*: The emendation from NJ retains the parallelism of structure.

116/9. *saf*: 'sans'.

116/10–11. *likewise . . . enhaunced*: RJ, rather than N, follow Fr. 'ainsi toutes les voyes de Dieu sont exaulcees'.

116/15. *estimacion*: Like BRo, which omit '& faut qu'à luy obeisse' added in D (Cl has only 'obeisse').

116/17. *though . . . streight*: om. Fr.

116/17. *it*: 'toutes les choses qui luy aduiengnent'.

116/20. *to man*: Fr. adds '& l'a plus en grant chierté'.

116/21–2. *or . . . Him*: R follows Fr. 'ains que l'homme l'aimast' more closely than do NJ.

116/22. *His . . . loves*: In this mistranslation of 'naist & procede toute loyalle [om. BClRo] amour & charité', R probably uses *procedith* in the sense 'surpasses, excels', in confusion with *precedith*.

116/23. *so sure*: '[le add. Ro] plus seure oroison'.

116/23. *confirmed . . . wille*: 'conformee [confermee BRo] au vouloir'.

116/29. *is confirmed in*: 'se conforme à' DBCl; 'se conferme a' Ro.

117/16–17. *and essencially and*: R is like BClRo in placing the modifier. D, which omits the equivalent of the second *and*, places the modifier with 'aux hommes'.

117/17–18. *dependaunt . . . wisedam*: R is like BClRoD₁, which have 'deppendences' for D's 'disposition'. Fr. has 'Bonté & sapience' as subjects of the next sentence.

117/19. *condicion*: Like Cl, which omits 'a, &', added in DB.

117/20. *trwe*: 'veritable' (followed by erasure) Cl; 'veritablement' BRo; om. D.

117/27. *neythir*: Fr. has 'iamais'. *neythir* in RNJ may be an error for *neuir*. Note N's variant *neyper* for *neuir* (RJ) at 118/21.

118/12–13. *saf . . . humanite*: Fr. reads 'sinon entant que se puet estendre [entendre Ro] le iugement de ton [sa Ro] humanité'. The English means 'except in that which your human judgement extends far enough to know'.

118/15–16. *and . . . scourge*: J's omission indicates that RN were not copied from J.

118/16. *Good frendis*: Chartier, followed by the translator, forgot that in the dialogue Hope is speaking only to Understanding, and hence the sermon-like address is out of place.

118/25–6. *which . . . self*: 'Dont le mouuement est en toy' BClRo; 'dont l'emolument est en toy' D.

118/26. *yn Hym*: Since Fr. has 'à luy', J's *yn* suggests that the original reading was *yn Hym*, omitted by R. N's *yet* indicates that an exemplar was probably difficult to read here.

118/28 ff.: Cf. the discussion of God's providence and man's free will with Boethius, Lib. v, Prosae 2–6.

118/29–30. *He . . . it*: The NJ reading is supported by Fr. 'eternellement il ait voulu & sceu toutes choses, sans changier vouloir'.

119/7. *traversable*: Fr. has 'entreuerchiez'. *traversable* is not given in *OED* in the figurative meaning 'moving to and fro, hence confused'. The earliest record (1534) is in the legal meaning 'capable of being formally denied'. The use in R may be compared with the first recorded figurative use of the verb *traverse*, from Painter, *Pal. Pleas.*, i. 90 (1566): 'This miserable lover, trauersing in seuerall mindes . . . chaunged his mynde a thousand times in an hower'. R also may use the word with overtones of the meaning 'dispute, discuss', recorded in *OED* from *c*.1440 from *Partonope* 1772.

119/8–9. *him . . . hym*: DBCl support the addition from NJ here: 'le respondant, & les argumens retournent contre'. It is interesting, however, that Ro omits exactly the same passage as does R.

119/14. *thiself*: 'toy meismes' ClD_1; 'soy mesmes' DBRo.

119/20–1. *What . . . stedeffast*: N twice on this page, here and in ll. 27–8, omits sentences of transition.

119/23. *and . . . thingis*: '& toutes choses inuariable science'.

119/31–2. *which . . . thingis*: Fr. reads 'qui par soy mesmes & en soy mesmes comme tout parfait congnoist toutes choses'. With omission of the superfluous *and* after *perfecte* in RNJ, the sentence follows Fr. exactly. *and* was probably picked up by an earlier scribe because of its occurrence after *inperfecte* at 120/2.

120/2. *and . . . thingis*: '& qui mendie dehors la congnoissance des choses par leurs especes'.

120/7. *knowest*: Like Cl, which omits 'de luy', which clarifies the idea in DBRo.

120/8–10. *vpon . . . vndirstondinge*: 'de sa science. Elles sont pour ce quil les scet: Et tu les scez par ce quelles sont/leur mutacion ne peut muer sa science' Cl; 'de sa science absoluë. Elles sont de luy par eternelle congnoissance & sapience sceuës clerement, & parce qu'il les sçait [fait Ro] de luy; & de sa grace tu le [les Ro] scez, pourtant qu'elles font leur mutation. Doncques pour ce ne se peut muer sa science' DBRo.

120/10–11. *for . . . vndirstonding*: 'Car de sa science procede leur estre' D_1; 'Car sa science precede leur estre' DBClRo.

120/16. *of . . . fallible*: 'sa science est necessaire, eternelle [*om.* ClRo], & infalible'.

120/17. *principally*: 'principalment' BRo; 'presentialment' DCl.

120/20–1. *nor . . . contingence*: 'ne force leur contingence' Ro; 'ne sa science ne force leur contingence' DBCl.

120/23. *necessary*: R is like BRo, which scribally omit part of Fr. because of the repetition of 'necessaire' in this reading of DCl: 'establement necessaire./Il les scet necessairement par soy mesmes qui est necessaire,/ telles qu'elles seront'.

120/24. *Him*: 'soy' here stands for 'itself' (i.e., their nature) in Fr.

120/25–32: Cf. Boethius, Lib. v, Prosa 6.

121/5. *mesured*: Fr. has 'mesme'. R's *mesured* must mean 'fixed'. This passage is the only example quoted in this meaning for the participial adjective in *MED*.

121/21. *promysed*: 'promis' Cl; 'permis' D; 'monstre' BRo.

121/30. *reprocheth*: ClRo have 'reprouche'; DB 'rapprouche'. *reprocheth* has no meaning in a clause which should mean 'if some blessed combination does not find a plan whereby man may approach the divine clemency'.

122/2. *Who . . . be*: 'Qui sera celui' BClRoD$_1$; 'Ov est celuy' D.

122/15. *of seeke soules*: 'des ames malades' Cl; 'des maladies des ames' DBRo.

122/18. *ben ordeined*: 'sont' BRo; *om.* DCl.

122/24. *by . . . blissidhod*: R is like Cl, which has 'par louenge chose qui acroisse sa beatitude'. D has 'louënge ne chose qui accroisse sa beatitude'; BRo 'loenge acrut sa beatitude'. *breke* is a serious mistranslation of 'acroisse'.

122/25. *kyndenes*: 'gratitude' ClD$_1$; 'creature' DRo.

123/1. *a* (1) *. . . regoinessaunce*: 'peage & recongnoissance'.

123/5. *the prynte*: 'la mienne'.

123/30. *dewly*: 'druëment'.

124/2–4. *For . . . prayer*: Either this passage is mistranslated, or RNJ are corrupt. Fr. has 'Car oroison est si attrayant à Dieu, que ceulx mesmes qui ont attribué deité aux choses mues, leur ont tantost rendu le deuoir d'oroison'. The variant readings in NJ are not satisfactory here. If in N, however, *fo* is an error for *so*, as seems likely, then it is possible that N has the intended reading: *Deite* then would be the object of *gave* and *such as* the subject.

124/4–9: See Valerius Maximus, i. 1–2.

124/11. *comon*: 'commis'.

124/12. *obseruacions*: 'obsecracions' BClRo; 'oblations' D.

124/17. *execracions*: DCl have 'expiations'; BRo 'expiracions'. *execracions* (RN) has little meaning here, whereas *expracions* (J) might be a scribal error for either *expiations* (the best reading) or *expiracions*.

124/17. *this . . . stones*: The mistranslation of 'vserent en sacrifiant de aucunes prieres', caused by confusion of 'prieres' and 'pierres', muddles the meaning of *obsecracions*, which in Fr. refers to 'prieres'.

124/23. *Eolus*: The correct reading from N is like that in D. The corrupt *Colus* (RJ) is, however, in BRo and probably in the uncorrected Cl.

124/28. *emprise . . . Troye*: Fr. has 'prise que les Grecs [gens Ro] eussent recousse du feu de Troye'. N has *emperrise*, J *emperise*, suggesting that these two scribes at least thought of 'empress'. Fr. 'prise' and R's *emprise*, however, suggest that the translator meant 'spoil, prize', a meaning not in *MED* and questioned in *OED*.

125/2. *shulde . . . prayer*: Fr. has only 'deuoient aorer'. Since NJ omit *shulde pray to or*, it may be the addition of the R scribe.

125/2-3. *in . . . them*: Fr. has 'De elle [celle Ro] firent ilz preambule en toutes grans choses'. Thus *sent* (RJ) is superior to *sought* (N).

125/3-11: See Valerius Maximus, i. 2. 2.

125/5. *the Caves*: DBCl have 'Cannes'; Ro 'Capue'. Twice in *The Quadrilogue Invective*, at 158/28 and 192/14, this same change of 'Cannes' to *Caves* occurs.

125/15-16. *as . . . dedis*: This clause follows Fr. exactly except for the omission of 'contient' after 'Bible', an omission which completely alters the sense of the passage. Perhaps some verb, possibly *offers*, has been scribally omitted before *of* in a manuscript lying behind RNJ.

125/19. *And . . . that*: om. Fr.

125/25. *the people*: Fr. has 'les batailleurs [batailles Ro] du peuple'. In l. 26 R has *in playne batailes*, not in Fr.

125/27. *hevynne*: Like Cl, which omits 'par deuote oroison pour ses combatans', added in DBRo.

125/29-30. *the . . . Dauid*: Fr. has 'la promesse [promission Ro] à Dauid'. *provisione* in RNJ may be a scribal error.

125/33. *lawdes and praysingis*: 'loenges' BRo; *sing.* DCl.

126/5-6: *Clouis* is Clovis I, King of the Franks (*c*.466–511), whose spectacular conversion to Christianity was a popular medieval story. See G. Kurth, *Clovis* (Bruxelles, 1923), ii. 170–209. *Clottorye* is Clotaire II, King of the Franks, son of Chilperic, in contrast to Clotaire I, son of Clovis, who was reputed to be a cruel king. *Dagonbert* may refer to any one of the three Dagoberts, all Kings of the Franks. Dagobert I, son of Clotaire II, protected the Church and placed illustrious men in high positions in it. See *Gesta Dagoberti I, regis Francorum*, in *MGH: Scriptores Rerum Merovingicarum*, ed. B. Krusch (1888), ii. 401–25. Dagobert III, son of Childebert III, as king and martyr, is supposedly the subject of *Vita Dagoberti III, regis Francorum* (*ibid.*, 507–24), but Krusch believed that in reality the saint and martyr was Dagobert II, son of Sighebert III.

126/7. *good Kyng Robert*: Robert II, called 'the Pious'.

126/23. *Him*: Fr. adds 'il puisse'.

126/24. *erred*: Fr. adds:

> Luy mesmes tout vif s'enterre,
> Et parà [pert Ro] toute sa defferre,
> Et le bien qu'il deuoit querre.

126/25. *sekyng*: Fr. has 'cesser'. Cf. 93/4, where both R and J have *sykyng* for 'ceasing'.

126/26. *ernest peny*: 'euuerre' D; 'verre erre' ('erre' a form of 'arrhes') uncorrected Cl; 'mierre' corrected Cl; 'verre' B; 'voiore' Ro.

126/27. *for . . . way*: 'pour erre De le remettre en son erre'.

127/2. *sideling*: Fr. has 'lateral'. This is an interesting early occurrence of *sideling*, which in *OED* appears in a non-figurative use in 1548, but in the figurative meaning 'oblique' only in 1611.

127/2. *the askyng*: 'la demande' BClRo; 'ta demande' D.

127/3. *traversing discrecion*: Fr. has 'transuersaine digression'. The ppl. adj. *traversing* is listed as rare in *OED* and is not recorded in the meaning 'digressing'. The first record in any sense is from 1561. But Palsgrave, 761/2, uses the verb in this sense in 1530. *discrecion* is certainly an incorrect spelling for *digression* (see *MED*). R also has *degre* for *decree* at 24/5.

127/8–9. *furst* (2) . . . *perfeccion* (1): See Introduction, p. 50.

127/15. *that*: Like Cl, which omits 'au premier', added in D (BRo add the phrase after 'gent').

127/16–18. *and . . . enchayned*: Fr. has '& comme l'estre des choses est enchaine'. There is no Fr. equivalent for *and . . . them*. The construction *hough the beeng of thingis and hough the crafte of thingis* suggests perhaps that again two attempts to render the passage were copied from the author's draft.

127/20. *the . . . them*: 'les parfaictes'.

127/23–4. *which . . . newe-founde*: 'que ils n'eurent pas faiz, mais trouuez'.

127/29–31. *in . . . above*: In Fr. this goes with the next sentence.

128/1–3. *and . . . Deite*: Fr. reads 'De là en auant ne furent gens qui ne recogneussent sur eux aucune souueraine puissance, ou goustassent quelque pou de la cognoissance de deité'. R's scribal omission was caused by the repetition of *man*.

128/4. *ooned*: 'vnies' BClD$_1$; 'venuës' D; 'veues' Ro.

128/4–5. *and . . . is*: R is like Ro, which has 'tous entendemens en gros que dieu est'. DBCl have 'Toutes entendent en gros, que Dieu est'. 'que' here means 'that', and the entire phrase means 'understanding in a general sense that God exists'.

128/6. *what . . . is*: 'que Dieu est' B; 'qui Dieu est' ClRo; 'quel Dieu il est' D.

128/12. *sacrifices*: RJ are like BClRo, which omit '&' after this. N, like D, has *and*.

128/17–19. *And . . . Him*: 'pour recongnoistre que tousiours auoient ils & auroient mestier de celuy qui les leur auoit donné' (Ro omits 'ils & auroient').

128/20–2. *wer . . . temple*: Cl has 'firent emplier/lordre des ministres du temple par qui commenca par ceste introduction'. BRo have 'acomplis' for 'emplier' and omit 'par qui'. D has 'furent aussi plus amplement faits & accomplis. L'ordre des ministres du temple commença par ceste introduction'.

128/23. *all*: 'toutes autres' Cl; 'autres' DBRo.

128/24. *offeryngis*: 'offre' Cl; 'offertes & oblations' D; 'offiert oblacions' Ro; 'oblacions' B.

128/28–9. *the hoole*: Like BClRo, which omit 'ne sur partie d'iceluy heritage', added in D.

128/30. *Israell*: Like Cl, which omits 'excepté celle de Leui', added in D; 'excepte celles de leurs prestres', added in Ro; 'excepte la leur', added in B.

128/33. *all . . . necessary*: 'tout'.

128/33–129/2. *His . . . Him*: Fr. has 'ses ministres deuoient de tout prendre'. N's *shulde be rewarded* follows Fr. sense more closely than RJ's *shulde rewarde*.

129/2–4. *but . . . othir*: R is like Cl, which reads 'quil fut mis en equalite de partaige auec les autres qui le tout auoient departi entre les autres'. DBRo have 'qu'ils fussent mis' for 'quil fut mis' and 'entr'eux' for 'entre les autres'. D also adds 'diuisé &' after 'auoient'.

129/4–5. *in . . . Him*: R is like Cl, which has 'Dont en seigne que tout estoit sien· de toutes choses lui estoit fait offerte'. D has 'Doncques en signe que tout procedoit de luy, & que tout estoit sien, de toutes choses luy estoit & deuoit estre faite offerte, disme, ou oblation'. BRo follow D in the first clause, but omit '& deuoit estre' and 'disme' in the second.

129/7–8. *to be . . . noted*: 'notoire'.

129/15–16. *The . . . offeringis*: R is like Cl, which has 'Le createur qui se repaist nest pas nourri de la pasture de tes offrandes'. D has 'Le Createur de toutes choses n'a mestier d'estre nourry de la pasture d'icelles offrandes'. BRo have 'Ton' for 'Le' and omit 'de toutes choses' in D's reading.

129/18. *nor . . . beestis*: om. Fr.

129/25–6. *Through . . . therth*: R is like Cl, which has 'Par tel sacriffice feuz Ie enuoye en terre'. DBRo insert the passage after *hoope* in l. 27. DRo, however, have the third person, like R.

129/28–30. *For . . . hoope*: 'Sacrifiez [Sacrifie BRo] à Dieu [en *add*. Ro] sacrifice de iustice, & lors esperez [espere BRo] en luy'.

130/6. *what . . . which*: 'Bien est deceüe la folle fiance de ceulx qui cuident faire grant euure [offre Ro] quant ils'.

130/9. *evil*: 'mal' Cl; *om*. DBRo.

130/29–31. *which . . . aultar*: 'Lesquelz sont en ces Iours plus loingtains de son obeissance que les plus prouchains de son autel' Cl; 'Et croy qu'en ces presens iours les plus lointains de son obeyssance sont les plus prouchains de son aultier' DRo (B breaks off after 'iours' and omits the rest of the treatise).

130/33. *mystery*: 'mistere' ClD$_1$; 'maistre' DRo.

131/1–2. *make . . . repreveable*: 'furent leur mistere esperituel Comme oeuure reprouchable' Cl; 'fuyent leurs [les Ro] mysteres & offices espirituels, comme euures reprouchables' DRo.

131/6–9. *the . . . chirche*: 'les constitucions plaines de barat et de questions prouffit triumphe et les sainctes doctrines des peres anciens pouoient souffire a vng chascun ministre en leglise' Cl; 'les constitutions sont desrogues, & exercice de barat [font *add*. Ro] & de questueux proufit à present est trimphant; & les sainctes doctrines des Peres rejettees [sont degettees Ro] & arriere mises, lesquelles [Aucuns Ro] pouoient & deuoient souffire à vn chascun ministere [auoir mistere Ro] en l'Eglise' DRo (Ro has only 'triumphal' for 'à . . . trimphant').

131/12–13. *shall . . . preesthode*: Fr. has 'desseura l'ordre du sainct mariage d'auec la dignité de Prestrise'. The prepositions in R (*from* and *vnto*) make the English unclear, and the omission of *from* and the change of *vnto* to *than* in NJ do not improve the sense. One would expect *depart þe ordre . . . from the dignite*.

131/13. *clennesse*: Like Cl, which omits '& chasteté sans souilleurs', added in D.

131/13–15. *Now . . . temporalles*: R is like Cl, which has 'Maintenant court le statut qui les a actrais aux estas mondains et souilles de cures temporelles'. DRo have the following longer passage: 'Maintenant court le statut de concubinage au contraire, qui les a attraits aux estats mondains, & aux deliz sensuels & corporels. Et qui plus est, se sont rendus à immoderee auarice, en procurant par symonie & par autres voyes illicites, litigieuses, & processiues en corruption, & autrement, benefices & prelatures espirituelles. Et auec ce se sont souillez & occupez és affaires citoyens, & és negoces & cures temporelles'.

131/16–17. *anon . . . departe*: D reads 'ores la desordonnance auaricieuse des Prestres a fait separer'. Perhaps R did the best he could with an exemplar like Cl, which omits 'a fait'.

131/18. *3a*: 'mais de'.

131/22. *straungenes*: 'estrangete' ClRo; 'dissolution' D.

131/23. *nowadays*: Like Cl, which omits 'comme dit est', added in DRo.

131/24–6. *Forasmuche . . . take*: Fr. reads 'Car tant ont telles Constitu-tions de lieu, comme on y prent de plaisir'. R means 'Because they have whatever constitutions of place give them pleasure'. Chartier's 'Constitu-tions de lieu', followed by R, is an equivalent of the Latin 'constitutum locorum' or 'statutum locale', referring to particular local laws or orders of priests as they add to or extend by interpretation, for their own use, the scope of the general constitutions of the church.

131/27–8. *of . . . sclaunder*: 'd'escande luxure'.

131/29. *men . . . doubte*: R is like Cl, which has 'on pourroit doubter'. In light of N's variant *I* for *men*, however, D's reading is interesting: 'ie diroye plainement'. Ro combines the two in 'on pourroit penser ou doubter voire plainement dire'.

132/6–8. *Yet . . . chirche*: 'ne blasmons pas pour tant les bons hommes seculiers qui ont donne a leglise les possessions' Cl; 'Si n'entens-ie pas pourtant blasmer les preudes hommes d'Eglise de bonnes meurs & honneste conuersation: ne aussi les seculiers, qui de deuotion parfaite ont donné à l'Eglise les possessions' D; 'Ne Ie nentens pas pourtant a blasmer les preudhommes seculiers qui de deuocion par faicte ont donne a leglise les possessions' Ro.

132/8–9. *for . . . clergie*: Fr. reads 'Car ils se sont deschargez pour monter vers Dieu en esperit plus legierement'. 'Et la Clergié' then becomes the subject of 'a prins' in the next sentence.

132/11. *hevyn*: Like Cl, which omits the following passage from DRo: 'Car l'appetit auaricieux des Ecclesiastiques a si surmonté leur raison, que leur damnation y gist manifestement, & si fait la destruction temporelle d'vn chacun: qui est & peut estre vitupere à l'honneur vniuersel de l'Eglise deça bas, & ou deprimement de soy, & principalement des Ecclesiastiques, qui tels maux commettent'.

132/12–13. *am . . . stroke*: 'suis deffié de leur duree qui à bien iuger approche hastiuement sur eux en toute desesperance'.

132/16. *indignite*: Fr. has 'indignite'. I have emended *dignite* despite its appearance in RNJ, and despite the fact that *OED* has not found *in-dignite* elsewhere in this meaning earlier than 1589. At 49/29, R also uses the word to mean 'contemptuous or insolent usage', the first record of which is from 1584. *MED* omits the word.

132/19. *men*: Like Cl, which omits '& especialement sur les sacrifians. Dont pour leur iniquité il faut qu'autres l'achaptent & comparent, qui est double damnation ausdits sacrifians, & misere diuerse à autruy', added in DRo.

132/24. *desirith*: DCl have 'designe'; Ro 'descripst'. Perhaps *desirith* is a scribal error in RNJ for *descrivith*. See 64/27.

132/31–3: See Valerius Maximus, i. 1–2. The quotation is indirect in Fr.

[THE QUADRILOGUE INVECTIVE]

134/5–6, 135/8–9: The King of France at this time was Charles VI. The Dauphin, later Charles VII, carried the title of Regent after 30 December 1418.

134/6. *ferre . . . oratours*, 135/9. *verey . . . oratours*: Chartier's style was notably influenced by the Roman orators, especially Cicero. See E. J. Hoffman, *Alain Chartier, His Work and Reputation* (New York, 1942), pp. 138–44.

134/7. *with . . . and*: om. Fr.

134/23. *atemprate*: See Introduction, p. 17.

134/27–8. *vpon . . . punyshed*, 135/31. *is . . . men*: 'the people are punished'.

134/28–30. *which . . . lordeshippes*, 135/31–3. *And . . . lordys*: 'que aprés bon amendement et loiale [louable B] correction [il *add*. ABH] a renvoyé et redrecié les seigneuries' (ABH have present tense verbs).

135/7. *comon*: Fr. has 'françois'. This is the first of U's fairly consistent omissions of direct reference to France. See Introduction, p. 47.

135/15. *fame and*: om. Fr.

135/18. *determined*: 'et leur determinement' H; 'et leur detriment' DAB.

135/20. *reuerseth . . . down*: 'verse'.

135/21. *and dominacion*: om. Fr.

135/22. *and destruccion*: om. Fr.

135/22–3. *the . . . ouyrthrowen*: 'des vainqueurs vaincus'.

135/26–8. *the* (2) *. . . abated*: Mistranslation of 'le decret de plus attrempee punicion, l'orgueil de trop oultrecuidié povoir qui se descognoist est rabaissié [abaissie BH]'.

135/30. *rod*: 'nourreture'.

136/2–3, 137/3. *and as . . . lorde*: R is like D, which has 'et, comme maistre seigneur', whereas U is like ABH, which add 'et' after 'maistre'.

136/5. *may deceve*: The corrector of R who changed *deceve* to *deceiveth* did not see the real scribal error, the omission of *may* after *man*, as shown by NS. Fr. has 'puet decevoir'.

136/8. *as*: 'comme' BH; om. DA (like U).

136/11–12. *the . . . abydinge*: Fr. has 'le cours et la duree'. R confused 'cours' and 'court'.

136/13–14. *and* (1) *. . . ayre*: Fr. has 'et que elles ont leurs maladies et leur mort comme les hommes en leur endroit'. *in the ayre* may be corrupt since N has *in them* and S *in theyr*.

136/23–6. *And . . . principaliteys*, 137/25–9. *Whiche . . . lordshipps*: 'Et se memoire vous [nous ABH] puet aucune chose ramentevoir et les anciens livres de noz peres apprendre a cognoistre noz faiz par les leurs, toutes anciennes escriptures sont pleines de mutacions, subversions et changemens des royaumes et des principautez'.

136/31. *the . . . of*: om. Fr.

136/31–3. *by . . . failed*, 137/33–4. *of . . . lastinge*: See Introduction, p. 68.

137/5. *pleasire and*: om. Fr.

137/7–13. *aftir . . . knowen*: See Introduction, pp. 57–8. *corages* in l. 9 is a mistranslation of 'ouvraige' or perhaps the result of a corrupt Fr. exemplar.

137/20. *and . . . ensaumple*: om. Fr.

137/20–1. *by* (2) . . . *molde*: 'a tour de sa roe . . . d'une mesme masse'.

137/22. *bothe . . . lesse*: om. Fr.

137/31. *finall declynnyng*: 'declin' DAB; 'fin' H.

138/3–6. *shall . . . people*: 'reste le pié des fondemens que les haulx buissons forcloent de la veue des hommes'.

138/6–9. *Thebes . . . releued*, 139/5–8. *Thebes . . . sed*: Fr. has 'Thebes, qui fut fondee de Cadmus, fils d'Agenor, et la plus peuplee de dessus la terre en son temps, en quelle part pourroit l'en trouver tant de reliques de son nom que gens se puissent monstrer nez de sa semence'. Both R and U are free in translation here. Because of the story of Cadmus' sowing of the dragon's seed from which armed men grew, 'semence' is significant. U's *seth* is thus probably a scribal error for *sed*, since *seth* does not occur elsewhere in U as a spelling of the adv. or conj. *sith*.

138/11–12. *whereof . . . extincte*: 'desquelles encores nous usons, ne pout oncques tant estroictement garder les lois de Ligurgus le droicturier, qui furent faictes pour sa perpetuation [perpetracion B], que sa vertu ne soit estaincte et aneantie [et aneantie om. B]'.

138/16–19. *The . . . asshes*, 139/14–17. *Cartage . . . fyre*: R is much freer than U in rendering Fr. 'Cartage la batailleresse, qui avoit dompté [donctoit A; domptoit H; ne doubtoit B] les elephans a batailler et qui jadis fut tant redoutable aux Rommains, ou a elle tourné sa grant gloire sinon en la cendre du feu dont elle fut arse et embrasee'. Worcester, who has 'redoubtee des' for 'redoutable aux', is perhaps somewhat more nearly like R and U than are the Fr. manuscripts.

138/19–20. *of* (2) . . . *cite*: om. Fr.

138/21, 139/18–19. *excellent vertue*: Both R and U are like B, which omits 'en' in 'excellente en vertu' (DAH).

138/22–3. *the* (1) . . . *falles*, 139/19–21. *the* (2) . . . *falles*: Fr. has 'd'elle mesmes, par sa pesanteur, elle decheut, car les trop pesants fais font les griefves choistes'. See Lucan, *Pharsalia*, i. 71–3.

138/23–6, 139/21–4. *And . . . realmys*: See Introduction, p. 54. *OED* quotes *rebate* intr. only from Foxe, 1570.

138/32–3. *though . . . yghen*: 'en racontant les faiz qu'ilz cognoiscent a l'oeil'.

138/34–5. *nothing . . . vndirstonde*: 'riens ne se fait, sont une abisme parfonde ou nul entendement humain ne sceit [ou peut *add*. H; ne ne puet *add*. B] prendre fons'.

138/36–140/1. *so . . . so . . . to*: Fr. has 'trop' and after 'fraelles' adds 'a les comprendre' to complete the structure.

139/11. *his*: Lacedomone's.

139/11. *attained*: Fr. has 'estaincte'. U seems to mean 'corrupted, tainted', but since the *i* is not ticked, the scribe may have thought the word was *attamed* (injured, damaged).

139/24. *and* (2): This structurally awkward *and* is not in Fr.

139/26. *Perciens*: Fr. adds 'et [*om*. ABH] des Persans'. The phrase may be scribally omitted in U.

140/1–5, 141/1–5. *we . . . peyne*: Fr. has 'nous imputons a Fortune, qui est chose faincte et vaine et ne se peut revencher, la juste venjance que Dieu prent de noz faultes, laquelle, ainsi que dit Vallere, vient bien a tart, mais la longue attente est recompensee par aggravement de peine'. Both R and U have faulty translations here: U has not understood that 'venjance' goes with the verb 'imputons a'; and if R understood the structure, then *compleyne vpon* has the unusual meaning 'blame upon', not recorded in *OED* and recorded in only two fifteenth-century examples in *MED*. R seems to have misunderstood entirely the first part of the saying from Valerius Maximus, in which 'laquelle' refers back to 'venjance'.

140/6, 141/6: Like U, Fr. has 1422, the year of the deaths of Henry V of England and Charles VI of France, upon which Henry VI was proclaimed by the English King of France. After his father's death Charles VII, because of his own timidity and apathy and because of the selfish counsellors who surrounded him and who blocked any efforts to make peace with the Burgundians, allowed the fortunes of France to fall to an unprecedentedly low ebb. As E. Perroy, *The Hundred Years War*, writes: 'Charles consistently disappointed all those . . . who regarded him as the legitimate heir of a glorious dynasty'. Chartier was one of the disappointed, and out of his disappointment grew *Le Quadrilogue*.

140/9–11. *and* (1) . . . *allyaunce*, 141/8–10. *enriche . . . aliaunce*: Fr. has 'enrichir de noz despoilles et [*om*. B, like U] despriser noz faiz et noz couraiges et des nostres, qu'il a vers soy atraiz, fortifier les voulentez a son aliance'. In the changed structure of R, the subject of *made* and *dispreisid* must be understood from the context.

140/11, 141/10. *I se*: It is interesting that both R and U have this reading not in Fr.

140/12. *growe*: Fr. adds 'et a noz aveuglees affections adjouster tousjours quelque chose'.

140/13–14. *and . . . displesaunce*: 'et que sa fureur a mis en oevre'.

140/16, 141/16. *of oure forefaders*: Like BH, which omit 'et des' in 'de noz peres et des primerains' (DA).

140/17. *punycion*, 141/17. *affliccion*: 'pugnition' H; 'affliction' DAB.

140/21. *multitude of*: om. Fr.

140/22. *ben*: The subject *which* refers to the singular *stroke*. Fr., however, has 'les coups'. The reading in R may come from careless translation or scribal error (*stroke* for *strokes*).

140/22. *wourthi*, 141/22. *digne*: All the Fr. manuscripts I have seen have 'signes de'. The similarity of R and U, however, suggests that 'digne' may have been in the translators' Fr. exemplars.

140/30. *in . . . plee*: R's legal rendering of 'et est dit *invectif*' would perhaps come naturally to such a translator as Sir John Fortescue.

140/31. *trauersing wourdis*, 141/31. *plesaunt woordes*: Fr. has 'envaïssement [amatissement B; inuisement H] de paroles'. In light of the legal language *moote or plee* in R, *trauersing* may be used here in the legal sense 'contradicting formally a previous pleading'.

140/31–3. *Wherfor . . . persones*, 141/31–5. *and* (1) *. . . surpluse*: 'Si ne vueille aucun lire l'une partie sans l'autre, afin que l'en ne cuide que tout le blasme soit mis [*om.* BH] sur ung estat [*om.* B]. Mais s'aucune chose y a digne de lecture, si vaille pour attrait a donner aucune espace de temps a visiter et lire le sourplus'.

141/16–17. *troubled and conquestioned*: Fr. has 'debatu'. *conquestion* (from L. *conquestio*) is listed in *OED* only as a noun. The only example cited is from Blount, *Glossogr.* (1656): '*Conquestion*, a complaining'. U may mean 'questioned' in the sense of 'debated'.

141/23. *remedie and*: om. Fr.

141/29–30. *in . . . comprehendid*: 'en quatre personnages est ceste oeuvre comprise'.

142/3. *The Auctour*: J begins here. The names of the speakers are omitted in R and have been taken from N. From here to 144/15, some readings are not in J since the top of f. 1 has been torn away.

142/4–6. *whanne . . . labour*, 143/4–6. *whan . . . laboures*: Both R and U are awkward in translation of Fr. 'lors que la premiere clarté du soleil et nature contente du repos de la nuit nous rappelent aux mondains labours'. The awkward *and* which follows in R has no Fr. equivalent. U's rendering of the adj. 'contente' as *is content* confuses the structure of the clause. See Introduction, p. 57.

142/7. *the . . . presentith*, 143/7. *vndirstanding . . . first*: It is interesting that both R and U similarly change Fr. 'a l'entendement . . . se presente'.

142/16. *causith*: If R followed Fr. structure as in the rest of the sentence, the relative pronoun subject of *causith* is omitted.

142/17. *thanne ... ageinward*, 143/16–17. *I ... contrarie*: 'je contrepensoye et pensoye [comparoye ABH] a l'encontre'.

142/24. *witty policie*: Fr. has 'industrie'. See Introduction, p. 30.

142/28. *goode ordre*, 143/25. *ordre of*: R is like DAH, which have 'ordre'. U is like B, which adds 'de'.

142/28–9. *hath ... cause*, 143/25–6. *set ... cause*: Fr. has 'a mettre en oeuvre le povoir que Dieu nous a laissié, est cause'. *set* in U either begins an adjective clause, the relative pronoun of which is omitted, or is an infinitive (as in Fr.) with *to* omitted. See Introduction, p. 50.

142/30. *that*: In this section of N a corrector has changed certain readings, making N different from RSJ. Here *þat* has been changed to *lesse*. See also 144/2 *fayled* RSJ–*fayling* N; 144/14 *ye* RSJ–*I* N; 146/16 *come to* RSJ–*shuld* N; 146/17 *vsid in* RSJ–*browth to* N; 146/31 *envirouned* RSJ–*bylyd* N; 148/25 *forlynyd* RS–*forlyvyd* J–*far* N; 148/28 *your* RSJ–*þat he* N. The same corrector may also have inserted *h*s in *wer*, a common spelling in N for *where*.

143/25. *regle*: U has *regle*, listed as rare in *OED*, four times in various meanings of 'rule'. At 171/16, in the phrase *out of regle*, U is not borrowing directly from Fr., which has 'françois'.

143/31. *disconisaunce*: Fr. has 'descongnoissance'. The scribe of U, perhaps not familiar with this rare English word, wrote *discorusaunce*. At 207/10, however, it is correctly written. *MED* does not list the word, and the only *OED* record is from Caxton in the meaning 'non-recognition'. U here and at 207/10 means 'ignorance, lack of knowledge'.

144/9. *that ... lygne*: 'sa [la B] tresexcellente extraction [de France *add*. BH]'.

144/14–15. *hir ... vnarayed*, 145/13–15. *hire ... shulders*: 'ses blons cheveulx, qui a fin or estrivoient de couleur ... espanduz et degetiez sans aournement au travers de ses espaules'.

144/17–18. *hynge ... syde*: R's exemplar may have been like A, which omits 'enclinee' in 'ja penchoit de coste, enclinee moult durement' (DH). Following *syde*, there is probably a scribal omission in RNSJ; Fr. adds 'De sa vesture ne me puis je pas passer ne taire'.

144/19–20. *for ... werkis*: 'De trois paires d'ouvraiges sembloit avoir esté tissu et assemblé'.

144/27, 145/27–8. *and ... men*: 'et adreçoyent les oeuvres des homes'.

145/3. *and manhoode*: om. Fr.

145/19. *merueylous ... remembred*: Fr. has 'merveilleux artifice fait a ramentevoir'. *MED* does not list *artificieuse*. The first *OED* record is from Palsgrave, 1530.

145/24. *auncient*: Fr. adds 'françois'.

146/1–5. *Thenne ... freschnes*, 147/1–6. *What ... remayn*: R misunderstood Fr. structure here: 'Qu'en diroy je plus? De si precieux et riche ouvraige estoit basty cellui mantel et de si longue main avoit on mis paine a y ouvrer et faire l'assemblee des parties dont il estoit composé que, dessoubz le ciel, ne fut veu le pareil, se Fortune, envieuse de longue prosperité, l'eust souffert en sa beauté demourer'. In l. 2, following *was*, the R scribe picked up the words *so displesaunt* (*om.* NSJ) from l. 6, where the wording is similar. In U, I have emended *hire* to *his* in l. 4 on the strength of *his* in l. 5. The scribal error may have occurred because of *piere* which follows *hire*.

146/9. *wisedome*: Fr. has 'industrie'. See Introduction, p. 30.

146/10. *into . . . pecis*, 147/10. *and defouled*: 'et aucunes pieces violente-ment arrachees'.

146/12–16. *And . . . same*, 147/10–14. *And . . . sentence*: Fr. has 'Ne demande nul se la partie moyenne estoit neantmoins [*om.* H] demouree entiere ne conjointe, et les lectres formees et assises en leur ordre, car si [*om.* B] separees, decharpies [estoient B; *om.* H] et [si *add.* B] desordonnees furent que pou s'en povoit assembler qui portast proufitable sentence'. U may have used a manuscript like B.

146/19–21. *semyd . . . hepis*, 147/18–19. *lyke . . . palles*: Fr. has 'comme desracinees, gectees et pendans au travers par paleteaux'. R did not understand 'paleteaux' (shreds, bits), and in U *palles* may be related to *palt* = 'a piece of strong, coarse cloth, or of a thick dirty dress; anything waste or dirty, trash' (*OED*), or to the Scottish *pell*, not recorded in *OED*, but noted in the plural in Wright's *English Dialect Dictionary*, in the meaning 'rags, tatters'.

146/25–7. *But . . . 'Quadrilogue'*, 147/24–5. *Of . . . 'Quadriloge'*: 'Du mantel me deporteray a tant [quant B] de present pour ce que trop [*om.* H] longuement ne vueil sur [la *add.* BH] description demourer, ne ce n'est la fin de ce present quadrilogue'.

146/28. *entent*, 147/25–6. *principall intencion*: DAB have 'principale', like U; but H omits the modifier, like R.

146/29–30. *And . . . paleys*: Fr. has 'Ung riche palais ancien avoit de coste soy'. The palace symbolizes royalty.

146/30. *solempnely*, 147/27. *curiously*: 'somptueusement'.

146/32. *soueraigne . . . werkmen*: Fr. has 'engins de souverains ouvriers'. Cf. the use of *wittes* to translate 'engins' at 80/19, 142/24, 160/9.

146/32–3. *richely . . . thingis*: 'enrichy d'entailleures, paintures, armoeries et [de *add.* BH] autres menueries [menuyseries B; menues H]'.

147/11. *the* (1) *. . . othir*: *om.* Fr.

147/15. *it . . . for*: Mistranslation of 'ceste chose seule en peut on dire, que'.

147/18. *naked and*: *om.* Fr.

147/25. *dispoose and*: 'appliquer'.

148/4–5. *in ... nygh*, 149/3–7. *soo ... moost*: U is more literal in rendering Fr.: 'n'y apparoit refection sinon aucuns appuys de foibles et petites estaies que pour passer temps et a la haste, non pas a durer, on avoit ça et la assises ou et quant la ruyne sembloit greigneur et le peril plus prouchain'. U's *refeccion*, borrowed from Fr., is listed in *OED* as rare in this sense, and the first record is from Blount, *Glossogr.* (1656).

148/9. *enbrowdered*: 'couvert et paré'.

148/10–12. *with* (2) ... *same*, 149/12–18. *that* (1) ... *trauaile*: Compared with the more literal U, R presents a much shortened translation here: 'et estaioit [estriuoit contre BH] le costé qui plus penchoit et par pesanteur s'enclinoit et tiroit grant partie du sourplus a [*om*. B] tendre [*om*. B] en ruyne, et contretenoit [contrement H] de cellui bras le plus [*om*. H] principal pan de [dun B] mur et [*om*. B] qui portoit le branle du seurplus, et neantmoins [*om*. H] se desmentoit et decrevoit [decheoit B; *om*. H] en pluseurs lieux [endrois BH] et des [les BH; plus *add*. H] principaulx piliers s'enclinoient [*om*. B] aux fais des aucuns [autres H]. Or fut moult fort grevée de si long travail'.

148/18. *poor*: 'vil' DAB; 'vil & poure' H.

148/19–22. *But ... syghes*: Free translation of 'Comme doncques elle les eust choisiz a l'ueil, indignee en son hault couraige, vers eulx les prist a reprendre de leur oiseuse lacheté par parolles entrerompues souvent de douloureux soupirs qui de cuer adollé lui mouvoient'. *queinte and straunge* seems to be a misunderstanding of 'entrerompues'. *queinte* because of its position with *straunge* may mean 'unusual', but modifying *wordis* it may mean 'wise' or 'highly refined'. It is also possible that *straunge* is an error for *strang*, 'strong'. At 11/31, in a similar context, R has *straungely* for *strangly* (S). Cf. also 237/18 in U.

148/31. *herbergage*, 149/36. *herbrurgh and*: Fr. has 'heberge et retrait'. Following *and*, a blank space in U probably indicates that the scribe could not read the English word for 'retrait' in his original.

148/31–2. *shall ... subuerte*: 'versera'.

149/6. *ruine and trouble*: 'ruyne'.

149/7. *all ther moost*: See *OED* under *all* D. 3b. for other instances of this later form of *alther most*, when the nature of its construction had been forgotten but the meaning 'greatest of all' retained.

149/32. *musinge*: Since Fr. has 'musardie', *musinge* may be a scribal anticipation of the word in l. 34.

149/33. *and ... ferfulnesse*: 'que vous bastez'.

150/3. *blame*: Like B, which omits 'ou reprendre', added in DAH.

150/3. *slow*, 151/4. *slaughfull*: 'paresseuses' ABH; 'piteuses' D.

150/4–5. *yet ... same*: 'y voulez envieillir'.

150/7. *yow* (2): Fr. adds 'devant toute autre chose'.

150/9–10. *hath . . . lyfe*: Fr. has 'a fait naistre et avoir vie'. *ordeynd you* (N, *ins.* J) may be the correct reading to translate 'fait'. The R scribe, faced with an omission (as in S) may have added *lent the grace*. Following *lyfe*, RNSJ omit a sentence of Fr.: 'Encore dy je que peu doit priser sa naissance et mains desirer la continuation de sa vie qui passe ses jours, ainsi que fait homme nez pour soy seulement, sans fructifier a la commune utilité, et comme cellui qui estaint sa memoire avecques sa vie'. The omission may have been in R's Fr. exemplar because of the repetition of 'vie', or in an English manuscript behind RNSJ because of the repetition of *lyfe*.

150/10. *hough grete*: 'tant . . . prouchaine et si inseparablement'.

150/12. *in*: 'de'.

150/14. *him*: *him* here may be a form of *hem*, as it is elsewhere in RNSJ. However, since the Fr. equivalents of *bodyes* in l. 11 and *hartis* in l. 13 are singular, and are in series with *his lyff and helth* and *the man* in l. 14, the translator may carelessly have changed from his own plural to the Fr. singular one pronoun too early.

150/24. *for . . . wele*, 151/29–30. *to . . . cuntree*: 'au commun besoing et pour le salut de leur païz et seigneurie'.

150/27. *hevyn*: Fr. adds 'par lien indissoluble'.

150/28. *accomplisshid*, 151/33. *fulfilled*: 'acomplie' ABH; *om.* D.

150/30. *of the eyre*: *om.* Fr.

150/32. *defending them*: Since NSJ and Fr. do not support this reading, it may be a scribal addition in R.

150/33. *Nough*: 'Or' H; *om.* DAB.

151/1–2. *at . . . mischeeuys*: *om.* Fr.

151/6. *and bittyr*: *om.* Fr.

151/8. *and bounde*: *om.* Fr.

151/9. *of . . . wele*: *om.* Fr.

151/20. *encreecith*: U is like BH, which have a full stop here.

151/26. *to . . . norisshing*: 'envers vous a toute soustenance, et qui vous repaist et nourrit'.

151/30–1. *haue . . . othir*: 'mieulx veulent soy laisser perdre avecques la chose publique'.

152/4–11, 153/4–10: See Valerius Maximus, v. 4. ext. 5.

152/13. *thyng*: 'chose' B; *om.* DAH.

152/15. *most*: Omitted in NSJ and Fr., *most* may be a scribal recall in R from l. 14.

152/16. *for*: 'en' ABH; 'et' D.

152/17, 153/15. *enemys*: Both R and U are like B, which omits 'et adversaires', which follows 'ennemis' in DA. H has only 'aduersaires'.

152/18. *vnstaunchable*: *om.* Fr.

152/19–20. *and kepe me*, 153/18. *for . . . it*: 'pour tenir' DA; 'pour moy tenir' B; 'pour moy mettre' H.

152/22. *Myne . . . enemyes*: 'Ilz'.

152/25–6. *ye . . . enheritaunce*: 'parachevez [permettez BH] ma perte et desertion'.

152/27. *thes*, 153/25. *my*: 'cestes mes' DA; 'mes' BH.

152/29. *cruellenesse*, 153/26–7. *auctoritee and sharpnesse*: 'austerité [auctorite H] et aspresse'.

152/30, 153/27. *suffirth*: Since both R and U thus rendered 's'i offre', there may have been scribal error in their Fr. exemplars.

152/32. *steren and*: *om.* Fr., NSJ.

153/2. *and suffred*: *om.* Fr.

153/4. *Scithiens*: Fr. adds 'en'. *in* may be scribally omitted in U.

153/7. *where they taryed*: *om.* Fr.

153/9. *thaire*: 'leur' B; 'la' DA.

153/11. *most*: Here and elsewhere in U, *o* in the verb *most* has been changed to *v* by a rough upward stroke. I have followed the original spelling since *most* is the usual U form.

153/17. *and laboure*: *om.* Fr.

153/19. *serue*: Fr. has 'asservicez'. It is unclear whether U means 'put me in bondage' (a meaning not in *OED*) or 'treat' here.

153/19. *disordinate laschenesse*: 'desordonnances et lachetez'.

154/1. *and . . . fortune*: 'exposee a toute fortune'.

154/2. *is . . . thidir*: 'degetee'.

154/3–4. *and . . . as*: 'ou' DAH; 'la ou' B.

154/5. *and greve*: *om.* Fr.

154/6. *purchasse*: Fr. adds 'la vostre'.

154/13–15. *our . . . worshippis*, 155/10–12. *to . . . releevys*: R is typically much freer in translation than U: 'aux travaillans saiges et curieux adviennent de don des cieulx et de leur pourchaz les prosperitez et les ressourses'.

154/15–17. *wille . . . hurtis*: Fr. has 'rien ne suffist vouloir le salut et liberté publique et desirer la confusion de son ennemi'. Even with the emendation of *hath* to *helth* from NSJ, there may still be scribal error here.

154/17. *but . . . atcheue*: *om.* Fr.

154/20–3. *whanne . . . preysing*, 155/17–20. *whan . . . price*: 'quant ilz ne se apparoissent et mettent avant en besoigne et que entre les autres en peut on si pou choisir pour telz, donc ceulx qui bien font sont dignes de plus grant los'.

154/26. *constaunce*, 155/23. *constaunt trouth*: 'constance et loyauté'.

154/27. *have perseuerid*: Fr. has 'a eu [si grande *add.* H] renom de perseverer'. *in grete wurship* in l. 28 may translate 'grande renom'.

154/29. *shal be subdewed*: Fr. has 'soient rabaissez et avillez'. *OED* lists only two examples of *subdued* in the meaning 'reduced, brought down', both from Shakespeare.

154/31-2. *seeche . . . goodis*, 155/28. *renne . . . siluer*: Fr. has 'courent [queurent A; plustost *add.* H] a l'argent'. It is interesting that both R and U introduce the word *couetice*. In R either *seeche* or *serch* (NSJ) might be the original reading.

155/3. *wedyr*: 'les vagues'.

155/15. *the* (3) . . . *rewarde*: 'la louenge et le guerdon'.

155/27. *Many*: Fr. adds 'de la chevalerie et'.

155/29-30. *passe . . . lyues*: 'vivent avecques les vivans'.

156/1 ff., 157/1 ff.: There was continual protest about the ways of the French court during this period. Droz cites quotations from sermons of Jean Gerson, chancellor of Notre-Dame during Chartier's life, and of Jacques Legrand for comparison with Chartier's passage here.

156/2. *O . . . delices*: 'o envieillie et enracinee norreture de pompes et de delices'.

156/4-8, 157/4-8. *this . . . customes*: Fr. has 'ceste subversion, dont Fortune nous [leur B] fait ciseau de si prez, nous [vous BH] avez couvee [atournee H; conduite B] et mise sus, [que *add.* B] et toutes voies sont et demeurent par vous les [leurs B] cuers si envelopez que le peril de la seigneurie et d'eulx mesmes et la doubte de leur prouchaine desercion ne les peut retraire de leurs delicatives acoustumances'. *MED* does not list the adj. *delicative*, and *OED* gives the meaning 'dainty' only as applied to food, a meaning which occurs in Caxton. But here and at 177/18, U uses the word to mean 'luxurious, indolent'.

156/10. *willis and werkis*, 157/10. *werkes*: D has 'courage et ouvraige'. U, however, is like ABH, which omit 'courage et'. BH also have the plural 'ouuraiges', but H introduces the phrase with '&' rather than 'a'.

156/12. *lees them*: Fr. adds 'elles vous font et laissent perir et si ne les voulez laisser'.

156/16. *vse*: Fr. adds 'et endurcir'.

156/17-18. *suche . . . of*: Fr. supports the emendation of R's *a* to *as* (NSJ): 'comme celluy dont l'onneur et la renommee naissent aux vertueux'.

156/18-21, 157/20-3: See Livy, xxix.

156/18, 157/21. *had*: It is interesting that both R and U render 'demena' as *had*.

156/21. *cast . . . hoost*, 157/23. *put . . . out*: 'degeteez'.

156/21-6, 157/23-6: See Livy, xxiii. 18.

156/22-5. *wherin . . . chaungid*: R's structural change of Fr. leaves the English sentence incomplete: 'et qu'il ot esté haultement receu et delicativement traictié, trouva les cuers de ses chevaliers changez et matiz'. Note R's combination of the NS and the J readings in *delicatis or delicacyes*.

156/26-30. *And . . . lordshippis*, 157/27-9. *And . . . lyf*: R mistranslated here, and U, though nearer to Fr., is awkward: 'Et pour exemple de hault prince adjouster, le [en A] pareil cas en avint a Alixandre aprés la conqueste de la grant Babilone et Sardanapalus en perdy sa seigneurie et vie'. Alexander's luxurious living is treated by Vincent of Beauvais, iv. 42. Sardanapallus, the last king of the Assyrians, is described as corrupt and effeminate in Vincent, ii. 93.

156/31. *ouirthrowen*: 'avillez et amendriz'.

156/34-158/8. *Yet . . . mysease*, 157/33-159/6. *And . . . herburgh*: R is much freer in translation than U: 'Et telz y a qui jour et nuit sont par les bois et par les champs a chacer les bestes et au gibier des [les BH] oiseaulx, et les aultres rompent chevaulz au pourchaz des offices, des estaz, [et *add.* H] des chevances et de leurs autres plaisirs, qui pour honneur acquerir [conquerre H] et [de *add.* A] leur naturel devoir acquiter ne laisseroient le repos d'une nuit ne ne souffreroient le dangier, [dun *add.* ABH] estroit ou messaisé hebergement'. The omission of 'dun' in D (Droz's text) must certainly be a corruption.

157/3-4. *of the men*: 'françois'.

157/9. *voluntees*: 'voluntez' H; 'voluptez' DAB.

157/10. *whiche is*: Fr. has no equivalent for this confusing addition.

157/11. *superfluite*: 'pusillanimité'.

157/16. *euer . . . more*: om. Fr.

157/16. *hard*: Like B, which omits 'chose' in 'forte chose' (DAH).

157/17. *continuaunce and*: om. Fr.

157/17-18. *dispose . . . to*: om. Fr.

157/18. *endure*: U, or his Fr. exemplar, confused 'endurcir' with 'endurer'.

157/22. *thinges*: Fr. adds 'qui . . . seroient trouvees'.

158/9. *which seke owte*, 159/7. *Than ye seeke*: Neither R nor U understood Chartier's complete satirical intention here, although in l. 12 (*Stoppe*), U changed to the direct address of Fr. Chartier has here an ironic series of direct addresses to Frenchmen, telling them to do all the things that will be most disastrous to them.

158/10. *of* (1) *. . . day*: 'empruntez de la nuit sur le jour'.

158/13. *of the . . . delices*, 159/10. *the . . . femynyns*: Neither R nor U understood that 'les blandices et delices feminins' is in series with 'saveurs', 'repoz', and 'oultraiges'. R seems to mean 'because of the fair showings of feminine delights ye sleep as hogs', whereas U makes the phrase the subject of *causeth*.

158/17. *in . . . rehercid*: 'y'.

158/18. *dredfull*: I have added *dredfull* from NSJ since DA have 'douloureux'. It should be noted, however, that BH omit the Fr. modifier.

158/19–20. *so* (1) . . . *daunger*, 159/15–16. *so . . . perpetuite*: 'pourrez tant user et si longuement vous y aouiller [oublier B; auiler H] que trop en avoir prins vous en fera souffreteux a tousjours'.

158/20–7, 159/17–20: See Valerius Maximus, ix. 3. ext. 4.

158/20. *the . . . of*: This is omitted in the Fr. manuscripts, but Worcester has inserted 'royne'.

158/21–3. *while . . . hir*, 159/18. *whan . . . hir* (2): 'quant les en peignant on lui denonça la rebellion de sa cité'.

158/23–4. *and . . . closette*: om. Fr.

158/26. *veray force and*: om. Fr.

158/28. *Bataile of Caves*, 159/21. *Bataile of Cannes*: The reference is, of course, to the Battle of Cannae. I have not emended R's *Caves* either here or at 192/13–14, because at 125/5, *Batell of the Caves* occurs, *the* perhaps being a scribal error, along with *v* for *u* or *n*; but the phrasing may suggest that the R translator did not recognize the battle referred to by Chartier. The state of Rome after the defeat at Cannae is described by Livy, xxii. 43–57, but there seems to be no reference to the renouncement of richness of array of the kind described here. The wearing of mourning is described in 57.

158/29, 159/22: See Droz's note for a description of the renunciation of finery in Languedoc in 1356.

158/29–30. *whanne . . . Iohn*: 'en la prise du roy Jehan'.

158/34. *perdicion*: Fr. adds 'et vous tire a perdicion [la mort ABH] les bras au col'.

159/9. *to* (1): Fr. adds 'difference des'.

159/24. *demonstraunce*: 'demonstrance' BH; 'remonstrance' DA.

159/27. *deth*: 'la mort' ABH; 'perdicion' D.

160/9. *maner of goodnes*: 'chose'.

160/12–13. *ye . . . entent*: 'vostre sens est perdu quant a les emploier'.

160/17. *fauour of*, 161/15. *folowinge*: 'suivre le bruit ou'.

160/18. *evill doars*, 161/16. *yll doing*: 'mal faire' B; 'mal' DAH.

160/20. *people*: Fr. adds 'qui peu voulentiers empressent'. Note U's rendering.

160/20. *eville*: Fr. adds 'qui se ingerent rebouter est celle qui'. Note U's rendering.

160/22-4. *the . . . and,* 161/22-6. *for . . . augmente*: DA have 'pour louenge et memoire, les Rommains faisoient ymages de divers metaulx, ars et curres triumphans a ceulx qui vertueusement se portoient pour accroistre la seigneurie rommaine et augmenter'. U seems to have used a manuscript like DA, although he probably had a corrupt reading for 'curres', perhaps 'oeuvres', the reading in Worcester. R, however, may have used a manuscript like BH, which have 'dor et de cuiures' for 'ars et curres'. B also omits 'rommaine'.

160/27-8. *For . . . poynte*: 'si venons'.

160/28-9. *the . . . yow*: 'que la justice de querelle, posé que ja autre ochoison n'y trouvissez, vous doit rebouter'.

160/32, 161/33. *Forgestus and Engestus*: Note that N has *horgestus* for *Forgestus*, but RSJ follow Fr. Droz says that Chartier probably knew the history of Hengist and Horsa from a version of the *Brut*.

161/5. *lettid and lest*: Fr. has 'delaissent'. *lest* may be a scribal error for *left*.

161/6. *tydinges*: There is probably a scribal omission here in U, caused by the repetition of *tydinges*. Fr. reads 'Toutes bonnes nouvelles vous semblent victoire et toutes mauvaises vous esbahissent'. Since 'nouvelles' is not repeated, the omission is probably in U rather than in U's Fr. exemplar.

161/8. *ferme ner stable*: 'affermez'.

161/17. *of . . . goodnesse*: 'des bons est le redoublement de leurs biensfaiz'.

161/20-1. *the . . . that*: 'celle qui souverainement'.

162/2. *and*: Fr. adds 'par traïson'.

162/4, 163/4. *of him*: R and U both are like ABH, which have 'de celui', omitted in D. The reference is to Richard II.

162/5, 163/5. *tyrauntly*: Both R and U use this word, described as rare in *OED*.

162/7-8. *and* (4) *. . . desiyrd,* 163/7-8. *And . . . is*: 'et [ceulx *add.* B] qui de tele ligne sont issuz que [*om.* B] naturelment [desirent et *add.* BH] convoitent'.

162/10-12. *and in . . . subgettis,* 163/10-12. *and . . . felawys*: 'dont a la desraison de leur querelle [a leur desraisonnable querelle B] ilz ont adjousté desloiauté, en soustenant les oeuvres desloialles de leurs alliez et compaignons'.

162/14-16. *Remembir . . . yow,* 163/14-15. *Your . . . cuntree*: Fr. has 'Voz ennemis anciens et naturelz vous assaillent a leur entreprise et viennent chalengier vostre terre et vostre pays'. *assailing* in RNSJ may be a scribal error for *assailin*. N's *come chalengyng* is a nearer rendering of 'viennent chalengier' than the RSJ readings. But the sentence is structurally so confused that it is impossible to be sure of the original reading.

162/16–17. *the . . . asawlte*: 'assaillans'.

162/20–2. *Thei . . . substaunce*: Fr. has 'ilz se efforcent d'oster et ravir par force la vie et la substance'. R's scribal omission was caused by the repetition of *lyfe*.

162/25. *ye . . . goodis*, 163/23–4. *your . . . defende*: 'voz vies et voz corps sont tenuz defendre'.

162/26–7. *puttyng . . . tyrannye*, 163/25. *for . . . tirannye*: DAH have 'pour vous defouler soubz leur tirannie'; B has 'desoller par voye tirannicque'. *defende* in error for *defoule* in U was probably caused by scribal recall of *defende* in l. 24.

162/27. *Now . . . yow*: 'Enviz entreprendriez'.

162/29. *and brought it*: om. Fr.

162/31–2. *Yet . . . yourself*, 163/28–30. *And* (2) *. . . defende*: 'quant la terre, sur quoy vous habitez et qui vous soustient et donne pasture vous ne povez pas secourir ne defendre'.

162/33. *a people*: om. Fr.

162/33. *from*: R's change of preposition here changes Chartier's meaning, which U retains. DAH have 'sur'; B has 'en'.

162/34. *and . . . it*, 163/31–2. *nor . . . it*: 'ne [et BH] garder vous ne [le *add.* A] savez'.

162/36. *Parde your*: 'Voz' BH; 'Les' DA.

162/36. *nat*: Fr. adds 'de fer'.

162/36–164/1. *lengar of lyfe*: 'indiviables' D; 'inuincibles' A; 'inuisibles' BH.

163/2. *fortune*: 'guerre'.

163/10. *vntrue rebellys*: Like H, which omits 'et' in 'desloiaulx et rebelles' (DAB).

164/5. *have . . . haue*, 165/6. *haue . . . us*: 'ont riens d'avance qui les eslieve sur vous'.

164/7. *nothinge ellis but*: om. Fr.

164/9–10. *to be . . . of* (1): 'estaindre . . . et destruire'.

164/10. *lordeshippis*: Fr. adds 'devant voz yeulx'.

164/11. *Almighty . . . hand*: 'la grace de Dieu y euvre de soy'.

164/11–12. *me thinckith*: om. Fr.

164/12. *to . . . grace*, 165/13. *deserue*: Fr. has 'deservir', supporting the emendation in U. Cf. 219/4.

164/16–21. *This . . . namely*, 165/17–22. *Theise . . . tyme*: Again R is much freer in translation than U: 'Ces parolles moult aigrement et de cuer

couroucié disoit au [trois *add.* ABH] dessus escrips celle dame tresadoulee
et de ses beaulx yeux, dont les ruisseaulx de larmes couroient, regardoit si
effroiement leur desroyé [desnoye BH] maintien que bien sembloit soy
sentir d'eulx injuries ou mescogneue. Et aprés ce que chascun se fu
longuement tenu de parler'.

164/22. *nor strength*: om. Fr.

164/23. *sympill*: om. Fr.

164/27. *hertely*: om. Fr.

164/28. *and . . . ligne*, 165/28–9. *for . . . lyne*: 'du declin de ta lignee'.

164/28–9. *beleve . . . and*: om. Fr.

164/30–4. *Wherfor . . . personis*, 165/30–3. *But . . . penaunce*: Cf. R's free,
somewhat inaccurate rendering with U's extremely literal, somewhat
awkward translation. Fr. reads 'maiz trop m'est amere desplaisance que
j'aye de [*om.* H] ce [*om.* BH] meschief la perte et le reproche ensemble et
que m'en doiez en riens tenir suspect quant d'autruy coulpe je porte la
tresaspre penitance'.

165/6–7. *manhode and*: om. Fr.

165/7–8. *ye . . . enmyes*: 'vous avez riens qui soubz eulx vous deprime'.

165/9. *and turneth*: om. Fr.

165/9. *cowarde*: om. Fr.

165/10. *skonched*: This verb is probably a variant of *squench* (from
quench), perhaps influenced by the verb *sconce*. Here and at 209/2, where
Fr. has 'estaindre', *skonch* means 'extinguish'; but at 229/1, where Fr.
has 'effacier', it may mean either 'blot out' or 'hide, screen from view'
(note R's *hide*).

165/13. *ne deuoire*: om. Fr.

165/24. *importable . . . care*: 'mal'.

165/25. *speke*: Like H, which omits 'et respondre', added in DAB.

166/1. *I . . . whom*: See Introduction, pp. 19–20.

166/2. *O . . . and*: R probably used a manuscript which combined the
readings of B and H. B has 'O' rather than 'Haa' (DAH), whereas H adds
'maleureux', not in DAB.

166/3. *false*: om. Fr.

166/4. *which*: See Introduction, p. 50.

166/6–7. *rewarde . . . persecucion*: 'me persecutent'.

166/10. *and diffende*: om. Fr.

166/13. *persecucion*: The modifier *perfight* in RNSJ has no Fr. equivalent.
It is probably a scribal error carried down from an earlier English manuscript. Note *perfight pacience* earlier in the line.

166/15. *defaulte*: Fr. adds 'et necessité'.

166/15. *Also . . . that*: om. Fr.

166/16–17. *canne . . . course*: Fr. has 'ne treuve chemin qui la puisse sauvement adrecier'. *redy way* seems to mean 'near or direct way'.

166/17–18. *all . . . sworde*: Fr. has 'Tout est proye ce que le glaive ou l'espee ne defend'. U omits the sentence.

166/19. *othir of hoope*: Fr. has 'autre esperance'. *trest*, inserted in J after *othir*, omitted in RNS, may be the original reading, since the wording *othir of* is unusual in the translation.

166/19. *and*: 'et' H; 'pour' DAB.

166/20. *that . . . me*: 'qui [que A] ma despoille enrichit'.

166/21. *werre*: Here an equivalent of 'Que appelle je guerre? Ce n'est pas guerre' is omitted in RNSJ. The repetition of *werre* may have caused the omission in an earlier English manuscript, or the repetition of 'guerre' might indicate that the omission was in R's Fr. exemplar.

166/22–4. *a . . . gouernaunce*, 167/20–2. *a (2) . . . ordinaunce*: U's literal rendering is much clearer than R's changed version: 'ung larrecin habandonné, force publique soubz umbre d'armes et violente rapine que [par *add.* B] faulte de justice et de bonne ordonnance [ont *add.* AH; en *add.* B] fait estre [om. H] loisibles'. In R the understood subject of *is ravischid* is *the comon wele of realme*.

166/28. *langage and wordis*: 'parolle' DA; 'parolles' BH.

166/31. *comfortis and helpis*: 'refuges'.

166/34–168/4. *Alle . . . hevinesse*, 167/31–169/6. *All . . . lifes*: Again R translated more loosely than U: 'Tout est en autres mains acquis ce que force [om. H] de [om. H] murs et de [om. H] fossez n'environne et encores en meilleures gardes a il souvent [om. ABH] de [moult *add.* AH] grans pertes que chascun voit. Or convendra il les champs demourer desers, [et *add.* B, like U] inhabitez et habandonnez aux bestes sauvaiges, et ceulx qui par travail de loial marchandise ont les aucuns en leur necessitéz secouruz demourer despourveuz et esgarez et perdre [om. A] par courroux la vie aprés les biens'. In view of Fr., R's reading is better than that in NSJ: *for hevinesse* translates 'par courroux', and *The schare and cultre* is the subject of the next sentence. In U some word to render 'esgarez' may have been scribally omitted after *stande* at 169/5; the original may have read, for example, *stande astonied with the losse*.

167/1. *constrained*: 'aguillonné'.

167/1. *do*: DB add 'et souffrir'; A adds 'et soustenir'.

167/4–5. *right . . . power*: 'tant de droit comme sa force lui en donne'.

167/8. *werre*: Fr. adds 'par leurs outraiges'.

167/11. *I*: 'homme'.

167/12. *likned*: 'adjouster'.

167/12. *dye*: Fr. adds 'et transiz'.

167/15. *and . . . stablenesse*: om. Fr.

167/16. *to lyue . . . dispeire*: 'par desespoir laissier mon estat'.

167/27. *A, a*: om. Fr.

167/28. *at neede*: om. Fr.

167/29. *more*: 'plus' ABH; om. D.

167/30. *theym*: Fr. adds 'ne fournir'.

168/5. *which . . . londe*: om. Fr.

168/7–8. *takyn . . . gete*: R changed the Fr. structure and left the sentence incomplete. DA have 'en habondance, sont souvent estraintes jusques au sang espandre pour ce que je n'ay baillié ce que j'ay et ce que je n'ay mie'. In place of 'espandre . . . j'ay', B has 'pour rauir'. R is most nearly like H, however, which adds 'rauir' after 'pour' and omits 'je n'ay baillié ce que'. N's omission occurred because of the repetition of *haue*.

168/9. *fall . . . myserye*: 'decline'.

168/12. *powr*: Fr. has 'povre' modifying 'femme' and uses 'petis' here, like U.

168/12–15. *which . . . day*, 169/13–16. *and* (2) *. . . day*: R is free, somewhat inaccurate and awkward here. Fr. has 'et [om. B] desirant la mienne, que tant me tarde que je la regrete chascun jour, comme cellui qui couroux, fain et [om. BH] defiance de confort [et desconfort BH], mainent douloureusement a son derrenier jour'. *laid* in U, past participle of 'lead', may be a reverse spelling arising from monophthongization of the diphthong *ai* to slack *e*. Cf. *rayneth* and *rayne* in l. 19. *MED* cites this passage to exemplify *laid* in the meaning 'afflicted', but Fr. suggests that the word means 'brought'.

168/15–17. *a . . . people*, 169/17–19. *it . . . man*: Fr. has 'ne fault faire enqueste ne demande, les oeuvres sont publiques et le tesmoing en est intollerable famine, qui encourt et courra sus a ung chascun'. It is difficult to be certain what U intended in *rayneth and shall rayne*. 'run', 'rain', and 'reign' are all adequate in the context. Fr. is literally 'run', but use in this sense is not idiomatic English, and *rayn-* would be a very eccentric reverse spelling for *renn-* (despite *laid* in l. 16). 'Reign' renders the meaning well, and was in use by this time: cf. *OED*, 3c. See also 208/27, 209/26 n.

168/19. *passid*: Fr. adds 'et vouloir par raison departir le demourant des choses consumees par oultraiges'. A scribal omission either in the English or in R's Fr. exemplar seems possible here.

168/21. *to* (1) *. . . it*: 'ravir' DAH; 'prendre' B.

168/22. *thei goo*: 'il sera'.

168/26. *O*: om. Fr.

168/26. *thing*: 'chose' A; om. DBH.

168/27–30. *I . . . goodis*, 169/29–31. *I . . . castell*: Fr. has 'je suys en exil en ma maison, prisonnier de mes amis, assailli de mes defendeurs et guerroyé aux souldees [des soldoyers H, like R] dont le paiement est fait de mon propre chatel'. Note that the past participle 'guerroyé' is translated 'I werre' (spaced thus in RNSJ). In U *handes* may be a scribal error for *friends*. *castell*, omitted in *MED* and *OED*, appears in U here and at 185/27, 187/18, 191/10, and in the plural at 181/23, as an eccentric spelling of *catell*. The same confusion occurs in MS. Bodley 34 in *Sawles Warde*. See note to l. 34 of this work in *Early Middle English Verse and Prose*, ed. J. A. W. Bennett and G. V. Smithers, 2nd ed. (Oxford, 1968), p. 420. *MED* lists *chasteus* as a plural of *chatel*.

168/32. *exploit*, 169/32. *weye actuell*: 'demourant ou exploit'.

169/10–12. *And . . . lyf*: Fr. has 'Si fault que le corps decline en default des biens et que en languour soubz seigneurie dissipee et [*om.* B] chargee de famille mendie [mendiant BH; mendient A]. Je vif'. Having changed the sentence structure to eliminate 'fault', U then literally translated 'que' as *that* in l. 11. Further awkwardness occurs because U linked the next Fr. sentence, beginning with 'Je vif', with the preceding one by the infinitive. The phrase *beggyng hunger* is also not clear. U evidently used a manuscript like BH, which have the present participle 'mendiant', but he either had before him a corrupt manuscript with 'faim' for 'famille' or changed the thought deliberately. The phrase means either 'hunger which causes begging' or 'hunger which accompanies begging'; neither meaning of *beggyng* is recorded in *MED* or *OED*.

169/24. *force*: Fr. adds 'ou il sera' (*thei goo* R).

169/28. *Right . . . is*: Fr. has 'Ennuyeuse chose est a raconter et plus griefve a soustenir'. There may be scribal omission here in U.

169/32. *I*: Preceding *I*, Fr. adds 'Et pour faire une abhominable somme de mes males mescheances infinies'.

169/33. *in* (2): *om.* Fr.

170/1–3. *from . . . men*, 171/2–3. *taken . . . rauysshers*: 'qui des mains de ceulx qui les ont gaignez sont transportéz aux plus fors et [*om.* BH] ravissans'.

170/3–4. *is . . . course*: Fr. has 'est la chose menee [muee B] et changee de sa nature'. R understood 'chose' to refer to the common weal.

170/6–7. *wherin . . . makith*, 171/6. *wherynne . . . made*: 'ouquel se siet et preside Voulenté. Si a fait'.

170/8–10. *what . . . punyschith*, 171/7–9. *that* (2) . . . *vnpunisshid*: Fr. has 'ce que Fortune [force ABH] veult elle peut, ce qu'elle peut elle accomplit, ce qu'elle accomplit elle appreuve, ce qu'elle appreuve est essaucié, loé et non pugny'. Both R and U used a manuscript like ABH in the reading 'force'.

170/11–13. *may . . . growe*: 'semble maintenant l'ostel d'ung mauvais mesnagier qui dissippe sa presente substance avant qu'il pourvoye a celle a venir, menjut sa vigne en verjus'.

170/16–17. *colde wynter*, 171/15. *hard . . . ceason*: 'froide saison' ABH; 'froidure et saison de l'yver' D.

170/17. *nede come*, 171/16. *he . . . neede*: 'elle [besoing H] le sourpreigne'.

170/18. *and spende*: om. Fr.

170/21–2. *in . . . fortunes*: 'entier comme une espargne pour secourir aux extremitez et pour avoir recours en perverse fortune'.

170/25. *my . . . susteyned*: Fr. has 'le mien en seroit plus aisié à soustenir'. *herte* may mean 'hurt'; cf. U's *hurtes*.

170/32–3, 171/28. *turneth . . . confusion*: Both R and U retain the inverted sentence order of Chartier. *ordir* is the subject.

170/34–172/2. *which . . . half*: Fr. has 'qui, pour les oppressions de son peuple qu'il ne voult amendrir ne cesser en delaissant le conseil des saiges anciens et ensuivant la sote oppinion des jounes et [om. H] non saichans, perdy de sa seigneurie dix lignies et demie'. R's reading, after addition of *of* at 172/1, follows Fr. more closely than does that of NSJ. Worcester has 'hommes' after 'jounes'; both English works have *men*. See 2 Chronicles.

171/4. *thrugh the impediment*: 'entre l'impetuosité'.

171/14. *porueieth himself*: 'se pouruoit et fournit' H; 'se fournit et espargne' DAB.

171/17. *me*: This has no Fr. equivalent, and although it fits the context well enough, it may be a scribal error for *the*, a reading which follows Fr. (see R).

171/20. *and sounde*: om. Fr.

171/26. *pacience*: U has an omission here, probably derived from a Fr. manuscript. The omitted Fr. passage reads: 'Et quant pacience fault, qui soustient les courages contre la durté de fortune et qui tient les autres vertuz alieez et conjoincetes, ne doubtez que elles se separent et departent'. It will be noted that the English continues *And yf so be that pacience faile*. Fr. continues 'Si avient souvent que, pacience faillie'. The English clause is probably a rendering of the last quoted Fr. clause, rather than of 'quant pacience fault'. Hence, it would appear that the scribe of U's Fr. exemplar jumped in his copying from the beginning of one clause about 'pacience' to a later clause. If the omission is one by the U scribe, we must assume that *And yf so be that pacience faile* is a translation of 'Et quant pacience fault' and that the scribe jumped from *pacience faile* to a similar phrase which rendered 'pacience faillie'.

171/27. *obeisaunce*: Fr. adds 'subjection'.

171/29. *good*: om. Fr.

171/29. *be*: Fr. adds 'noter et'.

172/3–4. *The . . . body*: R changed the idea of Fr.: 'Le peuple si est membre notable d'un royaume, sans lequel les nobles ne le clergé ne pevent suffire a faire corps'.

172/5. *it*: Refers to *people*, treated as singular in Fr.

172/6. *infelicite*: Fr. adds 'et persecuté par les autres membres subgiez a son mesmes chief', as in U.

172/6. *no*: Fr. adds 'meilleur'.

172/6. *body*: Fr. has 'propos'. *body* may be a scribal error in RNSJ recalling the phrase *the body of policie* in l. 4.

172/10–12, 173/12–13. *for . . . people*: Fr. has 'quant, pour garder les parties de leur communité chascune en sa dignité et en son ordre, ilz establirent les tribuns [tribus D *before emendation*, H; tributz B] du pueuple'. R follows Fr. except for the omission of 'quant' and 'ilz', also omitted in Worcester. R also follows the corrupt reading of D (before emendation by Droz), H, and Worcester in *tribus*, whereas U follows B in *tributys*.

172/12. *defende and kepe*: 'defendre'.

172/13–14. *But her*: R added this unclear relating element, as he also untied some of the structural knots of the preceding Fr. sentence, while retaining the meaning of Chartier.

172/17. *for . . . helpe*: This seems to be a translation of 'sans aide ne secours', which occurs earlier in Fr. before 'je suis' (*I am*) in l. 14.

172/18–19. *the* (3) . . . *suffur*: 'gemissemens des souffreteux'.

172/19. *iugementis*: 'justice'.

172/20. *and sharpe*: om. Fr.

172/20–2. *Wherfor . . . bewar*: 'Or s'en gard qui en coulpe s'en sent'.

172/22–3. *the . . . voice*, 173/23. *so . . . piteable*: Fr. has 'tant de couraiges tormentez et de voix trespiteables'. R's *voice* and U's *vois* both seem to be plural.

172/23. *which*: Fr. adds 'comme par desespoir'.

172/24. *wepyngis*: om. Fr.

172/30–1. *from . . . blame*, 173/30–1. *of* (1) . . . *harmys*: 'de la coulpe de griefz maulz'.

172/32–3. *and . . . blame*, 173/33–4. *and . . . reproche*: 'delaissié pour si [*om*. H] chetif que je suis, sans adjouster a ma misere blasme ou reproche'.

173/6–7. *sorow and*: om. Fr.

173/9. *of this lande*: 'françoise'.

173/10. *in a woodnesse*: Omitted in Fr., which adds 'de ses dens'.

173/15. *with me*: om. Fr.

173/17–18. *aftir . . . vengeaunce*: 'a crier [decrire H] a Dieu venjance'.

174/1. *am . . . brest*, 175/1. *drye standing*: See Introduction, p. 50.

174/3. *cruelle*: *om*. Fr.

174/3. *hert sorow*: Fr. has 'grant douleur'. Although *hert* may be a scribal error in RNSJ for *grete*, I have not emended since *hert* is much more vivid in the context. Also note *hertely sorow* at 164/27.

174/4–5. *sende . . . ende*: 'me vueille gectier et [*om*. BH] mectre [*om*. BH] briefment hors de ceste langoureuse vie'.

174/5–6. *as . . . conforte*, 175/5–6. *in . . . orphente*: Fr. has 'en orphanté'. In U I have emended *orphent* to *orphente*, a word probably taken directly from Fr., in accordance with the common practice of U. The word *orphente* is not listed in *OED* (cf. *orphanity*).

174/10. *speke*: Fr. adds 'et commença lors a respondre [reprendre B]'.

174/16. *const*: This spelling occurs only here in R.

174/16. *ner ber*: *om*. Fr.

174/19. *blamyng thi bettirs*, 175/19. *blaspheme*: 'blapheme' DAH; 'blasme' B.

174/20. *which*: This awkward relative has no Fr. equivalent.

174/21. *nor bere*: *om*. Fr.

174/21. *theim*: 'les' ABH; 'le' D.

174/22. *but . . . wey*: 'sans forvoyer'.

174/28. *hough many vnkyndnes*: Fr. has 'combien grant ingratitude'. *vnkyndnes* may be intended as plural here. SJ have *vnkyndenesses*.

174/29. *willes*, 175/27–8. *volunte madly*: 'voulenté . . . follement affectee'.

174/30. *which*: Fr. adds 'depuis trante ans'.

174/31. *by long processe*: *om*. Fr.

175/2. *curse and banne*: 'maudire'.

175/8. *And . . . complaynte*: 'Atant'.

175/10. *engraiued*: *engraiued* translates 'aggravanté', and at 181/18 it translates 'aggravez'. The word is related to *engreven* (*MED*), *engrieve* (*OED*), 'vexed, troubled, aggrieved', but is influenced by Fr. 'aggravanté' and 'aggravez', and perhaps also by English *engraved*, 'impressed deeply'. Cf. *agraued* 177/30.

175/11. *a woorde more*: *om*. Fr.

175/17–18. *nor . . . werre*: The negative depends on that in the preceding clause and on the connective *nor*. Cf. 177/30.

175/20. *werres*: Fr. adds 'que tu pourchasses'.

175/21. *whiche*: Refers to 'guerres' in Fr.

176/3, 177/3. *suerte*: Like ABH, which omit D's 'chascun jour'.

176/4–5. *which . . . pleasaunces*: Fr. 'comblé de tous biens' refers to 'tu, ta femme et tes enfans'.

176/7. *what*: Like BH, which omit 'bruit', added in DA.

176/9. *which . . . vnkyndenesse*: Fr. has 'Icellui temps detestoies et tenoies a mauvais, en tresgrant ingratitude'. 'Icellui temps' is translated earlier as *at that tyme*. Cf. its position in U.

176/10. *must*: DA add 'regreter et'; B 'regracier et'; H 'regrauer et'.

176/15–16. *the eases*: 'les'.

176/20. *the* (1) *. . . discordis*, 177/20. *the* (1) *. . . dissencions*: Fr. has '[l]es batailles intestines, guerres [et grans BH] et discors'. Worcester adds '&' after 'batailles'.

176/22–4. *through . . . lordeship*, 177/21–4. *wherof . . . it*: 'dont la seigneurie rommaine, plus par eulx-mesmes que par estranges ennemis, est decheue du tout et sans ressource, qui fut tele et si haulte comme les ruines le demonstrent'.

176/29–31. *through . . . werre*, 177/28–30. *And . . . agraued*: Fr. has '[Car *add.* H] Par toy et par les partiz que tu as choisiz folement et soustenuz de obstinee voulenté est ceste guerre sourse et aggravee'. U's *agraued* is a blend of *aggrieve* and *aggravate*. *MED* has *agreven* = 'affect (sth.) adversely, aggravate', but no use like that here in U; and it does not list *agraued*. *OED* under *aggrave* gives no examples of this rare word in the meaning here, but records Palsgrave, 419/1 (1530): 'I agrudge, I am agraved, *Je suis greué*'.

176/33. *now*: Fr. adds 'assez et'.

177/2. *aknowe*: Fr. adds 'au moins'.

177/4. *place*: Fr. adds 'et soubz la seigneurie'.

177/7. *reuled and*: om. Fr.

177/9–10. *that* (1) *. . . desire*: Fr. begins a new sentence: 'Or le [*om.* AH] te fault a present regreter [regracier B; regrauer H] et loer'.

177/26. *him*: This refers to *peeple*. That U elsewhere thought of *peeple* as plural, however, is indicated by the verb *desiren* in l. 25.

178/1. *this myschief*: 'le'.

178/6. *and true*: om. Fr.

178/10. *man*: Following this R omits Fr. 'car tous ceulz de mauvais vouloir, qui en temps de paix ne l'osent mectre en oeuvre, prennent hardement de soy mectre sus soubz umbre de guerre'. It may have been omitted in R's Fr. exemplar since the Fr. word preceding the omitted part is 'grever', similar graphically to 'guerre' at the end of the omitted passage.

178/17–18. *and rewlars*: om. Fr.

178/18. *evyn quycke*, 179/19. *sodeynlye*: 'vifs'.

178/19–20. *and* (2) *. . . powdir*, 179/20–1. *and . . . heuyn*: DAB have 'et embrasez du feu qui du ciel descendy'. U is like H, however, which has 'les autres ars & embrasez' for 'embrasez'.

178/21-2. *beate . . . in*, 179/22. *bete . . . synnes*: Fr. has 'bat ta coulpe de tes mauvais pechiez'. *bete thy culpe* in U means 'atone for your guilt'.

178/24. *that . . . prosperite*: *om*. Fr.

178/25-6. *'Alas' . . . the*: RSJ follow Fr. more closely than does N: ' "Helas" cent fois le jour, et requier Dieu qu'il te pardonne'.

178/27. *not*: Fr. is not negative; hence the entire idea is different in R.

178/29. *ben*: Fr. adds 'tant horriblement'.

178/33. *and goodnes*, 179/31. *goodnesse and*: *om*. Fr.

179/7. *ordre*: 'tout [*om*. BH] ordre'.

179/25. *and*: 'et' B; *om*. DAH.

179/28. *townes*: Fr. adds 'par aucuns des tiens'.

179/29. *skaundre*: *OED* quotes *skander* as 'Obs. rare' from Manning and Trevisa.

179/30. *of this land*: 'françois'.

180/1. *full*, 181/1. *so*: 'trop' H; *om*. DAB.

180/9. *our . . . see*: 'mieulx ne se fait'.

180/10. *takith . . . grettely*: Fr. has 'se donroit aussi grant garde'. The S reading *takith not as grete hede* follows Fr. somewhat more closely in word order than does R. J's *a grete hede*, though perhaps corrupt in *a*, supports S. This entire sentence is omitted in N, probably because of the similarity of *For* in l. 9 and *Fertheremore* in l. 13.

180/14. *hathe*: Fr. adds 'douleur ou'.

180/15. *sorowfull*: *om*. Fr.

180/15. *othirs*, 181/14. *othir*: Both R and U are like ABH, which omit 'qui souvent aviennent a ung chascun, et', added in D.

180/16. *thinke*: A question follows in Fr.

180/17. *and moche more*: *om*. Fr.

180/18. *O*: *om*. Fr.

180/20. *that ben dispurveid*: In Fr., the participle 'despourveus' refers back to *worshipfull men and grette ladyes*.

180/20-1. *and goodnesse*: *om*. Fr.

180/21-2. *fer . . . treuthe*: N is corrupt here in its omission. Fr. has 'souffreteux de confort et [*om*. B, like R] aggravez de douleur pour leur loiauté acquiter et garder'.

180/21. *fulled*, 181/18. *engraiued*: Fr. has 'aggravez'. *fulfylled* (SJ) may be the correct reading instead of R's *fulled*. At 174/10, 'aggravanté' is rendered *fulfilled*. For U's *engraiued* see 175/10 n.

180/22. *O*: *om*. Fr.

180/26. *iuberte*: See Introduction, p. 19.

180/27–8. *And . . . morgage*: 'Et dont les pluseurs pour se mectre en point [paine B] de bien [faire a *add*. B] servir [faire H] ont leurs terres vendues et engaigees'.

180/31. *drynke*, 181/29. *drinkinge*: Since both R and U add this to Fr., there may have been Fr. manuscript support that I have not seen. See also 182/1, 183/1 n.

181/5. *boldenesse nor*: *om*. Fr.

181/7–8. *infirmite is*: U's Fr. exemplar may have had 'est' rather than 'et' (DABH); or *is* may be a scribal error for *and*.

181/9. *parties*: Fr. adds 'non pas en tous'.

181/21. *weight of*: *om*. Fr.

182/1. *and asche vs*, 183/1. *askyng*: *om*. Fr.

182/2. *from a*, 183/2. *out of a*: Both R and U are like BH, which omit 'cheneviere ou d'une', added in DA.

182/3. *as to . . . therof*: 'comme a le [*om*. H] deviser sur le coute [cendres BH], coste le vin'.

182/4. *werris*: Fr. adds 'en leur fouyer'.

182/5–6, 183/6–7. *with . . . lost*: 'et en le plaignant comme chose perdue'.

182/11. *liven . . . ease*, 183/10–11. *ben . . . be*: 'sont plus fourniz et plus aises que nous ne sommes'.

182/14–15. *thei . . . rumours*: 'les meurs que je dy sont plus souvent trouvez en ceulx qui plus mectent avant de plaintes et de murmures'.

182/18. *many of them*: *om*. Fr.

182/19. *for*: Like H, which omits 'garder et', added in DAB.

182/20. *of goodis*: *om*. Fr.

182/21. *had vsid*: Fr. has 'eust toujours eu . . . devant les yeulx'. *vsid* probably means 'practised, carried into effect', in the sense of 'upheld', a meaning not recorded in *OED*.

182/22. *stablischid*, 183/22. *stablelye confermed*: 'fermes et arrestez'.

182/23. *of right*: *om*. Fr.

182/24. *O*: Fr. has 'ou'. *O* may be a scribal error for *Or*, although it is not unusual for R to begin with an exclamation when Fr. does not.

182/28–9. *semblable . . . affliccions*: N is corrupt here. RSJ follow Fr. 'ainsi viennent les afflictions'.

182/29–30. *whanne . . . clere*, 183/29–30. *in . . . knowen*: DA have 'd'une mutacion. En plus grant l'exemple en est cler'. Like U, BH place 'en plus grant' with the preceding sentence.

182/31. *owrself*: Fr. adds 'pour trouver mutacion de gouvernement entre nous, et d'entre nous'. The omission is probably scribal, either in an English manuscript behind RNSJ or in R's Fr. exemplar.

182/31–2. *we . . . vs* (2): RSJ follow Fr. more closely than does N: 'l'avons de rechief mis dehors de nous et de hors nous contre nous'.

183/1–2. *saying . . . dooues*: U misinterpreted Fr.: 'et que nous ne chaçons les ennemis comme l'en chaçeroit les [*om.* H] coulons'. Chartier means that the *burgeys* and the *preest* think that it should be as easy to chase the enemies as it is to chase doves out of a field.

183/5. *wold nat leese*: Fr. has 'n'en laisseroient'. *leese* may be a scribal error for *leeue*.

183/12. *to us*: 'a nous' ABH; 'avons' D, like R.

183/13. *and stable*: *om.* Fr.

183/20. *and worship*: *om.* Fr.

183/27. *But elas*: *om.* Fr.

184/7. *fulfillid*: 'ensuye'.

184/9–10. *haue . . . warres*: 'se sont maintenuz'.

184/10–11. *in this seasons*: 'ou temps passé'.

184/18–19. *thei . . . worship*: 'de tant se ressourdoient ilz plus vertueuse-ment comme le besoing les rendoit plus contrains a ce [a ce *om.* BH; bien A]'.

184/20–2, 185/18–20. *thei* (2) *. . . armes*: DAB have 'ilz en establissoient de nouueaux et mettoient sus des gens [fors *add.* A; fres et nouueaulx *add.* B] de tous estas, mesmes des serfs, et les apprenoient et faisoient exerciter aux armes'. H changes the structure and is not like the English. Worcester, like U, has '&' before 'mesmes'.

184/22. *the*: Fr. adds 'cure et'.

184/22. *good*: 'bonne' ABH; *om.* D.

184/24. *in their dedis*: *om.* Fr.

184/25. *sevre*, 185/23. *seure and ferme*: R probably used a manuscript like A, which has only 'seurs'. D adds 'et hardiz', and BH have only 'saiges'. All the manuscripts add 'et arrestez'.

184/25–7. *thei . . . failid*: 'le tresor de Romme estoit desgarny de pecune'.

184/27–31. *euery . . . cite*, 185/24–9. *yche . . . citee*: Fr. has 'chacun bailloit liberalment le sien et [*om.* H] mesmement les dames leurs precieux joyaulx [et *add.* H; et ce *add.* B] pour secourir a la necessité publique et reacheter le temps de prosperité commune [comme BH] de leur propre chatel, ne riens ne leur estoit [*om.* A] plus chier que ce qu'ilz exposoient pour la seigneurie et bien publique de leur cité'. Note that both R and U omit an equivalent for 'mesmement les dames', perhaps indicating its omission in a Fr. manuscript. For 'le sien' Worcester has 'du sien'.

185/4. *skape*: Fr. adds 'a honneur'.

185/5. *and*: 'de'.

185/5–6. *in this land*: Fr. has 'françois', modifying 'couraiges'.

185/7. *daungers*: Like H, which omits 'de guerre', added in DAB.

185/10. *reforme*: 'reformer' B; 'rafermer' DAH.

185/16. *releue*: May be a scribal error for past tense.

185/21–2. *preeuid . . . bataile*: 's'en aidoient en leurs batailles et devenoient vaillans et hardiz'.

186/1. *the . . . callid*: om. Fr.

186/1, 187/1: See Vegetius, *Instituta rei militaris*, iv. 9, *Quid faciendum sit, si nervorum defuerit copia*, translated into French in the Middle Ages by both Christine de Pisan and Jean de Meun.

186/1–2. *how . . . nede*, 187/1–3. *that . . . cordage*: Fr. has 'que, comme aux engins de guerre, dont les Rommains defendoient le Capitole de Romme, feust defailli le cordage'. Cf. the awkward literalness of U with the better rendering of R.

186/3. *and . . . all*: This is not in Fr. *forthewithall* as one word may be intended.

186/4. *toke . . . workemen*: 'bailler'.

186/5–8. *and . . . cite*: See Introduction, p. 49.

186/12–13. *I . . . but*: om. Fr.

186/14–15. *all . . . by*: 'noz chevances'.

186/15. *What . . . but*: 'Qu'est ce [*om.* A] autre chose a dire si non que'.

186/21. *chargith*: Fr. has 'en charge ou accusation d'autruy ne soit ja chose trop louable'. There may be scribal omission in RNSJ.

186/22–3. *of . . . lordeship*, 187/21–2. *of* (1) *. . . comonte*: 'de la communité de la seigneurie'.

186/25. *maners*: Like B, which omits 'des hommes', added in DAH.

186/26–7. *in . . . twelth*, 187/25–6. *to . . . saluacion*: 'une singuliere forme de querir leur salut'.

186/28–9. *muse . . . themself*: 'se soubtillent'.

186/31. *the* (1) *. . . welthe*, 187/28. *to . . . saluacion*: Both R and U are like ABH, which have 'commune' for D's 'comme' in 'a la prosperité comme le salut'.

186/32–3. *wheras . . . pardicion*, 187/29–30. *the . . . perdicion*: Fr. has 'quant [que B; qui H] par leurs parciaulx desirs ilz le [*om.* BH] perdent avecques la seigneurie qu'ilz [ilz *om.* A] delaissent en perdicion'. U used a manuscript like BH. *lyue* at 187/30 in U is obviously a spelling of *leave* ('delaissent').

187/4. *heedys*: Fr. adds 'et [*om.* B] bailler [*om.* B] pour faire cordes et secourir'.

187/12. *falle and*: om. Fr.

187/15. *his*: This may be a scribal error for *their*; or the translator may refer back to *fadir* and *neyghbour* in ll. 9–10, ignoring his change to *thaimself* earlier and his own use of plural pronouns later in the paragraph.

187/17. *and abused*: om. Fr.

187/18. *and goodys*: om. Fr.

188/6. *all their pleasuris*: 'les biens a leur part'.

188/6. *of any disease*, 189/6. *of disease*: Although this has no Fr. equivalent in any manuscript I have seen, its appearance in both R and U probably indicates that the translators used a Fr. manuscript with this phrase.

188/7. *and* (2) . . . *therto*, 189/7. *and* (2) . . . *good*: 'sans riens [autre chose en *add*. H] avoir'.

188/9. *mereveillous*: om. Fr.

188/10. *for* (1) . . . *seruice*: 'dont il nous puisse paier, et en servant a la communité'.

188/10–11. *of very necessite*: om. Fr.

188/11–12. *with . . . God*: 'a Dieu m'en rapporte d'avoir noz consciences excusees'.

188/17. *and reuenewis*: om. Fr.

188/24. *force*: Like ABH, which omit 'est et', added in D.

188/25–6. *who . . . case*: 'a bien enquerir'.

188/27. *a man of*: om. Fr.

188/31. *in their howses*: Like BH, which omit 'sur le leur', or like A, which omits 'le leur, en' in D's 'sur le leur, en leurs maisons'.

188/32. *in diseasis*: 'a regret'.

189/15–16. *we* (2) . . . *goon* (1): 'l'on se plaint de nous ou nous allons'.

189/17. *nor dommages*: om. Fr.

189/26. *and gilty*: om. Fr.

189/28. *redondeth*: It seems likely that *redouteth* is a scribal error for *redondeth*, a direct borrowing in U's customary way from Fr. 'redonde'. The scribe may not have been familiar with the word since the first *OED* record in the meaning 'fall' is from Nashe, 1589.

189/30. *goodes*: Fr. adds 'en leurs maisons'.

190/3. *watirs*: DA add 'et les agoutz'; B 'et les degoutz'; H 'et les gouttes'.

190/6–9. *makit . . . richesses*: 'leur a diminué le paiement des devoirs [*om*. H] et [*om*. H] des rentes qu'ilz nous doivent, et l'outrageuse chierté qu'ilz ont mise es vivres et ouvraiges leur a creu l'avoir [leur avoir H] que par chascun jour ilz recueillent et amassent'.

190/10. *and goodis*: om. Fr.

190/12–14. *For . . . aftir*, 191/12–14. *For . . . aftirward*: Fr. has a clause in conjunction with *that doubte* in l. 11: 'et qui feroient assez [aussi H] grant marchié du sang des nòbles hommes [comme *add.* H] dont, s'ilz estoient perduz, le royaume ploureroit la [leur BH] mort puis après'. Note the similarity of translation in R and U at the beginning of the sentence.

190/15, 191/15–16. *God . . . enemyes*: 'Dieu me gard que je defende ou debate qu'il ne soit bon de grever et guerroyer ses ennemis'.

190/18–19, 191/18–20. *wolde . . . devoir*: 'ne demanderoient pas plus grant eur que soy y trouver pour faire leur devoir'.

190/20, 191/20–1. *for . . . avauntage*: 'pour attendre son bon et delay pour faire son preu en son avantaige'.

190/22–3. *at the ende*: Fr. has 'au chief'. Note that U has *in a chief*, 191/22, but also *in the ende*, 191/23.

190/25–6. *leve . . . mesur*: Fr. has 'exposer a perte et laisser atrempance et mesure'. 'a perte' has been confused with 'a part'.

190/26–7. *right . . . name*, 191/26–7. *the . . . prowesse*: 'le nom de vaillance'.

190/28. *And . . . purpose*: om. Fr.

190/31–2. *the* (1) . . . *Agyncourt*, 191/30. *the . . . bataill*: 'fait de la maleureuse bataille d'Agincourt'.

190/33. *fortune*: 'infortune'.

191/2. *that* (1): Fr. adds 'leur bourse'. There may be scribal omission in U.

191/22. *othir*: Like H, which omits 'mendres', added in DAB.

191/28. *seeke*: A adds 'aucunes'; DBH 'anciennes'.

191/29. *late*: Fr. adds 'et de noz jours'.

192/4. *difference*: Fr. adds 'ou doit avoir'.

192/4. *counseill*: Fr. adds 'et en oeuvre'.

192/6–7. *fortune . . . ageyne*: 'de perverse fortune se veult ressourdre'.

192/8–9. *To . . . buffettis*, 193/7–9. *Suche . . . corage*: 'Telle oeuvre avons nous a mener, en quoy plus chiet d'aguet et de sens que d'ouvraige de chaude colle'.

192/9–10. *as . . . Romayne*, 193/9–10. *And . . . Romayn*: 'En pareil cas le monstra bien le saige Rommain'.

192/10 ff., 193/10 ff.: See Valerius Maximus, v. 2. 4, and Livy, xxii. 10 ff.

192/13. *which . . . Rome*: 'le consul'.

192/13–14. *Bataile of Caves*: See 158/28 n.

192/18. *of dede bodyes*: om. Fr.

192/19. *this noble*: om. Fr.

192/23–7. *yet . . . horsemen*, 193/22–7. *neuyrtheles . . . horsmen*: Fr. has 'neantmoins oncques ne voult souffrir que la chevallerie rommaine, deprimee par les victoires des adversaires, feust a ung coup et comme [pour ABH] la derreniere foiz exposee es perilz de Fortune, qui moult estoit favorable au vainqueur, et tant y contrestat que le peuple, en derogant au tiltre de son honneur, esleva en dictature et comme son compagnon Minicius, le maistre des gens de cheval'. B omits 'feust . . . coup' and 'et comme . . . compagnon'. Like U, B has the spelling 'Municus'.

192/32. *yeve*: Perhaps *yelde* (NSJ) more nearly translates Fr. 'rendre'.

192/33. *thankingis*, 193/33. *laude and thanke*: 'graces de son secours'.

192/35–6. *But . . . knyghtis*, 193/35–195/1. *by . . . victories*: R is much freer than U in rendering Fr.: 'par laquelle le dictateur Fabius mena Hannibal si durement que, [peu ABH] a peu et sans dommaige de la chevallerie de Romme [Rommaine ABH], que a tresg[r]ans et dures pertes aprés toutes ses victoires'.

193/17. *in the bataile*: om. Fr.

193/18–19. *keped . . . domage*: 'costoioit ses ennemis et les dommagoit'.

193/33–4. *and blasphemyd*: om. Fr.

194/4. *if . . . ourself*, 195/4. *but . . . oureself*: 's'en nous ne tient'.

194/5. *vs, Frenschmen*, 195/5. *vs*: Fr. has 'nous, François'. As usual, U omitted reference to the French.

194/7–8. *our . . . daunger*, 195/6–7. *thaire . . . meruailous*: 'ses pertes ont esté et sont grandes et ses [en BH] dangiers merveilleux'.

194/9. *to . . . tribulacion*, 195/8–9. *paciently to suffre*: 'avoir pacience de souffrir'.

194/10. *lightar*, 195/9. *lighter and easier*: 'legiere chose'.

194/10. *vs*: Fr. adds 'si fortunez que nous sommes'.

194/10. *for them*: Fr. adds 'si exaucié comme il cuide'.

194/11. *conquere us*: *wynne on vs* seems to be an inferior correction in R since NSJ have *conquere us* for Fr. 'de nous conquerir'.

194/13. *own*: Like B, which omits 'bon', added in DAH.

194/22, 195/22. *and grette*: om. Fr.

194/23. *and . . . do*, 195/23–4. *vpon . . . it*: Fr. has 'sur ceulx qui mais n'en pevent'. The addition of *put* from NSJ seems to retain R's intended structure and meaning.

194/23. *O good*, 195/24. *A*: om. Fr.

194/24–7. *whanneas . . . it*: Fr. has 'quant celle desloiale voye a mise Fortune en ses variables oeuvres, que, des ce qu'il meschiet aux chetiz, on leur met sus que c'est par leurs dessertes'. R's *chaungeable* in l. 25 in place of *varyable* (NSJ) may be a scribal error recalling l. 24.

194/29–30. *haue . . . myself*, 195/30. *haue . . . it*: R is like DAB, which have 'l'ay pourchacee et bastie', while U is like H, which omits 'et bastie'.

195/4. *shall it be*: Fr. has 'fera', easily confused with 'sera'.

195/17. *toke the langage*: Fr. has 'print a repliquer'. This English phrase is not recorded in *OED*, and its two occurrences in U are the only examples cited in *MED*. At 175/12, this unusual phrase is used to translate 'prist les parolles'. *OED* under *speech* 2d. gives one example of *take the speech* from 1612.

195/21–2. *put . . . destrue*: 'confundre'.

195/25. *so*: 'telle' BH; 'celle' DA.

195/32. *haue*: Fr. adds 'desloiaument'.

196/7. *that*: Like BH, which omit 'de', added in DA.

196/8. *passed . . . vs*: 'paisible'.

196/9, 197/8. *them*: om. Fr.

196/10. *in . . . mysknowlege*, 197/9–10. *in . . . ingratitude*: 'en [*om.* BH] ingratitude et [de BH] descongnoissance'.

196/11–13. *which . . . evile*: 'Si est vostre desmesuree vie et vostre desordonné gouvernement cause de nostre impacience et commencement de noz maulx'.

196/14–15. *with haboundaunce*: 'et que les finances y habondoient'.

196/15–16. *right so*: om. Fr.

196/16. *ydill . . . to*, 197/15–16. *tendre . . . with*: 'oisivetez aouillees [acueilluz H] de'.

196/17–18. *hathe . . . sheldis*, 197/17. *hath . . . wyttes*: DA have 'vous avoit ja et a bestourné le sens'. Both R and U are like BH, which omit 'et a'. How *sheldis* in R occurs as the rendering of 'sens' is difficult to explain. The translator may perhaps have misread 'sens' as 'ecus' in his exemplar.

196/20. *thingis*, 197/19. *myscheevys*: Fr. has no equivalent. U omits 'estoit et', which follows in Fr.

196/23. *which . . . come*, 197/22. *comyng and growinge*: 'lors sourvenant'.

196/26–7. *nor . . . in*, 197/25–6. *at . . . receyued*: 'pour son besoing ne a pourveoir que tout ne soit avant despendu que receu'.

196/30. *voice of tyteleris*: Fr. has 'mouetes'. *tyteleris* suggests R's association of *tit*, a prefix used in denoting a small bird (cf. *titlark* and *titling*) with *tittlers*, 'whisperers, telltales', suggested by *tales*, l. 31.

196/31. *see floode*: N's *flode of þe see* is closer to Fr. 'les floz de la mer'.

196/32. *war*: Fr. adds 'pour ces causes'.

197/24. *som . . . goodys*: om. Fr.

197/28. *richesse*: om. Fr.

198/2. *of the sequeles*, 199/2. *of . . . folowinge*: Both R and U used a manuscript like ABH, which have 'des sequeles'. D, certainly corrupt, has 'desquelles'. It is difficult to understand why Droz did not emend here.

198/2–7. *Thanne . . . myne* (1), 199/3–6. *Therfore . . . myn*: Fr. has 'se tu me blasmes que en si dure adversité je ne puis pacience garder et en tes haultes prosperitez tu n'as peu retenir atrempance ne moderacion, ton inconstance [ta constance BH] doit estre dicte mendre que la mienne'. U seems to have followed blindly the inferior reading of DA, while R, though retaining 'inconstance' of DA, improved the sense by changing 'mendre' to *more*.

198/7. *receueable . . . myne*, 199/6. *resonable*: Fr. has 'recevable', like RNS. It is interesting that J's *resoynable* agrees with U's *resonable*; both, however, are probably scribal errors.

198/9–10. *thou . . . them*, 199/9. *thou . . . susteyne*: 'tu m'acuses d'avoir soustenuz'.

198/12. *I . . . say*: om. Fr.

198/12–13. *ther . . . that* (2): 'aucuns des tiens'.

198/13. *wasche . . . therfrom*, 199/11–12. *might . . . excuse*: Fr. has 'ne s'en sauroient laver'. The first *OED* record of R's phrase *wasche ther handis therfrom* is from 1554, but in 1465 Margaret Paston also used the phrase; see N. Davis, 'The Language of the Pastons', Sir Israel Gollancz Memorial Lecture, *Proc. Brit. Acad.*, xl (1954), 135.

198/17. *lettirs*: Fr. adds 'par renommee et par'.

198/25–6. *by . . . thyne*, 199/21–2. *suspect . . . thyn*: 'de souppeçon, de faulte d'aide et [ou BH] de reffuz [refuge B, like U] ou [et BH] doubte de recueil de toy et des tiens'.

198/28. *delytes*: The plural, meaning 'crimes, violations of law and right', in Fr. and NSJ seems better in the context than R's singular.

198/31 ff., 199/27 ff.: According to Droz's note, this passage refers to the abandonment in 1418 of Rouen and other places in France to the English.

198/33. *and abyden*: om. Fr.

198/33–200/1. *as . . . goon*, 199/29–31. *as* (1) *. . . failed*: 'tant come [les biens et *add.* H] les vivres et les rappines de des biens [et . . . biens *om.* H] qu'ilz [nont ne H] n'avoient pas acquiz les ont peu soustenir, mais ilz ont failly aux places quant la proye leur a failly'.

199/17. *Therfore . . . blame*: Fr. has 'S'ilz ont erré, a eulx en doit on demander le retour'. There may be scribal error in U here, but U's rendering as it stands makes emphatic the point of the preceding sentence.

200/3. *kepe*: Fr. adds 'aux amis'.

200/4 ff., 201/3 ff.: See Droz's note, which illustrates historically these typical charges and countercharges exchanged between the people and the army in France during this period.

200/6. *them*: Fr. adds 'et de ce qu'ilz font tu dois porter le faiz'. This passage may have been omitted in R's Fr. exemplar since immediately before it the verb 'faiz' occurs.

200/10–11. *thi . . . wourthi*, 201/10–12. *they . . . vnworthy*: See Introduction, pp. 54–5.

200/12. *but . . . discoragid*: 'deffiez et descouragez' DAB; 'deffient desconfortent & descouragent' H.

200/16–17. *sodeinly . . . followith*: 'puis reprist en ceste maniere [ainsi B] a parler'.

200/22–3. *of . . . thiself*: 'pour tousjours courre sus par detraction a meilleur de toy'.

200/29–30. *that . . . mesur*, 201/30–1. *to us . . . vs*: 'a nous de abuser des estas oultre ce que mesure donne quant ilz nous appartiennent'.

200/31. *þe*: 'du'.

200/32–202/1. *thow . . . be*, 201/34–203/1. *thou . . . we*: 'tu t'es selon toy desroyé en tes [*om.* ABH] estaz trop [*om.* B] plus que nous'.

201/3. *And . . . me*: 'Assez me vueil de ceste chose [ce H] taire a poy de parler [paroles BH]'.

201/4. *and committe*: *om.* Fr.

201/5–6. *for . . . misdeedys*: 'de ce qu'ilz font'.

201/7. *membre*: D has 'umbre'; AB have 'nombre'; H omits the clause. *membre* may be a scribal error.

201/24. *the . . . pompes*: 'la vanité des pompes'.

201/25–6. *by . . . greeuys*: 'trop fort te dueilles'.

201/30–1. *and maynteyne*: *om.* Fr.

201/33. *vpon . . . tyme*: Fr. has 'sur ce point du temps dont tu parles et de cestui'. The U scribe, after copying *this*, may have looked back to *this present tyme* rather than to *this point* and thus omitted the intervening passage.

202/1–6. *Whervpon . . . arrayed*, 203/1–5. *And . . . prince*: R is much freer in translation than U: 'et tu en vois encores les ensaignes, quant ung varlet cousturier et la femme d'un homme de bas estat osent porter l'abit d'ung vaillant chevalier et d'une noble dame et dont ilz souloient estre en court de prince tresbien parez'. U is like A, which omits 'et dont ilz' after 'dame'.

202/7–10, 203/6–8. *thei . . . owtward*: 'ceulx qui ont eu a departir les guerredons des biensfaiz et des honneurs les ont donnez aux robes et aux apparences de dehors'.

202/10–11. *suche . . . conseite*: 'prins tele instruction'.

202/17, 203/15. *the cite*: Chartier was, of course, thinking of Paris. See Droz's note.

202/17, 203/15–16. *aboue . . . be*: D reads 'a esté sur toutes les autres a esté'. B omits the first 'a esté' and 'les autres'. H omits 'a . . . autres' and substitutes 'tant'. R and U may have used a manuscript which omitted only the first 'a esté'.

202/22. *in . . . parte*: 'et [ou AH] l'abisme'.

202/25. *castyng owte*: Fr. has 'et a respandu' and adds 'le venin et'.

202/28. *puttist by fore*: Fr. has 'mes au devant pour'. There may be scribal omission in RNSJ. Note that NSJ have *be fore*. Perhaps the original reading was *puttist byfore for*.

202/32. *rebukyng*: 'obprobrieuse'.

202/33. *place*: R confused 'lien' with 'lieu'.

203/10–11. *a* (2) *. . . iourneyman*: 'ung ouvrier mecanique'.

203/18. *entowned*: Fr. has 'entonné' (absorbed, engulfed). Neither *MED* nor *OED* records this verb, but *MED* has the verbal noun *entunning*, 'putting of a liquid into a cask'.

203/19. *and* (2): This has no Fr. equivalent and may be a scribal addition.

203/24. *venym*: Fr. adds 'et la poison'.

203/27–8. *to* (2) *. . . couere*: U used a manuscript like B, which has 'pollir'; DAH have 'palier'. *pollisch* in this sense is quoted by *OED* only from the earlier translation of *The Book of the Knight of La Tour-Landry*.

204/6. *obstinate . . . that*: 'obstinacion y a mis en aucun temps celle loy avant la main que'.

204/7. *and pleasur*: om. Fr.

204/8–9. *the . . . of*: om. Fr.

204/10–11. *to* (1) *. . . ougtht*, 205/10–11. *to* (1) *. . . be*: Fr. has 'aux publieurs du dire et a toy du croire, si en demeure le tort a qui il devra [demorer *add*. H; demouree *add*. B]'. R's *caused* (*the*), with *the* inserted, follows Fr. more closely than *caused them* (NSJ).

204/12–14. *he . . . disseyvid*, 205/13–14. *it . . . thoughtys*: Fr. reads 'se peut aidier a decevoir par parolles d'autruy qui dedans soy mesmes est desja corrumpu par mauvaise pensee'.

204/17. *will*: Like H, which omits 'tousjours', added in DAB.

204/23. *sette . . . poynte*: Fr. has 'mise avant'. R's phrase, not in *OED*, seems to mean 'begun and put in way of development'.

204/25–6. *grette . . . doubtis*, 205/25–6. *payne . . . doutes*: ABH have 'les douleurs des confors [desconfors B] et des doubtes'. D has 'les douloureux desconforts de doubtes'. R may have used a manuscript which combined these two readings. U is like AH.

204/29–30. *full . . . myghtely*: 'moult puissamment'.

204/33. *that . . . that*: Since NSJ omit the first *that* it may be a scribal addition in R. *at all tymys* has no Fr. equivalent.

204/34–6. *whethir . . . necligence*: 'se honte y a, [ne *add*. BH] qui plus en doit rougir ou ceulx qui faillent a leurs gardes defendre ou ceulx qui leur faillent de bon secours'.

204/36–206/9. *But . . . them,* 205/35–207/7. *And . . . trouth* (1): The freedom with which R changed the Fr. structure is clear here. Fr reads 'Et sur tous en est plus la vergoigne a ceulx qui les defaillans et les bien-faicteurs mectent tout [comme B] en ung raeng, que se n'est ce que vertu en donne aux bons le contentement de leur cuer, au jugement des hommes y a peu de difference. A qui tu t'en prendras? je ne scay, fors que a faulte de cognoissance, et a ce que les haulx et puissans hommes, entre les grans abondances qu'ilz ont de toutes choses, ont le plus de souffrete et de despit de ouir dire verité et que par leur puissance ilz finent de toutes autres besoignes, de langues veritables sont ilz tousjours diseteux'. (There are some changes in BH, which, however, do not seem to have influenced the English.) Note U's mistranslation of 'au jugement des hommes y a peu de difference' and omission of 'et que par . . . diseteux'.

205/3. *vntestable*: Fr. has 'detestables'. *vntestable* is not in *OED*.

205/4. *ruine*: Fr. has 'ruineux'. *ruine* seems to be the noun used attributively. In *OED*, under the noun *ruin*, 2c., a predicative use meaning 'ruinous' comes nearest to the meaning here.

205/6. *suche*: 'telle' BH; 'celle' DA.

205/25. *payne and*: om. Fr.

205/30. *and defended*: om. Fr.

205/31. *entermedled*: Fr. adds 'et dangereuse'.

205/34. *kepe . . . and*: om. Fr.

206/10. *it* (2) . . . *himself,* 207/9. *it . . . releeuid*: 'se ressourt'.

206/11. *and suffre*: om. Fr.

206/12. *swet*: om. Fr.

206/12–13. *wilfull . . . estates*: Fr. has 'descongnoissance des haultes seigneuries'. *wilfull mysknowlege* seems to mean 'obstinate refusal to know, obstinate lack of knowledge', still another shade of meaning given in R to *mysknowlege*. See 5/11–17 n., 89/32 n., and Glossary.

206/14. *the* (1) . . . *same,* 207/12. *the* (1) . . . *conclusion*: 'le fruit de l'issue'.

206/16. *the,* 207/14. *his*: 'la' BH; 'sa' DA.

206/20–1. *The . . . them,* 207/17–19. *Longe . . . hate*: Fr. has 'Longue fut et trop [plus H; plus *add.* B; et plus *add.* A] attaigneuse que il n'affiert la contention de ces deux, qui estrivoient ensemble par parolles mordans treshaineusement'. *and sharpe* in R, omitted in NSJ, may be a scribal addition (note *sharpe* later in l. 21 and in l. 11); but NS are corrupt after *sharpe* (*for he* instead of *for the*), and thus R may have the original reading in the passage. *annouse* in U may be a scribal error for *anniouse*.

206/22. *thrid*: Fr. adds 'les escoutoit'.

206/24. *wourdis*: The R scribe picked up *that ware bytwene them* (om. NSJ) from l. 21 following *wourdes*.

206/24. *hym*: Fr. adds 'point et'.

206/25–6. *and . . . charge*: 'pour verser sur lui couvertement'.

206/26–7. *he . . . followeith*: Fr. has 'et fut l'entrée de son parler tele'. I have added *hereafter* from NSJ in accordance with the usual practice of the translator.

206/30. *pursued*: 'persecutez'.

206/32–208/1, 207/30–1. *that . . . questions*: 'qui voient le feu embrasé et esprins par leurs lieux et habitacions et sont en question pour debatre'.

207/9. *his*: 'ses' H; 'les' DAB.

207/21. *touche him*: 'approucher aux faiz'.

207/22. *sharply*: Fr. has no equivalent, but adds 'point et'.

207/28. *ouermiche*: om. Fr.

208/1–2. *to . . . dede, 209/1–2. who . . . it*: Fr. has 'a qui le devoir de l'estaindre appartient'. For U's *skonche* see 165/10 n.

208/3–5. *the . . . distruccion, 209/2–6. the (2) . . . house*: Fr. has 'se brulle la maison par leurs difficultez et negligences, que [quoy ABH] que chascun y deust comme au feu courir et eviter la destruction de son hostel en pourchassant le salut [saluacion B] de [om. B] cellui [om. B] a [de B] son voisin'. In U *and* in l. 5 may be a scribal error for *in*.

208/6. *debatis*: om. Fr.

208/8. *as, 209/9. yf*: 'comme' B; 'se' DAH.

208/10. *chargis and lodes*: Fr. has 'voitures' and adds 'des effondrez et'.

208/12. *to . . . move*: 'esmouver'.

208/13. *put*: *cast* (NSJ) may be the original rendering of 'gecter', although, as the Glossary shows, *put* is a much used utility word in R.

208/13–18. *Let . . . vs, 209/14–17. He . . . haue*: Fr. has 'Entreprengne Cellui [En gre prengne cellui ABH] qui en a le povoir [de *add.* BH] l'adversité que nous souffrons et plus en gré que nous ne la recevons ou congnoissons, car, quoy qu'elle suffise pour punir noz maulx selon sa pitié, je doubte que assez grande ne soit elle pas selon noz faultes et la descongnoissance que nous [en *add.* AB] avons d'elles [om. ABH]'. R had difficulty here with an inferior manuscript like D, while U used a better exemplar like ABH: the parallel structure of 'En gre prengne' and 'et plus en gré' is typical of Chartier's style and fits the context better than D's reading. Even U, with a better examplar, had some difficulty with the passage.

208/18–19. *nat . . . God, 209/17–18. withoute . . . God*: 'sans avoir congnoissance de Dieu'.

208/19. *perilles, 209/18. mischeef*: om. Fr.

208/21. *to returne*: With the infinitive reading of NSJ (R omits *to*), the passage follows Fr. 'et dy pour retourner'.

208/22–3. *like . . . retourne*, 209/21–2. *as . . . retourne*: Both R and U used
a manuscript like BH: 'ainsi que de longue maladie dont les membres
sont alterez et corrumpuz ne peut on recouvrer [retourner BH]'.

208/23. *actes*, 209/23. *accesse*: A has 'actes'; B 'acces'; H 'acez'; D
'assez'. *actes* is presumably a copying error for *acces*.

208/24–9. *likewise . . . nature*, 209/23–8. *also . . . kynde*: See Introduction,
p. 54.

208/27. *reynith*, 209/26. *reigneth*: Fr. has 'court', but *reigne* is the idiomatic English equivalent of this. Cf. 168/15–17 n.

208/28–9. *and* (2) *. . . nature*: Fr. has 'si que par aprés les choses retournent [tournent B] a leur nature'. The English variants here probably
indicate a copy text difficult to read somewhere in the manuscript history.
Inasmuch as R omits *þat the thyng hyt* and NSJ omit one word (*hyt* SJ,
the N), the four words may have been a marginal insertion in an earlier
manuscript.

208/31–2. *withowte . . . man*, 209/29–30. *withoute . . . men*: Fr. has 'sans
plaintes et [*om.* B] au contentement [detriment B] d'un chascun'. *contemptes*
in U may be a scribal error for an equivalent of Fr. 'contentement'.

209/13. *shall*: 'doye'.

209/20. *cesse*: By omitting Fr. 'et dy' here, U disrupted the structure of
the rest of the sentence, leaving the clause beginning *that as of* in l. 21
without connection to the first part. Some scribal error may be involved.

209/23. *paynes*: 'recidives'.

209/28. *and that*: In all the Fr. manuscripts I have seen, a new sentence
begins here with 'Si ne'. Perhaps U, however, used a manuscript which
had 'si que', which he assumed was in series with the preceding 'si que'
(*so that*, l. 27).

210/4. *and*: 'de la'.

210/4. *putte*: Fr. has 'mectre fin en'. *end to* may have been scribally
omitted in an earlier manuscript; otherwise, this is an unusual use of
put alone to mean 'expel, remove'.

210/5. *answer . . . men*, 211/5–6. *restith . . . men*: 'ne correspont pas en
fait ne en oeuvre a ce qu'en est es voulentez et desirs hastiz des homes'.

210/10. *warre*: 'aidans'.

210/13. *thes poyntis*, 211/13–14. *theise .iij. thinges*: 'les'.

210/17 ff., 211/19 ff.: See Isaiah 29: 14–15.

210/18. *ouerthrowe*: Fr. adds 'de Dieu', and in l. 19, where R has *of God*,
Fr. has 'de lui'.

210/19–24. *Anothir . . . werke*, 211/21–6. *The . . . comprehende*: See
Introduction, p. 53.

210/27. *yoke*: The omission of *yoke* after *yevin* probably indicates a
corrupt text, not the author's copy, behind the extant manuscripts.

210/30. *and thurst down*: *om.* Fr.

210/33. *the grette*: 'quans' (probably confused with 'grans').

211/2. *and woode*: *om.* Fr.

211/11. *his*: 'ses' B; *om.* DA.

211/11–12. *to* (2) . . . *deedys*: 'esploicter'.

211/15. *demeene thaim*: 'nous en aidier'.

211/20. *withdrawen and taken*: 'irrité ou [et BH] precipité'.

211/20. *well . . . grace*: 'de bien recognoistre [cognoistre BH; tenir *add.*
ABH] de lui'.

211/28. *vnhappy batailes*: Fr. has 'batailles civilles et plus que civilles'.
U may have had a Fr. exemplar that had a gap between the two occurrences of 'civilles'.

211/28. *it*: This awkward pronoun has no Fr. equivalent.

212/1. *of* (1) . . . *vs*: Fr. has 'd'ennemis'. Since NSJ have *that oure
enemyes* for *of . . . thei*, two different readings in the author's copy may be
reflected here, NSJ representing one rendering and R a second attempt.

212/2. *that . . . payde*: 'mal contens'.

212/3. *that . . . owte*: 'escondiz ou reboutez'.

212/4, 213/3–4. *diuerse . . . ryotes*: DA have 'rappors divers et souspeçonneux, ligues et riotes'; H has 'et langage rioteux' and B has 'et
langaiges rehoteux' for 'ligues et riotes'.

212/5, 213/5. *constreynid*: 'contraint' ABH; 'tenu' D.

212/7. *more*: Fr. adds 'd'eur'.

212/7. *a man*: *om.* Fr.

212/8. *powere*: *om.* Fr.

212/9. *grette and*: *om.* Fr.

212/9–12. *for . . . same*, 213/8–9. *the* (3) . . . *thrall*: Fr. has 'que grant
autorité de seigneurie a fait estre serfz a plusieurs pour icelle avoir, mais
plus que serfz quant le besoing contraint a la defendre'. R's omission,
emended from NSJ, occurred because of the repetition of *bondage*.
Note U's omission of the end of the Fr. passage.

212/13. *hough*: This awkward connective is omitted in Fr. See Introduction, p. 59.

212/16. *wille*: Fr. adds 'et a pourveoir et avoir l'ueil a choses repugnans
et aux cas qui soudainement leur sourviennent soit en leur avantaige,
quant bien en veulent user, ou en leur préjudice, se obvier n'y scevent'.

212/17. *grettest and*: *om.* Fr.

212/18. *grette and*: *om.* Fr.

212/18. *prikkid*: *om.* Fr.

212/19. *to . . . lordship*: 'qui pour relever ceste seigneurie opprimee sourviennent en chascun jour'.

212/20. *a remedy*: *om*. Fr.

212/21. *follow . . . people*: 'aux divers appetiz des hommes'.

212/22. *and knowlege*: *om*. Fr.

212/22. *of long lyvyng*: 'et la longue vie' is in conjunction with 'experiences' in Fr.

212/27. *medlid with experiens*: *om*. Fr.

212/27-8. *in . . . past*: 'des oeuvres passees en ce temps de guerre'.

212/29. *of . . . princes*: *om*. Fr.

212/30 ff., 213/28 ff.: On 17 January 1420 Charles VI forbade the citizens of Paris to obey the Dauphin, who he said was not worthy of succession or of any honour or aid. See Droz's note.

212/31. *from . . . house*: 'de la maison royal dont il est filz et heritier'.

212/32. *sowing of discorde*: 'sedicion'.

212/32. *he was also*: *om*. Fr.

212/33. *evile*: *om*. Fr.

212/34. *obeyid*: Like H, which omits 'du sourplus', added in DAB.

213/8. *gardeyne*: Strange rendering of 'bergier', presumably misread as *verger*.

213/14. *to* (1) *. . . cas*: 'a choses repugnans et aux cas'.

213/15-16. *they . . . it* (1): 'bien en veulent user'.

213/26. *and kunnynge*: *om*. Fr.

213/27. *auauntynge*: Like H, which omits 'et sans arrogance', added in DAB.

213/30. *and* (2): *om*. Fr.

214/1. *which . . . him*: 'ou il se devoit fier'.

214/3. *vndirstonde and comparid*, 215/2-3. *weyed and remembred*: DA have 'comparé et remembré'. R may have used a manuscript like BH, which add 'sceu'.

214/6-7. *but . . . labour*: *om*. Fr.

214/9. *And*, 215/7. *God*: Both R and U seem to have used a manuscript like H, which has a definite stop before this clause. AB have no stop, and D places a full stop after 'tesmoing'.

214/9-10. *of the realme*: *om*. Fr.

214/12. *diuerse . . . enpouerisched*, 215/9-10. *diuers . . . feith*: Fr. has 'en pluseurs hommes de tous estas si enferme et [de *add*. A] petite foy'. A seems superior, but note U's slavish rendering of 'petite foy' in DBH.

214/13-14. *the* (2) *. . . lorde*, 215/11-12. *the . . . lord*: 'l'adhesion de leur seigneur'.

214/15. *that war*, 215/12. *that is cleerly*: om. Fr.

214/17. *which*, 215/14. *the whiche*: The relative goes back to *the most parte of them* (R, l. 13) and *diuers men* (U, l. 9).

214/17–18. *of . . . releef*: om. Fr.

214/18–20. *Lo . . . notwithstondyng*, 215/14–17. *There . . . amonge*: Fr. has 'La est trouvee la fermeté et esprouvee la vertu ou sont les extremes perilz, quant le sens demeure entre'. *as whanne* (NSJ) seems to be a more likely rendering of 'quant' than *and whanne* (R). In U it is difficult to know whether *extreemys* is a scribal slip, a plural noun, or an inflected adjective.

214/21–2. *and . . . aventures*: 'et la constance ou mylieu des terribles aventures'.

214/23. *me . . . that*: om. Fr.

214/24–5. *though . . . might*, 215/19–20. *whan . . . socours*: 'quant l'in-fortune [la fortune B] d'icelle la rent plus besongneuse de bon [son BH] secours'.

214/27–8. *to . . . requierith*, 215/22–3. *to . . . neede*: 'les infortunes de son adversité aider a [& BH] soustenir et non lui defaillir de fait ne de couraige en necessité'.

214/29–30. *And . . . Mathathias*, 215/23–4. *This . . . Mathathias*: Fr. has 'Ceste maniere tint le vertueux homme et d'entier courage Mathathias'.

214/30. *as whanne*: This has no Fr. equivalent. Again R may have begun the sentence in one way and changed the structure in the middle.

214/32. *instaunce and*: om. Fr.

214/33. *certeyne*: Fr. adds 'pervers hommes'.

215/2. *rebellions*: 'forteresses rebellans'.

215/4. *so well*: om. Fr.

215/21. *redondeth*: Cf. 189/28.

216/2. *robbid, pillid*, 217/1. *taken, robbed*: 'destruite [om. ABH], prinse, pillee'.

216/2–3. *of . . . in*, 217/2–3. *and (2) . . . dispeire*: Fr. has 'et le peuple en servitute et dispertion'. Note U's *dispeire* for 'dispertion'; Worcester has 'desesperacion'.

216/4–5. *this wourshipfull*: om. Fr.

216/11. *whanne . . . togedir*: om. Fr.

216/16 ff., 217/11 ff.: See Livy, xxii. 53.

216/17–21. *which . . . cite*, 217/11–15. *which . . . that*: 'qui bien fait a ramentevoir comme, ou temps que la seigneurie romaine estoit si dure-ment foulee par Hannibal, aprés [et B] ses grans victoires, que es [des H] couraiges des Rommains n'avoit plus [om. B] comme nulle esperance de salut de leur cité et que'.

216/22. *the cite*, 217/16. *the . . . Rome*: 'la cite' B; 'leur cite' H; 'Romme' DA.

216/23–35. *Thanne . . . auctorite*, 217/17–26. *he . . . auctoritee*: See Introduction, p. 52.

217/2. *confusion*: This is not in the Fr. manuscripts I have seen, but Worcester has 'confusion'.

217/4. *the woofull fliers*: The Fr. manuscripts have 'les fuitiz et les desolez', but Worcester has 'douloureux' for 'desolez'.

217/7–8. *redemyd and bought*: 'racheterent'.

217/9. *by . . . agayne*: 'remistrent'.

218/3. *the . . . tyme*: 'tel estat'.

218/3–4. *haue . . . deserued*, 219/3–4. *haue* (2) *. . . deserue*: Fr. has 'en avons eu et avons bien besoing de plus que Dieu ne nous en donne et que nous n'en desservons'. R may have used a Fr. exemplar which omitted 'que Dieu . . . et'. Note again U's confusion between *desire* and *deserue*, which is probably scribal. Cf. 165/13.

218/4–9. *But . . . mortall*, 219/4–8. *And . . . mortall*: Fr. has 'mais, se nous en avons usé aucunement es [en nos H] plus grans besoings et maintenant aprés ung pou de amandement de la premiere infelicité, nous y defaillons, les meschiefz ou nous nous sommes trouvez ont esté [sont BH] tresmauvaiz, mais de [le ABH] rencheoir nous sera mortel'. In U *us* was probably omitted scribally after *to* (2) in l. 8.

218/13. *derke*: R is like B, which has 'obscures'; DAH have 'obstinee'. BH are plural here, however.

218/14–16. *don . . . ageyne*, 219/13–15. *which . . . custumes*: 'qui les ont a telz meschiefz asserviz, ains retournent des qu'ilz se sentent quelque peu deschargiez a leurs premieres acoustumances'.

218/16. *as . . . vomyte*, 219/15–16. *like . . . vomyte*: See Proverbs 26: 11.

218/17. *hopyng . . . prosperite*, 219/17. *and . . . prosperite*: 'pour l'esperance qui est de meilleur prosperité'.

218/18–19. *to . . . fortune*: 'en pis que le bruit de la premiere [? ceste H; telle B] confusion que nous avons a tel douleur passee, ce que ja Dieu ne vueille avenir' (B omits 'a tel douleur' and adds '& dolleur' after 'confusion').

218/20 ff., 219/20 ff.: Here Chartier launches into a discussion of finance in France. Sir John Fortescue might well have been interested in this passage, since he wrote of French finances and taxes in *The Governance of England*, chaps. 3–7, where he frequently compared England and France.

218/26. *For*: 'Ce puis je savoir que'.

218/26. *the prince*, 219/25. *our prince*: 'le Prince' BH; 'nostre prince' DA.

218/27. *nor levied*: om. Fr.

218/30. *the goodis*: om. Fr.

219/5. *it*: 'en' in Fr. refers to 'savance et constance'.

219/24. *yll*: Fr. has 'bien'. *yll* may be a scribal error.

219/26. *reuenues*: Cf. 189/8, where the U scribe also mistakenly wrote *reames* for *reuenues*.

219/26. *policye*: 'industrie'.

219/28. *more like*: om. Fr.

219/31. *the handes of*: om. Fr.

220/1. *by thes meanis*: om. Fr.

220/2. *and . . . away*: om. Fr.

220/8–9. *tyme* (3) . . . *season*, 221/7. *this . . . needfull*: 'ce temps besongneux'.

220/9–11. *Yet . . . tyme*: 'Et se plus large estoit la finance, l'aide et la revenue'.

220/12–13. *keping . . . the* (1): om. Fr.

220/17 ff., 221/13 ff.: The comment beginning here may refer to Louvet, who exercised great influence over the Dauphin and to whom Charles VII later gave many gifts. See Droz's note.

220/18–19. *takeyng . . . trouthe*, 221/14–16. *and . . . therto*: 'et convient traire par largesse les pluseurs a faire leur devoir ou loiauté ne les povoit mener'.

220/19–20. *longyng . . . werkis*: 'sur ce point'.

220/22. *the reason of*: 'les droiz et'.

220/23, 221/20. *case*: 'cas' BH; 'pas' DA.

220/23. *I suppose*: om. Fr.

220/24–6. *in to . . . deseruid*, 221/21–3. *by . . . it*: 'par trop despendre et se eslargir ou il n'affiert et mal recompenser ou donner a qui dessert'.

220/28. *be . . . egally*: 'soy tenir droicte'.

220/31–3. *wharas . . . prosperite*, 221/28–9. *there . . . deserued*: Fr. has 'n'eust des services mal congneuz et des biensfaiz mal deserviz'. U's rendering is awkward. 'des' means 'some', not *of the*, for example; only careless translation can account for this error, since U passed over 'des' the first time without difficulty. U has a double rendering for 'deserviz', which in Fr. can mean either 'rewarded' or 'deserved'. Perhaps two attempts of U to translate the Fr. word have been copied into the English text.

220/34. *reason*, 221/30. *abusion*: 'raison' H; 'evasion' DAB.

220/34–222/1. *suche . . . place*, 221/30–223/1. *euer . . . preiudice*: 'tousjours en est il mal prins, si ne doit l'usaige avoir lieu dont l'user porte prejudice'.

221/2. *all is*: 'du tout'.

221/6. *aides*: Fr. adds 'faiz au prince'.

221/7. *passed*: Fr. has 'paisible'. *passed* may be a scribal error picked up from l. 5.

221/8. *needfull besinesse*: 'gens et besoingnes'.

221/18–19. *by mesure*: 'et mesurent'.

222/2–3. *the . . . large*: Fr. has 'ce que la planté des biens et l'oiseux esloingnement de grans cures avoit fait ouvert et abandoné'. Note the easy confusion between 'cuers' and 'cures'.

222/4–6. *shewe . . . honour*, 223/4–7. *aught . . . prince*: 'ne s'i doye donner que la vertu de liberalité, qui tant bien siet en hault seigneur, n'ait tousjours vers le prince son effect'.

222/6–7. *right welle*: om. Fr.

222/7–12. *hath . . . prodigalite*: 'regarde lieu et temps de donner, et que en temps d'abondance et de oisiveté tele domnacion seroit dicte oeuvre de largesse qui maintenant se devroit appeler prodigalité'.

222/12–14. *Wherefor . . . themself* (1), 223/11–13. *Well . . . thaim*: 'Bien doivent avoir regard a ce que dit est ceulx qui trop pour eulx y pour-chacent, et plus en est sur eulx le pechié et la charge'.

222/16. *nay*: Fr. adds 'des siens'.

222/16–19. *For . . . prospere*, 223/15–18. *And . . . seruise*: Fr. has 'et qui se veult enrichir avecques ung prince necessiteux et accroistre trop grandement sa substance et son estat des biens de cellui qui peu en a pour la sienne sauver monstre par sa privee affection que son couraige est indigne de service publique'. Either R used an inferior Fr. manuscript, of which I have found no evidence, or he badly misunderstood the passage. *endeinith* seems to represent some confusion in rendering 'indigne'. The variants in RNSJ, especially the repetitive *and is in necessite* in NS, may reflect several attempts to render Fr.

222/19. *war*, 223/18. *were . . . gouerned*: 'se gouvernerent'.

222/20. *householdis*: Fr. adds 'et povoir'.

222/23. *but . . . speke*: om. Fr.

222/24–7. *for . . . people*, 223/22–5. *that . . . peeple*: 'c'est que aucuns chiefs et conditeurs de gens [de guerre *add.* B] prennent l'argent des gaiges de leurs souldoiers sans le leur departir, en les faisant vivre sur le peuple'.

222/27–8. *vpon* (2) *. . . renne*, 223/25. *folowith*: 'encourent'.

222/29–30. *so . . . for*: 'en soy continuant comme les grans larrons qui emblent a la seigneurie'.

223/14. *nobles*: 'franchise et noblesce'.

223/20. *diminued*: om. Fr.

223/28. *and reue*: This is omitted in Fr. although B adds 'et viure'.

224/1-4. *And . . . wele*, 223/31–225/3. *And . . . deede: wherefor thei* in l. 3 seems to be a scribal addition in R. For discussion of this passage, see Introduction, p. 53.

224/8-9. *to . . . profite*, 225/7-8. *for . . . lorde*: 'a leurs vies exposer pour le salut publique'.

224/12. *prosperite*: See Introduction, p. 17.

224/13 ff., 225/11 ff.: See Valerius Maximus, v. 6. ext. 1.

224/15. *that he ledde*, 225/12. *where . . . to*: Fr. has 'qu'il menoit'. Following this, both R and U are like ABH, which omit a superfluous 'que' added in D.

224/16-18. *The . . . bataile*, 225/13-14. *And . . . Codrus*: 'et combien que ceste responce feust venue a la cognoissance de ses ennemis et que defence feust faicte que nul ne se embatist a ferir Codrus'.

224/19. *havyng . . . wele*: om. Fr.

224/20. *his . . . harneys*, 225/15. *his . . . aray*: 'son abit royal en abit [vesture ABH] de saquement'.

224/21. *more . . . anothir*: om. Fr.

224/24. *Marcius Currius*, 225/17. *Marcus Tulius*: I have not emended the name in either R or U, since the Fr. manuscripts disagree. N's *Cursius* may be superior to *Currius* (RSJ), since D has 'Curcius' and AH have 'Cursius'. U is somewhat like B, which has 'tucius', but exactly like Worcester's 'Tulius'. For the story of Curtius, see Valerius Maximus, v. 6. 2.

224/24-5. *the . . . came*, 225/18. *the* (1) . . . *open*: 'la tresparfonde ouverture de la terre qui advint'.

224/27. *be remedied*: 'combler'.

224/28. *most*: Fr. adds 'digne et'.

224/29-30. *this . . . youthe*: 'le jouvencel'.

224/31. *that myght be*: om. Fr.

224/31. *toke . . . lepte*: 'saillit a cheval et tout armé'.

225/23. *of . . . thinges*: 'chose'.

226/1 ff., 225/25 ff.: This reference is to Decius Mus, who in 340 B.C. was supposed to have given Rome victory by devoting himself and his enemies to the gods below and then charging into the enemy ranks to his death. See Livy, vii. 34 ff. and viii. 9, and Valerius Maximus, v. 6. 5.

226/2-4. *Sampson . . . Israel*, 227/2-3. *And . . . Israel*: DB have 'et [om. H] Sanson le fort, pour les Philistiens ennemis du peuple d'Israël acravanter et confondre'. H, like R, omits 'et confondre'. Worcester, like R, has the uninverted structure: 'pour crauenter & confondre les philistiens'. See Introduction, p. 55.

226/12. *we . . . werkis*, 227/12. *this . . . susteyne*: 'ne povons ceste oeuvre bien mener'.

226/12–14. *in . . . profight*: 'toutesvoies elles nous deffaillent de fournir a suffisance et nous leur defaillons de les esploiter a prouffit'.

226/15. *woll we go to*, 227/15. *goo we to*: 'Reste'.

226/18 ff., 227/18 ff.: See Valerius Maximus, ii. 7.

226/18, 227/18. *which saith*: 'disant' BH; *om*. DA.

226/21–2. *Now . . . but*: See Introduction, p. 31.

226/22–3. *to . . . ordeigned*: 'loy ordonnee et gardee'.

226/25. *laboured . . . gette*: 'acquirent'.

226/27–30. *contrary . . . therfor*: 'contre droit de chevalerie ou contre le commandement du chief dont la punicion ne feust capitale ou mortelle'.

226/30. *Mavlius*, 227/29. *Manlius*: RSJ definitely corrupt the name to *Mavlius*; N has either *Manlius* or *Maulius*, like U. H seems to have 'Maulius', but DAB have it correct as 'Manlius'. See Valerius Maximus, ii. 7. 6, and Livy, viii. 7.

226/33. *of his fadir*, 227/31. *fadirs*: Fr. has only 'son'.

226/34–228/2. *and . . . lawe*, 227/33–229/2. *And . . . transgressoure*: Fr. has 'et en ce cas la victoire que fist le [ce B] vaillant [*om*. B] jouvencel comme vainqueur ne peut effacier la desobeissance qu'il fist comme transgresseur'. NSJ are less like Fr. than R, where *victorye* remains the subject. For U's *skonche* see 165/10 n.

227/1–2. *had . . . guydinge*: 'menoit et conduisoit' B; 'menoit' H; 'conduisoit' DA.

227/8. *vertu*: Like BH, which omit 'et' added in DA.

227/9. *the richesses*: *om*. Fr.

227/16. *had and*: *om*. Fr.

227/20. *that . . . possession*: 'acquises'.

228/4. *nature . . . be*: For the significance of the variants here, see Introduction, p. 20.

228/4. *mercifull*: Fr. adds 'pour le devoir de sang acquiter'.

228/5. *at that tyme*: *om*. Fr.

228/5–6. *egrely . . . armes*: Fr. has 'pour la loy d'armes aigrement [acomplu & *add*. H] observer'. *obserued* seems to mean 'observant', a meaning not in *OED*.

228/9. *notable lawe*: 'honnourable mestier'.

228/9–13. *Moreouir . . . roddis*: 'et, oultre de ceulx qui pour ces causes [*sing*. BH] ont esté capitalment punis, trouveroit on pluseurs es rommaines escriptures qui pour menues et petites negligences [dilligences BH] ont esté batuz de verges a l'estache'.

228/14 ff., 229/15 ff.: See Valerius Maximus, ii. 7. 4.

228/15, 229/15. *counseile of Cocta*: 'conseil Cocta' DA; 'conseil toca' H; 'conseil de Torca' B.

228/17, 229/17. *parte*: Like ABH and Worcester, which omit 'de la chose publique et', added in D.

228/18. *of . . . gouernaunce*: 'du logeis qu'il devoit garder'.

228/18, 229/18. *Lucius Tucius*: The reference is to C. Titius. See Valerius Maximus, ii. 7. 9.

228/20–1. *war* (2) . . . *werkis*, 229/20–1. *for . . . werkemen*: 'a servir de [*om.* H] pierres ceulx qui gettoient des [les B] fondes'.

228/24. *fynde and perceyve*: 'appercevons'.

228/26–8. *for . . . iustis*: The J omission was caused by the scribe's leap from *iustice* in l. 26 to *iustis* in l. 28. Here is one clear piece of evidence that RNS were not copied from J. See Introduction, p. 18.

228/27–9. *ther . . . matir*, 229/26–7. *they . . . iustice*: 'fault il une maniere de justice garder et [*om.* ABH] l'un vers l'autre, combien que justice ne soit ce pas, pour faulceté [faulte ABH] de la matiere et [*om.* H] de l'entencion'.

228/30–1. *the . . . faile*: 'en une famille faille'.

228/33–230/1. *the . . . lordis*: 'leur sceurté'.

229/9–10. *and deedys*: om. Fr.

229/19. *commaunded*: 'condempné'.

229/23. *the grete defautes*: 'les plus grans et difficilles choses'.

229/29. *obeisaunce*: Fr. adds 'vers ung chief'.

230/1, 229/31. *their enemyes*: 'leurs ennemis' B; 'les ennemis' DAH.

230/3–4. *vndir* (2) . . . *commaundour*, 231/3. *to . . . him*: 'a l'obeissance du [dun BH] commandeur [commandement H]'.

230/8. *iustice*: Fr. adds 'd'armes'.

230/9. *gouernaunce*: 'gouvernail' (rudder).

230/10. *O*, 231/9. *A*: om. Fr.

230/11–12. *if . . . othirwise*, 231/10–12. *that . . . correctours*: 'que qui vouldroit les abuz corriger en ceste partie plus y avroit de coulpables que de corrigeurs'.

230/12. *ouir his maister*: 'du maistre' B; 'du mestier' DAH.

230/13. *and . . . serchid*: om. Fr.

230/13–15. *and* (2) . . . *capiteynes*, 231/14–15. *and . . . himself*: 'mais chascun veult faire compaignie et [estre *add.* B] chief a part soy'.

230/16–17. *But . . . man*: 'Nul ne souloit estre'.

230/18. *On . . . side*: om. Fr.

230/22–8, 231/21–7. *And . . . abydyng*: Cf. R's freedom with U's more literal rendering: 'Or avient que sont faictes entreprinses ou sieges assis ou le ban des princes est crié et le jour souvent nommé pour les champs tenir, mais plusieurs y viennent par maniere plus que pour doubte d'y faillir et pour paour de avoir honte et de reprouche plus que pour vouloir de bien faire, et si est en leur chois le tost ou le tart venir, le retour ou la demeure'. R's *as it were* at 230/27 makes better sense than *is* (NSJ), but without *thei make* NSJ would follow Fr. exactly. Perhaps here again two attempts to translate the passage have come down in the manuscripts.

230/29. *thei loue*: om. Fr.

230/30. *noblesse and wourship*, 231/28. *the* (1) . . . *nobles*: Fr. has 'l'onneur de noblesse'. After this R and U are like B, which omits 'dont ilz les tiennent', added in DAH.

230/31-2. *they* . . . *goo*, 231/29-31. *right* . . . *restith*: 'voulentiers les portassent avecques eulx, comme les limaz qui tousjours trainent la coquille ou ilz se hebergent'.

230/33. *as* . . . *do*, 231/32. *in* . . . *goten*: 'par la maniere que elles leur furent acquises'.

231/5. *or trust*: om. Fr.

231/7. *and obserued*: om. Fr.

231/8-9. *in the see*: om. Fr.

231/11. *and giltye*: om. Fr.

231/14. *thenmyes*: Fr. adds 'par guerre'.

232/1. *olde awncientes*: 'anciens nobles [om. H] hommes [om. B]'.

232/2-3. *noblesses . . . right*: 'et les drois des noblesces'.

232/4-5. *to . . . abyding*: 'de voiager sans guaires de repos ne d'arrest'.

232/5 ff., 233/4 ff.: See Droz's notes about the foreign troops whose help the Dauphin obtained.

232/6. *put . . . passe*: 'passent'.

232/9-10. *hough . . . strokis*: Fr. has 'quel en sera le bruit, et se laisseroient avant chacer et charger du [om. BH] fais [om. BH] de la guerre jusques a estre deboutez de leurs maisons qu'ilz meissent paine de prevenir ne de chacer la guerre loing de soy'. R's Fr. exemplar may have omitted 'et charger . . . chacer', because of the repetition of 'chacer'. *hough the werkis shal be guydede* seems to mean 'what course the deeds will take'.

232/12. *and . . . honde*: om. Fr.

232/12-18. *we . . . people*, 233/14-19. *neede . . . men*: Cf. R's free rendering here with U: 'a convenu [faillu ABH] prendre ceulx que on a peu finer et faire sa [la H] guerre de gens acquis par dons et par prieres ou lieu de ceulx qui leur devoir et loiaulté y semonnoit. Si est faicte la guerre par gens sans terre et sans maison ou que [om. A; pour BH] la greigneur part, que necessité a contrains de vivre sur autrui'. At 232/15 note that NSJ add *of verray ryghtwysnes*; unless this is a rendering of 'et loiaulté', it has no Fr. equivalent.

232/19–20. *suche . . . suffre*: 'souffrir'.

232/20. *that . . . this*: 'de ce pechié'.

232/21. *sufficiauntly*: om. Fr.

232/23–8. *and . . . entent*, 233/22–8. *doo . . . performed*: Fr. has 'mectent [veullent mettre B] paine de tirer sur [les *add*. BH] champs les nobles pour aucun bien faire, ilz delaient [mettent H] si longuement a partir bien enviz et s'avancent bien [si AB; *om*. H] tost [*om*. H] de retourner voulentiers [*om*. B] que a paine se peut [pouent B] riens bien commencer, mais a plus grant paine entretenir ne [de H] parfaire'. B also replaces 'ilz . . . partir' with 'Aucuns sy mettent treslonguement et les pluseurs ne voullent partir au moins que'. The awkward *and* preceding *wold* in R has no Fr. equivalent.

232/29. *notwithstonding*: 'avecques'.

232/30. *that . . . them*: 'de pluseurs'.

232/30. *is founde*, 233/30. *is . . . a*: 'se treuve souvent [*om*. H] une [*om*. H]'.

232/31–4. *which . . . more*, 233/31–4. *that* (1) *. . . polecye*: R is much freer than U: 'que ceulx qui ne sauroient rien conduire par eulx ne vouldroient armes porter soubz autrui et tiennent a deshonneur estre subgiez a cellui soubz qui leur peut venir la renommee d'onneur que par eulx ilz ne vouldroient acquerir'.

233/1. *with . . . rest*: 'on y [*om*. BH] reposant'.

233/12. *that we suffre*: om. Fr.

234/1–6, 235/1–5. *O . . . opinyon*: Fr. has 'O arrogance aveuglee, folie et petite cognoissance de vertu, o tresperilleuse erreur en fait d'armes et de batailles, par ta malediction sont desroutees et desordonnees les puissances et les armes desjoinctes et divisees, quant chascun veult croire son sens et suivre son oppinion'. A combination of the reading in R with that in NSJ to produce *and of batailes* in ll. 2–3 follows Fr. *of the grette powers* in l. 4 in RSJ, omitted in N, may be a scribal error. In U note *constaunce* for Fr. 'cognoissance'.

234/6–7. *wanne . . . bettirs*, 235/5–6. *for . . . best*: 'pour soy cuider equiparer aux meilleurs'.

234/9. *I haue hard*: NSJ follow Fr. 'ay . . . ouy'.

234/9–10. *thei . . . an suche*: This is direct quotation in Fr.: 'Je n'yroie pour riens soubz le panon d'ung tel'.

234/10. *hym*: Fr. has 'le sien'. *hym* may be a scribal error in RSJ for *hys*; N's *men* is corrupt.

234/11–12. *But . . . it* (2): 'Et ceste parolle n'est pas assez pesee avant que dicte'.

234/12–13. *the* (1) *. . . warris*, 235/11. *the . . . heritage*: 'les lignaiges ne font [sont H] pas les chiefs des guerres [*sing*. BH]'.

234/13–15, 235/11–13. *suche . . . obeyed*: 'ceulz a qui Dieu, leurs sens ou leurs vaillances [*sing.* H] et l'auctorité du prince, en donnent [donne B] la grace doivent estre pour telz obeiz'.

234/15–16, 235/14. *is . . . yevin*: Fr. has 'n'est mie rendue'. The reference to the order of chivalry is interesting here. Both R and U translate the more emphatic Fr. negative with a more cautious phrase. Cf. S's *yolden*, with *yeuen* cancelled, with R's *yevin* and NJ's *yolden*.

234/17, 235/16. *proferre*: Fr. has 'preferer'. *OED* lists *proferre* as a by-form of (or error for) *prefer*, but only in the meaning 'promote, advance'. Here, however, the meaning is 'favour or esteem more'.

234/19–21. *And . . . obeisaunce*, 235/17–20. *We . . . yien*: Fr. has 'Mouvoir nous pevent a ce faire moult d'anciennes histoires, mais avec ce nous doivent contraindre [a ceste obeissance *add.* ABH] les maulx qui par oultrecuidance et faulte d'obeir sont avenuz et aviennent en noz vies [et *add.* ABH] devant noz yeulx'. The SJ scribes seem to have had difficulty reading *our yen* at 234/21; N also reflects the difficulty in *þer yen*. In l. 21 also, *foliship* (*MED folship, OED foolship*) in RSJ is replaced in N by *felyshipp*, meaningless in this context.

234/22. *reding of*: om. Fr.

234/22–3. *may . . . pryde*, 235/20. *ben . . . pride*: 'prouffitent a regectier [regreter A; reciter BH] ung pou [pour amatir B; contre *add.* H] cest orgueil'.

234/24. *of Rome*: om. Fr.

234/25–6. *and . . . labours*: 'a Romme de vaillanz hommes que on envoioit querre es champs ou ilz faisoient les [leurs BH] labours des terres'.

234/26 ff., 235/24 ff.: See Livy, iii. 26 ff., and Valerius Maximus, i. 8. 6, and iv. 4. 3, 7.

234/27–8. *streightly . . . faulte*: 'si craintivement obeiz que, ou les faultes'.

235/22. *senatours*: 'conseulz'.

236/2. *þat . . . dowbte*: om. Fr.

236/2. *peynes*: Like ABH, which omit 'honteux' added in D.

236/3. *defawtes*: Fr. adds 'plus cruelles'.

236/7, 237/7. *redde*: 'leu' BH; 'levé' DA.

236/9. *we . . . knyghthode*, 237/8–9. *is . . . cheualrye*: Fr. has 'nous disons tenir sur nostre chevalerie'. Even with the addition of *we* from NSJ, there may be scribal error in the English. *see* here may be intended as a form of *say*.

236/9–12. *Who . . . vsid*: 'Qui sera cellui qui me puist mectre avant ung hault honneur rendu pour vertueux service ne une seule correction pour deliz infiniz commiz en chief'.

236/14–15. *ther . . . people*, 237/13–14. *any . . . ignore*: Fr. has 'aucun en enquiert pour savoir ce que nul ne peut ignorer'. R's mistranslation is serious here. U's use of *ignore* is interesting: *OED* records the verb first in 1611 in the sense 'not to know', and *MED* does not list the verb. Godefroy says that Froissart used Fr. 'ignorer' = 'negliger' = 'disregard'; and this may be the meaning intended here, although *OED* records this meaning first from 1801 and says that it was regarded with disfavour and used with apology until *c.*1850.

236/16. *of the capiteynes*, 237/15. *of the prince*: There is no equivalent in any Fr. manuscript I have seen, but since both R and U add a phrase here, they may have Fr. support. R omits 'enfraindre les deffenses' following this.

236/17–18. *whanne . . . displesaunce*: Fr. has 'a qui qu'en desplaise'. N's omission was probably caused by the repetition of *liste*.

236/18. *and*: Fr. has 'pour garder choses abandonnees', not 'et'.

236/18–19. *withowte leve*: R seems to have used a manuscript like BH, which place 'sans cause' with 'livrer les forteresces' rather than with the preceding phrase, of which it is part in DA. Since *leve* is inserted in J and omitted in RNS, it may be a corrector's guess, not the original rendering.

236/19. *þemself*: Fr. adds 'de force'.

236/19–21. *At . . . profight*, 237/19–21. *at . . . aparte*: Fr. has 'au besoing faillir et soy rendre sans besoing, faire departir les compaignies [compaignons BH] et tenir [faire BH] compaignie a part'. 'sans besoing' might in DAB be interpreted as U does with 'faire departir', but H definitely places it with 'soy rendre'.

236/22. *any*: 'aucune' BH; 'une' DA.

236/25–6. *and . . . it is*, 237/25–6. *hou . . . it* (1): Fr. has 'de ce qu'il en est, [et add. ABH] a chascun de ce qu'il en congnoist'. *and* added from NSJ improves R's reading, although it does not exactly follow Fr.

236/27–8. *and wourshipfull*: om. Fr.

236/28. *to themself*: om. Fr.

236/28–31. *that . . . gette*, 237/27–30. *that . . . renoun*: Fr. has 'que a peu [paine BH] se laissent ja les pluseurs couller [contre H] en l'ordonnance des autres, sans difference de meurs ne de voulentez, et ne craingnent aucuns encourre male renommee'. Note U's easy confusion between 'contraignent' and 'craingnent'.

236/33. *for . . . hemself*, 237/31–2. *for . . . marke*: 'et doivent contre [entre AB] les autres celle [telle ABH] merche porter'.

237/5. *of the*: 'des' B; 'et' DAH.

237/14. *han be seen*: Fr. has 'avons nous veu'. *be* may be a scribal error for *we*.

237/17. *and leue*: om. Fr.

237/17. *left and*: om. Fr.

237/22. *defautes*: 'choses'.

237/23–4. *and redresse*: om. Fr.

238/1. *mysgouerned people*: om. Fr.

238/1. *in . . . founde*: 'nul d'eulx en son semblable ne laisse'.

238/2. *in . . . remedye*, 239/2. *withoute remedie*: 'sans y donner le [*om.* BH] remede'.

238/3 ff., 239/2 ff.: See Valerius Maximus, iii. 5. 1.

238/4. *rynge*: Fr. adds 'qu'il portoit'.

238/6–7, 239/6. *Marcus Staurus*: AH have 'staurus'; D has 'Scaurus'; B is unclear. See Valerius Maximus, v. 8. 4.

238/7. *hough . . . answer*: 'une responce de vertueux pere'.

238/12–13. *if . . . faute*, 239/10–12. *and . . . reproche*: 's'il lui feust rapporté mort par vaillance, [et *add.* H] qu'il ne le recevroit en sa maison aprés une faulte si deshonnourable'.

238/14–16. *Lo . . . man*, 239/12–14. *This . . . hert*: 'Ce fut dit de pere constant et entierement ferme de garder l'onneur de sa maison et de sa noblesce et fut sentence d'omme [donnee H] de grant gravité [crainte BH]'.

238/16–18. *Also . . . childern*, 239/14–17. *But . . . sonnes*: 'mais par la bouche de femme et [*om.* BH] de fraelle sexe fut en semblable cas seurmontée ceste parolle, quant une dame de haulte renommee vint a l'encontre de ses enfans'.

238/21–3. *Syn . . . yow*: This quotation is indirect in Fr.: 'puis que fouir vouloient, qu'ilz rentrassent ou ventre qui les avoit portez et que autre lieu n'avoit [nauoient ABH] pour les sauver'. Where R has *and entre*, N has *entre* and J has *reentre*. The S reading, however, is especially interesting in that the first letter *r* looks somewhat like the ampersand and the second letter is unclear, unlike the scribe's other *es*. R might easily have taken *and entre* from such a manuscript.

238/26–7. *Suche . . . prynces*, 239/25–6. *Than . . . prince*: Fr. has 'Si doit estre discipline de chevalerie et crainte d'onneur gardee es maisons des nobles comme en l'ost du [dun B] prince'. The addition of *be kept* from NSJ makes R's reading follow Fr. more closely, but the rendering is still awkward.

238/28. *savable*, 239/27. *saluable*: Fr. has 'salvable'. Both English words, and *soluable* at 225/3, seem to mean 'saving, protecting from anything undesirable', a meaning not given in *OED*. 'conducive to salvation', a later meaning under *savable*, comes nearest to the meaning required in the context here. *OED* quotes only Evelyn, a. 1706.

238/30–1. *For . . . that*, 239/29. *And . . . somme*: 'Et comme se' H; 'En somme, se' DA; 'Et somme se' B.

238/33. *which . . . by*: 'de'.

238/34. *Ostomyen*, 241/1. *Octauien*: Fr. has 'Octovien', referring to the Emperor Augustus, a favourite figure in Charlemagne and other romances. Droz says that Chartier was thinking of *L'histoire des Sept Sages de Rome*, where 'Octoviain César . . . très riche et convoiteux' appears. R may have misread the name and assumed that it was Osman, leader of the Ottoman Turks.

238/34. *that is*: 'qui fust' H; *om.* DAB.

239/5. *folowed . . . steppes*: 'ne faisoit pas les oeuvres'.

239/7. *reproche*: *om.* Fr.

239/8. *hertys and*: *om.* Fr.

239/29. *it . . . dreede*: 'la peur'.

240/2. *may . . . voide*: 'seroit au paraller irritee'.

240/4. *aneantisid*: Cf. 65/2, where *avauntise* occurs in error for *aneauntise*, as *andantisid* does here. The R scribe may not have been familiar with this word.

240/5. *is more by*, 241/6. *shuld . . . by* (1): 'devroit estre imputé a'.

240/7-8. *to . . . debate*, 241/7-8. *to* (1) . . . *strif*: 'a raconter pour entrer en contempcion [contencion BH; entencion A]'.

240/8-9. *vttirly . . . vse*, 241/8-9. *rather . . . thaim*: 'seroient [feroient A] du tout a traire [taire AH] a qui n'en vouldroit plus user'.

240/11-12. *So . . . say*, 241/11-12. *and . . . man*: 'et a tant suffise a chascun ce peu que j'en scay [say AH] dire'.

240/21. *of . . . thingis*: *om.* Fr.

240/22. *at this tyme*: *om.* Fr.

240/22-3. *that . . . therof*, 241/20-1. *that . . . daungers*: 'a qui [en *add.* ABH] sont [font H] les faiz et les dangiers'.

240/23. *But*, 241/21. *but of mageste*: 'mais je m'arreste' DBH; 'mais de maieste' A.

240/27-8. *in . . . mainteyned*: Fr. has 's'elle ne lui est baillee et maintenue'. Perhaps the omission of *wrongfully* in NSJ indicates that it is a scribal addition in R, but with the idea in the following sentence it does carry some significance here.

240/30-242/1. *But . . . come*: With the addition of *þat of* from NSJ, R slavishly follows Fr., which joins the two thoughts with 'et que des maistres viengne'.

241/4. *distiped*: Fr. has 'dissipee'. *distiped* may be a scribal error for the rare word *dissiped*, listed with examples only from 1597 and 1612 in *OED* and omitted in *MED*. Worcester may have 'distipee', although *t* is somewhat unclear and may be intended as *c*.

241/5. *good and haueure*: 'avoir'.

241/15. *replike*: *replique* is described as rare in *OED*, with the first example from 1549.

241/17. *The Knight*: This heading, not originally in U, was inserted by another hand. It is also omitted in B, which otherwise consistently names the speakers, as does U.

241/18. *the princes*: 'la magesté des princes'.

241/26. *leest*: 'mendres' B; 'membres' DAH.

241/26. *fallen*: Fr. has 'defaillie'. *fallen* may be a scribal error for *failen*.

241/26. *amonge the*: 'entre les' BH; 'es' DA.

242/4. *subiectis*: Fr. adds 'et seurmontables'.

242/8. *Alpees*, 243/8. *streyghtes*: Fr. has 'Alpees'.

242/11–12. *the . . . looke*, 243/12. *the . . . noblesse*: 'le meur adrecement et hault esgard'.

242/12 ff., 243/12 ff.: Perroy, 148–9, says that at the time Chartier was writing, Bertrand Duguesclin, referred to here, was a 'mediocre captain . . . swollen with self-importance and at the same time punctilious about chivalrous honour' and 'enjoyed a popularity out of all proportion to his talents and his exploits'. Perroy adds, 'he surpassed his fellows by his iron authority and the strict discipline he imposed on his mercenaries'. For the custom of cutting the cloth, Droz refers to G. L. Hamilton, 'The Descendants of Ganelon and of Others', *Romanic Review*, x (1919), 149, 156. This reference to Charles V, along with the reference to 1422 earlier, indicates that Chartier wrote in 1422 before the death of Charles VI on October 22.

242/13. *which*: 'qui' is in BH, which, however, change and expand the preceding passage.

242/13. *Bertrame*: Fr. adds 'le bon'.

242/13–15. *ouircome . . . peace*, 243/13–15. *vainquyssh . . . felicite*: 'vaincre les ennemis glorieusement et le royaume de grief maleur soy ressourdre en paisible bieneureté'.

242/16. *suche*: Fr. adds 'remonstrance en'.

242/16–17. *of . . . day*, 243/16. *of . . . discipline*: 'de discipline et [*om.* BH] de chevalerie, dont nous parlons'.

242/20. *Wherby . . . that*: *om.* Fr.

242/20, 243/19. *wourship*: Fr. adds 'et de sceurté [discipline militaire H]'.

242/22–6. *for . . . cruelte*, 243/20–5. *and (2) . . . cruelte*: Note R's greater freedom of rendering here: 'et ceste ouverture de [*om.* H] vengence rigoureuse forclouy toutes voyes aux faiz [de fait B] deshonnourables. [Et *add.* ABH] En cest endroit l'aspresse [la poeste B] de vengier chaudement teles [les H; manieres de *add.* B] honteuses offenses est tenue [a faire B] aux princes et haulx hommes a equité, qui en autre [aucuns B] cas seroit [pourroit estre B] pour cruaulté reputee'. (B also has 'Mais' for 'et haulx . . . qui'.)

242/28. *their grette*, 243/26. *grete*: *om.* Fr.

242/29. *and mekenesse*: *om.* Fr.

242/30–1. *disconfidence . . . hardines*: R misunderstood Chartier's intention here. Fr. has 'de confidence sceurté, de sceurté hardement'.

242/33. *growith*: om. Fr.

243/4. *surmountable*: The first record of this word in *OED* is from Cotgrave (1611).

243/10. *excercites*: Fr. adds 'd'armes'.

243/12. *destressid*: Fr. has 'mort'. *destressid* may be a scribal error for *decessid*. If not, it is a peculiar use of the word to mean 'exhausted', hence 'dead', or perhaps 'overwhelmed, crushed in battle'.

243/30. *good . . . guydinge*: 'conduire'.

243/32. *of rancore*: 'de rancune' B; om. DAH.

244/1. *at this tyme*: om. Fr.

244/1. *in this mater*: 'es debas de ceste matiere'.

244/2–4. *suche . . . trouthe*, 245/2–4. *thaim . . . maner*: 'ceulx qui ont les faiz publiques a conseillier d'en acquitter leurs loiaultez plainement'.

244/5. *the* (1) *. . . lordis*: 'les choses proufitables aux communitez et aux seigneuries'.

244/5–6, 245/6–7. *And . . . reason*: 'qui [ne add. ABH] donne conseil [si non add. ABH] a l'appetit, non pas a la raison'.

244/7. *certainly*: om. Fr.

244/9. *defaultes*: 'difficultez'.

244/13. *to . . . thingis*, 245/14. *to speke more*: 'de adjouster aucune autre chose [a ses parolles descripti add. A; a ses parolles add. B; a parolles add. H]'.

244/17. *offences*: Fr. has 'deffences'. Since *defense* is sometimes used in R (34/6, 35/6) and elsewhere in Middle English to mean 'offence', it would be interesting if here 'offences' were used to mean 'defences'. I have found no record of such use elsewhere, however, and R may mean only 'attacks' or 'faults', both of which fit the context.

244/20–1. *the . . . neyghboure*, 245/21. *the* (1) *. . . othir*: 'vitupere de son prouchain'.

244/23. *infortune*: 'fortune'.

244/24–6. *ye . . . founde*, 245/25–6. *to . . . remedies*: 'peut a tous ensemble venir ce [le AB; de H] bon eur que chascun veult [et doit add. B] querir par divers remedes'.

244/27–8. *me . . . that*: om. Fr.

244/28–9. *but . . . to*: 'ne plus negligens [moins dilligens B] ou [et B] mains [om. B] enclinez a'.

244/29. *own*: 'commune'.

244/29–30. *lyke as don*, 245/30. *than*: 'que font' H; 'que sont' DAB.

244/30. *iustely*, 245/30–1. *in . . . swarme*: 'en leur essaim' D; 'en leur exam' A; 'en leur examen' H; 'en leur endroit' B.

244/31–246/3. *and . . . right*: Note R's free translation here: 'et mectent leur vie pour deffendre et entretenir leur assemblee et leur petite pollice et pour garder la seigneurie de leur roy qui regne entre elles soubz une petite ruche, que moult de foiz, quant il est navrez en leurs batailles contre une autre compaignie d'autres mouchetes, elles portent et soustiennent a leurs eles et se laissent mourir pour luy maintenir sa seigneurie et sa vie'. *litill praty roofe* obviously means 'little beehive'. *OED* records *praty* in one instance as an error for 'petty', and it may be so here.

245/4. *they*: om. Fr.

245/7. *playn*: om. Fr.

245/19. *discharges*: Like BH, which omit 'l'un vers l'autre', added in DA.

245/20. *oonly*: Like BH, which omit 'en tant', added in DA.

245/31. *kepe* (1): Fr. adds 'leurs offices et'.

246/4. *So . . . tyme*: om. Fr.

246/4. *chiding and debate*, 247/3. *chidinges and debates*: It is interesting that both R and U translate 'tençons' with this doublet.

246/5. *holde your peace*: Like BH, which omit 'souffrez ou' in 'souffrez ou surseés' (DA).

246/10. *neyburs*: Fr. adds 'en la lectre'.

246/10–11. *Wherfor . . . fruytfull*, 247/10–11. *and . . . frutefull*: 'et que cy en droit n'aiez pas disputacion haineuse, mais fructueuse'.

246/13–14. *their saying*, 247/14. *that was said*: om. Fr.

246/17. *in . . . processe*, 247/16. *in . . . memorye*: 'a memoire et a fruit'.

246/19. *I woll that*: Fr. has 'sers' in the imperative, translated in R as *thou serue*.

246/21. *Rome*: Fr. adds 'et renforça leurs couraiges a vertu'.

246/21. *did the feighters*: 'les glaives des combatans'.

246/25. *euery man*: 'chascun' BH; 'chascun lecteur' DA.

246/25–7. *that . . . werke*, 247/25–6. *tendrely . . . operacion*: 'le voulloir interpreter favourablement et y jugier a [et ABH] cognoistre la bonne affection plus que la gloire de l'ouvraige'.

THE GLOSSARY

In accordance with EETS practice, *y* when it represents a vowel is treated as a variant of *i*; *i* when it represents a consonant has the place of modern *j*; *u* and *v* when they represent consonants have the place of *v*, and when they represent vowels the place of modern *u*; and initial *ʒ* is treated as *y* except in the few proper names in which it is a form of *Z*. References are to page and line numbers; in *The Quadrilogue Invective* even page numbers occur in the R version and odd numbers in the U version. Usual verb forms (i.e., *-eth*, *-ith* in present third singular, *-est*, *-ist* in present second singular, *-en* in present plural, *-ed*, *-id* in past tense and past participle, and *-ing* in present participle) are not recorded unless variant forms occur in the treatises. An asterisk beside a page/line reference indicates an editorial emendation not found in the English manuscripts. Abbreviations of grammatical terms are those of *OED* except that *n.* is used for 'noun' unless *sb.* is contrasted with other functions.

a ? *prep.* in 99/14 (yn NJ; see note).
aback *adv.* back 192/25; *see* **drawe**, **putte**.
abasche *imp. refl.* be upset or surprised 43/26. **abas(c)hith** (R), **abaisshith** (U) *pr. 3 sg.*, *pl.* disconcert(s), make(s) afraid 160/7, 161/6. ~ *your co(u)rages* makes your hearts afraid 154/9, 155/7, 162/35. **abaisshed** *ppl. adj.* upset, afraid 149/21.
abate *v.* destroy 14/19; humble 49/25; *pp.* diminished 13/9; diminished in power and vigour 19/7. *abatid of* brought down from 155/26.
abating *vbl. n.* destruction 157/14.
aba(u)ndo(u)ne, habando(u)ne *v.* surrender 216/29, 237/16; depart from 217/16; discard 85/17 (*MED*, *OED* meaning om.); *pp.* yielded utterly 172/6, 173/6; given away without restraint 223/4 (*MED*, *OED* meaning om.); given up as lost 214/16, 215/13. ~ *the bridyll to let* (sth.) run unrestrained 93/31.

abandened *pp.* 70/29; **abondoned** 214/16; *see* **bandon**.
abbregement *n.* epitome 122/31.
abhominacion *n.* defilement 205/1; *pl.* vile practices 18/8.
abide *v. tr.* hope for 74/17; await 43/12, 191/20; *intr.* hope 79/27; wait 190/20; remain 16/4, 159/19, 230/33; dwell 198/33; face 8/4. ~ *vpon* hold to 119/28. ~ *with* tolerate 57/27. **abyde** *pr. pl.* 68/8; **abyden** 83/20. **abo(o)de** *pa. t. sg.* 4/27, 21/3 (**aboyd** J), 159/19. **abyde** *pp.* 52/24; **abydin** 6/7; **abydyn** 146/5. **abiding** *pr. p.* submitting to 81/11.
abiding(e), abydyng *vbl. n.* existence 68/19, 113/7; permanence, continuance 30/4, 212/14; remaining 81/23, 230/28, 231/27; delay 43/9, 74/31; waiting for 7/27; expectation 42/6, 68/19; *pl.* 68/20. ~ *vpon* expectation of 123/17. *toke his* ~ *vpon* gained his position by 96/23.
abilementis *n. pl.* warlike supplies 220/13.

abisme *n.* deep chasm 203/21.

abled *pp.* enabled 55/12; endowed with fitting strength 57/22.

abode *n.* delay 141/4.

above *prep.* superior to 28/22; more than 41/4, 66/1, 202/17, 203/15; not exposed to the influence of 106/19. ∼ *alle this* in addition to all this 179/12; *see* **reason.**

abregge *v.* shorten the coming of 17/23; **abreggein** shorten 17/18. **abriggid** *pp.* removed 61/30.

abrode *see* **alle, caste, springe.**

absentid *pp.* withheld 66/9 (*MED* meaning om.; *OED* 1530).

abused *pa. t.* misguided, deceived 93/10; *pp.* 47/20, 187/17.

abusing *vbl. n.* deceiving 90/31.

abusion *n.* corrupt practice 48/1; falsification, especially heresy 82/5, 221/30.

accessaryes *n. pl.* things assisting, but subordinate 226/7, 227/7.

accesse *n.* fever 209/23.

accidence *n.* in *by the* ∼ through secondary means, incidentally 62/12.

accompenied, accompanyed *pp.* ∼ *to* joined with 76/11. ∼ *with* allied with 110/33; attended by 96/4 (**ac(c)ompayned** N).

ac(c)ompte *n.* answering for conduct or discharge of responsibilities 30/22. *make* ∼ *of* compute 218/31. *yelde* ∼ render account 45/31.

accompten *pr. pl.* count 180/29.

accorde *v.* agree 40/10; be suitable or proper 81/7. ∼ *to* agree concerning 97/16. ∼ *with* be consistent with 90/24. **according** (*to*) *pr. p.* corresponding 61/25.

accroche *v.* acquire 160/10.

acerteyned *ppl. adj.* secure 40/31.

achyved *see* **atcheue.**

acquitaill *see* **aquitale.**

acquite *v.* fulfil, act according to 159/4, 245/3; *refl.* discharge one's duties 244/3.

acquyting *vbl. n.* acting according to 180/21.

acte *n.* edict 171/6; *pl.* see 208/23 note.

actuelly *adv.* actively 155/14.

ad- *see* **a-.**

ad(d)ressid *pa. t.* directed 29/25; *pp.* 134/14, 135/17.

addressinge *vbl. n.* directing 24/25.

adhesion *n.* attaching oneself as a supporter 89/18, 215/11 (*MED* om.; *OED* 1624).

ado *see* **haue.**

aduersite *n.* perversity 99/16 (see note).

advoutrye *n.* adultery 131/27.

afer(re) *adv.* from afar 71/6. ∼ *out of* far away from 213/28.

affection (-cion) *n.* influence 66/14; loving feeling 108/8; good will toward 143/30, 244/21, 245/21; *pl.* 142/33; partiality 161/15; *pl.* 160/17; state of mind, nature, inclination 33/18, 194/24, 195/24; *pl.* 139/34, 140/1; *pl.* wills, wishes 110/26, 222/18, 223/17; intentions 40/3.

affectuelly *adv.* so as to answer the purpose (confused with *effectually*) 233/28.

affrayingly *adv.* with alarm 165/19 (*MED, OED* word om.; related to Sc. *affrayitly*).

aftir *prep.* in imitation of 38/17, 77/14; according to 16/24, 22/5, 210/17, 211/18. ∼ *that* (*conj.*) according as 167/4; *see* **looke.**

agains *see* **ayeinst.**

agaynsaide *pp.* denied 34/24.

age *n.* lifetime 18/11, 103/25.

ageyne *prep.* with regard to 121/5. **agayn** to meet 239/17; cf. **ayeinste.**

ageinward *adv.* on the other hand 142/17; **agaynewarde** 143/16.

agraued *pp.* made more grievous or serious 177/30 (*MED* om.; *OED* rare; see note).

agreable *adj.* fitting 122/3.

agreably *adv.* willingly 101/11.

agreuid *pp.* distressed 149/18.

ai *adv.* always 227/7.

aydes *n. pl.* grants to a king, as in war 219/32, 220/1.

aknowe *pp.* in *be* ∼ acknowledge 177/2.

alerion *n.* eagle without beak or feet 68/6 (*MED* om.; *OED* 1605).

alightid *pp.* relieved 25/6 (**alyghthed** N).

alightyngys *vbl. n. pl.* alleviations 74/32.

all(e) *adv.* completely, fully 25/24, 194/10, 215/2. ~ *abrode* over the entire surface 144/22.

al(l)day *adv.* always 42/18, 114/1, 136/24.

allegeaunce *n.* relief 67/11.

al(l)iaunce *n.* harmony 31/13; allies 140/11, 141/10. **alliauneces** *pl.* bonds of affection, trust, etc. 24/4.

all ther moost *phr.* most of all 149/7 (see note).

allthough *conj.* as if 183/8.

alone *adj.* without an equal 147/15.

along *adv.* ~ *from* far from 232/10.

alowable *adj.* praiseworthy 15/31.

alowe *v.* praise 46/27, 170/9. **alowed** *pp.* 10/18; **alloude** 171/9.

also that *adv. conj.* in the same way as 87/24.

altrid *pp.* deteriorated 208/22; **alterned** 209/22 (? scribal error or confusion with *alternen* = 'vary, alternate').

amate *v.* dismay 63/5.

amynushith *pr. 3 sg.* diminishes 136/3 (**amynuseth** NS). **admynusid** *pa. t.* 222/20. **amynusid** *pp.* 190/5.

ampte *n.* ant 170/15.

anaged *adj.* inveterate 157/2 (*MED* om.; *OED enaged* 1593).

anamowrid vpon *pp.* in love with 67/6.

and *conj.* with 72/3, 118/22.

aneauntise *pr. pl.* bring to nought, destroy *65/2. **aneantisid** *pp.* *240/4.

anempst(e) *prep.* against, toward 65/6; in preparation for 170/16.

angre *n.* grief 18/10; **angur** 74/26.

annyed *pp.* vexed 147/4.

annoye *n.* discomfort, trouble 73/11, 104/18.

an(n)oye *v.* molest, vex 4/12, 9/3, 190/15. **anoyeng** *ppl. adj.* troublesome 11/13.

annouse *adj.* disturbing, vexatious 207/17 (? scribal spelling error for *anniouse*); cf. **ennoyouse**.

anoynted *pp.* lit., besmeared, hence glutted 197/16 (*MED*, *OED* fig. meaning om.; Fr. 'aouillees').

anon *adv.* again at this time 131/16.

anuncied *pp.* made known to 159/18.

apayred *pp.* impaired 49/29.

aparte *adv.* aside 123/13; individually 10/2, 153/29, 186/16, 187/14.

aplying of *vbl. n.* achieving 146/27.

apparence *n.* probability 42/7; sign to sight or understanding 70/27 (*MED* meaning om.; *OED* rare 1587; see note). **apparaunce** appearance 202/10.

apperceyue *pr. pl.* observe 229/23; *pa. t.* 149/20. *pr. 2 sg.* recognize 32/22.

appere *v.* be discovered 67/34. **appeerid** *pa. t.* was shown 227/28.

apperteyneth *pr. 3 sg.* befits 203/13. **apperteyne** *pl.* belong 201/32. *pa. t.* was proper 21/2.

appesing *vbl. n.* ? satisfaction, placating 202/28 (Fr. 'palier' = 'disguise the enormity of').

ap(p)etite *n.* fancy, preference 34/17, 52/20; inclination 72/6; desire, will 22/2; *pl.* 212/21, 213/21. *aftir the* ~ just as one pleases 244/6; sim. *to the* ~ *and pleasir* 245/6. ~ *sensitif* see 21/18 note.

applie *v.* adapt 100/13; devote 65/15, 196/16; use 93/12. ~ *of* use in 81/16. ~ *to* use 52/19; *refl.* set oneself to achieve 44/16, 61/27.

appostomed *ppl. adj.* fig., festered, swollen 7/25 (*MED* only noun fig.; *OED* 1626).

appropird *pp.* attributed as proper 113/26; **appropred** 117/23.

approwith *pr. 3 sg.* commends 170/9. **appro(o)ued** *pp.* tested, made sure 215/15, 233/22; **apprevid** 232/23.

aquitale *n.* fulfilment 4/4. *true acquitaill* dutiful or faithful conduct 181/18–19.

arayed *ppl. adj.* in *in poynte* ~ properly made ready for battle 181/25.

arbitracion *n.* deciding according to one's will 119/5.

arbytriment *n.* freedom of will 112/29.

arche *n.* ark 27/5.

areste *n.* moral restraint 64/25.

arestid *pa. t.* resided, waited 76/36 (see note).

argue *v. tr.* consider 100/16.

argument *n.* proof 67/33; subject 127/2 (*MED* meaning om.; *OED* 1570).

Aristogracye *n.* government by those best fitted to rule 55/26, 56/8 (*MED* om.; *OED* 1531, spelling om.).

armories *n. pl.* armorial bearings 147/30 (*MED* meaning om.).

arte *n.* in *the divine* ∼ skill resulting from divine knowledge 28/16-17. **artes** *pl.* ? skills, craftsmanship (*MED*, *OED* om. in pl.), ? scribal error for *arces* 161/24 (Fr. 'ars' = 'arches').

artificiall *adj.* skilfully made 137/34.

artificieuse *adj.* artful, skilful 145/19 (*MED* om.; *OED* 1530).

aruspices *n. pl.* ancient Roman soothsayers 225/20 (*MED* om.; *OED* 1584).

as *adv.* likewise 60/28, 231/7; used to introduce a contracted question 117/4 (*MED* om.; *OED* 1579). *is* ∼ *moche to say* ∼ means 55/1-2.

as *conj.* as if 7/1, 10/3; so as (with inf. of result or purpose) 88/24; that 63/18; when 187/1; *see* whanne.

asche *see* axe.

askyng *vbl. n.* question 127/2.

assayith *pr. 3 sg.* tries 80/22, 94/1. **asaiyd** *pp.* tested by experience 8/15.

assemble *n.* union 29/3, 95/24; group 244/32; **assemblees** *pl.* 245/32.

assemble *v.* collect, gather 147/14; *pa. t.* 58/23; *pp.* made 147/8; made up, composed 145/20.

assigned *pp.* ordained 85/18; allotted 128/28.

Assimylatyve *n.* see 21/23 note.

assistid *pa. t.* gave support to 76/36 (Fr. 'assirent' = 'fix'; see note).

as(s)oile *v. tr.* answer 33/4, 45/27; refute 220/29; *pp.* 76/26; *v. intr.* absolve from sin 48/25.

assottid *adj.* foolish 173/1.

assur(e) *imp.* make secure 107/14; *refl.* have confidence 99/19; *pr. subj. refl.* 79/30. **assured** *pp.* secure 99/25; *ppl. adj.* 99/24; **aswryyd** reassured 66/23 (Fr. 'assoulagié').

astate *see* estate.

astonied *pp.* dulled, benumbed 12/8.

aswagith *pr. 3 sg.* alleviates 69/21.

at *prep.* from 114/24; with 198/28, 199/24; in a condition of 242/14.

atcheue *v. abs.* perform successfully 154/17 (*MED* meaning om.; *OED* 1607). **achyved** *pp. tr.* gained 77/13.

atte *prep.+art.* at the 176/2.

attey(g)ne *v.* obtain, reach 76/28, 233/34; fig., come as far as 140/25, 141/26. **atteyned** *pa. t.* arrived at 73/11. ∼ *to* get to know 58/15, 139/33; ∼ *to knowe* 101/13; ∼ *to vndirstonde* 71/2; ∼ *to the knowlage* 98/7. **atteynte** *pp.* ? achieved, ? condemned 96/28 (see note); affected 164/22; **ataint** 165/23. **attained** fig., corrupted, tainted 139/11.

attemp(e)raunce *n.* temperance 93/28; proper care 40/20.

attempte *v.* violate 108/31 (see note).

attendaunce *n.* attention 7/12 (Fr. 'vent'). *yeve attendence* accompany or wait upon 58/3.

attende *v. intr.* give heed (to) 15/29; *pa. t. tr.* expected 87/8; looked forward to 107/9.

attribucions *n. pl.* attributes 117/7 (*MED* om.; *OED* 1596).

attribute *v.* assign 121/31; *pp.* ascribed as belonging or appropriate (to) 117/16 (*MED* om.; *OED* 1538); ascribed (to an author) 58/23.

auctorysith *pr. 3 sg.* sanctions 170/10. **auctorisid** *pp.* 44/12; made legally valid 128/14; *ppl. adj.* highly esteemed 21/5, 47/12.

auctorite(e) *n.* power to inspire belief 21/5; divine authority 25/24; power to influence others 153/26; supremacy 216/35, 217/26. *in* ∼ in position of power 86/26.

audience *n.* opportunity to be heard 51/35. *gat* ∼ obtained hearing, 'got followers' 89/34-5.

auncientis *n. pl.* ancient Greeks and Romans 10/14 (*MED* meaning om.; *OED* 1541).

availe *n.* profit 10/10.

availe *v. intr.* be effectual 141/34, 240/2; *pr. 3 sg. tr.* profits 10/20. *what* ∼ (*it*) of what use is it 14/17, 119/20.

avaunce *v.* help 214/25; *pr. 3 sg.* raises 31/16; *imp.* hasten 30/34; *pa. t. refl.* 17/18; *refl.* came forward 16/5; *pp.* profited 8/2; presented (as a gift) 62/1 (*MED* meaning om.; *OED* 1509).

avaunte *n.* in *madest* ∼ boasted 94/10.

auauntynge *vbl. n.* boasting 213/27.

avauntyst *pr. 2 sg. refl.* boast 95/7.

auenterous *adj.* rashly daring 191/25; **aduenturous** 190/25.

aventur(e), aduenture, a(d)ventour *n.* fortune 10/4; *pl.* 100/16; peril, loss 150/18, 151/24; *pl.* 155/22; happenings 103/21; hazardous enterprises 204/20, 205/20. *put in* ∼ put in jeopardy 18/30, 224/6, 225/5; *sett(yng) in* ∼ 181/23, 191/11.

aventured *ppl. adj.* perilous 77/26.

avise, advise, aduyce *n.* judgement, opinion 81/17, 98/11; counsel 100/12; wisdom 184/13, 185/11. *take* ∼ deliberate 241/11. *take good* ∼ consider well 240/11.

avise *v.* counsel 13/32; *imp.* consider 19/29, 166/30; *refl.* 15/3.

avisement *n.* counsel 81/26. *take good* ∼ consider well 97/35.

avoide *v.* put an end to 119/29, 245/22. **auoideth** *pr. 3 sg.* empties 171/13. **avoydid** *pp.* cleared out 7/10.

avoued *pa. t.* made a vow of 225/25. **avowed** *pa. t. refl.* took a vow 226/1. ∼ (*vpon*) *pp.* made good (against) 130/26.

avowes *n. pl.* vows 71/13.

awaiting *pr. p.* watching for a chance (to do something) 193/18; **awaytinge** *ppl. adj.* 193/8.

awaitinges *n. pl.* ambushes, plots 213/1.

awaytis *n. pl.* ambushes, plots 210/33.

axe *v.* ask for 46/17; *pr. subj.* inquire about, wonder 188/16. *axeth his way* asks directions 116/2. **askethe** *pr. 3 sg.* 122/26. **axe** *pr. subj.* 51/35. **asche** *pl.* 182/1; **aschyn** 168/12. **asked** *pa. t.* 115/23. **axid** *pp.* 198/20.

axtre *n.* axle 121/2.

ayein *adv.* again 168/18; **aȝeine** 134/15.

aye(i)nst(e) (R), **ageinst** (R), **agains(t)** (U) *prep.* against 3/14, 166/25, 167/23; counter to 103/29, 110/22; to meet 238/18; to 118/20; towards, in regard to 151/7, 156/10, 177/9; in preparation for 171/15, 185/10; in the sight or presence of 173/30; cf. **ageyne.**

ayel *n.* grandfather 111/16.

bablid *pa. t.* stammered 7/23.

bayne *n.* bath 10/31.

bandon *n.* in *a* ∼ at one's own free will, unrestrainedly 94/22.

banne *n.* summons to arms 231/22.

banne *v.* curse 175/2.

bapteme *n.* baptism 18/35.

barat *n.* contention 131/7.

bare *see* **bere.**

barris *n. pl.* pieces of wood making fast the head of a wine cask 7/12 (*MED* meaning om.; *OED* 1520).

bastard *adj.* counterfeit 78/13.

bataileuse *adj.* warlike 139/14 (*MED, OED* spelling om.).

batail(li)s, batelles, batallis *n. pl.* armies 50/22, 104/4, 105/28, 234/25, 235/22.

bathid *pp.* fig., immersed 65/17 (*OED* 1526, *MED* related uses earlier).

bawme *n.* fig., healing influence 69/20.

be *v.* be *am pr. 1 sg.* 164/35, 165/34; *is* 173/28. *art(e) 2 sg.* 8/2, 174/20, 175/20. *is 3 sg.* 3/27, 143/7. *be pl.* 3/29, 139/4; *by* 5/22, 227/9; *ben(e)* 13/14, 153/13; *benne* 106/27; *been* 156/12; *is* 159/1, 218/29; *ar* 113/16; *arn* 97/2, 155/19. *be subj.* 11/20. *was pa. t. 1, 3 sg.* 4/4, 145/16; *vas* 178/9. *war(re) 2 sg.* 9/27; *wer* 174/32; *was* 175/31. *war(re) pl.* 3/6, 214/33; *wer(e)* 3/12, 191/3; *weren* 33/23; *was* 220/7. *be pp.* 7/1, 157/13; *ben(e)* 5/21, 199/16.

be *see* **by, bye.**

become, bycome *v.* in *is* ∼ has become 77/2. *wher(e) is* ∼ what has

become of 28/5, 154/25–6, 155/22–3;
whereynne is ∼ 137/33. *wher shall
we* ∼ what shall become of us 67/
17.
been *n. pl.* bees 247/1.
before, bifore *adv.* ahead of time 30/
31; in front 6/20, 238/20, 239/19.
so ferr ∼ so deeply 30/32 (Fr. 'si
auant').
beforn *prep.* before 165/11.
beggernesse *n.* beggary 167/8 (*MED,
OED* word om.).
beggyng *ppl. adj.* ? causing begging,
? accompanied by begging 169/12
(*MED, OED* meaning om.; see
note).
begilith *pr. 3 sg.* disappoints 78/14.
beholden *v.* take note 105/7. **be-
holde** *pp.* morally obliged 221/14.
behovefull *adj.* necessary, expedient
71/6, 113/28.
being *n.* state 40/8, 119/15; existence
72/9.
belding *n.* building 27/33; **bilding**
40/7.
belongith *pr. 3 sg. impers.* (it) is
appropriate 96/15.
benefice *n.* favour 68/13; ecclesiastical living 131/3.
ber(e) *v.* endure, suffer 37/19, 151/
24; have 66/31, 104/7; yield 114/
25, 147/14; wear 145/15, 238/6, 239/
6; hold (office) 43/33; carry 6/19,
164/34, 165/34; harbour 221/31;
support 149/15; *abs.* bear fruit 40/
18. ∼ *awey* get 8/15. ∼ *oute*
support, abet 90/10, 200/6; thrust
out 214/27; pay for 218/22; bear
232/16. ∼ *vp* exalt 9/12; support
79/25, 148/10. ∼ *recorde* testify
48/9. ∼ *witnesse* is evident 61/19
(*MED, OED* meaning om.; Fr.
'se manifeste'). ∼ *on honde* maintain (falsely) 194/26, 194/28; ?
make known 17/14 (see note). **ber**
pr. pl. 194/26; **berith** 48/9; **beren**
40/18. **bar(e)** *pa. t. 1, 3 sg., pl.*
9/12, 69/16, 238/6, 239/6; **bore** 6/
17. **barest** *pa. t. 2 sg.* 66/31 (see
note). **born(e)** *pp.* 8/15.
beseen *pp.* dressed 203/4.
besege *n.* saddle-bag 6/19.
besely *adv.* diligently 154/14.

besette rounde *pp.* surrounded,
assailed 214/2.
beshynyng *pr. p.* illuminating 21/11.
besyde of *prep.* near, but not in
direct contact with 193/18.
besines(se) *n.* trouble 186/16; occupation 191/22; affairs 206/8; matters
demanding attention 221/8.
best *adv.* most largely 139/6.
beste *n.* in *take it to the* ∼ make the
best of it, accept it goodnaturedly
116/17 (*MED for the best*).
bestiche *adj.* beastlike, hence primi-
tive 127/15 (**beestysshe** J; **bees-
tyhsse** N).
betake *v.* take 243/1.
bete *imp.* atone for 179/22. ∼ *down
(inf.*)? build, in sense of 'write'
(*MED, OED* meaning om.), ? suppress 95/27 (Fr. 'bastir'; see note).
betokene *pr. pl.* symbolize 24/14.
bettyr *adv.* rather 111/20.
bewepte *ppl. adj.* disfigured by weep-
ing 144/10.
by *see* be.
by, be *prep.* by means of 32/28, 167/
8; from 171/29, 221/3; with 207/
18; because of 44/11, 79/11; according to 24/7, 45/12; as a means of,
for 74/29, 86/17; during, for 107/
23; in 159/1. ∼ *this day* now 162/
29–30. ∼ *as moch as* to the degree
that 117/6.
bidin *pa. t. pl.* remained 216/34.
bye *v.* pay for 181/11; procure by
sacrifice 184/29; **be** 185/26. **bought**
pa. t. redeemed 216/13, 217/8.
bignesse *n.* size 137/21 (*MED* om.;
OED 1529).
bygvnne *pa. t.* began 164/20. **bygon-
ne** *pp.* started in office 55/11.
byhilde *pa. t.* beheld 148/6.
bilafte *pp.* abandoned 173/16; **bileft**
213/31.
bynde *v. intr.* condemn for sin 24/30,
41/15, 48/25; *tr.* control, restrain
34/29, 150/27, 151/32; oblige 150/
7, 151/8. **bounde** *pp.* 97/28, 151/
8; **bounden** 220/17; **bownden**
232/8; *see* **bounde.**
byndyng *vbl. n.* confining 84/22.
bytinge *ppl. adj.* bitter 201/23, 206/
21; **byghting** 207/18.

blandisch *pr. pl.* ? act or speak with flattery 44/5 (see note).

blaspheme *n.* evil speaking 175/19.

blasphemyd *pp.* slandered 193/34.

blaundischynge *vbl. n.* flattery 69/7.

blaundisshing *ppl. adj.* flattering 9/13.

blemeshid *ppl. adj.* disfigured 4/28.

bloo *adj.* livid, leaden-coloured 4/31.

blood *n.* parentage 229/5; lineage 88/1.

bodeneth *pr. 3 sg.* fig., buds, begins to grow 85/16 (*MED* meaning om.; *OED* 1566).

body *n.* ? scribal error 172/6 (see note). ~ *of policie* body politic, government 172/4, 173/4.

boistous *adj.* rough in sound 152/28; coarse 186/7.

bonchef *n.* good fortune 113/27. **boncheves** *pl.* 103/29.

bonde *n.* fig., constraining force 205/1; *pl.* shackles 109/23.

bong *n.* stopper 7/13.

boord clothe *n.* table cloth 243/18.

bordure *n.* ornamental work round a garment 145/31; **bordwr** 144/31.

bostingis *vbl. n. pl.* menacing language 96/3 (*MED* meaning om.; *OED* 1600).

bothe *adv.* ? also 24/31 (see note).

botoume *n.* fig., foundation 244/9 (*MED* fig. meaning om.; *OED* 1577).

bounde *ppl. adj.* fig., in service or slavery 22/31, 39/6, 226/7; **bonde** 36/12. **boonde** not free 3/28.

bountevousnes *n.* bounteousness 242/27.

bourieneth *pr. 3 sg.* buds, begins to grow 85/16.

brayde owte *pa. t.* cried out 200/16.

braunle *n.* tottering, wavering 149/15 (*MED* om.; *OED* one ex. 1581; Fr. 'branle').

breedith *pr. 3 sg. intr.* arises 243/28; *pr. pl.* 189/27.

bref *adj.* quick to come 141/23 (*MED, OED* only related meanings).

breke *v.* defeat 125/34, 235/3; frustrate (a purpose or act) 29/26, 161/3, 234/3; bring to an end 18/15, 139/14, 240/3, 241/3; fig., destroy 18/26, 80/8, 202/33; ? reveal, disclose 122/24 (mistranslation of Fr. 'acroisse'; see note). **bracke** *pa. t.* made way through 106/1. **broken** *pp.* torn apart 146/10, 147/10; burst 7/10; violated 17/26. *brake hir voice* disrupted her speech 7/22.

bren(ne) *v.* burn 206/33, 229/17. **brende** ? *pa. t., pp.* 178/20. **brent(e)** *pp.* 109/14, 179/20.

brennyng *vbl. n.* burning 109/10.

brennyng(e) *ppl. adj.* burning 207/30; ardent 3/14, 123/9.

brestinge oute *vbl. n.* bursting forth 169/9.

breue *n.* in *in* ~ in brief 147/26.

bryng *v.* cause to come 77/10 (see Introd., p. 50); cause 224/7; give 171/3. ~ *forth* bring into being 72/7. ~ *in* cause to come 66/19; introduce 96/8, 121/26. ~ *lowe* overthrow 82/28, 157/31; withdraw 95/3. ~ *owt of* free from 82/30. ~ *owte of knowlage* take away the understanding 6/2. ~ *vndir* bring into subjection 82/28. ~ *vp* originate, give utterance to 182/14; exalt 90/29. **bringith** *pr. pl.* 224/7; **bringin** 182/14; **brought** *pa. t.* 90/29; *pp.* 72/7; **browght** 95/3.

brosten out(e) *pp.* cracked 149/16; burst 203/23.

brotill *adj.* brittle 126/16.

bruyt(e), brute *n.* fame, reputation 40/15, 138/25, 139/24; tumult 54/34, 170/24, 171/23; rumour 177/6.

brwsid *pp.* crushed out of shape, broken in pieces 144/17, 146/10; **brusid** 146/14; **brosid** 147/10.

buffettis *n. pl.* blows 192/9.

busshement *n.* fig., things concealed, as in ambush 85/6 (*MED, OED* reference only to troops in ambush).

but *adv.* only 89/2. *conj.* ~ *yf* unless 141/23, 195/4. ~ *that* unless 129/2, 223/5; without (followed by clause) 94/24; before (after negative) 111/11 (*MED* meaning om.; *OED* 1523). ~*(that)* otherwise than (after 'think', 'doubt' with negative) 65/34, 110/16, 146/13.

caytyf *adj.* vile, wretched 5/33, 65/27.
caitifnes(se) *n.* captivity 61/15;

misery 105/3; wickedness 148/27, 149/32.

call *v.* appeal to 54/12; invite 89/8, 179/1; call back 15/5, 30/34, 156/8. ∼ *ageyne* recall 162/27.

can(ne) *inf.* know how to, be able to 191/23, 231/20; *pr. 1 sg.* 174/2, 175/1; *pl.* have knowledge of 232/31. **canste** *2 sg.* 174/18; **const** 174/16.

capacite *n.* mental ability 30/25, 211/23.

capitally *adv.* involving loss of life 229/11 (*MED* adv. om.; *OED* 1619).

carectis *n. pl.* signs, characters 144/26, 145/26.

careyne *n.* flesh 92/25.

cas(se), caas(e), cace *n.* condition, plight 10/25, 62/27, 103/32, 152/30, 153/27, 180/9; matter 106/30, 188/16, 216/16, 217/11; cause 47/11; law case 204/9, 205/9.

cast(e), kest *v.* throw with force, violence, haste, etc. 5/10; intend 7/33. ∼ *abrode* throw carelessly, with strands (of hair) widely scattered 145/14; fig., throw violently 203/24. ∼ *away* squander 78/32; reject 7/31, 47/21; throw away as worthless 147/19. ∼ *downe* demolish 109/13, 226/4; overthrow 22/26, 36/9; turn downward 20/34. ∼ *owte* exile 7/30; reject 212/3. ∼ *owte of* set free from, deliver from 25/5, 209/7. *was* ∼ had fallen 144/15. **kest** *pa. t.* 45/28. **cast(e)** *pp.* 5/10, 145/14; **casten** 146/20, 203/24.

castell *n.¹* fortress 138/1, 139/2.

castell *n.²* wealth, goods 169/31, 185/27, 187/18, 191/10; *pl.* 181/23 (*MED, OED* word om.; eccentric spelling of *catell*; see 168/27-30 note); cf. **catall.**

catall *n.* wealth, goods 190/9.

cause *n.* case 101/20; *pl.* conditions 101/16. *for* ∼ *of* because 158/22.

cautele *n.* crafty device 91/25; cunning 239/31. **caute(e)les** *pl.* stratagems 211/24, 241/4; **cawteles** 210/23.

cenefye *n.* mustard plant 89/28 (*OED senvy*, spelling om.; see note).

ceryously *adv.* in due sequence 23/28.

certeyne *n.* fixed sum of money 123/1.

cesse, ceasse, seese *v.* stop, discontinue 177/30. **cessid** *pp.* 171/5; **sessed** 220/2; **ceessid** 233/4; **seced** 125/7.

chaffyng *ppl. adj.* reprimanding 11/31.

chalenge *v.* lay claim to, demand as a right 201/1; *pr. pl.* 162/16; *pr. p.* 163/15. **chalence** *inf.* demand 29/5. **chalaungid** *pp.* reproved 240/25.

chalenging of *vbl. n.* demanding 79/5.

champaine *adj.* level and open 13/18.

chaungeably *adv.* alternately, in regard to position 121/4.

chapitle *n.* chapter 141/20, 141/24.

chapitre *n.* ecclesiastical court 36/20.

charge *n.* burden of trouble 92/3, 179/2, 188/7; burden of sin 222/13, 223/13; *pl.* burdens of weight 164/35; expense 220/13; *pl.* 170/20; office 35/4; *pl.* 131/15; duty 54/3; *pl.* 128/23; responsibility 168/10; accusation 64/2, 187/19; *pl.* 188/30. *in the* ∼ *of* as a responsibility of 171/19. *to be out of* ∼ *in* not to be a burden on 223/20-1. *taken in* ∼ assumed the responsibility 201/2.

charge *v.* burden (financially) 222/22; burden (a part of the body) in a physical sense 38/25; accuse, blame 179/12, 186/21; lay 74/3. ∼ *with* blame 240/10. *pp.* laden 180/24, 181/21; fig. 23/2, 169/12; burdened with guilt and sin 198/16, 199/14; entrusted 200/3.

chargeable *adj.* troublesome 98/33; accusing 205/27 (*MED, OED* meaning om.).

charging *ppl. adj.* accusing 204/27.

charpith *pr. 3 sg.* makes more acute 105/15 (*OED sharp*, spelling om.).

chase, chace *v.* drive forcibly 154/7, 233/11; fig. 172/33, 173/34; rout 155/6; persecute, harass 233/9. ∼ *away* drive out 14/12. **chase** *pr. pl.* 154/8; **chasen** 172/33; **chacen** 173/34.

chastesing *vbl. n.* amending 192/2.

chaumberer *n.* chambermaid, chamberlain 226/8; *pl.* concubines 94/14.

chaunge *n.* in *newe* ~ mutation 182/29–30; *pl.* 176/25.

chaungid *pa. t.* shifted, transferred 36/29; *pp.* 35/27, 61/4.

chavefith *pr. 3 sg.* inflames 38/25 (*MED, OED* spelling om.).

cheef *n.* ? masterpiece, ? important thing 27/19 (*OED* cf. *a great*; Fr. 'chief d'euure'). *in chefe* in the highest position 237/11 (*MED* phr. om.; *OED* 1607–12).

che(e)pe *quasi-adv.* in *gret(t)e* ~ at a very low price, very easily 190/13, 191/13 (*MED, OED* only as adj.; *OED* rare; modelled on *good-cheap*).

che(e)se, chose *v.* choose 12/30, 81/7, 183/18; pick out, know 203/10. **cheese** *pr. pl.* 148/26, 149/31; **chesen** 14/27. **chase** *pa. t. sg.* 17/27. **chesin** *pa. t. pl.* 16/36. **chosen** *pp.* perceived 149/24.

chere *n.* countenance 78/10.

cherisch *pr. pl.* encourage 44/29 (see note). **cherischid** *pp.* treated with favour 8/33.

cherte *see* **chyerte.**

chesell *n.* chisel 157/4.

chesinges *vbl. n. pl.* elections 56/2.

chiding *vbl. n.* contention 246/4; *pl.* 247/3.

ch(y)erte *n.* dearness, affection 116/22. *haue in* ~ hold dear 77/21.

chirte *n.* shirt 105/27.

chose *n.* choice 230/27.

circute *n.* compass 31/18.

cysmes *n. pl.* schisms 47/15.

cites *n. pl.* ? cities 104/6 (? scribal error; Fr. 'occis'; see note).

clarifien *pr. pl.* clear from ignorance 145/27.

cleerte *n.* brightness 143/4.

clees *n. pl.* claws 151/36.

clemence *n.* (divine) mercy 45/5, 173/25.

clene *adv.* ~ *armyd* fully armed 224/31 (*MED, OED* meaning questioned).

clennesse *n.* moral innocence 46/1; clean uses 30/12 (*MED, OED* meaning om.).

cler(e) *adj.* bright 20/30, 89/17; free from any trouble 188/35 (*MED* only in phr. *quit and* ~ = 'unscathed'; *OED* 1635).

clerenes(se) *n.* brightness 20/21, 21/16.

clergy *n.* learning 95/25.

cleving *vbl. n.* remaining faithful 68/2, 99/17.

close *v.* enclose, confine 41/6, 105/34. ~ *away from* (*refl.*) exclude oneself 73/19. ~ *from* shut out from, exclude from 36/22, 51/17, 110/16. ~ *from you* exclude you 50/11 (*MED, OED* no use exactly like this; see note). ~ *owte of* exclude from 62/14. ~ *within* encompass by 69/24, 166/34. **closed** *pp.* concealed 85/7. **close** rolled up (as a scroll), shut 23/28 (see note). *have your hondis* ~ take no action 148/28. *kepte* ~ concealed 85/4.

closette *n.* bower 158/24.

closyng *n.* enclosed place 228/17.

closture *n.* enclosed place 229/17 (*MED, OED cloister*; spelling om.; Fr. 'closture').

clowde *n.* ~ *of thi mortale body* moral darkness of the body 22/24–5.

col(l)er *n.* part of a harness 208/8, 209/8.

colour *v.* excuse 194/28, 195/28.

colourable *adj.* specious 198/22.

colour(e) *n.* fig., cloak 201/7; *pl.* rhetorical figures, allegories 84/32. *vnder* (*the, a*) ~ under the pretext 131/13, 153/22, 162/2, 199/18; under the alleged authority 166/23, 198/27, 199/23, 200/5, 201/4–5.

colouryng of *vbl. n.* giving a fair appearance to 91/33.

comaunded *pa. t.* ordained 92/12.

combraunce *n.* destructive influence (of the flesh) 25/15.

come *v.* come into existence 55/10, 235/11; attain 219/26. ~ *in* grasp by 103/16 (*MED* cf. *come by*). ~ *forthe* be born 110/23. ~ *vp* originate 86/16. *for to* ~ forthcoming 196/24; coming forth, arising 196/23 (Fr. 'sourvenant'). **come** *pr. pl.* 55/10; **comyth** 235/11; **comon** 154/18. **come** *pa. t. sg.*

110/23; *pl.* 152/6; **comen** 160/32; came 86/16.

comen *adj.* possessed alike 92/22. **comown** generally known 101/14; *see* **counceyll, well.**

comensales *n. pl.* those who eat at the same table 81/18.

coment *n.* ? commentator (*MED, OED* meaning om.); ? scribal error 58/17 (Fr. 'commentateur'; see note).

comyng(e) *vbl. n.* ∼ *in* entrance 20/27. ∼ *oute of* outcome 143/16. ∼ *vpon* attacking 181/4; *pl.* 180/5. **comynges** *pl.* coming events 13/14 (*MED* 'event'; *OED* meaning om.).

commiccion *n.* mixed state 71/26. **commyxtions** *pl.* parts, substances mixed 71/28 (*MED, OED* meaning om.; Fr. 'mixtions').

commission(e) *n.* authority 21/19, 23/14, 55/7.

commyssioner *n.* representative of the supreme authority 55/6 (*OED* 1535).

committe *pr. pl.* entrust 46/11. **committid** *pa. t.* 86/1; *pp.* appointed 234/14; fig., delivered over 44/21.

comonalte *n.* common people 190/7; commonwealth 55/30. **comunalte** community 228/25.

comons *see* **comune.**

comonte *n.* community 229/24; common people 173/12; commonwealth 186/22, 187/22; **commynte** 172/10; *pl.* 55/20.

comowned *pp.* discussed 81/1.

compace *see* **compas.**

compacite *n.* ability to grasp ideas or knowledge 210/22 (*MED, OED* word om.; combination of *capacity* and *compass*; Fr. 'capacité').

compacte *pr. pl.* are suitable or applicable 117/26 (*MED* om.; *OED* rare, only ex. 1541; **compecte** NJ; Fr. 'competent').

compare *v.* vie 234/6; *refl.* 235/5.

compas *n.* circle 121/1; area, measurement round 136/30. **compace** proper proportion 137/21.

compassid *pa. t.* planned 29/27; *pp.* surrounded 146/31; **compaced** 147/28.

compassion *n.* ? passion 79/14 (*MED, OED* meaning om.; Fr. 'passion').

compileth *pr. 3 sg.* (? scribal error for pa. t. *compiled*) writes 88/9. **compiled** *pa. t.* 11/4; *pp.* 140/28; *ppl. adj.* composed (of constituent parts), in contrast with the single essence of God 120/1.

comprehendid *pp.* accomplished 141/30; encompassed 147/28.

comprised *pa. t.* comprehended 58/26; *pp.* conceived 31/20; composed 140/29.

compte *n.* account of stewardship 30/20; calculation 219/29.

comune *n.* common people 212/4. **comons** *pl.* community 245/5.

comunycacion *n.* association 88/22.

comunycant *adj.* ∼ *beyng with* shared existence with, existence unified with 71/26 (*MED* om.; *OED* rare as adj., 1557).

conages *n. pl.* coins 123/3.

concience *n.* in *with* ∼ in conformity to what is right 188/11.

condicion *n.* nature, character 20/6, 35/29, 156/9, 157/9; circumstance 176/13, 177/13; *pl.* 38/28; manners 53/28, 157/33. *by suche* ∼ on condition that 179/3; *on a* ∼ *that* 93/2–3; *vndir s(h)uche* ∼ *that* 158/16–17, 178/3; *vpon suche* ∼ *that* 159/13.

condicioned *pa. t.* made dependent (upon conditions to be fulfilled) 84/31; *pp.* governed, limited 94/19 (*MED* meaning om.; *OED* 1619).

condidith *see* **coundite.**

condiscendid *pp.* agreed 216/21.

conditor *n.* leader 212/5; **conditours** *pl.* 222/24.

conduyting *vbl. n.* spiritual control 113/14 (*MED* v. *conduiten*).

confecte *pp.* compounded 69/18.

confiaunce *n.* confidence 67/29, 198/31 (*MED* om.; *OED* rare).

confydence of *n.* firm trust in 79/11.

confirme, conferme *v.* verify 65/29, 191/28; establish firmly 96/22, 161/21; fig., strengthen spiritually 69/32, 71/19. ∼ *aftir* 'conform after' = form or shape according to 95/31. *confirmed in* (*pp.*) 'conformed in' = adapted to 116/23, 116/29 (Fr. 'conformer').

confirmyng *vbl. n.* uniting 72/16.

conformeable *adj.* agreeable 108/9.

confortatyve *adj.* strengthening 112/15.

conforted *pp.* supported 110/33.

confound(e) *v.* overthrow, destroy 38/10, 50/21, 194/21, 227/2; discomfit in argument 27/16.

confo(u)rm(e) to (vnto) *v.* bring into harmony with 67/1; *pp.* 41/17; cf. **confirme.**

confuce *ppl. adj.* disorderly 69/10.

confused *pp.* routed 90/15; *ppl. adj.* brought into ruin 3/28; overthrown 97/3.

confusion *n.* overthrow, ruin, destruction 48/10, 78/10, 172/26, 173/27.

conioyned *pp.* joined 67/23, 147/11; **conyoined** 245/23.

conquestioned *pp.* ? bewailed (*MED* om.; *OED* only ex. 1656); ? debated 141/17 (see note).

consecrat *pa. t. 2 sg.* dedicated 26/10. **consecrate** *pp.* made holy 87/29.

conseite *n.* idea, action 202/11.

consented *pa. t.* allowed 187/4.

consentement *n.* consent 44/25.

conseruatours *n. pl.* guardians 58/32.

conserue *v.* preserve from destruction 21/21, 169/23.

consolatyve *adj.* consolatory 99/33 (*MED* om.; *OED* rare).

conspiracions *n. pl.* conspiracies 204/3, 205/3.

constitucion *n.* statute 131/26; *pl.* 131/7. ∼ *of place* statutes of particular religious houses 131/25.

constreyne, constrayne *v.* restrain 27/1, 237/29; oblige, compel 17/26, 27/1, 96/19, 172/15; impel, prompt 113/15, 162/23, 163/21, 194/12, 195/12; afflict 173/17; *pp.* violated 41/29 (*MED* meaning om.; *OED* 1588).

constreynt(e), constraynt(e) *n.* coercion, force 13/26, 87/18, 135/24; affliction 61/21.

consumith *pr. 3 sg. intr.* wastes away 21/26.

consumpcion *n.* wasteful use 201/26, 202/14, 203/12 (*MED* meaning om.; *OED* 1677).

contagiousenes *n.* communication of moral corruption 45/1.

contemplatour *n.* one who meditates upon divine works 127/29.

contemptes *n. pl.* scornful or hateful actions 209/29.

content *n.* contentment 9/30 (*MED* meaning om.; *OED* 1579).

contentinge *vbl. n.* contentment 207/3 (*MED* meaning om.; *OED* a1541).

contentith *pr. 3 sg. intr.* gives satisfaction 85/11.

contingence *n.* freedom from necessity 120/21.

contingent *adj.* not fixed by necessity 120/19.

contingently *adv.* dependent upon circumstances, not necessarily 120/24 (*MED* a1500).

continuaunce, contenuaunce *n.* preservation 228/26; continued existence 240/32; duration 190/5, 191/5. *by (of) long(e)* ∼ for a long time 56/13, 87/17.

contractes *n. pl.* marriages 49/4.

contrarie *n.* in *in the* ∼ on the other hand 143/17; in opposition 227/21.

contrary(e) *adj.* opposed 79/9; changeable 212/16, 213/13; harmful, perverse 28/30, 43/21, 177/26. ∼ *ayeinst* diametrically opposed to 91/17; ∼ *to* 69/29; against 237/30. *in* ∼ *wise* on the other hand 36/11, 38/13.

contrarious *adj.* hostile, perverse, harmful 156/33, 170/22, 176/26, 184/6. ∼ *to* at variance with 99/24.

contrariousnes(se) *n.* self-willed perversity 16/3, 23/19; antagonism 69/3.

contrever *n.* initiator, deviser 91/22.

contryue *v.* fabricate 82/10; *pa. t.* devised 107/33; *pp.* composed 84/12.

conuenable *adj.* suitable 222/8.

conuenient *adj.* proper 30/14.

conuersacion *n.* mode of life 47/1, 97/18.

conuersaunt *adj.* living and associating (with) 82/22; **conuersaund** 98/4.

conuerte v. direct 241/19; *imp.* 152/
31, 153/28. *conuerted into* applied to
(a specific use) 187/5.

coope n. cope, ecclesiastical vestment
126/8.

cordage n. cords or ropes 187/3
(*MED* om.; *OED* 1598 in literal
sense).

corporellis *adj. pl.* material 120/28.

correct v. chastise 237/29.

corrupcion n. corrupting influence
72/15, 92/26; infection 38/24; *pl.*
fig., moral infections 38/3.

corrupte v. tr. bribe 221/12; *pr. 3 sg.*
intr. goes bad 95/26. ~ *the humours*
distempers the humours 5/19.
corrupt(e) *ppl. adj.* infected with
evil 56/19, 205/14; full of errors (of
a text) 38/23.

cor(r)uptible (-able) *adj.* perish-
able, mortal 15/16, 74/18; sinful
157/33.

corvyn *pp.* carved 146/32.

costeyed *pa. t.* attacked 192/19 (*MED*
meaning om.; *OED* 1531).

co(u)ndite, conduit(e), cunduyte
n. guidance, leadership, command
19/21, 90/10, 226/2, 227/1, 232/31;
skill, discretion 191/20; fountain,
well 97/9.

co(u)ndite, condyt, conduit(e) v.
guide, lead 102/17, 112/7, 210/22,
233/31; manage 7/33. **conditeth** *pr.
3 sg.* puts together 40/5; **condidith**
40/3. **coundited** *pa. t.* commanded
226/31; *pp.* 238/33.

counforte n. ease 205/26 (see 204/
25–6 note).

counsaile n. assembly 227/5. *comen
counceyll* family council called for
advice 81/16. **Counseiles** assem-
blies of ecclesiastics 48/21.

**co(u)nseil(le), counsaile, counsell,
counce(y)ll** n. advice 66/16, 228/
15, 229/15; prudence, judgement
35/3, 64/17, 192/4, 193/4; intention,
opinion 101/5; *pl.* 64/24; plan 7/32;
pl. 64/20; private or secret design
50/9; *pl.* (divine) secrets 77/4.

counstaunce n. constance 171/27,
175/15 (*MED, OED* spelling om.).

countenaunce n. show 56/16; appearance, bearing 144/9, 145/8;

mode of behaviour 146/29; *pl.* 147/
26. **cownthenaunce** control 134/
9 (Fr. 'pointure').

countirfeted *ppl. adj.* false 78/9.

countrepeise n. counterweight 220/
27, 221/24.

co(u)rage n. heart, spirit 7/25, 170/
27, 171/26; *pl.* 3/23, 154/9, 155/8;
boldness, confidence 9/13, 56/17;
nature, disposition 53/32, 174/15,
175/16; *pl.* 164/6 (**coraugys** N);
thought 149/25; *pl.* 101/16; see 137/
9 note.

couraged *pa. t.* encouraged 104/17.

cours(e) n. life span 4/14; development 137/13; course (of a disease)
208/28, 209/27; drift (of a narrative)
140/15 (Fr. 'discours'); opportunity
for existence 189/24. ~ *of their age*
rest of their lives 3/22. *in* ~ in succession 139/22. *make thi* ~ make
your way (to) 33/10.

courtyne n. fig., curtain 85/21; *pl.*
85/20.

couenable *adj.* appropriate 61/19,
152/26, 153/24.

covenablely *adv.* appropriately 93/
34.

couer(e) v. hide 95/10, 203/28.
couerid *pa. t.* covered 144/18;
cured 145/18.

covert n. in *vndir* ~ *of* under the
authority and disguise of 85/4.

covert *adj.* hidden, secret 99/27;
cowert 202/29. **cowarte** indirect
206/25.

couert(e)ly *adv.* secretly, closely 84/
23; indirectly 207/23.

couertoure n. hiding place, refuge 57/
34.

cowardes n. cowardice 193/35 (*MED,
OED* spelling om.).

cowarte, cowert see **covert.**

cownte n. reckoning 115/33.

cownthenaunce see **countenaunce.**

crafte n. profession 46/20, 229/9;
trade 231/12; special skill or
knowledge 87/2, 136/32; ? making,
planning 127/18 (see note); *pl.*
crafts, arts 86/32.

crafty *adj.* learned 28/15; skilfully
wrought 29/27.

cratures n. *pl.* creatures 127/28.

creat(e) *pa. t.* created 121/8; *pp.* 21/13, 113/11; *ppl. adj.* 68/19.

Creature *n.* Creator 15/10.

creaunce *n.* belief 107/14.

creme *n.* consecrated oil 18/35.

crepyng *ppl. adj.* moving stealthily 79/32.

crye *n.* proclamation 230/24. **krye** cry 197/29.

crye, krye *v.* ~ *ageinst* (*agains*), *vpon* condemn 181/29; *pr. pl.* 190/10, 191/10; **cryen** 182/1. **cried** *pp.* proclaimed 166/25, 231/22.

cruellenesse *n.* severity 152/29.

culpe *n.* guilt 179/22.

cured *see* couer(e).

curiosite *n.* carefulness 125/14.

curious(e) *adj.* zealous (of persons) 155/11; painstaking (of activity) 185/20.

curiously *adv.* carefully 140/15, 141/14; skilfully 147/27.

cursidnes *n.* wickedness 95/20, 234/3.

cursing *vbl. n.* excommunication 48/23.

curteis *adj.* gracious, gentle 20/24, 28/7.

custome *see* take.

customed, custumed *pa. t.* trained 91/1; *pp.* accustomed 106/19. ~ *in* in the habit of 58/1.

daung(i)er(e) *n.* peril 22/6, 158/20; mischief, harm 152/23; *pl.* 152/22, 153/20; bondage 63/28; power 188/33, 189/31. *vnder* (*in*) *the* ~ at the mercy, within the power 14/16, 156/33; sim. *vndir their* ~ 4/9; *pl. vnder the* ~ 157/32.

debate *n.* discussion 132/23.

debonairte *n.* meekness 243/26.

decesse *see* dissease.

declare *v.* interpret 59/7, 246/26; show 224/8; expound 227/15. **declaren** *pr. pl.* 177/24.

decline *n.* degeneration 165/28; misfortune 217/6. *fall into* ~ deteriorate 168/9; *falleth into* ~ see 16/17 note. *in maner of* ~ degenerated 164/28.

decline *v.* deteriorate 169/10.

dede *n.* in *in* ~ in fact 113/9.

dedeifyed *pp.* dedicated 45/19 (*MED,*

OED spelling om. under *dedify*; see note).

dedicat *pp.* dedicated 51/9.

deduccion *n.* conclusion 121/19 (*MED* meaning om.; *OED* 1532).

deed(e) *adj.* dead 86/5, 179/28.

de(e)pe *adj.* profound 41/19; grave, heinous 132/2; very great 69/24, 198/23; **diepe** 138/35; deep 134/18. **depper** *comp.* 30/28; **depest** *sup.* 202/22.

deeply *adv.* with deep feeling 181/12.

def- *see* dif-.

default(e), defaute, defaw(l)te, diffaulte, diffawte *n.* fault, sin 15/15, 30/20, 203/5; *pl.* 32/22; lack 114/21, 148/1; lack of food 11/11, 168/14. *in* ~ in the wrong 207/4. *in* ~ *of* through the failure of, in the absence of 149/1, 232/11–12, 233/13.

defencers *n. pl.* defenders 153/23.

defensable (-ible) *adj.* able to defend a country 142/22, 143/19.

degre *n.* decree 24/5 (Fr. 'decret').

degreis *n. pl.* steps 24/11.

deyne *pr. pl.* condescend 82/8.

dele *v.* distribute 203/7.

delectacion *n.* delight 9/28.

delicacyes *n. pl.* luxuries 156/23.

delicat(e) *adj.* pleasing to the taste 92/18; luxurious, voluptuous 92/29, 150/3, 156/8.

delicatis *n. pl.* luxuries 156/23.

delicatyue *adj.* indolent 177/18. **delicatiues** *pl.* luxurious, voluptuous 157/6 (*MED* om.; *OED* only meaning 'dainty' applied to food, 1491).

delices *n. pl.* worldly pleasures 45/3, 156/2, 177/1.

delicious(e) *adj.* luxurious, voluptuous 86/30, 148/26, 151/4.

deliciously *adv.* luxuriously, voluptuously 149/31.

delictes *n. pl.* crimes, violations of law or right 236/12; **delites** 198/28, 237/11.

delyte *pr. 2 sg. subj.* ~ *of* are highly pleased with 79/33. **delited in** (*refl.*) took pleasure in 49/22.

deliueryng *vbl. n.* saving 236/19.

deliuir, deliure *v.* surrender 236/19, 237/18; save 237/19.

demaynes *n. pl.* lands subject to a king 218/33, 219/31.

demaunde *n.* question 66/28, 169/17; *pl.* 25/34.

demeene *v.* use 211/15.

demerytes *n. pl.* sins 53/22.

demonstracion *n.* process of making evident by reason 62/12.

Demonstratyue *n.* logical demonstration proving conclusively 23/15 (see note).

denouncen *pr. pl.* proclaim 196/30; **denonceth** 197/29.

departe(n) *v.* divide, share 55/3, 229/26; distribute 78/32, 161/13, 203/6; separate 131/17, 147/12, 170/30; take away 9/7. ∼ *from* sever 131/12. ∼ *outwarde* go forth 233/24. **departed** *ppl. adj.* terminated 99/9.

departing *vbl. n.* sharing 169/21, 228/27; distributing 160/15.

dependaunt *adj.* relying on something else, here on God 117/17 (**dyspendaunt** J).

dependith *pr. 3 sg.* is pertinent (to) 132/28 (*MED* meaning om.; *OED* 1525); relies (upon) 120/7. **dependen** *pl.* 120/8.

deprimed *pp.* abased, overthrown 165/7, *193/23, 235/7 (*MED*, *OED* word om.; Fr. 'deprimer').

deprivith *pr. 3 sg.* takes away 45/2. **deprived** *pp.* deposed 37/10.

derk(e) *adj.* blind 140/20, 141/21; hard to understand 32/25; little regarded 77/29; lacking intellectual or spiritual light 5/23, 128/4.

derogacion *n.* ∼ *to* disparagement of 98/23. *deregacion of* infringement upon 193/26.

derogate of *pp.* disparaging of 97/22.

derth(e) *n.* high price 190/8, 191/7.

descendid *pp.* sent down 224/28.

desercion *n.* destruction 149/34 (*MED*, *OED* meaning om.; Fr. 'desertion' = 'destruction').

desert(e) *n.*[1] action that deserves its appropriate reward, here punishment 67/11. *withowt* (*any*) ∼ without deserving (something) 11/11, 42/1. *aftir his desertis* according to his merits or worth 236/11; sim. *aftir*

the qualite of theire ∼ 41/1; *aftir the reason of mennys* ∼ 220/22.

deserte *n.*[2] desolation 13/23. *in* ∼ desolate 3/32.

deserte *adj.* uninhabited 108/2; uncultivated 168/2, 169/2.

deservingis *vbl. n. pl.* merits 121/16, 121/22.

desirith *pr. 3 sg.* ? asks, ? scribal error for *descrieth* = 'proclaims' 132/24 (see note).

desirous *adj.* earnest 67/29.

desolate *adj.* laid waste 47/11, 103/34.

desperable *adj.* hopeless 104/25.

desperate *adj.* hopeless 100/7.

despite *n.* indignation, contempt 7/9, 206/7, 207/7. *had in dispite* held in contempt 131/20.

destitucion *n.* deprivation of office 108/20 (*MED* meaning om.; *OED* 1554).

destressid *see* **distressid**.

destrue *v.* bring to nought, destroy 195/22, 227/3; consume 171/11.

determinacion *n.* opinion 119/29; conclusion 132/3, 132/17; extermination 141/19, 159/15. ∼ *substantyve* judgement that is not subsidiary, here of God 79/28.

determined *pp.* declared authoritatively 85/20; ordained 113/25; settled 126/31. ∼ *in* judged or decided by 25/18.

dethe *n.* in *furst* ∼ as distinguished from the 'second death', which is the punishment of lost souls after death 113/25.

detraccion *n.* slander 77/29, 200/22, *201/23.

devilrye *n.* devilish behaviour 95/18 (*MED*, *OED* meaning om.; see note).

devoir(e), devour(e), devir *n.* duty 22/30, 190/19, 191/20. *put* (oneself) *in* ∼ endeavour 151/2, 209/1–2. *in no* ∼ make no effort 164/12. *seet litle* ∼ make little effort 165/13.

dewly *adv.* sufficiently 123/30.

dewte, du(e)te(e) *n.* performance of prescribed services of the church 46/22; *pl.* fees 191/6. *of* ∼ out of reverence 86/22.

Dialetique *n.* method of probable reasoning, as opposed to Demonstrative 23/15 (**Dealetyque** N; see note).

diche *n.* moat 9/17; *pl.* 168/1.

dictature *n.* dictatorship 193/10, 193/27 (*MED* om.; *OED* 1553).

dictees *n. pl.* verses 4/5.

diepe *see* **deepe.**

difface, disface, deface *v.* blot out of existence, memory, etc. 106/24; *pa. t.* 61/17; *pp.* 28/1; transformed for the worse 91/32; marred, made ugly 146/13.

diffame *n.* disgrace 178/32, 179/30.

diffame *pr. pl.* dishonour 8/26.

diffaulte *see* **defaulte.**

diffence, defence *n.* offence 35/6; *pl.* 34/6 (see note); laws of prohibition 237/15; defences against criticism 245/18. *made* ~ prohibited by law 225/14.

diffende, defende *pr. 3 sg. subj.* forbid 31/25, 190/15, 191/15; *pr. pl.* 80/14; *pp.* 45/24.

diffiaunce, defiaunce *n.* distrust 198/30, 199/26; *pl.* breaches of trust 63/16. **Deffyaunce** character's name 12/5.

difficultee *n.* ? reluctance, unwillingness (*MED* a1425, meaning questioned; *OED* 1513); ? quarrel (*MED*, *OED* meaning om.) 209/3 (see note).

Diffidence *n.* character 'Deffyaunce', distrust 20/7, 69/28.

diffyeng *vbl. n.* lack of trust 102/15.

diffyith *pr. 3 sg.* revolts at 80/6.

defied *ppl. adj.* mistrusting 201/12.

diffinityue *adj.* final 51/23.

difforme *v.* turn into an evil or ugly form 72/14.

diffoule, diffowle, defoule, defowle *v.* profane 50/4, 82/12; trample down, oppress 4/21, 46/3, 188/34, 189/32; make dirty, ugly 147/10.

diffowlit *pp.* 11/17.

diffoullers *n. pl.* oppressors 106/32.

digne *adj.* worthy of reverence 96/21; deserving 141/22.

dignite(e) *n.* nobleness 32/10; excellence 138/27, 139/25; *pl.* 66/31; high office, honourable position 49/13, 154/30, 155/26; *pl.* 134/10, 135/13.

dykes *n. pl.* moats 167/31.

dymes *n. pl.* tithes 128/27.

diminuacion *n.* diminution 161/2 (*MED* om.; *OED* rare).

diminued *pa. t.* decreased 223/20; *pp.* 191/6.

disapoynte *v.* dispossess (of an office) 108/23.

disceve, disceyve, dissave, deceyve *v.* deceive 69/7, 174/15, 175/16; mislead into sin 66/6, 204/14, 205/13; frustrate, prove false 136/5, 137/6. **disseyvith** *pr. 3 sg.* 80/17.

discharge *v. refl.* exculpate (oneself) 194/22, 195/22; *pr. 1 sg.* unburden (the heart) 172/30, 173/29; *pp.* cleared of blame 194/14, 195/14, 198/2; *ppl. adj.* freed from adversity 219/15.

discharges *n. pl.* exculpations 244/18, 245/19.

discheuele *ppl. adj.* carelessly dressed, especially with the hair hanging in disorder 7/15.

discipline *n.* knowledge, training 81/11, 107/5, 127/21.

discomfit(e), discounfit(e) *v.* overthrow, defeat 103/9; *pa. t.* 105/6. **discomfited** *pp.* 104/3; **discomfite** 104/4; **discounfite** 135/23, 161/7.

discomfit(o)ure *n.* defeat 104/7; *pl.* 50/28; physical injury 18/25 (*MED* meaning om.; *OED* rare, only ex. 1599).

discomfort(e) *n.* discouragement 71/8; grief 78/3.

disconfidence *n.* distrust 242/30 (*MED* om.; *OED* 1621).

disconisaunce *n.* ignorance, lack of knowledge *143/31, 207/10 (*MED* om.; *OED* rare, only ex. *c.*1477, not in this meaning).

discordable *adj.* discordant 99/8.

discorde from *pr. pl.* are inconsistent with 97/23.

discordes *n. pl.* ? disagreements of opinion; ? fig., harsh, unpleasing sounds; ? scribal error 62/14, 77/10, 141/15 (Fr. 'discours'; see 62/13–14 note).

discouer(i)d *pa. t.* disclosed to view, uncovered 7/4, 148/8, 149/10; *pp.* revealed 51/28, 202/30; *ppl. adj.* bare 147/18. **discoured** *pa. t.* 239/19.

discounfite *see* **discomfite.**

discrecion *see* **disgression.**

dyscreecith *pr. 3 sg.* diminishes 137/4.

discryvith *pr. 3 sg.* proclaims 64/27.

disdayne *n.* in *had in* ~ held in scorn 9/12. *haue disdeyne* take offence 207/6–7.

disdeyne *pr. subj.* treat with contempt 46/26. **disdeyneth** *pr. 3 sg.* scorns 46/20, 207/12. ~ *ayeinst* is contemptuous of 114/20. ~ *at* (*pl.*) take offence at 95/8.

disease *n.* suffering 175/9, 177/15; annoyance, trouble 76/6, 188/6, 189/6; *pl.* 180/16; uncomfortable conditions 188/32.

diseasid *ppl. adj.* uncomfortable 159/6.

disencresce *n.* decrease, fall 134/15.

disenhabited *ppl. adj.* uninhabited 168/33 (*MED* om.; *OED* v. 1530, ppl. adj. 1600).

Disesperaunce *n.* Despair, character's name 69/28.

disfigurid *pp.* deformed, defaced 18/31 (disfugered N), 77/28.

disgression *n.* digression 132/28; **discrecion** 127/3.

disguysid *ppl. adj.* altered in fashion for modish display 53/33.

disherited *pp.* disinherited 65/8; *ppl. adj.* 3/32.

dysheryteson *n.* disinheritance 156/7.

disioyned *pp.* disunited, divided 234/4, 235/4.

disiounte *n.* position of perplexity 71/23 (disioynte N; **dysyunte** J).

disknoweth *pr. 3 sg.* fails to know or acknowledge 177/12 (*MED* om.; *OED* nonce-word, only ex. 1605). **disknowen** *pp.* unrecognized, scorned 165/21 (Fr. 'mescogneue').

disknowing *vbl. n.* failing to know or acknowledge 197/9.

disknowlege (-lage) *n.* lack of knowledge (? through heedlessness) 62/26 (Fr. 'nonchalence'). ~ *of* failure to acknowledge 50/19 (see note).

disknowlegyng of *vbl. n.* failure to know 196/17 (*MED* om.; *OED* vbl. n. om.; only ex. of v. 1576, not in this meaning).

disordeyned *pp.* brought into disorder 235/3.

disordinat(e), desordinat *adj.* unfitting, improper, unreasonable 53/31, 152/21, 153/19; disorderly 69/11, 170/33, 171/28.

disordinaunce *n.* confusion 113/4; dissoluteness 97/14.

disparple *v.* throw into confusion 50/22. **disparpulid** *pp.* scattered abroad, dispersed 202/24; **disperpuled** 3/29, 102/28, 216/3; *ppl. adj.* divided, thrown into confusion 168/10 (disperpluyd N).

dispeyred, dispaired *ppl. adj.* despairing 3/28, 173/28; hopeless 85/25.

dispence, dispense *n.* expenditure, sometimes wasteful or over-generous 184/15, 220/24; *pl.* 202/30, 218/28; burden of expenditure, cost 189/19; *pl.* 188/20, 200/26.

dispendid *pp.* consumed 218/30.

dispice *v.* despise 11/26. **dispiseth** *pr. 3 sg.* disregards 123/20 (dyspyteth J).

dispite *see* **despite.**

dispitouse *adj.* insulting, vexing 141/8.

disple(a)sur(e) *n.* offence 72/28; sorrow 76/17. *take it for no displeasire* do not be displeased 201/28.

displesaunce *n.* displeasure 140/14, 165/31. *for no* ~ despite anyone's displeasure 236/17–18 (*MED, OED* phr. om.). *take a* ~ am displeased 164/30.

dispoyled *see* **dispuyle.**

dispoyler *n.* plunderer 50/31.

dispo(o)se *v. tr.* govern 77/23; bestow, dispense 185/28, 240/20; expose 193/24 (*MED, OED* meaning om.; Fr. 'exposee'); *refl.* expose oneself 150/25, 151/31 (*MED, OED* meaning om.; Fr. 'soy exposer'); *refl.* incline one's mind 53/30, 64/9, 157/17; *abs.* ordain 85/10.

dispo(o)sing(e) *vbl. n.* expenditure 161/11; use of 227/14 (*MED* meaning om.; *OED* 1638).

disporte *n.* pleasure 8/31.

dysportes *pr. 3 sg. refl.* amuses herself 8/29.

disposicion *n.* relative position 121/5 (*MED* meaning om.; *OED* 1541); *pl.* 121/7; plan 121/30; dispensation 115/8; intention 179/10; condition 136/1, 137/1; *pl.* 4/24; uses 241/19 (*MED, OED* no ex. exactly like this).

dispraysing ayeinst *vbl. n.* depreciation or scorning of 88/1.

dispreysable *adj.* worthy of blame 27/19.

dispreyse, disprayse *v.* speak contemptuously of, despise 46/4, 53/5, 81/17, 141/9; *pa. t.* 140/9; blamed 53/11; *pp.* 53/5.

dispuyle *pr. pl. refl.* undress 93/14. **dispoyled** *pp.* stripped of possessions 104/33; destroyed 61/4; robbed 166/20; *ppl. adj.* fig., naked 54/24.

dispurve(y)id, dispurveyd, dispo(u)rveyed *pp., ppl. adj.* destitute 64/7, 168/3, 169/5; unprepared 100/18; unprepared for 13/13, 61/27. ~ *of* lacking 12/18, 162/1, 163/1.

dissaiveable *n.* used as synonym for **Sophistique** 23/16.

dissave *see* **disceve**.

dissclaundir *n.* slander 52/4.

dissease *n.* death 34/9; **decesse** 3/8.

disseyte *n.* deception 80/22; *pl.* 90/2.

disseurte *n.* lack of security 242/31 (*MED, OED* word om.).

dissimelid *pa. t.* concealed 40/26. **dissimiled** *pp.* pretended not to see 44/10.

dissimelynge *vbl. n.* ignoring 44/25. **dissimulacion** *n.* dishonesty 8/18. **dissol(l)ucion** *n.* excess, extravagance 39/11, 201/25; *pl.* 200/24; dissolute living 93/20; *pl.* dissolute practices 47/3, 202/27, 203/27.

distaunce *n.* extent of space 143/17. *grette* ~ remoteness 142/18.

distinccion *n.* separation 24/16.

distiped *pp.* scattered in defeat 241/4 (*MED, OED* word om.; ? scribal error for *dissiped, OED* rare; Fr. 'dissipee'; see note).

distraccion *n.* misappropriation 132/26 (*MED, OED* meaning om.; Fr. 'distraction').

distressid *pp.* afflicted with pain 169/9. **destressid** *ppl. adj.* ? exhausted, i.e., fig., dead; ? overwhelmed, crushed in battle; ? scribal error for *descessid* 243/12 (Fr. 'mort').

distribue *v.* distribute 227/10. **dystrybueth** (NJ) *pr. 3 sg.* 112/25.

distryneth *pr. 3 sg.* afflicts 66/1 (*MED, OED* spelling om.; **destreyneth** NJ).

diuers(e) *adj.* perverse, adverse 212/15, 213/13.

diuidith, deuideth *pr. 3 sg.* distributes 136/1, 137/2; breaks asunder 136/14, 137/16 (Fr. 'retranche'). **diuidid** *pp.* 234/5, 235/4; see 71/32 note.

dyvision *n.* severance 67/2.

doctrinable *adj.* instructive 33/6 (*MED* om.; *OED* rare, only ex. 1581).

doloreux *adj.* dolorous 143/8, 169/16, 177/15; **dolereux** 179/23; **doloreus** 149/26 (*MED, OED* spellings om.).

dolours *n. pl.* griefs 205/25.

Dominicall *adj.* in *Prayere* ~ Lord's Prayer 122/10 (*MED* om.; *OED* 1553).

dompte *v.* subdue *22/1 (see note).

do(o) *v.* achieve 100/33, 139/32, 227/33; administer 32/13; impart 114/23; provide 219/27; give 220/8. ~ *armes* go to war 167/22. *nat* ~ *withall* not do anything about it 14/15. ~ *vpon* put on 231/20. *hath all don* is finished 80/29. **doon** *inf* 193/18. **doo** *pr. pl.* 153/20; **don(e)** 37/31; **doon** 96/25, 199/23. **did** *pa. t. 1, 3 sg., pl.* 87/2, 102/20; **dede** 78/28, 225/17. **dedist** *2 sg.* 48/3. **do(o)** *pp.* 7/3, 139/32; **don(e)** 107/20, 236/12; **doon** 31/26, 227/33; *see* **amysse, power**.

doolefull *adj.* sorrowful 159/15.

doubtable *adj.* uncertain, to be feared 10/26, 156/1; redoubtable 82/24 (**doutetable** N).

dou(b)te *n.* in *putteth litle* ~ have little hesitation 191/11. *sette no* ~ *vpon* not be uncertain about 31/15.

dou(b)te, dowbte *v.* hesitate 190/11; fear 6/24, 212/6, 213/5; *refl.* 130/27, 154/29, 155/26; be feared 142/30, 143/27; conjecture, suspect 220/22, 221/20 (*MED* meaning om.; *OED* only as tr. v., 1574; Fr. 'se douter'). **doubtyn** *pr. pl. subj.* 39/2. **doubtid** *pp.* respected 3/11; *ppl. adj.* 104/35; worthy of reverence 134/6.

douteouslye *adv.* uncertainly 213/31.

dowe *n.* dove 91/1.

dowtfull *n.* used as synonym for Dialetique 23/15.

drawe *v.* lead 30/2; attract by moral force 22/28, 127/9; write out 132/23; go 7/34; *refl.* 13/7; turn one's attention 4/5, 20/19; come 69/12. ~ *aba(c)k(e)* withdraw 69/30, 77/20. ~ *along* (*refl.*) retreat 232/9. ~ *bak* retreat 161/20. ~ *owte* extract, derive 31/15, 224/10. **drawen** *pr. pl.* 30/2. **drough** *pa. t.* 69/12; **drowgh** 20/19; **drwe** 217/20; **drowe** 16/1. **drawen** *pp.* 132/23; **drawe** 130/17.

dreed(e), dred(d)e *n.* deep awe or reverence 35/12, 134/7, 135/10; fear 90/28, 134/20, 141/16; danger 191/30; *pl.* 71/17; see 67/30 note.

dreede *v.* fear 143/15. **dredde** *pp.* 48/22; **drad(de)** 218/10, 219/9; **dred** revered 88/28.

dreedfully *adv.* with fear 235/26.

dreme *pr. pl.* speculate 186/26; **dremen** 187/25.

dremyng *ppl. adj.* dreamlike 19/20 (*MED* adj. om.; *OED* 1552).

dresse *v.* direct 112/9; *pr. 3 sg. abs.* prepares 85/11; *pa. t. tr.* prepared 67/28; *refl.* raised oneself 69/14; *pp.* combed 144/15.

drye *pr. 1 sg.* wither (*MED*), pine away 175/1. *dryed vp in þe brest* (*pp.*) withered, pined away 174/1 (*MED*, *OED* phr. om.; Fr. 'seiché sur le pié').

dryfte *n.* meaning, scope 68/4 (*MED* meaning om.; *OED* 1526).

drynesse *n.* thirst 196/28.

dryuinge oute of *vbl. n.* expulsion from 233/9.

dronken *pp.* drunk 35/9 (**drounken** N; **drongen** C).

droppinges *vbl. n. pl.* rain, etc. 191/3.

duete *see* **dewte**.

duke *n.* leader 104/20; Doge of Venice 55/28.

dull *adj.* dispirited 4/26; exhausted 15/8.

dulnesse *n.* sluggishness 148/27.

dure *v.* last 76/2. **durith** *pr. 3 sg.* 4/11 (**doryth** J). **dureth** *pl.* 52/9; **dure** 40/19. **dueringe** *pr. p.* 18/34.

during(e), dueryng *vbl. n.* endurance, permanence 31/13, 132/12, 146/6.

dwelle(n) *v.* remain 153/20, 175/5; *pr. pl.* 138/33, 142/34; persist 158/17, 159/14.

eary *v.* plough 168/5 (*MED eren*; *OED ear*; **eery** SJ, **eeryth** N).

ease *n.* in *do* ~ give assistance 182/8. *take their preve* ~*s* selfishly make themselves comfortable 56/29.

eche (R), **iche** (U) *pron., adj.* each 53/27, 173/12, 181/14. **ichone** each one 139/22. **echon othir** each other 7/25.

edifie *v.* build 102/29; *pp.* 136/31, 137/33.

effect(e) *n.* execution, fulfilment 37/12, 73/2, 223/6; *pl.* attributes regarded as the observable manifestation of essential nature, here of humanity 62/13.

efficient *adj.* that makes a thing what it is 62/11, 67/23.

effusion *n.* ~ *of bloode* bloodshed 202/33; ~*s of the blood* 203/32. ~ *of his propir bloode* suicide 17/20.

eftirward *adv.* afterward 160/34.

eftis *adv.* again 94/29.

eftsones *adv.* likewise 181/12, 182/31.

egall *adj.* fair 42/12; equal 57/15; *n.* 193/28.

egally(e) *adv.* equitably 51/26, 220/21, 221/19; evenly 220/28.

egalnesse *n.* equality 129/3.

egir, egre *adj.* sharp 200/22, 201/23; severe, harsh 45/3, 172/20, 173/21.

egyrly, egrely *adv.* angrily 164/16, 165/17; harshly 176/11, 177/11.

egrith *pr. 3 sg.* sours 95/26 (*MED*, *OED* meaning om.; Fr. 'aigrist').

eyded *pp.* aided 214/1.

eyre *n.* air 68/8, 150/30.

ell *adv.* else 141/18.

em- *see* **en-**.

embraced *pp.* inflamed 67/4.

empeche *v.* prevent 14/19.

empeyrith *pr. 3 sg.* makes weaker, damages 11/28; *pl.* 38/28.

employed *pp.* bestowed 128/20 (*MED* meaning om.; *OED* 1548). **enployed** used 220/12 (empleyed J).

empreent, enprentid *see* **inprynte**.

emprise *n.* will 78/4; spoil, prize 124/28 (*MED* meaning om.; *OED* questioned; Fr. 'prise'; see note); *pl.* undertakings 105/23.

enbrace, embrace *v.* embrace 71/5; acquire 53/23; undertake 67/20; grasp with the mind 30/36 (*MED* Chaucer, *Boethius* [*c.*1380]; *OED* 1831).

enbracementis *n. pl.* undertakings 208/30 (*MED* om.; *OED* 1630).

enbrasing *vbl. n.* undertaking 209/28.

enbrowdered *pp.* embroidered 148/9 (enbrowded NSJ).

enbrowdour *n.* embroidered work or material 144/21 (*MED*, *OED* noun om. in this meaning).

enbrowdringe *vbl. n.* embroidered ornamentation 145/21 (*MED* om.; *OED* 1536).

encerched *pp.* made search 141/15.

enchayned *pp.* linked together 127/18.

encheson *n.* cause, motive 160/28, 161/30; *pl.* 219/13.

encline *v. tr.* bow (the body and head) 59/26; bend 82/8; fig., cause to bow or obey 25/12; *intr.* sag 149/13; fall 40/7; be favourably inclined, be disposed 74/15, 92/3; ? bow down, ? turn in feeling or action 44/29; apply oneself to 244/29; turn aside 34/10; *pr. p.* sloping 145/17; *see* **inclyne**.

encreece *pr. pl.* grow 137/29; **encresin** 136/26.

encreecinge *vbl. n.* growth 137/31; **encresing** 136/29.

encroche *v.* seize wrongfully 154/31.

ende *n.* utmost limit 105/26. *maketh an* ∼ completes 85/12. *make an* ∼ *of* put an end to 110/17; finish off, complete 153/23. *toke their* ∼ were fulfilled 83/35.

endeinith *pr. pl.* deign, think fit (with n. cl. as obj.) 222/18 (*MED* with inf.; *OED* rare, only in refl.; see note).

enforce *v. tr.* compel 105/10, 127/10; exert 151/29; *refl.* (with inf.) exert oneself, strive 7/24, 27/29, 244/12, 245/13; *refl. abs.* exert oneself 19/13; *refl.* strengthen oneself, grow stronger 16/16, 102/14 (*MED*, *OED* refl. om. in this meaning); *intr.* grow stronger 105/9. ∼ *to* strengthen in 247/20. **enforcet** *pr. 3 sg.* 105/9.

enforme *v.* learn 123/6.

engendringe *vbl. n.* copulation 99/5 (engendreure J).

engynes *n. pl.* wits, skills, talents 143/21, 147/29, 161/8; instruments (of war) 187/1, 221/10.

englouted *pp.* swallowed 203/16.

engraiued *pp.* impressed deeply, greatly troubled 175/10, 181/18 (*MED engreven* = 'vexed, troubled, aggrieved'; Fr. 'aggravante', 'aggravez'; see 175/10 note).

engrosse, engroce vp *v.* amass 41/10, 190/8.

engruggement *n.* increase 43/10 (*MED*, *OED* word om.; see note).

enhabite *v. tr.* furnish with a dwelling place 83/8; *pr. pl. intr.* dwell 163/29.

enhaunce *v. tr.* praise 39/12; increase 27/31; lift 68/8; exalt in wealth 47/3; elevate spiritually 77/9, 115/3; *abs.* 115/1; *refl.* lift oneself up with pride 89/1. **enhaunsith** *pr. 3 sg.* 170/10.

enhaunceyng *vbl. n.* raised position 35/16.

enlapped with *pp.* fig., wrapped in 157/6.

P

enlarge v. make less strict 92/4; pp. 93/30.

enlonge v. extend 103/25 (*MED* only one ex., ? 1440; *OED* rare, 1509).

enlowed pp. brought low from a higher position 139/23, 155/26 (*MED*, *OED* word om.).

enlumynith pr. 3 sg. enlightens 21/12 (**enlymyneth** SJ). **enlumyneste** 2 sg. 25/13.

ennake imp. fig., void 153/28 (*MED*, *OED* word om.; Fr. 'denuez').

ennoyouse adj. troublesome 169/28 (*MED anoious*; *OED* rare).

enpartith pr. 3 sg. gives a part of 117/19.

enpeirynge vbl. n. damaging 147/21.

enpoysoned pp. steeped in poison 105/27.

enposteme n. fig., moral sore 203/22 (*MED emposteme = aposteme*; *OED* 1565).

enquest n. inquiry 169/17.

enrichid pp. made splendid by decoration 144/21, 145/22, 147/30 (*MED* meaning om.; *OED* 1601).

enroote pr. pl. fix firmly in custom 157/33; ppl. adj. 157/2 (*MED* meaning om.; *OED* 1595).

ensignes n. pl. symbols of dignity 145/23.

enstablischid pp. established 55/29.

enstraunged pp. removed far (from) 116/11, 131/21.

ensue v. intr. (impers. with virtual subj. cl.) follow as a logical consequence 169/22; **enswe** 213/17 (*MED* use om.; *OED* 1581).

entailed ppl. adj. portrayed by carving 147/30; transf., with reference to embroidery 145/26.

ente(e)r(e), entier adj. complete 67/30; sincere 129/24; honest 182/25, 183/24.

entermedled, entremedled pp., ppl. adj. intermingled 23/28, 30/2, 144/29, 145/30; fig., mixed up, confused 204/31, 205/31, 208/25 (*MED*, *OED* fig. meaning om.).

entier adv. entirely 239/13.

entyrditid pp. cut off (with shades of ecclesiastical meaning) 70/31.

entowned pp. engulfed 203/18 (*MED*, *OED* word om.; Fr. 'entonne'; see note).

entrailes n. pl. inward parts (seat of emotions, etc.) 63/6.

entre v. ~ in consider 97/4 (*MED* meaning om.; *OED* 1553). **entird** pa. t. made a beginning (in understanding) 127/18.

entre(e) n. entrance 8/20, 9/19; right of entering 8/13; beginning 75/32, 206/13, 207/11; opening (of a speech) 207/24.

entremedelynges vbl. n. pl. impertinent interferences 8/30 (*MED* om.; *OED* 1531).

entreprenours n. pl. those willing to engage in risky undertakings 232/21.

entrete v. deal with, treat 32/9. **entreetid** pp. 157/25.

entvned pa. t. chanted 126/9.

envy(e) n. malice 11/1, 53/22; rivalry 196/19, 197/18; pl. injuries 56/6.

envyous adj. malicious 146/4; hostile 58/17 (see note).

environith pr. pl. surround, envelope 4/8. **enviro(u)ned** pp. 4/22, 146/31, 147/29.

er(e)ly adv. early 230/28, 231/26. ~ or late sooner or later 18/19, 42/18.

ernest see **peny.**

esclaue n. slave 14/15 (see note).

especiall n. in in ~ especially 207/1.

esperable adj. to be hoped for 67/33 (*MED*, *OED* word om.; Fr. 'esperables').

esperaunce n. hope 167/13.

essence n. substance, denoting unity of the Trinity 88/25, 119/31.

essenciall adj. that is such by essence 45/12; cf. **essence.**

essencially adv. as an essential attribute 117/17.

estable ppl. adj. fixed permanently 15/11.

establisshe pp. founded 135/13.

estayinges n. pl. supports 149/4 (*MED esta- = sta-*; *OED* om.; Fr. 'estaies').

estate, astate n. condition (material or moral, bodily or mental) 42/26, 142/10, 143/9; existence 143/23,

196/5, 197/5; status, especially exalted rank 40/24; *pl.* 196/18, 197/17; physical position 121/3. *of* ~ of rank 63/32.

esteme *v.* estimate (the number of) 58/24.

estimacion(e) *n.* comprehension 30/ 25; judgement, opinion 27/20, 103/ 29.

estimatiffe *adj.* ~ *vertue* faculty of judgement 5/26 (see note).

estraungeth *pr. 3 sg.* moves away 9/4; *pp.* removed 212/31.

ete, eete, eyte *v.* eat 91/1, 129/17, 177/3. **ete** *pr. pl.* 170/13; **etyn** 129/ 10. **ete** *pa. t.* 50/32.

eureuse *adj.* prosperous 185/7; **vrous** 192/4.

euerych *pron.* each one 24/11; *adj.* each 176/3.

evill(e) *adj.* defective 95/26; miserable 124/13.

evil(le), evell *adv.* insufficiently 42/ 11, 212/2; wickedly 42/22; with hostility, cruelly 180/19; *see* **founded.**

evyn(e) *adv.* quite, fully 170/18, 178/ 18; just then 126/11.

exalteth *pr. 3 sg.* raises in power, estimation, wealth, etc. 135/14. **exalted** *pp.* 207/9; elevated (to high office) 55/25; extolled 171/9; *ppl. adj.* raised aloft 147/28; successful, powerful 195/10. ~ *in pride* swollen with pride 193/13.

examined *pp.* proven 61/17.

excellentes *n. pl.* excellent actions 64/3 (*MED* om.; *OED* sb. rare, only in meaning 'excellencies'; **excellences** J, **excellence** N; see note).

excercinge *vbl. n.* performing 227/23 (*MED, OED* vbl. n. om.).

excercise (-sice, -cice) *n.* education, experience, skill 57/17; habitual practice of warfare 107/2 (*MED* meaning om.; *OED* 1551); use (of arms) 184/22, 247/17; actual performance 24/31, 53/16. *witty* ~ wise and skilful effort or performance 10/32, 83/19, 103/19, 113/10, 134/4; *pl.* 64/3 (Fr. 'industrie'). *yeveth* ~ allows some freedom 94/2-3.

ex(c)ercise *v.* use 22/1; perform 54/ 28, 185/20; *pp.* afflicted, in sense of 'proved' 73/29. ~ *of* afflicted by 16/35.

excersyseing *vbl. n.* performance (in war) 226/23.

excercites *n. pl.* practices 243/10.

excited *pa. t.* urged 229/4.

execracions *n. pl.* ? actions of removing a curse 124/17 (*MED, OED* meaning om.; **expracions** J; see note).

execucion *n.* in *put in* ~ bring into operation 141/13-14; carry out 179/ 10-11.

execute *v.* carry out the duties of 46/18; bring into operation 29/7. **execute** *pp.* carried out 46/6.

exemple *n.* in *in* ~ as an example 60/18.

Exemplier *n.* example, model for imitation 126/13 (*MED, OED* spelling om.; **exampler** NJ).

exempt(e) *pr. 1 sg. refl.* free myself (from blame to which others are subject) 172/30 (**exempe** J); *pp., ppl. adj.* free of hardship, suffering, etc. 188/16, 189/15. ~ *from* not liable to the duty of 48/29; not subject to 63/29, 128/23. ~ *of* free from blame (to which others are subject) 173/30.

expense, expence *n.* spending 185/ 13; wasteful spending 221/21; *pl.* 203/30; costs 201/27.

experient *adj.* experienced, tried 9/ 23 (*MED* only in Latinate phr. *ben* ~ = 'to test'; *OED* adj. om., only ex. as sb. 1605; Fr. 'experimenté').

experte *adj.* experienced 3/29.

expertely *adv.* by actual experience 51/31.

exploit(e) *n.* achievement 168/32; fulfilment 75/6; undertaking 166/26.

exposid *pp.* explained in detail 63/4.

exteynte *pp.* annihilated 61/10 (**extyncte** N).

exterminacion *n.* utter destruction 61/20, 158/18 (*MED* meaning om.; *OED* 1549).

extincte *pp.* brought to an end 138/ 12.

extort *ppl. adj.* wrongfully obtained 102/23.

extraccion *n.* lineage 145/8.

extreemys ? *n., adj. pl.* extremities, hardships; extreme 215/16 (*MED* noun om.; *OED* 1546–7).

extremite *n.* extreme degree (as opposed to the mean) 91/25; extravagance in behaviour 93/29 (*MED* meaning om.; *OED* 1533).

faade *adj.* that has lost the sense of taste 6/8 (*MED* om.; *OED* 1715; Fr. 'fade').

facions *n. pl.* shapes 137/22; **factiones** 136/20 (**fassions** NS).

factours *n. pl.* adherents 90/28 (*MED fautour*).

faculte(e) *n.* power 57/20; opportunity 213/7.

fadid *ppl. adj.* pale, wan 7/17 (**fade** NSJ).

faile *v. intr.* be at fault 21/13, 115/34; go astray 81/28, 219/6; come to an end 65/20, 170/28, 171/27, 199/31; be wanting at need 22/12, 37/25; be lacking 170/15, 218/6; sim. (with dat. of person) 15/8, 166/31, 167/28; be inadequate or insufficient (with dat. of person) 226/13, 227/13; not render expected service or aid (with dat. of person) 205/35; come short of performing one's duty 231/24; pass away 18/10, 34/25; fig., lose power or strength (with dat. of person) 85/32; *pass.* come to an end 187/2. ~ *of* lack 101/25, 129/27; lose 9/30. **fail(l)e** *pr. pl.* 85/32, 167/28; **failleth** 205/35; **failyn** 166/31, 170/32. **fayled** *ppl. adj.* come to an end 6/8; inadequate, lost 144/2, 145/1.

fayne *adj.* glad under the circumstances, obliged 17/12, 232/13; **feyne** 192/32.

fayne *adv.* gladly, willingly 127/27, 230/31, 231/29.

fayre, feyr *adj.* eloquent 58/15; noble 205/20; sound 59/2. **fayier** pleasing to hear 41/19 (*MED*, *OED* spelling om.).

fall(e) *v.* turn out 187/12; come as a consequence 13/31, 198/12; occur, happen 109/24; *impers.* 64/32, 231/21; come to ruin 18/4; vanish 77/27;

fall (into false belief) 78/4, 83/34; be forced 124/13. ~ *in* belong in classification under 58/8 (*MED* ~ *into*). ~ *of* happen to 103/7. ~ *to* befall 64/26, 195/26. ~ *vndir* be subjected to 115/26. ~ *in age* grow old 3/31. ~ *in my memorye* occur to me 235/7–8. *happid* ~ chanced to occur 156/27. **fall(e)** *pr. pl.* 3/31, 235/19; **fallith** 41/3; **fallen** 58/8, 213/19. **falle** *subj.* 231/21. **fellest** *pa. t. 2 sg.* 95/10. **fell** *3 sg.* 61/5, 144/5. **fall** *pp.* 3/25, 78/4; **fallen** 95/16 (**ifalle** J), 184/17, 185/9.

falling *ppl. adj.* degenerating, decaying 35/29 (Fr. 'caduque'). ~ *evill* epilepsy 95/11.

famylier *adj.* intimate 76/9; too free 95/32.

familiers *n. pl.* members (of a household) 228/30.

fande *see* **fynde**.

fantasie *n.* mental apprehension, or faculty by which it is formed 6/13, 15/34; false supposition, deluded notion 82/27; *pl.* 79/5, 83/1, 86/20; inclination, desire 90/29; *pl.* 19/20.

fantasied *ppl. adj.* imagined 69/27.

farced *pp.* fig., overlaid thickly 222/28, 223/26.

fardell *n.* bundle 12/23; burden 165/34; burden of sin or sorrow 37/20.

fatt *n.* richest or choicest part 203/18 (*MED* only ex. *c.*1350; *OED* 1570–6).

fattenesse *n.* oily substance 47/18.

fau(l)te, fawte *n.* wrong, sin 30/21, 202/6; *pl.* 7/6, 220/19, 221/16; failure 235/19; lack 18/26, 232/10, 233/11; **favte** 50/19.

fauted *ppl. adj.* deficient, in sense of giving way before an enemy 239/8 (*MED* ppl. adj. om.; *OED* only record in meaning 'faulty', 1608).

fauty *adj.* sinful 207/1. **fawty** wrong 83/25.

fauorable to *adj.* inclined to countenance 93/33.

favour *v.* countenance 44/33.

fauo(u)r(e) *n.* favourable regard 110/1; liking 204/7, 205/7; partiality, personal sympathies as interfering with justice 160/17, 234/29, 235/28.

by ∼ through the goodwill of a superior 56/26. *toke them into his* ∼ brought them to his aid or support 102/5.

febelith *pr. 3 sg.* enfeebles 5/20.

feble *adj.* ineffective, deficient 30/19; miserable 172/3; weak 126/16, 149/4; lacking intellectual or moral strength 15/24, 117/19, 138/36, 139/34; inadequate, bad 170/11.

feblenes(se) *n.* lack of moral strength 67/12; scantiness 190/5, 191/5.

feblid *ppl. adj.* impaired 20/32.

feblischid *pp.* enfeebled 26/23, 240/3.

fed(d)irs *n. pl.* feathers 114/14, 123/15.

feding *vbl. n.* bringing up 99/9.

fedith *pr. 3 sg.* beguiles with flattery 9/9.

fee *n.* lordship 55/7.

feer(e) *n.* mingled feeling of dread and reverence toward a rightful authority 51/36, 55/18; formidableness 111/4 (*MED* meaning om.; *OED* 1601); object of fear 37/30.

feers, fe(e)rce *adj.* fierce 3/14; haughty 59/28, 210/30.

fe(e)te *n.* deeds 220/1, 234/2.

feyirnes *n.* beauty 146/23.

feyne *see* **fayne.**

feyned *ppl. adj.* deceitful, insincere 78/10, 162/2.

feynynge *vbl. n.* pretence 163/3.

feyr *see* **fayre.**

feith *see* **litle feith.**

felauship *v.* accompany 241/18.

felde *n.* fig., field of battle 70/15; *see* **kepe.**

felenouse *adj.* angry 11/31.

felle *v.* feel 179/9.

fellow(e), fel(l)awe *n.* equal 8/22, 192/28, 193/28; sharer 10/5; servant 230/16; *pl.* 231/16; companions, accomplices 16/7, 102/23, 163/12.

felony(e) *n.* anger 7/10; villainy 27/18, 199/31.

femynyne *adj.* effeminate 148/24, 158/13. **femenyns** *pl.* 149/29; **femynyns** 159/10.

ferce *see* **feers.**

ferde *adj.* afraid 14/5.

ferforth(e), ferfurth *adv.* in *so* ∼ so greatly 107/34. *as* ∼ *as* as much as

246/19–20. *to* ∼ to too advanced a stage (of discussion) 218/23.

fermed *pp.* fixed 29/20 (see note).

fer(re) *adj.* far away 85/31, 148/25, 149/30; remote in time or nature 134/6.

fer(re) *adv.* greatly 28/17, 147/16; far away 5/12. *so* ∼ so fully 181/6. *as* ∼ *as* as much as 200/19. **for** far 18/29; *see* **byfore.**

ferther *adv.* in *no* ∼ no more 172/28–9, 173/28–9. *no forther* no more fully 244/1.

fest *n.* in *makyng grete* ∼ *and ioye* rejoicing 178/23.

figur(e) *n.* image, likeness 18/27, 26/2; symbol 23/30, 129/21; *pl.* apparitions 6/15; emblems 23/28; letters 146/14; foreshadowings 84/33. *by* ∼ by figurative means 84/23.

figurid *pp.* presented as a symbol 24/12; foreshown 51/19; represented (in a picture) 144/22, 145/22; *ppl. adj.* symbolic 66/31.

filith *pr. 3 sg.* infects 38/26.

filth(e) *n.* unclean use 30/12; corrupt action 94/34; sin 18/29; *pl.* 97/2.

fynde *v.* find 123/32. **founde** *pa. t.* invented 86/32; **fande** 143/6, 157/26; **fonde** 14/33, 142/6; **foonde** 119/6. **fonde** *pp.* 27/26.

fyne *n.* end 105/22.

fyniall *adj.* final 67/23.

flaielinge *vbl. n.* scourging 209/10 (*MED, OED* vbl. n. om.).

flauour *n.* odour 69/29.

fled(de) *pa. t. tr.* forsook 215/11; *pp. intr.* driven away 106/22.

fleing *ppl. adj.* fickle 160/9 (*MED, OED* meaning om.; Fr. 'volages').

flesch(e)ly, flesshely *adj.* mortal 22/18; carnal 34/9; given up to carnal lusts 94/33 (*OED* rarely used of people).

flete *v.* drift 154/3.

flyen *pa. t. pl.* flew 119/6.

flyes *n. pl.* bees 244/30.

flitte *n.* flight 165/9.

floode *n.* tide 196/31; *pl.* 197/30.

florishyng youthe *n. phr.* the bloom of youth 224/29 (*MED* om.; *OED* 1562).

florisshith *pr. 3 sg.* flowers 85/16.

flouris *n. pl.* flowers 24/7. **flowres** prime of life 4/4.

folden *ppl. adj.* rolled up (as a scroll), shut 23/29.

foliship *n.* foolishness 234/21 (*MED folship*; see note).

followit *pr. 3 sg.* follows 218/1; **foles** 64/28 (**folowes** NJ).

foot(e) *n.* basis 68/1; lower part which supports 139/3.

for *see* **ferre**.

for *prep.* because of 11/2, 14/13, 140/13, 170/34, 171/30; as (with adj.) 58/9; as (with n.) 119/12; as regards 10/35; by 226/17; as equivalent to 120/6; for the purpose of 161/22, 181/18; in order to (with vbl. n.) 172/10, 180/21; in order (with inf.) 11/8, 149/31. ~ *bycause* because 86/30.

force *n.* military power 106/32. *of* (*veray*) ~ of necessity 13/27, 164/4–5. *of no* ~ of no effect 99/9. *it is* ~ it is inevitable 168/9, 189/14.

forced *ppl. adj.* imposed by force 195/20 (*MED* ppl. adj. om.; *OED* 1576).

fordoone *pp.* destroyed 19/12.

foreclooose *v.* stop, bar 187/14 (*MED* meaning om.; *OED* no use exactly like this). **foreclosed** *pa. t.* closed up 243/21 (*MED* meaning om.; *OED* 1547).

foreyne *adj.* foreign 63/11; **foren** 108/6.

forfeit *n.* offence 243/17.

forfettith *pr. 3 sg.* sins 18/34.

forge *n.* hearth for refining metals in making coins 123/3 (*MED* meaning om.; *OED* 1601).

forged *pp.* fig., made (as coins are made) 123/5.

forgetyn *see* **foryetyn**.

forgo *v.* lose 16/14.

forlynyd owte of *pp.* gone astray from, degenerated from 148/25 (Fr. 'forlignez').

forloyned of *pp.* gone astray from, degenerated from 149/30.

Formatyve *n.* see 21/23 note (*MED* om.; *OED* sb. om.).

formefadirs *n. pl.* forefathers 152/11.

forte *adj.* strong 226/3.

fortefying *vbl. n.* encouraging, aggravating 53/34.

forther *see* **ferther**.

fortifie *v.* confirm, corroborate 123/26, 222/7; strengthen 141/10. **fortefienge** *pr. p.* 140/11.

fortunable *adj.* favoured by fortune 164/3.

fortune *n.* condition 38/16; good fortune 85/31. *of* ~ by chance 104/26.

fortune *v.* happen 218/19; *pa. t.* chanced (with person as subj.) 224/16.

forvoied of *pp.* gone astray from 149/29.

foruoyeng of *vbl. n.* going astray from 175/21.

forwhy *conj.* for 72/9.

forwildid *ppl. adj.* laid waste 168/32 (*MED*, *OED* word om.; *for-* pref. denoting destructive effect+*wild*; Fr. 'en fresche').

foryetfull *adj.* forgetful 122/22; **forgetefull** 73/4 (**forgetyll** J).

foryetfullnes(se) *n.* state of being neglected 20/22 (**foryet(t)ylnes** NSJ); forgetfulness 77/29.

foryetyn, forget(t)yn *pr. pl. refl.* omit taking care of themselves 105/14; *pp.* forgotten 43/2, 205/19; omitted 126/32.

foryeuenesse *n.* forgiveness 32/11.

fotemen *n. pl.* foot-soldiers 228/14; **footmen** 229/14.

fotith *pr. 3 sg.* walks 79/29.

foule *adj.* sinful 54/24, 93/9; coarse 149/23; muddy 209/11.

foundament(e), fouendement *n.* foundation (of a building) 40/5; source 62/23; source of faith 25/20.

founded *pp.* originated 98/19. **fownded** provided for 128/23. *evell* ~ *ppl. adj.* insufficiently based 78/11 (*MED* om.; *OED* 1605).

foundir *v.* fall into ruins 148/3; *pp.* swallowed up 218/30.

founteigne *n.* source 122/33 (*MED*, *OED* spelling om.).

fo(u)rme *n.* logical arrangement of ideas 127/3 (*MED* meaning om.;

OED 1551); course, way 131/10; method 55/11. *vndir this* ~ as follows 16/8; in this way 55/31, 228/14. *vndir a singular* ~ in a private manner 186/26-7.

fo(u)rmed *pa. t.* stated formally 43/20; *pp.* arranged 147/12; made 245/27.

fourth *adv.* in the field of battle 232/25; *see* **norische, tellist.**

fowled *pp.* defiled 131/14.

fragilite(e) *n.* weakness 227/9; moral weakness 39/32.

fraunchise *n.* rights 173/14; sanctuary 167/29; freedom 9/30, 177/1; *pl.* 176/1.

frawded *pp.* deceived 79/7.

fredom(e) *n.* nobleness 23/17, 31/27 (see note), 222/15; sanctuary 166/32.

free *adj.* noble 96/11.

fre(e)le, freyle, fraile *adj.* weak, frail 17/22, 27/17, 238/17; subject to change 140/1, 141/1; transient 54/24; subject to injury or disease 5/34; easily overcome 63/20, 79/13.

freelnesse *n.* moral weakness 115/12.

freelte *n.* mortal nature 11/28; weakness 226/9.

frendis *n. pl.* kinsmen 55/16, 152/9, 153/8.

frendlyhode *n.* friendship 67/6.

frenesy(e) *n.* agitation of the mind, madness 5/14, 19/5; *pl.* 4/22; wild folly 83/6.

frequentacion *n.* performance 55/20 (*MED* meaning om.; *OED* 1525).

frequente *pr. pl.* practise 181/21.

fresch *adj.* gay 202/10. **fresshe** recent 107/13.

freschnes *n.* newness 146/5. **fresshnesse** elegance 159/22.

fryte *see* **fruyte.**

fro *prep.* from 25/15, 138/5, 187/7.

from *prep.* by 79/8; because of 131/28. ~ *hymself* out of his wits 5/17.

ꞃrowarde *adj.* perverse 105/8, 115/6.

ꞃrowardely *adv.* wickedly 167/3.

fructuouse *adj.* beneficial 207/10, 247/16.

fr(u)yte, frute *n.* profit, benefit 8/16, 78/15, 207/12; *pl.* 22/33.

frustratyve *adj.* fruitless 85/26, 89/5 (*MED* om.; *OED* rare, 1730).

fulfilling *ppl. adj.* pervading, perfect 21/10.

fulled *pp.* filled 180/21.

ful(l)fill *v.* fill, fill up 125/32, 127/27, 176/4; satisfy the appetite or desire of 94/20, 106/14, 129/16; accomplish, carry out 151/33, 170/9, 171/8; follow 184/7; *pp.* filled 96/20, 174/10.

fullfillyng *vbl. n.* carrying out 228/5.

ᵹaarde *n.* protector 55/5 (*MED, OED* spelling om.; **ᵹarde** NJ).

ᵹafe *see* **yeve.**

ᵹanne *pa. t.* began 19/17, 164/23.

ᵹarnischid, ᵹarnys(s)hid *pp.* equipped 27/2, 90/5, 229/30.

ᵹat(te) *see* **ᵹette.**

ᵹeynrestoryng *vbl. n.* restoring again 204/24.

ᵹeneracion *n.* descent 57/15; offspring, posterity 55/19, 65/30; *pl.* 84/10; nation 162/9, 163/9.

ᵹeneralite *n.* the greater part 41/4 (*MED* meaning om.; *OED* 1622).

ᵹentiles *n. pl.* those of noble birth 51/13.

ᵹestes *n. pl.* behaviour 147/26.

ᵹet(te) *v.* achieve 30/25; acquire 166/15, 167/13; receive 27/3; bring 163/26; bring to one's side 91/28. ~ *forewarde* advance 232/25. ~ *towarde* (*vnto*) bring (a person) to one's side 93/10, 96/2, 96/22. ~ *vpon* become possessed of 94/2. **ᵹat(te)** *pa. t. sg.* 27/3, 103/5; *pl.* 227/25; **ᵹetten** 53/16. **ᵹotin** *pp.* 170/2, 171/2; **ᵹetyn** 167/31; *see* **audience.**

ᵹif *see* **yeve.**

ᵹifte *see* **yefte.**

ᵹirdid *pp.* encircled round the waist 6/21 (**ᵹryd** J).

ᵹirdill *n.* carrying belt 6/21 (**ᵹrydyll** J); *pl.* 6/22.

ᵹladly *adv.* appropriately 53/4.

ᵹlayue *n.* spear, lance 153/16; *pl.* 165/1.

ᵹlorificacion *n.* investiture of the elect with heavenly bliss 26/7.

ᵹlorifie *v. refl.* exult 57/5, 140/8, 141/8.

ᵹlose *pr. pl.* interpret 83/24.

go *v.* walk 113/31; happen 44/4. ∼ *abowte* go to and fro 71/12; busy oneself 126/17. ∼ *byfore* be superior to 198/15, 199/12. ∼ *from the wey of* go astray from 174/22. ∼ *on* (*vpon*) *the erthe* live and move 50/33, 166/14. ∼ *owte of the fadirs ligne* degenerate 53/21 (see note). ∼ *owt of the way* digress 60/6. ∼ *owt(e) of the* (*right*) *way* go astray 45/33, 89/16, 100/10–11, 116/5. ∼ *vpon* attack 110/34. **goost** *pr. 2 sg.* 174/22. **goth** *3 sg.* 44/4, 199/12. **goo** *pl.* 168/22; **go(o)n** 71/12, 189/16. **went** *pa. t.* 89/16. **goon** *pp.* 45/33.

goyng *vbl. n.* in *at longe* ∼ in the end 106/34 (*MED* phr. om.; *OED* cf. *at long*).

good(e), god *n.* well-being 40/25; possessions, money, etc. 41/25, 174/18, 175/18; *pl.* 47/27, 199/29; grace 30/3, 78/14; *pl.* 68/18.

gossehawke *n.* large, short-winged hawk 69/23.

gouernaunce *n.* good order 29/23, behaviour, mode of living 152/26, 153/24. *haue the* ∼ *of* govern 244/2. *haue in thaire* ∼ control 245/2–3.

govern *pr. pl. refl.* conduct themselves 80/21. *be gouernid* (*pass.*) behave, act 196/4–5, 216/11–12. *uertuously gouernyd* (*ppl. adj.*) piously behaved 217/6–7.

gracious *adj.* fortunate 245/25.

grauntid *pa. t.* agreed 216/33.

gravell *n.* sand 73/6.

greable *adj.* fitting, pleasing 151/19.

grece *n.* fig., grease, i.e. the richest part 202/20.

gre(e) *n.* in *take in* ∼ accept willingly, take in good part 164/29, 194/12, 195/12, 209/14; *receyue in* ∼ 165/29.

gree *v.* consent 100/4.

greef, gref(f) *n.* sickness 114/3; distress, injury 44/17; *pl.* 48/7; sufferings 4/26. **greeuys** hardships, wrongs 201/26. *do* ∼ injure 126/23.

greef *adj.* grave, important 227/18; grievous 243/14.

gre(e)ue *v. tr.* injure, oppress, destroy 178/9, 194/8, 195/8, 231/14; *intr.* lament 154/4. **greve** *pr. pl.*

154/5; **greevyn** 155/4. **grevid** *pp.* distressed 73/3.

grefauntes *n. pl.* those who oppress or harm 221/12 (*MED, OED* word om.; Fr. 'nuisans').

grete *adv.* greatly 150/10; *see* **chepe.**

gret(e)nesse *n.* size 136/20, 143/17.

grette *n.* in *in* ∼ in a general way 127/32.

gret(te)ly *adv.* heartily 216/33; strongly 80/10.

greuaunce *n.* injury 179/9.

greuous(e) *adj.* troublesome, harmful 14/6, 66/2, 76/5; severe 141/5; important, grave 226/18.

greuouslye *adv.* oppressively 175/1.

grevousnesse *n.* seriousness 49/13.

groced vp *pp.* amassed 80/2.

grosse *n.* in *in* ∼ in a general way 128/5.

grosse *adj.* unclear and indefinite 81/17, 127/21 (*MED* meaning om.; *OED* 1534).

grossely *adv.* palpably, plainly 121/2 (*MED* adv. om.; *OED* 1526).

ground(e) *n.* fig., bottom, substance 139/33; earth; piece of cloth used as the basis for embroidery 146/18.

grounde *v. refl.* rely (on), especially in argument 226/18.

growe *v.* increase 44/11; originate 126/17. ∼ (*owte*) *of* originate from, issue from 39/9, 46/10, 69/9, 178/4, 187/17. ∼ *to* arise to the benefit or injury of 185/15, 224/22. **growen** *pr. pl.* 39/9, 46/10; *pp.* 44/11, 185/15.

growing(e) *vbl. n.* origin 72/3, 242/1.

gruge *n.* grumbling 116/18.

grugge *v.* grumble, complain 164/20; *pr. subj.* 43/13; *pr. 3 sg.* vexes mentally 236/26. ∼ *not at* have no scruples about 72/20.

grug(g)inge *vbl. n.* scruple 32/18; *pl.* complaints 66/24.

grutchyn *pr. pl.* are reluctant 188/4.

guerde *v.* fasten on with a belt 231/20 (*MED, OED* spelling om.).

guerdon *n.* reward 161/14.

guyde *v.* direct, lead 227/11, 233/31, 235/22; *refl.* conduct oneself (in walking) 63/9; *refl.* behave 236/33; *pp.* maintained 220/28. *be guydede* turn out 232/9 (see note).

guyding(e) *vbl. n.* behaviour 57/31; government 59/12, 81/15; command 227/2, 233/34.

habandoune *see* **abaundoune.**

haberioun *n.* coat of mail 230/21; **habirgeon** 231/20.

habitacions *n. pl.* mistranslation of 'habitudes' 30/1.

hab(o)undaunce *n.* abundance 52/19, 148/8, 149/9; *pl.* 206/6. ∼ *of his herte* overflow (of evil) from his heart 94/6.

habounde *v.* abound 143/21. **habunden** *pr. pl.* 142/23.

haynous *adj.* hateful 19/2.

halyng *vbl. n.* tearing in pieces 146/18.

hand(e), hond(e) *n.* hand 23/22. *afore the* ∼ beforehand 170/19. *bettir* ∼ victory 105/13. *the* ∼ *of God* vengeance 140/13, 141/13; *see* **close, ley, putte, take, wasche.**

hang *v.* hover (over), ready to fall 65/34, 140/13. ∼ *vpon* depend upon 112/33, 127/32; ∼ *in* 38/31. **hanghith** *pr. 3 sg.* 65/34. **hing** *pa. t.* 127/32; **hynge** 6/19; **honged** 38/31.

happe *n.* fortune 165/3; good fortune, prosperity 85/30, 213/6.

happe *v.* chance 244/24. **happith** *pr. 3 sg. impers.* 244/34; **happis** 230/23. **happid** *pa. t. impers.* 90/13, 156/27.

happy *adj.* blessed 42/9.

harburght *pr. 3 sg.* shelters himself 231/31 (*MED, OED* spelling om.). **harberowed** *pp.* lodged 188/32; cf. **herberow.**

hard *adv.* fiercely 193/37; severely 217/12.

harde *see* **here.**

hard(e) *adj.* cruel 36/9, 173/19; irksome, painful 206/11, 207/9; severe (winter) 171/15; violent 87/18; difficult to endure 152/13; firm, taut 94/2; stubborn 60/9. ∼ *iugement* severe punishment 39/21.

harden *pr. pl. refl.* become fixed 156/33.

hardy *adj.* daring 13/17, 184/24.

hardiment *n.* courage 181/5.

hardines(se) *n.* obstinacy 159/25; courage, boldness, resolution 155/8, 161/30, 164/6, 165/7.

hardnes(se) *n.* obstinacy 158/32; boldness 160/29; cruelty, harshness 104/17, 174/17, 175/17; severity (of winter) 170/16 (*OED* 1579).

harne(y)s, harneice *n.* armour 160/3, 161/3. *to* ∼ to arms 154/30–1, 155/27.

hasty *adj.* rash 69/6, 210/5, 211/6; imminent 28/31 (see note).

hastines(s)e *n.* rashness 14/27, 192/2, 193/2.

hastiuenesse *n.* rashness 193/9.

hauntyn *pr. pl.* practise habitually 180/23.

havntyng *vbl. n.* exercise 5/23.

haue, han (U) *v.* keep 183/21; lead 156/18, 157/21. ∼ *ado(o)* have to do 211/9; have to deal 101/20. **hast** *pr. 2 sg.* 10/7, 205/3; **has** 123/5. **haue** *pl.* 4/1, 142/25, 169/4; **han** 143/23, 157/30, 169/7; **hauen** 203/7; *see* **disdayne, remembraunce, suspeccion, suspecte.**

havure *n.* wealth 239/32; **haueure** 241/5.

hedy *adj.* violent 108/26.

he(e)de *see* **take.**

heele *n.* well-being 151/20; health 209/22.

heerdis *n. pl.* hards, coarser parts of flax 80/30.

he(e)r(e) *n.* hair 7/18, 158/21, 159/17; *pl.* 187/7.

helth(e) *n.* cure 9/20; well-being 150/14; salvation, spiritual well-being 6/4, 43/21.

helthfull *adj.* conducive to spiritual welfare 74/20 (**helefull** J).

hem *pron. pl. obj.* them 135/24, 137/23, 147/13; **him** 73/32, 129/12, 150/14, 196/11. **her** *gen.* their 35/4.

hemself *refl.* 101/31, 236/33; **hymself** 49/1, 56/25, 70/23, 152/5, 186/15, 232/9.

hepid *pp.* filled (with heaps of dirt) 225/20; fig., loaded 41/27, 177/4 (*MED* exact meaning om.; *OED* 1583); *ppl. adj.* heaped up to the brim 171/13.

hepis *n. pl.* fig., heaps 41/10. *on* ∼ in a prostrate mass 109/9.

herbergage *n.* lodging 148/31.

herberow *n.* abode, lodging 29/6;

herburgh 159/6; herbrurgh 149/
36 (*MED*, *OED* spelling om.); cf.
harburght.

her(e) *v.* hear 5/8. hard(e) *pa. t. sg.*
110/5; *pp.* 99/15, 234/9; herd(e)
88/24, 235/8.

herebefore *adv.* in time past 205/21.

hereon *adv.* herein 247/10.

heritage *n.* hereditary succession
235/11.

herken *v.* listen to 213/5; *pr. pl.* wait
233/7 (*MED* meaning om.; *OED*
1523). *harke(n) (vpon)* heed 22/32,
39/24.

herright *adv.* immediately 121/32.

herte *n.* hurt 170/25. hurtis *pl.*
injuries 170/25, 193/37; blows
causing damage 145/16.

hertely *adj.* severe 164/27.

hevy *adj.* dull 20/13; distressing,
sorrowful 4/17, 48/28, 206/16;
troublesome 28/28; grievous 138/23;
grave 213/18.

hevyly *adv.* mournfully 168/14.

hevines(se) *n.* grief 63/29, 164/21,
165/28; hevynesses *pl.* 214/3
(hyvenesse SJ).

hevinnes *n. pl.* heavens 21/15;
hevynes 15/15.

hid(d)ir *adv.* hither 70/33. ~ *and*
thiddir 146/20.

hiderto *adv.* before this 213/25.

high *pr. pl.* hasten 232/25; hyeth *refl.*
233/25.

high *adj.* great, exalted 5/22, 121/28,
144/8, 145/7; strong 25/22, 211/29;
difficult to perform 3/15; angry
148/20, 174/11; loud and angry 7/
28; haughty 194/22, 195/22. ~ *way*
way leading to spiritual grace 126/
27. *alle on* ~ very loudly 175/13.

highing *vbl. n.* exaltation 98/24.

highly *adv.* on high 25/12; greatly
48/34, 101/8; excellently 157/25.

highnes(se) *n.* loftiness of position
63/17; majesty 96/17; excellence
105/9; pride, greatness 192/15,
193/13.

hight *n.* in *on* ~ on high 166/25; fig.
42/20; *see* sette.

hym *see* hem.

hing *see* hang.

hyre *n.* reward 29/11.

histories *n. pl.* stories 229/7.

hit *pron.* it 29/12, 144/17. his *gen.*
125/15, 138/15, 139/14.

holde *v.* consider 173/33; *refl.* 36/22;
refl. remain 11/6; observe, abide by
33/3, 226/19; continue 123/26; have,
keep 39/28, 207/13; carry on (war)
152/5; support 195/32; keep faithful 81/20. ~ *as* consider as 172/32;
~ *for* 58/8, 193/34. ~ *right* remain
balanced (of a scale) 221/25. ~ *vp*
support 167/6. ~ *with* favour 49/5.
~ (one's) *pees* keep silent 164/20,
174/8, 175/8, 198/11. helde *pa. t.*
58/8, 152/5; heeld 175/8. holde *pp.*
149/14, 164/20; holden 81/20, 134/
13, 173/33; *see* parag, weye.

hol(l)y *adv.* completely 23/16; solely
163/8.

holpyn *pp.* helped 6/3, 169/4, 204/14.

honest *adj.* morally commendable 52/
18; honourable 105/22.

honeste(e) *n.* moral excellence 38/
12; decency 198/11, 199/10.

honestlye *adv.* honourably 231/19.

honged *see* hang.

ho(o) *see* who.

hoole *n.* in *ouir the* ~ completely (as
one's own) 128/28–9.

ho(o)le *adj.* complete 66/7; intact,
unharmed 191/24; well 114/2;
undamaged, uninjured 147/11, 189/
33; steadfast, loyal 99/17, 155/24,
215/24. ~ *thing* entire possession
128/29.

(h)o(o)ste *n.* army 104/5, 238/12,
238/27, 239/26; *pl.* 50/22.

hoote *adj.* zealous, furious 193/9.

hope of *n.* trust in, expectation of
55/15, 93/9.

hoste *n.* vassal 188/32; *pl.* 189/31
(*MED*, *OED* meaning om.; Fr.
'hostes' = 'vassals').

hough, howgh, how, hou, houg
adv. exclam. how 16/35, 41/22;
interr. 8/10, 18/21, 114/27; *conj.* why
52/9; as 135/13, 141/6, 143/12.

hough (how, hou) be it *adv.*
nevertheless 61/25; *conj.* although,
however much 121/13, 139/28; ~
that 161/27. *hough so it be* however
it may be 74/7.

household(e) *n.* maintaining of a

family 168/11; *pl.* household goods 222/20.

howirs *see* **our.**

humanite *n.* good behaviour 97/6; used as adj. 'human' 112/33 (*MED*, *OED* use om.).

humiliation *n.* humility 134/7, 135/10.

hurtelingis *n. pl.* violent thrustings down 22/27.

hurtis *see* **herte.**

iche, ichone *see* **eche.**

ydiotes *n. pl.* persons without learning 27/16.

ydolatrie *n.* immoderate veneration of persons 44/21. **ydolatre(e)s** *pl.* practices of idolatry 88/29, 93/18.

ydropique *n.* person with dropsy 196/28.

yese *n.* ice 79/29; **yse** 160/1.

if that . . . ne *conj.* unless 121/29–30.

yghe, yie *n.* eye 5/30, 146/33, 147/31. *at* (*the*) ~ with the eyes 149/24, 236/7. *haue an* ~ *to* pay attention to 213/14. **yghen** *pl.* 5/4, 138/33, 140/20; **yghes** 35/23; **yen** 234/21 (**yyn** S); **yien** 141/21, 165/11, 235/20.

ignora(u)nce *n.* offence caused by ignorance 232/10, 233/11.

ignore *v.* ? disregard, overlook (*MED* om.; *OED* 1801); ? not to know (*OED* 1611) 237/14.

ill *adv.* with hostility 181/17; inadequately 221/22.

ill(e) *adj.* wicked 153/17, 157/8; miserable 181/19; disastrous 185/14, 219/7; difficult 219/24, 227/9; inefficient 171/10. ~ *dooers* wrongdoers, criminals 161/15.

illusion *n.* deception 89/12.

im- *see* **in-.**

ymages *n. pl.* constellations 136/11, 137/13.

ymaginacions *n. pl.* thoughts about events not yet existing 4/26; untrue thoughts 202/29.

ymaginatiffe *n.* imagination 6/12. ~ *vertue* faculty of imagination 5/26 (see note).

immitatoure *n.* imitator *135/9 (*MED* om.; *OED* 1523).

immolacions *n. pl.* sacrificial slaughters 128/12.

impediment *n.* see 171/4 note.

importith *pr. 3 sg.* signifies 131/26.

impression *n.* influence 87/21.

in *prep.* in spiritual union with 24/26; in regard to 31/25; with 103/18, 140/29; by, by means of 20/12, 46/35, 57/20, 205/25; for 179/31, 247/25; as 84/9; into 171/26, 187/13, 215/6; in the hands of 169/33; in order to (before vbl. n.) 90/32, 110/11. ~ *them* (refl. pron.) in their own nature 121/6.

incerteyn *adj.* uncertain 62/28.

incerteyned of *pp.* certain about 42/31.

inclinable *adj.* disposed 119/26.

inclyne *adj.* favourably disposed 245/29.

incontinent *adv.* immediately 124/1, 157/23.

inconuenience (-iens) *n.* offence 222/24; misfortune 144/13, 182/24; *pl.* 172/10.

inconuenient *n.* offence 223/22; misfortune 173/11, 183/23; *pl.* 13/30, 58/2.

incredulite *n.* lack of religious faith 83/34.

indeuiable *adj.* immortal 165/1 (*MED*, *OED* word om.; Fr. 'indiviables' = 'immortal').

indignacion *n.* contemptuous behaviour 178/13, 179/14.

indigne *adj.* unworthy 223/17.

indignite *n.* contemptuous usage 49/29 (*MED* om.; *OED* 1584); unworthiness *132/16 (*OED* 1589; see note).

indissoluble *adj.* perpetually binding 151/33 (*MED* om.; *OED* 1542).

indulgence *n.* remission of sins 32/15.

inexpugnable *adj.* invincible 121/17 (*MED* inexpugnable, only ex. a1425; *OED* 1535).

infamye *n.* shameful vileness 91/23 (*MED* meaning om.; *OED* 1513).

infeccion *n.* moral contamination 38/3, 44/27, 208/27, 209/26; *pl.* 63/16.

infecte *pp.* morally contaminated 45/1, 89/27.

infynite *adj.* innumerable 236/12, 237/11.

infirmite *n.* moral flaw 181/7.

influence *n.* in *turnith the* ∼ influences the character and destiny of man 21/15 (see note).

infortunable *adj.* unfortunate 104/11, 179/4.

infortunat *adj.* unfortunate 11/12, 214/27.

infortune *n.* misfortune 14/18, 208/13, 209/13, 215/19; *pl.* 124/10, 214/24.

infusion *n.* infusing of a quality or idea into the mind or soul (esp. divine grace) 24/24, 71/30, 89/11.

ingendred *see* **engendirth**.

ingrate *adj.* ungrateful 177/18.

inhabitable *adj.* uninhabitable 36/30, 169/33.

iniquitees *n. pl.* sins 61/17; ? sinners 42/26 (*MED*, *OED* meaning om.; Fr. 'iniques'; see note).

iniquityf *adj.* grossly wicked 172/27 (*MED*, *OED* word om.; **inyquytes** N, **iniquytyse** S, **inquietyse** J).

iniuried *pp.* wronged 165/21.

iniurious *adj.* wilfully inflicting wrong 174/28, 175/27.

inmortall *adj.* immortal 162/36, 163/33; **inmortale** 210/29 (**inmortable** S, **immortable** J).

inpacience, impacience (-iens) *n.* inability to tolerate, irritability, resentment 196/13, 197/12; sim. (with inf.) 194/17, 195/17 (*MED* use om.; *OED* 1575). ∼ *of* 194/30, 195/30.

inpaciente *adj.* intolerable 18/13 (*MED*, *OED* meaning questioned; *OED* rare, 1590; Fr. 'impatient'; see note). *impacient of* unwilling to endure 157/10; cf. **vnpacient**.

inpacientes *n. pl.* annoyances 179/17.

inportable, importable *adj.* too heavy to be carried 164/34, 165/34; too painful to be borne 172/16, 173/18.

inportune *adj.* persistent 38/1.

inportunite *n.* burdensomeness 28/24.

inprynte *v.* lit., stamp 238/4, 239/4; fig., fix, impress 20/16, 186/23, 187/22. ∼ *in* impart to 74/7; move to 103/18. **enprynted** *pp.* 103/18; **enprentid** 238/4; **emprynted** 89/33; **empreent** 187/22; **empreentid** 239/4; *ppl. adj.* printed 137/12.

insomoche *conj.* to such an extent that 224/6. *insomiche that* inasmuch as 229/25.

inspiracions *n. pl.* influences under which the Bible was written 84/3.

instaunce *n.* instigation 214/32.

institucion *n.* in *naturall* ∼ inherent disposition, nature 86/22 (*MED c.* 1475, used of beasts; Fr. 'instinct').

institute *pr. pl.* appoint 55/32; *pp.* established 57/19.

instruccion *n.* knowledge, skill 135/7, 147/9; lesson 203/9.

instructe *pp.* taught 104/9.

into *prep.* up to 175/30, 215/3; for (a purpose) 187/5.

intollerable *adj.* unforgivable 83/6.

introduccion *n.* teaching 60/17, 96/23; *pl.* 97/3; preliminary steps 128/21; practice newly introduced *87/18, 131/4 (*MED* meaning om.; *OED* 1603).

invariable *adj.* unchangeable 115/7 (*MED* meaning om.; *OED* 1607).

invariablely *adv.* unchangingly 120/19 (*MED* adv. om.; *OED* 1646).

invariablenesse *n.* unchangeableness 119/23 (*MED* n. om.; *OED* 1654).

inuencion *n.* faculty of mental creation 97/33.

inwarde *adv.* internally 153/16.

yrouse *adj.* given to anger 117/28.

is *pron. gen.* his 141/13, 151/21, 173/26; see 68/13 note.

is(s)ewe *v.* take origin 67/16. **issewen** *pr. pl.* 186/18. **issued** *pa. t.* emerged 104/36. **issewid** *pp.* descended 73/7.

yss(e)we, yssue *n.* exit 9/19; end 75/32, 111/18; outcome, result 14/32, 105/22, 142/16, 206/12, 207/12; ? source; ? result 77/13 (Fr. 'source'); lineage 99/9.

ianglyng *vbl. n.* spiteful gossip, grumbling 57/26.

iape *n.* jest 95/15.

ientilnesse *n.* kindness 243/28.

ieoperdy *n.* jeopardy 58/5; iupardye 232/1; iuberte 180/26.

ioyne *v.* add 222/32. ioyneth *pr. 3 sg.* joins 98/28. ~ *to them* unites them with 73/30.

iointur *n.* union 18/26, 121/31.

ioyousetees *n. pl.* joyous behaviour 204/2.

iouglours *n. pl.* buffoons 53/31.

iuberte *see* ieoperdy.

iuell(i)s *n. pl.* jewels 158/11, 159/9.

iuge *v.* conclude 99/3; arrive at a sound conclusion about 214/10, 215/8. ~ *to knowe* believe 246/26, 247/25. *iugen of* appraise 182/4, 183/4. iuged *pp.* adjudged 214/16, 215/13.

iugement *n.* in *þe generall* ~ the last judgement 42/16.

iupardye *see* ieoperdy.

iupart *pr. pl.* risk 245/31.

iustice *n.* administrator of justice 37/24; infliction of punishment 238/30, 239/29; *pl.* 228/8, 229/8.

Iusticer *n.* administrator of justice, here God 67/14.

iustify *v.* prove the righteousness of, make righteous by infusion of grace 113/3; *pr. 3 sg.* 37/23; *pp.* 26/28, 96/35.

iustifiyng *vbl. n.* corroborating 111/27; administering of justice to 113/6.

kast *see* caste.

kembyng *vbl. n.* combing 158/22.

kende *n.* natural state 171/4. *naturall kynde* 209/28.

kepe *n.* care, heed: *take no* ~ *to* take no care in watching 181/9. *taking no* ~ *to* taking no heed of 159/9. *take so litle* ~ *therto* take so little heed to this 237/26–7.

kepe *v. tr.* guard, protect, defend 65/23, 142/20, 143/18, 152/10, 153/9; *refl.* 100/15; preserve, maintain 41/28, 53/34, 65/24; take care of 187/7; take care (with obj. cl.) 73/33; observe 97/20, 100/24, 226/16, 236/9; carry on 167/20; continue to cause 194/30; hold captive 152/20;

conceal 43/5, 199/10; *refl.* refrain 181/2; *intr.* continue (in a specified condition) 60/18. ~ *vndir* hold in subjection 28/2; conceal 84/23. ~ *vp the body of policie* preserve the body politic 172/4. ~ *the feeld* come to the field of battle 231/23; maintain one's position in battle, stand firm 160/5; ~ *feeldys* 161/4. kepe *pr. pl.* 53/34, 204/35; kepen 151/37. kepte *pa. t.* 68/32; keped 193/18. kept(e) *pp.* 41/28, 167/20; keped 189/4, 205/30; *see* close.

keping *vbl. n.* taking care 22/32; maintaining 172/10.

kest *see* caste.

kynd(e)ly *adj.* natural 55/10; pleasant 142/5.

kyndnes(se) *n.* friendship 10/12; gratitude 122/25.

kyndred *n.* family 55/18. kynderede line of descent 56/4. kindereddes *pl.* tribes 173/2.

kingly *adv.* of a king 81/15.

kytte *v.* cut 242/19. kut *pp.* 243/18.

knyt *pp.* fastened 93/15.

knowe *v. tr.* understand 31/7, 56/24, 210/8, 211/9; recognize 88/15, 236/34, 239/1; have experienced 120/7; *intr.* feel 4/11. *that is to* ~ that is to say 37/14–15. knowe *pp.* 88/15, 136/11; knowen 221/28, 239/1; ~ *to* familiar or intimate with 76/8.

knowing(e) *vbl. n.* understanding, knowledge, recognition 22/24, 26/3, 119/11; knowin 18/1.

knowlache (-lich, -lege), knawleghe (N) *n.* knowledge, understanding 135/11, 136/23, 148/24, 240/19; recognition 161/16.

knowlegyng *pr. p.* understanding 134/8.

kunnynge *see* connynge.

laave *v.* ladle out 31/5.

labo(u)r *v. tr.* till 167/30, 235/24; advocate strongly 90/27; produce with labour 246/28; take great pains with 187/8; *intr.* be troubled 145/4.

lach(e)nes(se), laschenesse *n.* slackness, remissness 149/25, 153/19, 181/7; cowardice 79/7 (lachessenes J), 239/18.

lachesse *adj.* remiss 78/26; **latches** 192/35.

ladyly *adj.* befitting a lady 145/8.

lay *see* **ley.**

lakketh *pr. 3 sg. intr.* is lacking 18/5. **lacked** *pa. t.* failed 126/24.

langour(e) *n.* sickness 5/21; sorrow 16/11, 148/19; woeful plight 103/11.

lang(u)age *n.* report, talk 57/1, 198/ 18; words 201/22; what has been said 201/3. *to(o)ke the* ∼ began speaking 175/12, 195/17.

languerous *adj.* sorrowful 175/4.

langustes *n. pl.* locusts 13/22 (*MED, OED* only one ex. besides this passage; see note).

langwisshing *pr. p.* pining away with grief 149/24; **languisshinge** 165/ 23.

large *adj.* not strict 94/1; great, capacious (of immaterial things) 108/33, 110/20; open of access 242/ 21, 243/19.

largely *adv.* greatly 48/13; liberally 112/26.

largesse *n.* liberality, munificence 29/23, 223/10; liberal bestowal of gifts 220/21, 221/15; *pl.* 221/18.

lasse *adj.* less 13/20, 189/17; less important 190/21, 228/24. **lesse** smaller in size 137/22. **lesser** *comp.* 189/20.

lasse *adv.* less 187/22, 198/7.

lasse than *conj.* unless 230/17; cf. **in lasse than.**

last *adj.* the greatest 138/20, 139/18 (*MED* these treatises only exs.). *the* ∼ *age* age immediately before present one 88/15.

lat *see* **lette.**

latche *n.* fig., snare 64/31 (**laithe** J).

latches *see* **lachesse.**

late *adv.* recently 190/30. *now* ∼ 191/ 29. *all to* ∼ much too late 169/19– 20, 207/15.

lately *adv.* tardily 140/4.

laughtir *n.* object of laughter 95/15.

lawe *see* **lough.**

lawfull *adj.* faithful, honourable 134/ 29.

leche *n.* physician 114/3.

lectoure *n.* one who reads a book 247/ 24.

le(e)de *v.* manage, conduct 193/8, 227/12. **lad** *pa. t. sg.* dealt with 193/ 37; *pp.* 171/4. **laid** *pp.* brought; afflicted (*MED*) 169/16 (see 168/ 12–15 note).

leef *adj.* agreeable 169/14.

leeffe *n.* leaf 85/18.

leene *adj.* ∼ *tyme* time of scarcity 8/8.

le(e)se *v.* allow oneself to be parted from 156/12, 157/12; *refl.* destroy oneself spiritually 81/24; *pr. pl.* lose, be deprived of 187/18; destroy, bring to perdition 156/11. **lest** *pp.* wasted 161/5; cf. **lo(o)se.**

leest *n.* selvage, band woven into fabric to mark end of a piece of cloth 74/4 (**lyest** NJ).

le(e)st(e) *adj.* in *at the* ∼ *wey(e)* at least 8/15, 48/29–30; *atte* ∼ *wey* 176/2, 182/26. *n.* those lowest in position 131/21, 241/26. *at the* ∼ at least 183/25.

le(e)ue *v.* abandon 65/28, 156/15, 157/16; ignore 191/26; lose, give up 182/4; *refl.* lose oneself (i.e. one's spiritual welfare) 70/23. ∼ *aparte* ignore 190/25. ∼ *in* abandon to 187/ 30. **leve** *pr. pl.* 70/23; **leuyth** 153/ 30; **levyn** 152/33; **lyue** 187/30.

lefte *imp.* lift 34/29. **lyfte** *pa. t.* 70/32, 125/26.

ley, lay *v.* cite (an example) 43/17, 199/27; add 223/29. ∼ *afore* bring to the attention of 76/19; ∼ *byfore* 150/6; ∼ *to* 151/7. ∼ *away* discard 54/9. ∼ *forthe* put forth in argument, cite an example 237/9. ∼ *vnto* cast upon 188/30. ∼ *to his hande* (*handis*) take action 182/7, 183/7. ∼ *to morgage* mortgage 180/ 28.

leiser *n.* ability, possibility 5/8; available time 106/27.

lenghe *n.* long period 73/17. *in* ∼ *of tyme* in the course of time 87/19.

lenyth to *pr. 3 sg.* supports oneself on 79/30.

lent *pp.* granted 150/9.

lepe *v.* leap 224/24, 225/17. **lepe** *pa. t.* 225/23; **lepte** 224/31.

lerne *v.* teach 111/33; *imp.* 71/19.

lernyng *vbl. n.* doctrine 98/21; *pl.* 99/ 15.

lesing *vbl. n.* fictitious story to be laughed at 95/9; *pl.* lies 57/26, 176/28.

lesinge *ppl. adj.* false 177/27.

lessed *pa. t.* diminished 35/1, 223/19; *pp.* 191/4.

lesson *n.* instructive example 190/30, 191/29.

let(te), lat(te) *v.* cause: ∼ *knowe* inform 78/8, ∼ *witte* 66/11; **let(te)** *pa. t.* ∼ *make* caused to be made 86/11, ∼ *purvey* prepared 27/4. as *impers. auxil.* let 67/11, 234/23; ∼ *it auaile* may it be profitable 141/34. leave: ∼ *alone* pay no attention, **letin** *pr. pl.* 46/16.

let(te) *v. tr.* hinder, stop 7/25, 244/5, 245/5; *pr. pl. intr.* prevent 161/5; refrain 236/17; impair, diminish 25/33. **lette** *pp.* 25/33; **lettid** 161/5.

letter, lettre *n.* Scripture 82/9, 91/32; text, writing 247/10; *pl.* 199/15. **lettur** literature in general, knowledge of books, etc. 57/2 (**lettrure** NJ).

lettinge *vbl. n.* opposition 233/30.

letturature *n.* learning 57/12 (**lettrure** NJ).

levied *pp.* raised 218/27; **leuyed** 220/1.

levir *adv.* rather 150/25, 151/30.

lewde *adj.* wicked 105/23.

liberall *adj.* bountiful 96/16.

liberte *n.* freedom from the bondage of sin 64/24.

lienage *n.* family 238/29. **li(g)nagis** *pl.* tribes 172/1; descendants 234/12.

lye *pr. pl.* exist 3/30, 4/3; **lyith** are appropriate 192/8.

lyer *n.* ∼ *vpon himself* deceiver, dissembler 99/32.

lyf *v.* live 149/31; **leve** 188/11. **lyve** *pr. pl.* 166/9; **lyven** 92/26; **lifen** 167/8. **lyuedin** *pa. t. pl.* 3/21, 76/31. **lyve** *pp.* 212/24; **lyued** 213/24.

lifte *see* **lefte**.

light *v.* fall and strike 141/21.

light *adj.* trivial 48/23, 160/6; unthinking, fickle 53/30, 85/27, 176/28, 177/27; easy 123/31, 174/15, 175/16. ∼ *to* moved readily by 86/13. **mor(e) lightar (-er)** easier 194/10, 195/9.

lightly *adv.* easily, readily 6/1, 22/22, 176/15, 177/15.

lightnese *n.* thoughtlessness 58/7.

lyke *v.* desire 10/3, 42/17, 154/4; do well 107/17; please 136/21; *impers.* 84/7, 237/16.

like *adj.* apt 148/3. *cace* ∼ similar situation 157/27, 239/16. *is* ∼ *for* seems 74/4.

like (wise) as, liche as *conj.* as if 6/26, 14/7, 147/18, 188/5, 189/5; as 36/7, 57/25, 128/19, 144/5, 145/5; *prep.* like 7/11, 155/1.

lyk(e)linesse *n.* in *by* ∼ seemingly 102/13. *as by* ∼ as might be expected 132/6.

lik(e)ned *pp.* compared 167/12 (Fr. 'adjouster'). ∼ *as* (*ppl. adj.*) similar to 57/5.

likenes(se) *n.* analogy 33/9; soul 89/33.

liking *vbl. n.* in *to your* ∼ in your opinion 153/25.

limitacion *n.* assigning within limits 128/31.

lymyted *pp.* assigned within limits 128/31; see 30/3 note.

lyne *n.* family 239/24; **ligne** 239/28. **lyeine** course 18/15. *by lyne* rightly 40/3; *see* **go**.

list(e) *v.* desire, choose (with inf.) 65/9, 111/28, 182/4, 206/14; *impers.* 30/12, 236/17.

litargie *n.* lethargy, mental or spiritual inertia 5/17.

litill *adv.* ∼ *and* ∼ a little at a time 192/20; *by litile and litle* 193/19.

litle feith *adj.* having little faith 215/10.

livelode *n.* livelihood, sustenance 13/17, 154/32.

lyuing(e) *vbl. n.* manner of life 196/5, 197/5; *pl.* possessions 141/8. *haue* ∼ live 151/12.

loenge *n.* praise 10/19 (**lowynge** J).

lokyng *vbl. n.* expression 7/8.

long on *adj.* because of 194/4.

long(e) to (vnto) *v.* be fitting or appropriate to 158/12, 159/10, 242/27; be prescribed for, be needed or used for 81/3, 211/25, 232/20; be the business, concern, or duty of 35/19, 81/8; pertain to as a right

243/23; belong to 47/5, 200/30, 201/ 33; be in the retinue of (a lord, etc.) 198/13; relate to 50/14. **longeth** *pr. pl.* 211/25; **long** 198/13; **longen** 242/27.

looge *n.* house occupied by a gardener, etc. 213/7.

looke *n.* in *high* ∼ noble appearance and bearing 69/16, 242/12.

lo(o)ke *imp.* take care 20/1, 66/6; behold 74/30. ∼ *afftir* expect 56/ 32. ∼ *wher* wherever 38/18, 96/12 (see 38/18 note).

loose *n.* renown 10/20.

lo(o)se *v.* lose, be deprived of 112/30, 186/19; destroy, bring to perdition 157/11. **lost** *pp.* damned 158/33, 159/26. *is lost* has disappeared 161/ 10; cf. **leese.**

lordeshippith *pr. 3 sg.* has power (over) 34/25.

lordly *adj.* having the appearance of a lord 144/9; suitable for a lord, magnificent 148/6, 149/7.

lothly *adv.* reluctantly 163/25.

lough *adv.* low 184/17; **lawe** 121/8; *see* **bryng.**

love *pr. pl.* like, enjoy, desire 188/31; **louen** 167/17. **louet** *pa. t.* 92/13.

loving *vbl. n.* praise 30/3, 122/24.

lowe *adj.* commonplace, base (of this world as opposed to heaven) 39/22, 68/25, 114/19; lowered 155/2; humble 37/4; **lawe** 203/2.

lowginge *n.* military quarters 229/18.

lowsith *pr. 3 sg.* sets loose 126/25.

luminarye *n.* ∼ *of your glorie* earthly glory 165/10.

lust(e) *pr. pl.* desire 240/9. *Him* ∼ *impers.* he wishes 129/17 (**lyste** J).

lustinesse *n.* merriment 205/2.

mad(e) *adj.* foolish, unwise 177/24, 193/12.

madly *adv.* foolishly 177/29.

mageste *n.* 241/21 (see 240/23 note).

magnanime *adj.* high-minded, courageous *217/11 (MED quotes only this ex.; OED 1523).

magnanymyte *n.* noble-mindedness, leading to great actions 76/31; courage 216/16.

maynte(i)ne *v.* defend, preserve,

keep control of 33/25, 142/20, 226/ 20, 227/19; rule, keep in good order 30/4, 134/14, 135/17; persevere in, carry on 14/6, 184/9; *refl.* conduct oneself, behave 109/26, 185/8, 197/4. **mainteignith** *pr. 3 sg.* cherishes 42/13.

mayntenaunce *n.* in *frendis of thy* ∼ friends that support you 10/15 (see note).

maiours *n. pl.* ? one's elders, ancestors 88/3.

maistre *n.* master workman 231/12; *pl.* 149/1.

ma(i)stres(se) *n.* sovereign lady 28/ 13; goddess 93/19; woman in control 170/7.

mayte *see* **mate.**

mak(e) *v.* make up, invent 92/23; exert 154/10; ask 201/29; build 51/ 9; enact 171/6; arrange 231/22; cause 49/13, 52/1; cause to be (with adj.) 110/8; sim. (with pp.) 106/13, 186/3; sim. (with pred. phr.) 156/ 5; *refl.* (with inf.) 14/30. ∼ *vp* build 83/18. ∼ *it not* does not prevent it 65/33. **makit** *pr. 3 sg.* 190/6; *see* **ende, reason, weye.**

maledic(c)ion(e) *n.* curse 165/15; wickedness 235/3 (*MED* cites only this ex.); God's punishment 62/9 (*MED* cites only this ex.).

malyson *n.* curse 164/14.

manace *v.* threaten 111/5; hold out as punishment to 49/2, 92/13.

manaces *n. pl.* threats 96/3.

maner(e) *n.* kind (of) 80/18, 136/19, 140/29; sim. (without 'of') 79/20, 114/5; *pl.* morals 95/22. *in* ∼ so to speak, in some degree 79/8. *in* ∼ *as* as if 28/25. *in* ∼ *of* after the fashion of 140/30; in a state of 164/ 28. *vndir this* ∼ in this way 36/20 (*OED* rare, 1523). *vndir suche* ∼ *a fourme* in such a way 218/7. *for the* ∼ *sake* for the sake of custom 231/ 24. *the* ∼ *of* the nature of 44/21. *no* ∼ (with n.) none at all 79/19, 92/24, 120/5. *one* ∼ *of* only one 111/ 9.

many oon *pron.* many 139/29.

marchaundise *n.* trading, commerce 166/16, 167/14, 190/21, 191/21.

marches *n. pl.* countries 99/14.

maresses *n. pl.* tracts of marshland 242/8; marreyses 243/8.

marke *n.* in *Goddis* ~ the tonsure 91/19. markis *pl.* that which marks a boundary or limit, limitations 31/18, 105/26; merkis 85/13.

mastres(se) *see* maistresse.

mate *n.* fig., checkmate, total powerlessness or defeat 19/5.

mate *pp.* drained (of) 157/26; rendered helpless or powerless, bewildered 149/33; mayte 148/29.

matir *n.* discourse 140/29. matere state of affairs 63/23. matyers *pl.* affairs 180/9.

ma(v)gre *prep.* in spite of 15/30, 102/14. ~ *thyn hede* in spite of you or all you can do 16/14, 54/12.

mawes *n. pl.* in *see* ~ seagulls 197/29.

may *pr. 3 sg.* may do 136/14.

meane, meene *n.* middle 137/19; trick 93/10; intermediary 121/27; condition, manner 238/10; way, course of action 91/29, 226/29; *pl.* 67/23; meyens 176/29. *by this* ~ in this way 99/23, 139/21-2, 217/9; *by thes meanys* 138/23-4.

meane *adj.* occupying a middle position 24/9; meeyne 147/10.

medle *v.* mix, mingle, blend 91/27. med(e)lid *pa. t.* 18/28; *pp.* 71/31, 95/25, 135/25, 148/10; fig., tempered (one attitude with another) 204/26, 205/26; fig., thrown into confusion 4/29 (*MED* cites this passage; *OED* meaning om.; Fr. 'meslé'). ~ *with* (*pa. t.*) dealt with 95/17.

medlyng *vbl. n.* uniting 77/3.

meke *v.* cause to be humble 82/2; *pp.* brought low 105/8; made receptive 52/7; *refl.* submitted 115/30.

mekenesse *n.* affliction, wretched state 27/24; timidity 79/7.

membre *n.* ? accomplice 201/7 (see note); *pl.* parts of the body 22/20, 99/28; privy members 93/16.

memoratiffe *adj.* ~ *vertue* faculty of memory 5/26 (see note).

memoriall *adj.* worthy to be remembered 227/28.

merite *n.* reward 112/30; virtue 109/17, 109/24; see 25/9 note.

meritorie *adj.* deserving of spiritual reward 73/32; praiseworthy 111/24.

merlion *n.* heraldic bird, often without feet or beak; ? confused with *merlete* 68/6.

mervaile (-eile) *n.* in *haue* ~ be astonished 16/12, 50/12, 94/3-4; *haue no* ~ 173/5-6. *take* ~ have admiration 104/32.

merueillous *adj.* terrifying, horrible 169/27; mervelous 96/27.

mesprision *n.* contempt 54/34.

mesurable *adj.* temperate 77/31.

mesur(e) *n.* moderation, temperance (in conduct, manners, etc.) 9/29, 18/28, 178/7, 179/7; measurement, reckoning 30/36, 219/29; fig. 115/34 (see note); size 29/29; quantity 171/13; *pl.* 170/14; balance 220/28, 221/25. *by* ~ by due proportion 221/18-19. *owt of (alle)* ~ excessively 94/15, 200/29-30; outrageously 167/20-1; intemperate 38/18. *vndir* ~ *of* within the limits or standards of 40/4.

mesuredest *pa. t. 2 sg.* measured out 30/29. *mesurd both by on mesure* (*pp.*) judged in duration by the same standard 10/16-17 (*MED* cites this passage; *OED* 1667). mesured *ppl. adj.* fixed 121/5 (see note).

mydde *adj.* middle 121/1. ~ *waye* middle 24/17.

myddis *n.* middle 6/11, 136/17. *in* (*the*) ~ in the midst 73/18, 103/2, 107/10, 215/17.

myghtily(e) *adv.* greatly 74/5; with powerful effect 185/16; with great effort, power, etc. 104/29, 204/30, 205/29 (myghtly NSJ).

mykell *adj.* great 183/6, 219/30.

mynde *n.* memory 15/21, 26/3.

ministour *n.* agent of a superior 55/6 (mynystrour NJ). ministers *pl.* 55/5; officers 106/1.

ministracion *n.* administration 47/30; instrumentality 33/9, 98/2.

ministre *v.* supply, furnish 167/29, 226/8, 227/8; *pp.* administered 51/26.

mysauenturis *n. pl.* misfortunes 10/28.

mysbeleve *n.* heresy 82/28.

Q

mysbeleving *pr. p.* disbelieving 89/19; *ppl. adj.* unbelieving 27/12.

myschevid *pp.* afflicted with misfortune and defeat 192/24.

misch(i)ef(f), mysche(e)ve, mischyff *n.* misfortune, evil plight 13/2, 174/27; *pl.* 3/29, 151/2; injury, harm 18/17, 164/31, 165/31; *pl.* 234/20; wickedness 11/23, 41/30; *pl.* evils 197/19. **to ~ into** great misfortune 50/21, 162/26-7.

mys(c)h(i)evous(e) *adj.* disastrous, miserable 18/2, 28/10, 41/29; wicked 170/3.

miscownted *pp. refl.* fig., made a wrong calculation 116/1 (*OED* 1530, fig. use om.).

myscreaunt *n.* infidel 109/30.

myscreauntes *adj. pl.* infidel 99/12.

mysdoing *vbl. n.* evil-doing 15/31.

mysdone ayeinst *pp.* violated, acted contrary to 98/25 (*OED* meaning om.).

mysease *n.* discomfort, extreme suffering 22/20, 158/8; *pl.* miseries 176/16.

misericorde *n.* mercy 75/7.

mysgouerned *ppl. adj.* ill-behaved 236/29.

mysguydid *pp. refl.* misbehaved 14/12.

mysguyding *vbl. n.* mismanagement, misapplication 48/14.

myshappen *impers. pr. 3 sg. subj.* happen unfortunately 194/26.

mysknowe *v.* refuse to recognize or acknowledge 35/5, 109/7, 111/23; *pr. pl.* 35/10 (**mysknowlegh** NSC). **mysknowe** *pp.* 8/9; **misknowen** 59/18, 81/31.

misknow(e)lage (-lege, -liche, N -leghe) *n.* failure to know, recognize or acknowledge 99/12, 196/10, 208/17; sim. implying scorn 60/14, 89/32 (*OED* 1533; see 89/32 note); lack of understanding 5/14, 21/3 (*OED* 1579; see 5/14 note); refusal to know, lack of knowledge 206/12 (see note).

mysknowlechinge *vbl. n.* ? refusing to acknowledge, here God; ? ignorance 37/3 (*OED* vbl. n. om.; see note).

mysmake *v.* undo 18/22.

mystaking *vbl. n.* wrong-doing 46/21.

mystakith *pr. 3 sg.* transgresses 36/11. **mistake** *pr. pl.* 47/20. **mystoke** *pa. t. refl.* wrongly viewed themselves as 77/8 (*OED* refl. om., tr. 1589; see note). **mystaken** *pp.* misunderstood the meaning of 81/35; *ppl. adj.* ? erring; ? misunderstood; ? scorned, despised (*OED* om.) 3/32 (Fr. 'despiz').

mysteppe owt of *v.* go astray from 71/24.

mystery(e) *n.* office 81/4; religious rite 129/22; *pl.* 131/1; religious truths 27/14.

mystye *adj.* fig., dark 13/33.

mystrust *n.* suspicion of others 80/3.

mystrust of *v.* lack faith in 81/22.

mysturned *pp.* perverted, turned in a wrong direction 157/3, 185/12, 197/17.

myxtion *n.* process of mixing 30/35.

moche, miche *adj.* much 187/19; many 89/30, 138/31, 203/23; *adv.* much 151/16, 163/32. **so ~** nearly 159/12 (*OED* 1560); *sb.* many 107/24; *see* by.

mocion *n.* cause 181/4; motive 246/28; *pl.* forces that prompt 115/4.

mocked *pp.* deceived 100/5.

moderacions *n. pl.* abatements of rigour 93/27 (*OED* 1598).

modre *v.* temper 91/34; *pp.* 116/31. **modered** *ppl. adj.* regulated 98/27 (*OED* ppl. adj. om.).

modulacion *n.* song 25/29.

mo(e)ve, me(e)ve *v.* move (physically) 121/7; prompt 125/13, 208/12, 209/13; stir up 206/32; disturb, trouble 126/19, 228/33, 229/30; put in regular motion 136/15; affect (with emotion) 172/24, 173/25; exist 24/14. **moeuid** *pa. t.* 47/13; **mevid** 127/25; **meeuid** 149/27; **moevit** 47/2; **meeve** 24/14. **moevid** *pp.* 7/34; **mouid** 140/26; **meeuid** 141/26; **mouevid** 204/9; **moevit** 228/33; **movet** 206/32.

mo(e)ving, meeuing *vbl. n.* inward prompting 118/25; cause 202/27, 203/26; *pl.* 180/4 (**moyevyngys** SJ);

stirring up 207/29; motion of the heavenly bodies 136/18, 137/20; *pl.* 137/9; changings 30/5, 120/28.

mokkerye (-arye) *n.* subject or action deserving derision 95/18; *pl.* 93/24.

mollified *pp.* lessened in harshness 236/25 (*OED* 1523); enervated 240/3.

monarche *n.* monarchy 139/24 (*OED* spelling om.).

Moneþe *n.* month 92/32.

mo(o) *adj.* more (of number) 106/26, 220/19; *sb.* 230/11.

mo(o)st(e) *adj.* greatest 152/14, 217/15; greatest amount of 152/15; *sb.* people of highest rank 131/21.

moote *n.* plea 140/30.

more *adj.* greater 36/6; larger in number 81/14; larger in size 137/22; more difficult 169/28; erroneously for 'most' 225/20.

more *adv.* nearer 159/14.

mortall (-ale) *adj.* deadly, fatal 3/3, 53/11, 168/6, 169/7; ? deadly in its effects; ? of a season: characterized by many deaths (*OED* 1649) 16/31.

mortifieng *vbl. n.* destroying the vigour of 24/20.

multiplicacion *n.* propagation 99/7.

multiplye *v.* add 106/26, 119/20.

musculles *n. pl.* muscles 19/14 (*OED* 1533).

musinge *vbl. n.* thoughts 149/32 (see note).

must *n.* new wine 7/11.

must (R), **most** (U) *v. auxil. pr. t.* must 150/17, 151/23.

mut *pr. pl.* may 184/8.

nayed *pp.* rejected 213/2; denied 231/8.

naked *adj.* destitute 3/32; devoid 7/31, 127/21; exposed to view 147/18.

name *n.* reputation 90/27, 155/24, 190/27, 191/26.

namely *adv.* especially 50/16, 53/23, 145/18, 222/1, 223/1.

naturale (-all, -ell) *adj.* native 14/9, 148/31, 149/36 (*OED* 1508); showing natural affection 109/1 (*OED* 1523); innate 152/8, 153/8; having a certain relationship by circum-

stance 152/19, 153/17, 177/23 (*OED* 1516). ~ *lorde* overlord or sovereign by birth 154/28, 155/25, 182/19, 183/18 (*OED* 1524).

natur(e) *n.* vital functions 98/31; natural feeling 26/29. *gothe for owte of* ~ makes himself unnatural 18/29.

naturiens *n. pl.* natural philosophers 137/14 (*OED* rare, 1390).

natwithstanding at *prep.* in spite of 151/1.

necessary(e) *adj.* inevitably fixed 120/14, 121/16.

necessaryly *adv.* of necessity (in regard to conflict between free will and providence) 120/19, 121/14.

necessite *n.* situation of hardship 41/30, 101/27; *pl.* needs for survival 170/17. *stondith in* ~ is financially poor 222/17.

necke *n.* in *vnto his* ~ ? completely 62/24 (*OED* phr. om.; Fr. 'iusques au col'; see note).

ne(e)de *n.* ~ *ys* it is necessary 5/28. *is no* ~ is not necessary 106/26. *at (a)* ~ in a crisis 236/19, 237/19.

ne(e)d(e)full *adj.* necessary 72/18, 221/8.

ne(e)dys *adv.* of necessity 13/29. ~ *most* it is inevitable 205/30.

ne(e)dith *impers. pr. 3 sg.* in *him* ~ is necessary to him 115/10. *intr.* in *it* ~ it is necessary 207/17. *nede nat* it is not necessary 236/20.

ner *conj.* nor 151/6, 157/7.

nerhand *adv.* nearly 131/19.

nest *n.* place where thieves gather 223/28.

neuir *adv.* not at all 182/17, 183/16.

n(e)we *adj.* recent 111/14; *sb.* in *of* ~ anew 66/27–8.

new(e) *adv.* anew 18/24, 104/6.

newe-founde *adj.* recently invented 98/19; newly found out 127/24.

newe-taught *adj.* recently taught 113/31.

next *adj.* nearest 183/17; *adv.* 24/19; *prep.* 130/30.

ney *see* **nyghe**.

nyce *adj.* wanton 38/18.

nycete *n.* wantonness, folly 17/34, 44/32; *pl.* excessive luxuries 56/21.

nygh(e), ney, nye *prep.* near 61/30, 105/5, 158/15; *adj.* near 100/25, 148/5, 157/7; nearly ready 148/6; *adv.* near 5/12, 151/16. *wel(l)* ∼ almost 149/8.

nygromancye *n.* necromancy 90/2.

no *conj.* nor 32/29.

nobles(se) *n.* nobility 3/26, 222/15, 223/14; persons of noble rank 190/12; noble birth 238/15; *pl.* honours 232/2.

nombir *v.* ascertain the amount of 218/31. **noumbrith** *pr. 3 sg.* fixes or knows the number of 31/6.

noo *adv.* not 51/32.

no(o)te *v.* accuse (one) (followed by n. cl.) 198/25; (followed by adj.) 199/21.

nor *conj.* ? and 77/18.

norischers (-ars) *n. pl.* fosterers 44/7, 47/17.

noris(c)h(e), noryssh, nurisch, noryce *v. tr.* provide with sustenance 18/14; bring up or educate 99/3, 148/7, 149/9; cherish (a person) 162/23, 163/22; foster (a feeling) 75/21 (*OED* 1560); fig., feed (a fire) 47/18; fig., encourage in growth 156/2; maintain, support 222/30, 223/27; strengthen 69/21, 73/20; *intr.* is encouraged and strengthened 105/9 (*OED* exact meaning om.). ∼ *forth* encourage 82/5.

noris(s)hing(e) *vbl. n.* rearing 99/6, 142/25; nourishment 98/31, 122/26. **norycing** fostering 157/2.

nortur, nurture *n.* upbringing 55/15; education 16/23.

note *n.* nut 84/18.

nothinge *n.* in *for* ∼ on no account 235/9.

nothinge *adv.* not at all 56/26, 160/4.

noughty *adj.* worthless 241/4; evil 41/26; *sb.* 167/6.

noumbre *n.* sum total 30/36. **numbur** company 228/16.

novellery *n.* novelty 87/16.

noyaunce *n.* annoyance, harmfulness 29/10, 51/17.

noye *n.* trouble, harm 41/11 (**noye-aunce** C).

noye *v. tr.* trouble, harm 6/2, 39/16; *refl.* 65/9; vex 52/28, 130/21; *intr.* cause annoyance (to) 61/28; *abs.* 18/4. **noyeth** *pr. pl.* 52/28; **noye** 78/20; **noyen** 61/28; **noyine** 130/21.

noyous(e) *adj.* vexatious 4/20, 6/7, 168/26.

nurture *see* **nortur.**

Nutrityve *n.* see 21/23 note.

obeis(s)aunce *n.* authority 23/17, 26/29, 35/1; obedience, submission 34/16, 170/31, 171/27.

obprobriouse, opprobriouse *adj.* shameful *177/6, 199/10; injuriously reproachful 203/31.

obscure *adj.* fig., gloomy 199/19.

obsecracions *n. pl.* earnest supplications 124/9, 126/29; see 124/18 note.

obseruacions *n. pl.* religious observances 124/12.

obserued *pp.* ? observant (*OED* meaning om.); ? perceived (*OED* 1560) 228/5 (Fr. 'observer', as interpreted in U).

obstinacion *n.* obstinacy 60/9, 205/6.

obstinates *n. pl.* stubborn persons 81/20.

occasion *n.* opportunity 94/29; cause 72/20, 161/5, 176/19; *pl.* 178/14, 179/15; pretexts 48/24. *for thoccasion of* on account of 37/27; *to thoccasion of* 39/1 (*OED* with *by*). *by the which* ∼ for which cause 99/10–11. *yiueth* ∼ gives rise 177/19; *gaue* ∼ 44/27. *were the* ∼ *of* have good cause for 105/8 (*OED* om.; Fr. 'ont . . . occasion de').

occision *n.* slaying 74/26, 216/2, 217/2.

occupacion *n.* exercise 12/31.

oc(c)upy (-ie) *v.* use 47/31; take up time 211/3; *pa. t.* performed 93/23; *pp.* been stationed at 8/18; taken possession of 40/30; busied 160/11, 161/10.

of *adv.* off 186/3, 193/16, 226/31, 227/30.

of *prep.* by 7/31, 36/23, 53/5, 168/28, 207/22, 212/34, 213/31; with 13/21, 72/32, 121/19, 165/18; from 33/28, 122/29, 136/19, 151/18, 225/17; out

of 209/11; by means of 35/7, 155/
11, 223/16, 247/18; because of 53/
19, 58/34, 72/17, 147/4, 196/10,
201/26; concerning 49/15, 73/8; for
72/18, 125/18, 148/21, 171/12, 178/
33; against 130/15, 200/24, 201/24;
in 79/12, 243/15; in (into) a state of
156/5, 183/25; to 81/16, 93/13, 137/1;
towards 245/21; over 119/17, 211/7.
offences *n. pl.* see 244/17 note
(**affenses** SJ).
offendid *pa. t.* violated 226/28.
office *n.* function 121/31; employ-
ment 90/24; duty, moral obligation
35/20, 60/1, 172/12; *pl.* performance of duties 30/20, 38/28.
oyn(n)ement *n.* ointment 69/18, 73/
30.
olifauntes *n. pl.* elephants 139/15.
Oligracie *n.* oligarchy 56/9 (*OED*
1577; see note).
on *prep.* in 90/33, 110/34; from 201/1;
among 207/27.
on(e)ly *adj.* preeminent 74/31; single
88/25, 245/23.
o(o) *adj.* one 97/19, 137/20.
ooned *pp.* unified 26/4, 67/22, 128/4.
o(o)n(e)ly *adv.* especially, preemi-
nently 24/23, 26/10 (see note). all ~
by itself 10/21.
ooste *see* **hooste**.
opening *vbl. n.* licence 95/29.
operacion *n.* work, treatise 141/29,
247/26; performance 199/12; performance of a mechanical nature
187/5; method of working 235/28;
pl. actions, deeds 131/1, 145/28.
opyn *n.* opening 22/17.
opyn *v.* reveal to (mental or spiritual)
view 39/11, 57/3; *refl.* reveal itself
206/10; fig., uncover 51/28, 85/7;
make accessible without restriction
222/3, 223/3; fig., provide free
access to 205/1. **openid** *pp.* 223/3;
open 205/1; *see* **weye**.
opyn *adj.* free of entrance to all 22/22;
public 25/7, 125/8, 204/9; fought
openly with full forces 34/13;
clear 103/16, 119/19, 202/2; gener-
ous 150/20, 151/26 (*OED* 1597). ~
wayes open roads, crossroads 12/10
(*OED* phr. om.; Fr. 'carrefours').
opinatiff(e), opinative *adj.* ~ *hope(s)*,

~ *wanhope* type of hope(s) common
to those who adhere obstinately to
their own opinion 80/18, 89/12, 100/
8 (*OED* 1530).
opynly *adv.* so that all may see and
take cognizance, publicly 63/14
(**apynly** N), 138/32, 168/16, 208/6,
209/7; clearly 77/13.
op(p)inion(e) *n.* judgement resting
on insufficient grounds 25/17, 80/
24, 118/8. ~ *holders* those who hold
obstinately to such a judgement 81/
19.
opprimed *ppl. adj.* oppressed 213/19
(*OED* om.; Fr. 'opprimee').
opprobriouse *see* **obprobriouse**.
opteyne *v.* obtain 85/2, 227/32.
or *conj.* before 52/29, 170/13, 171/11.
before ~ 83/34; *see* **afore**.
ordeigne, ordeyne *v.* order 125/5;
pr. 3 sg. provides 170/17; *pp.* predestined 23/9; destined 29/12;
instituted 124/18; enacted 205/6.
ordenary *adj.* having regular jurisdiction in spiritual matters 122/5.
ordinatly *adv.* in an ordered way 68/
32, 127/10.
ordinaunce *n.* predestined arrangement or order 31/2, 31/12, 69/1;
decree of Providence 113/6; order
56/15, 69/9, 146/21, 147/20; control, direction 167/22, 237/27; authoritative command 45/17, 224/
17; *pl.* 64/26; preparation 184/22,
185/21. *owt(e) of* ~ disarranged
158/25; devoid of order and proper
rule 240/1. *owt of all* ~ completely
unrestrained 98/12.
ordir, ordre *n.* fixed arrangement in
the spiritual or moral system 30/36,
56/3, 71/24; orderly condition 38/28;
form of divine service 128/21.
withowt ~ in a state of mental or
bodily disorder 16/5 (*OED out of*
~, a1548).
ordure *n.* filth 159/11.
orphelyns *n. pl.* orphans 168/33.
orphente *n.* orphanhood *175/6 (see
174/5–6 note).
othirwhile *adv.* at times 36/17, 73/29;
at another time 90/15. ~ . . . ~ at
one time . . . at another time 244/
35–246/2.

ouerferre *adv.* too far 219/22.

ouerseeth *pr. pl.* keep watch over 221/18.

ouerthwert *adv.* askew 147/19.

ouyr *adj.* upper 145/21.

ouir, ouere *prep.* in addition to 10/21, 37/6; in excess of 94/22, 201/31; above in authority 122/2.

ouirall *adv.* everywhere 48/20, 125/32.

ouirchargeid *pp.* overburdened 35/17.

ouirerenne *v.* overpower 46/4.

ouirlargely *adv.* to too great an extent 222/13 (*OED* 1576).

ouirmoche, ouermiche *adj.* too much 20/13; *adv.* too greatly 161/28, 207/21; *sb.* excess 220/26, 221/23 (*OED* sb. rare).

ouirpride *n.* excessive pride 31/17, 41/33 (*OED* rare).

ouirthrowe *v.* bring to nought 63/6. **ouerthrowe** *pp.* 210/18; **ouir-throwin** cast down in mental or bodily state 6/1, 31/30; vanquished 111/2; fig., humbled 134/24.

ouirthrowyng *vbl. n.* destruction 65/16.

ovirthwart *adj.* opposed, adverse 73/3

ouirtrowed *ppl. adj.* over-confident 134/23.

ou(l)tragiouse (-eous), owtra-giouse *adj.* excessive, extravagant 93/29 (outetragiouse N), 158/10, 159/8; excessively wrong 108/22; violent, fierce 106/32.

ourage *n.* work 147/2.

outereres *n. pl.* exposers 53/26.

outrage *see* **owltrage.**

owing *pr. p.* owed 190/7.

ow(l)trage, outrage *n.* violence, disorderly behaviour 41/30, 102/20, 196/33, 197/32; excess 105/21; *pl.* extravagances 169/22; violent deeds 166/9.

owt(e) of, out of *prep.* lacking 20/13, 56/25, 168/3; removed from 180/21; from 237/19; *see* **charge, yssewe, nature, ordinaunce, reason.**

owtrageousenesse *n.* flagrant wrong-fulness 44/32.

owtward(e), out(e)ward(e) *adv.* publicly 129/21; in outward appearance 145/11; from without 152/32 (Fr. 'a part'), 153/15; out of their houses 233/25.

pace *n.* fig., predicament 209/8.

payed *pp.* fulfilled 83/21.

paynefull *adj.* diligent 215/5.

paynem(e)s *n. pl.* pagans 51/6, 78/25; **paynemmys** 76/28.

palles *n. pl.* in *by* ~ ? in a state of wasteful disorder 147/19 (*OED* om.; see 146/19–21 note).

panyme *adj.* pagan 124/6.

papir *n.* coll., written documents 30/19.

parag *n.* in *holde by* ~ hold part of a fief without any service or homage 55/3 (see note).

parcialite *n.* rivalry 56/2.

parciall *adj.* personal, selfish 142/33, 143/30, 186/32, 187/29.

parfite, parfitely *see* **perfight, perfightly.**

paril(l)ous, perylous(e) *adj.* dangerous 78/34, 156/1, 157/1, 226/10 (perlyous J), 227/10, 234/2, 235/2.

part(e) *n.* way 15/3; side 221/24. *on (in) euery* ~ in every direction, everywhere 15/23, 196/23, 197/22, 203/23. *on the (that) othir* ~ on the other hand 43/7, 162/12. *for his* ~ as far as it is concerned 125/15; as his share 50/11; sim. 189/6, 190/1; *to oure* ~ 189/33–191/1; cf. **partye.**

parteable to *adj.* able to partake of 68/22 (*OED* with *in, of*).

parteners *n. pl.* sharers 50/1, 232/7.

particypacyon(e) *n.* partaking *22/30, 117/17.

particuler (-are) *adj.* individual 68/23; personal 160/6, 161/6, 176/27, 177/27; special 210/22. **particulers** *pl.* 211/24.

party(e), parti(e) *n.* part 107/25, 146/13, 147/15, 162/29; *pl.* 20/20, 142/18, 143/17; place 151/18; side 220/27; matter 123/25, 184/1; *pl.* 143/23, 231/10 (*OED* meaning questioned); plight, condition 111/23, 204/4, 205/4 (*OED* meaning questioned, rare); way of life 74/20

(see note), 204/4; *pl.* 194/32, 195/
32, 205/5; combatant 152/23; *pl.*
114/29; members 172/10, 173/12;
adv. or ellip. phr. partly 91/29. *on
the othir* ∼ on the other hand,
moreover 14/3-4, 80/9, 84/33, 163/
12, 185/23 (*OED* phr. only under
part). *on what* ∼ where 148/30.
what (*which*) ∼ *that euir* wherever
14/18, 114/9 (*OED* om.). *on euery* ∼
everywhere 91/28. *in no* ∼ in no way
173/29. *made a* ∼ *for the* caused
to take your side or act for you
122/6.

parting *vbl. n.* dividing 129/3.

passage *n.* journey 14/5; death 41/15;
pl. mountain passes 242/8, 243/9.

passed *see* **peesed.**

passe(n) *v.* go across 124/21, 242/7,
243/8; go beyond 24/13, 41/8;
transcend, overcome 41/16; surpass 28/17, 239/15; exceed 82/15;
go beyond the limits of 201/34;
experience, suffer 11/13, 232/6, 233/
5; disregard, neglect 88/2; establish
204/6. ∼ *ouir* make one's way 155/
29; pass by without notice 180/
1, 181/1. ∼ *ouyr tyme in haste* last
for only a little while 149/5.
passed *pa. t.* 88/2; **past** 204/6.

passible *adj.* liable to suffer change or
decay 71/29.

passid *n.* past 120/30.

patrimonye *n.* inherited property 47/
33; property belonging by ancient
right to the church 47/27.

patro(o)n *n.* likeness 26/2 (*OED* rare,
1557; Fr. 'image'); pattern, model
38/17, 77/17, 242/1, 243/2; *pl.* 53/
24.

peaced *see* **peesed.**

peacible, pe(a)sable (-ible) *adj.*
peaceful 41/23, 97/7, 109/5, 211/1,
220/8, 243/15.

peacibly *adv.* not subject to opposition 34/9; **pesibly** 108/4.

peaxce *n.* peace 170/5 (*OED* spelling
om.).

pecunie *n.* money 203/17.

peeple *n.* company or multitude 237/
20.

peeplid *ppl. adj.* in *best* ∼ most popu-
lous 139/6 (*OED well peopled* 1588).

peesed *pp.* set at rest 66/10. **peaced**
appeased 60/11. **passed** ? soothed,
alleviated; ? scribal error for
paised 11/8 (see note).

peesen *n. pl.* peas 91/1; *see* **reke.**

peice *see* **peyse.**

peyne, payn(e) *n.* punishment 39/6,
227/27; *pl.* 96/27, 236/2, 237/2;
sorrow, affliction 29/14, 172/31,
173/31; *pl.* 26/17, 189/7; difficulty
22/6, 232/27; effort 184/19. *do* ∼
exert oneself 194/8; sim. *doth not
his* ∼ 39/12; *put* ∼ 233/10; *put in*
∼ *refl.* 10/15-16; *sett* ∼ 195/8;
sim. *seet litle* ∼ 165/13. *vndir
grette* ∼ with severe threat of
punishment 224/17. *with* (*grete*) ∼
with difficulty, scarcely 147/22, 175/
11.

peynyn *pr. pl. refl.* ∼ *to* exert themselves in 180/27. ∼ *their bodies* ?
inflict pain upon their bodies; ?
for refl., exert themselves physically
158/4.

peynted *pp.* described 84/31.

peyse, peyce *n.* weigh 29/29; fig.
37/20, 138/22; burden of sin 29/
15.

peyse *imp.* fig., weigh 31/33; *pr. pl.*
220/21; *pp.* considered 234/11.

penaunce *n.* punishment 37/5, 232/
20, 233/20; *pl.* 52/31; suffering 164/
33, 165/33.

penetratif *adj.* piercing 125/34 (*OED*
all exs. before 1819 refer to senses;
penetrife N).

peny *n.* in *ernest* ∼ fig., customary
payment 126/26 (*OED* fig. 1533).

penyble *adj.* painful 13/4.

perfeccion *n.* height, supreme excellence 86/24; embodiment of perfection 86/28 (*OED* 1594).

perfight, perfite, perfect, parfite
adj. perfect 30/21, 134/30, 135/33;
adult 137/29; complete 166/13,
167/11. ∼ *age of man* adulthood
136/27.

perfightnes *n.* perfection 84/1;
perfictnesse 25/17.

perfiteth *pr. pl.* perfect 120/27.

perfourme *v.* achieve 32/29.

peryode *n.* time of duration 19/12;
a round of time marked by the

recurrence of astronomical coinci-
dences, used as a unit in chronology
136/13, 137/15 (*OED* 1613).

perpetuite *n.* endless duration 42/15,
139/11. *miserable* ∼ endless misery
159/16 (see 158/19–20 note).

persyd *pa. t.* pierced 24/8; **percid** 24/
15. **persyng** *ppl. adj.* piercing,
penetrating 67/2 (*OED* 1509).

persuasion *n.* in *by a* ∼ as a means
of persuasion 105/7.

perteigne *v.* belong 208/2. **pertey-
neth** *pr. pl.* are appropriate 243/25.
∼ *to* concern 80/35. **perteynyng to**
connected with 86/23.

peruerse *adj.* evil 215/26.

peruertible *adj.* capable of being perverted 34/22 (*OED* Cotgrave 1611).

peruertith *pr. 3 sg.* destroys, corrupts, turns away from right order
44/22; *pr. pl.* 38/27; *pa. t.* 34/10,
95/23; *pp.* 82/7.

pesible, pesibly *see* **peacible, peacibly.**

pestilence *n.* that which injures 63/
24; moral wickedness, fatal to
public well-being 35/15; *pl.* 44/10.

petyte *adj.* subordinate 68/16 (*OED*
1531).

Phisike *n.* medical science 58/16.

piete *n.* mercy 31/30, 43/5, 72/17;
affectionate loyalty between parents
and children 26/29 (*OED* 1579); cf.
pitee.

pyght *pa. t.* pitched 104/23.

pyleers *n. pl.* pillars 138/3; **pillers**
139/3.

pill *pr. pl.* despoil 8/26; *pp.* plundered
216/2.

pirischith *pr. 3 sg.* perishes 40/24
(*OED* spelling om.; **peryssheth**
N, **peryschet** S).

pyssemyre *n.* ant 171/14.

pite(e) *n.* affectionate loyalty and
respect, especially between parents
and children 152/9, 153/8, 228/3,
229/3 (*OED* 1579); cf. **piete.**

pit(e)ouse *adj.* merciful 108/34;
lamentable 145/14.

pla(a)ce *n.* dignity 25/23; office 68/
32; appropriate place 176/4, 177/4;
see **constitucion.**

plage *n.* divine punishment 61/13.

playn(e) *adj.* downright 245/7. *in* ∼
batailes in open or full battle 125/
26. *in* ∼ *maner* fully 245/4.

playne *see* **pleyne.**

playnynge *vbl. n.* utterance of grief
173/24; *pl.* 183/10.

plancke *n.* narrow footbridge 9/17.

platte *adv.* flat 148/18.

plee *n.* debate 140/30.

pleyasur *n.* pleasure 182/4 (*OED*
spelling om.). *to do pleasure* to
please 95/21.

pleyne, playne *v. tr.* deplore,
bewail 49/11, 191/31; *intr.* utter
feelings of injury or ill-usage 16/22,
180/13, 181/12; *refl.* lament 31/28.
∼ *vpon (on)* make complaint against
188/1, 189/1.

pleynnese *n.* plain truth 88/11.

pleintis *n. pl.* lamentations 12/9.

plenteouse *adj.* abundant 99/2 (**plen-
teueux** J); **plentuous** 176/8; abun-
dantly provided 174/18.

plentuousnes *n.* bountiful giving 74/
11.

plesaunce *n.* pleasure, joy 17/27, 54/
29, 92/3, 158/31; sensuous pleasure
53/34. **pleasaunces** *pl.* things that
cause pleasure 176/5. *aftir his* ∼ to
his liking 30/13. *take thy* ∼ are
pleased 16/11.

poignaunte *adj.* sharp (of words)
200/22 (*OED* 1542).

poynt(e) *n.* crisis (in affairs) 8/4; condition 4/29, 214/8; matter 61/26,
200/31, 221/17; thing 97/25; point
of discussion 226/15, 227/15; conclusion 119/28; *pl.* 65/33; characteristic, quality 23/9; *pl.* 97/34, 210/13;
kind 85/25 (*OED* meaning om.);
height 112/9; *pl.* aims 100/24. *in
the* ∼ *of the day* at daybreak 93/1.
no ∼ *of knowlage* no knowledge at
all 65/14. *sette at the* ∼ begun and
put in way of development 204/23
(*OED* om.; Fr. 'mis avant'). *in (at)
all poyntes* in every respect 70/30–1,
88/7–8; *see* **arayed.**

poyntelles *n. pl.* small, pointed
instruments 86/5.

polecy(e), pol(l)icie(-cey) *n.* government, conduct of affairs 44/22, 56/
6, 170/11, 171/10, 233/34, 245/32;

prudence in conduct of public affairs 219/26, 244/33. *witty ~* skilful and wise management 142/24. *The Polesyes* Aristotle's *Politics* 57/21.

poletik(e) *adj.* wise 21/18 (see note); civil 44/21.

polytykely *adv.* politically 55/33.

pollisch *v.* smooth or gloss over 203/28 (*OED* rare; see note).

polucion *n.* moral impurity 52/14; profanation 49/16.

polute *pp.* defiled 49/31.

pompe *n.* vain glory, ostentatious show 46/7; *pl.* 40/23, 156/2, 157/2; 'pompae diaboli', iniquitous shows of the devil, in baptismal formula 26/9.

po(o)rt(e) *n.* bearing 144/8, 145/8; social position 234/29, 235/27 (*OED* 1523).

poorte *n.* poverty 51/28.

portrayed *pp.* painted (with) 23/27.

portraturis *n. pl.* pictures 144/29, 145/29.

possessid *ppl. adj.* owned 170/12 (*OED* 1595).

possessioners *n. pl.* occupiers 3/8.

possid *pp.* tossed or dashed by waves 154/2.

postom *n.* fig., deep-seated abscess 202/23.

potence *n.* crutch 80/11 (**potente** NJ; see note).

poudrid *pp.* covered by ornamental figures here and there 149/11.

pouere *see* **powere**.

pourvey *see* **purveye**.

powdir *n.* ashes of a burned person 178/20.

power(e) *n.* in *do(o) thaire ~* do their best 163/19–20, 216/33.

pow(e)r(e), pouere, pore *adj.* poor 39/22, 166/27, 167/24, 212/8; mean-spirited 15/7; of inferior quality 224/20.

practi(c)ke *n.* practice 101/22, 242/3 (**praetyk** SJ).

practiked *pp.* put into practice 243/4.

praty *adj.* in *litill ~ roofe* ? skilfully made small hive 244/34 (see note).

precio(u)s(e) *adj.* of great spiritual worth 22/4; displaying careful delicacy in workmanship 146/1, 147/1.

predicacion *n.* exhortation 91/2; *pl.* 96/21, 198/17, 199/16.

preece *v.* push one's way presumptuously 161/19.

pre(e)f(fe), preif, profe, proef *n.* trial, test 61/18; demonstration, evidence 22/7, 26/27, 30/8, 31/22, 71/18, 202/2. **proves** *pl.* 28/8 (**prowes** N); **prevys** 109/12. *made a ~* had weight as evidence 58/11. *put hym in ~ of* attempt to examine, judge 30/30 (*OED* om.; Fr. 'iugera').

preent *see* **printe**.

pre(e)s(se) *n.* crowd 7/25; instrument for pressing 5/6; tribulation 175/20. *putt the in ~* set yourself or undertake ('to go' understood) 9/15 (see note).

pregnabull *adj.* used erroneously for **pregnaunt** (NJ) = containing a hidden sense 84/32 (Fr. 'enceintes'; see note).

preyse *v.* value, esteem 46/24, 151/12.

preysing *vbl. n.* praise 154/23; *pl.* 72/34.

preiudice *n.* wrong, harm 213/16, 220/36, 223/1.

prelacy *n.* ecclesiastical power 51/34.

premission *n.* sending before 68/11 (*OED* 1609; Fr. 'preuention' = 'prepossession').

prentid *see* **printe**.

prentishode *n.* fig., apprenticeship 14/7.

presence *n.* attendance 215/11.

presentes *n.* presence 101/9 (*OED* says this is probably an error; first citation 1578).

preseruyd *pp.* maintained 227/22.

presse *see* **preesse**.

preuaricacion *n.* violation, perversion 60/31, 96/30 (*OED* 1615; Fr. 'preuarication').

preuaricatours *n. pl.* traitors 102/22 (*OED* c.1555).

preve *v.* test, try 29/7, 43/8, 74/22. **prouueth** *pr. 3 sg.* approves 171/8. **preeuid** *pa. t.* proved trustworthy by trial 185/21. **preved** *pp.* 104/16; tested, made sure 214/19.

prevelage *n.* special benefit 54/23. **priuelege** special distinction 57/7.

prevys *see* **preeffe**.

pryce *n.* glory 3/25; praise 155/20.

prycke, prykke *n.* goad 53/4; pain, torment 13/25, 80/11 (see note); *pl.* 212/19.

pri(c)kid, prikked *pa. t.* caused mental pain to 25/5; *pp.* goaded 53/4; greatly tormented 212/18; fig., pierced 206/24, 207/22.

pricking, prik(k)yng(e) *vbl. n.* goading 208/10, 209/10; fig., urging forward 29/16; grief, distress 73/31; *pl.* 178/2, 179/2; inflictions of pain 45/6.

pryme-temps *n.* springtime 18/8.

principally *adv.* originally, primarily 117/16; from the beginning 120/17; see 55/26 note.

principle *n.* source 23/8, 40/2.

print(e), preent *n.* character 53/29; image, likeness 77/17, ? 123/5 (see note); printed design 147/17; *pl.* applied to constellations, *see* **ymages** 136/11.

printe *imp.* fig., impress 101/15. **prentid** *pp.* 14/9.

probacion *n.* ? trial, test; ? reprobation 96/29 (see note); *pl.* proofs 101/9.

procedith *pr. 3 sg. tr.* surpasses 116/22 (see note); *intr.* takes effect 172/26. ∼ *from (of, owt of)* results from, originates in, issues from 95/1, 117/2, 120/11; *pr. pl.* 112/33, 173/27. *procede forth* go on 117/14.

processe *n.* discussion 33/3; treatise 246/17; lapse (of time) 146/3. *by* ∼ *of tyme* at length 90/17; *in* ∼ *of yeris* 138/12. *by long* ∼ for a long time 174/31 (*OED* om.). *in shorte* ∼ briefly 146/28 (*OED* om.).

procureth *pr. 3 sg.* endeavours to bring about 122/27; causes 18/31, 55/16, 60/14; *pr. pl.* 49/8; *pa. t.* 60/23; *pp.* acquired 77/28.

prodiciouse *adj.* treasonable 74/26 (*OED* rare, only ex. 1635).

proesse *n.* prowess 227/25.

profecte *see* **profight**.

proferre *v.* esteem more 234/17, 235/16 (see note).

professione *n.* religious order 46/23.

profight (-fite, -figtht, -fecte) *n.* use 36/17; profit, benefit 30/16, 43/25, 210/12, 211/12; *pl.* 46/13, 182/18, 183/17. *comon* ∼ general well-being 186/8.

profitable *adj.* useful 36/15.

prof(o)undenesse *n.* depth of meaning 139/32 (*OED* 1525; Fr. 'abisme'); abyss 225/18, 225/24 (*OED* 1642; Fr. 'ouverture', 'abisme').

promission *n.* promise 60/25, 73/12.

prophetikis *adj. pl.* prophetic 84/3 (*OED* 1604).

propice *adj.* propitious 165/4.

propirly *adv.* accurately, exactly 9/14, 86/24, 117/28; completely 78/30; really 228/29.

propirte *n.* fig., property 51/35 (Fr. 'biens'); *pl.* essential qualities 80/23.

proporcion *n.* fig., comparative relation (in quantity) 120/5; relation, analogy 101/16, 121/28 (*OED* 1538); proportionate or harmonious regulation 84/30.

prouest *n.* officer 106/9.

provisio(u)n(e) *n.* foresight 25/27 (**prewysyn** NS); see 100/24 note. ∼ *of* ? previous arrangement with 125/30 (see note). *make his* ∼ provide the necessary things for sustenance 127/10.

provoketh *pr. 3 sg.* arouses 48/13. **prowok** *pr. pl.* incite 53/2. **provokid** *pp.* stirred up 178/1, 179/1.

prouueth *see* **preve**.

publique (-like) *adj.* open to general observation 169/18. **publikes** *pl.* civil 124/9. *wele (well)* ∼ common good or well-being 11/15, 143/31, 155/13; commonwealth, state 151/15, 245/9.

publiquers *n. pl.* disseminators, proclaimers 205/10 (*OED* om.; Fr. 'publieurs').

publischer *n.* proclaimer 22/9.

punchingis *n. pl.* blows 144/17 (*OED* 1530).

purchase *n.* bringing about 174/20.

purchasing *vbl. n.* acquirement by suffering, danger, etc. 155/12.

purchas(s)e (-chace, -chece), pourchase *v. tr.* procure (for oneself)

77/12, 223/12; win by suffering, danger, etc. 159/3, 169/1; bring about 154/14, 155/5; bring upon oneself 174/24, 175/23; *intr.* acquire possessions or success 154/6, 222/14.

pure *adj.* true 78/7.

pured *ppl. adj.* fig., purified 77/31.

purposith *pr. 3 sg.* proposes 85/9.

pursute *n.* continuation 112/12 (*OED* 1650; Fr. 'poursuite').

purve(y)aunce *n.* Providence 31/14; provision 171/12, 197/25.

purvey(e), po(u)rvey *v. tr.* provide 212/20 (purvoye SJ); *refl.* prepare oneself 171/14, 172/9; *intr.* take measures 66/17, 93/32; foreordain 89/9; make adequate provision (of goods, etc., for a person) 8/6, 196/26; make adequate provision (for some event, the commonwealth, etc.) 173/11, 213/13, 213/20 (*OED* rare); *see* **lette**.

put(te) *v. tr.* regard 41/22; start (a fire) 209/1; *intr.* cause to be 59/25; *refl.* 181/24; *refl.* continue (to speak) 244/1, 245/1; *refl.* apply oneself 232/23. ~ *aba(c)k(e)* reject 12/25; overcome, defeat 193/32; reduce to a lower position 28/1 (*OED* 1535). ~ *away* take away 34/6; dispel, put an end to 27/29, 62/4, 66/24, 108/33, 220/2, 239/18; reject 131/6; drive away, exile 102/11; overcome, defeat 193/32. ~ *bak* reject 81/30. ~ *bakke of* place back into 183/25. ~ *before* (one) dismiss from oneself 203/27. ~ *by* thrust aside 202/28. ~ *down(e)* suppress 59/20, 195/21; cast down, subdue 57/24, 59/21; *refl.* humble oneself 63/19. ~ *downe from* lower in rank 229/13. ~*fo(u)rth* further 214/25 (*OED* ~ *forward*); present 225/9; *refl.* come forward 189/26; exert oneself 102/28. ~ (*away*) *from* deprive of 62/21, 94/1, 152/19, 186/17. ~ *from* (oneself) dismiss, disregard 100/9, 207/23. ~ *in* introduce, allow in 66/26; *refl.* set oneself to do 190/19; place oneself in the power of 46/14; cause (one) to have 160/29, 163/13. ~ *in place* install in a position or

situation 191/19. ~ *in vre* practise 44/3; use 75/6; work 81/9; put in operation 140/13; cause 142/28; *refl.* set oneself to work, begin 99/22. ~ *into* give 182/25. ~ *on* (*vpon*) accuse 195/27, 195/28. ~ *out* exile 14/2; drive out 65/4; reject 66/26, 213/2; remove, get rid of 247/8; remove from office 162/24, 163/22. ~ *owt(e) of* free from (blame) 44/20; remove (oneself) from 208/13; deprive of 104/33, 154/1. ~ *owt fro* excommunicate 95/19. ~ *owt of your knowlage* forget 72/27. ~ *to* blame on 194/23; put forth to 240/27; send by command to 228/16; apply 65/15; *refl.* apply oneself to 46/14–15; apply oneself to practise 73/17. ~ *to* (one's) *honde* (*-is*) render assistance, set oneself to work 150/1, 164/11, 232/12. ~ *vndir* suppress 27/24; overthrow 46/3, 158/30; *refl.* humble oneself 110/7, 128/9. ~ *vnto* impose upon 172/16. ~ *vpon* inflict 37/5; urge, incite (*OED* 1602); assail (*OED* meaning om.; *Cloud of Unknowing* c.1350; see note) 19/15; *see* **aventure, devoire, preeffe, weye**.

putting *vbl. n.* ~ *of any heede to* paying any attention to 64/17. ~ *owt* driving out 65/5. ~ *to* adding to 173/33.

qualite *n.* ? nature 101/16 (see note).

quarell, querele *n.* hostile action 160/29, 161/29.

quarter *n.* particular place (of a building) 149/14; *pl.* measures of capacity (usually of grain) 193/16 (Fr. 'muys').

queinte *adj.* ? strange; ? wise; ? highly refined 148/21 (see note).

queyntise *n.* elegance 158/29.

queynttaunce *n.* acquaintance 5/13.

quenche *v.* extinguish 208/4; *pp.* fig. 164/9.

question *n.* dispute 209/4; *pl.* 131/7, 244/15, 245/16. *in questions* in controversy 207/31 (*OED* phr. sing.).

quy(c)ke, qwyk *adj.* running 196/15, 197/15; living 15/18, 178/18.

quier *n.* choir 126/8.
quykened *pp.* revived 104/6.
quykly *adv.* with vigour 59/10.
quyntyne *n.* object set up as a mark 167/1 (*OED* only in regard to darts and lances).
quyte *adj.* free (of suffering, etc.) 188/15. ~ (*owte*) *of* free from 63/28, 153/20.

racith *pr. 3 sg.* snatches 12/22. raseth tears 172/8.
radicall *adj.* ~ *humour* see 21/26 note.
rayne *v.* prevail, be current 169/19 (Fr. 'encourt et courra'; see 168/15–17 note). reynith *pr. 3 sg.* reigns 208/27 (Fr. 'court'; reigneth N; see note).
rape *n.* violent seizure 199/29; *pl.* cases of violent seizure 233/12.
rapoorte *n.* report 213/27.
raseth *see* racith.
rathest *adv.* soonest 39/5.
rathir *adv.* more truly 63/1; more readily 234/20; sooner 197/25. *the* ~ more readily 101/3.
ratified *pp.* confirmed as true 63/21.
raungis *n. pl.* rungs 24/13 (*OED* spelling om.; rungys S, rowndys N).
raunsoms *n. pl.* ? soldier's pay 169/31 (*OED* meaning om.; Fr. 'souldees').
raveyne *n.* rapine 54/35.
ravinours ? *n. pl., adj. pl.* plunderers; plundering 13/21 (ravenous NSJ).
ravissh(e), ravisch(e) *v.* seize (by force) 47/5; *pp.* 41/26; *ppl. adj.* 129/31; *pp.* drawn forcibly in a mystical sense 27/13; carried away by rapture 80/26. ~ *away* seized 166/23.
reason *n.* statement 190/29, 191/28, 195/16; *pl.* 123/27. *aftir the* ~ *of* because of 100/17 (*OED* with *by*); according to 220/22. *above* ~ more than reason can understand 84/27–8. *by* ~ according to the dictates of reason 35/13, 204/15, 205/15; *of* ~ 84/22. *owt of all* ~ completely immoderate 93/29. *to* ~ to a reasonable state 22/2. *it is* ~ *it is*

reasonable 39/8; ~ *wolde* 128/33. *mak reasons for* argue to justify 30/18.
reason *v.* question 7/27.
rebateth *pr. 3 sg. intr.* falls away (from) 138/25 (*OED* only ex. 1570; see note); *pa. t. tr.* diminished 17/10; *pp.* 13/9.
rebatyng *vbl. n.* destruction 156/12.
reboundith *pr. 3 sg.* arises 43/28, 214/26; fig., bounds back 188/29. rebounden *pl.* 38/27.
rebukyng *ppl. adj.* reproving 202/32 (*OED* as adj. 1611).
receyte *n.* prescription 122/14; amount received 219/30; *pl.* 218/32. *gaue receipt to* harboured (especially criminals) 102/6 (*OED* meaning om.; see note).
receyve *v.* accept 87/30.
recelled *pp.* hidden 187/1 (*OED* om.; Fr. 'recelee').
receueable *adj.* admissible 198/7 (*OED* 1581 of an excuse; see note).
recomended *pp.* praised 111/27.
reconsilenge *ppl. adj.* cleansing 51/21 (*OED* as adj. 1594).
recordacion *n.* remembrance 111/15.
recounforte *n.* comfort 153/12.
recours(e) *n.* in *haue (a)* ~ apply to for information 88/11; provide help 171/21.
recouer(e) *v. tr.* gain back 107/4, 224/12, 225/10; *intr.* regain position 149/17; *pp.* remedied 13/30, 51/28.
recoueriere *n.* recovery 172/29 (*OED* spelling om.: recouerere N).
recrayed *pa. t.* yielded in a cowardly way 14/24 (*OED* rare); *ppl. adj.* tired 72/25; recreant 76/3.
recreation *n.* nourishment 168/20, 169/23.
rede vp *pr. subj.* read 140/32.
redy *adj.* liable 35/26; inclined, willing 54/34, 95/30, 132/1, 201/23. ~ *way* fig., near or direct way 166/16 (see note).
redyly *adv.* without difficulty 211/11; redely 210/11 (rydely J).
redondeth *pr. 3 sg.* ~ *in* accrues to *215/21 (*OED* ~ *to*). ~ *vpon (pl.)* fall upon *189/28 (*OED* 1589; see note).

redoutable *adj.* to be feared 157/1, 169/26; to be revered 173/30.

redresse *n.* remedy 15/4, 135/33; amendment 237/24 (*OED* 1526).

redresse *v.* remove 22/14, 97/3; remedy 184/12, 185/11; direct aright 122/23, 145/27; repair 102/29; restore 134/29; settle (discords) 206/29, 207/26. *may nat ~ it* can do nothing about it 195/23–4 (Fr. 'mais n'en pevent'). **redressen** *pr. pl.* 145/27.

redressing *vbl. n.* directing aright 59/15, 113/19.

reduccion into *n.* state of giving obedience to 68/28.

reduce *v.* bring back again 72/8. *reduced in* (*pp.*) compelled to submit to *157/24.

refeccion *n.* repair 149/4 (*OED* rare, 1656; Fr. 'refection'; see 148/4–5 note).

referring *vbl. n.* returning 135/11.

reformacion *n.* correction 36/21 (*OED* 1509).

reforme *v.* ~ *oure corages* improve our conduct, character, etc. 185/10.

refreyn(e), **refrayne** *v.* check, restrain 71/25, 205/16, 212/6, 213/5.

refvit *n.* refuge 72/7.

regaltee *n.* sovereign jurisdiction 161/25.

regarde *n.* respect 88/8; *pl.* considerations of problems 211/24. *in ~* by comparison 108/27. *haue* (*a*) ~ *give* attention 29/33, 222/7–8, 223/11.

regimen *n.* rule 55/22.

regle *n.* order 143/25 (*OED* word rare; see note); principle governing conduct 197/6; rule 223/4. *out of ~* unruly 171/16.

regnault *adj.* reigning 111/16 (*OED* om.; Fr. 'regnant').

regoinessaunce *n.* recognition of a duty, with overtones of legal meaning (bond engaging to perform some act, as to pay a debt) 123/1 (*OED* spelling om.; **reconessaunce** J, **recognicyon** N).

reherce (-se) *v. tr.* recount 236/27; sim. (with om. of dir. obj.) 241/7; name 199/28; relate (how, that) 177/16, 187/1; *intr.* give an account (of)

145/18 (*OED* rare). **rehercen** *pr. pl.* 177/16. *afore rehercid* mentioned before 16/2, 142/27.

rehersinge *vbl. n.* recounting 139/29.

reigueur *see* **rigour**.

reysith *pr. 3 sg.* inspires 79/11. **reysed** *pp.* levied 221/1. ~ (*vp*) *ayeinst* raised in opposition to 36/7; **raysid** 56/6.

reioyse *pr. pl. refl.* exult 83/25.

reioysinges *vbl. n. pl.* expressions of rejoicing 203/30 (*OED* in pl. 1707; Fr. 'esbaudissemens').

reke *n.* in *pese* ~ pea field 182/2 (*OED* Palsgrave, 'Pease reke, *pesiere*', 1530).

rekke *pr. pl.* care 182/17; **rekken** 183/16.

relatif *adj.* existing only by relation to something else 79/27 (*OED* 1704; Fr. 'relatiue').

releced *pp.* relieved 105/16.

releef(e), **releue** *n.* deliverance from affliction or misfortune 143/10, 156/14, 157/15; ease from illness 214/18 (*OED* 1691). **releevys** *pl.* aids in time of need 155/12.

rele(e)ue *v. tr.* raise up again out of trouble or danger, succour 103/31, 152/14, 153/13, 183/26, 213/19; *refl.* 185/16; fig., feed 138/9; fig., lift higher 207/9; *intr.* rise again 193/6. ~ *in* (*refl.*) restore (oneself) into (some state) 217/26. **releue** ? *pr. pl.*, ? error for *pa. t.* 185/16.

rele(e)uing *vbl. n.* assistance in necessity 220/2, 221/2.

remembir (-re) *v.* mention 61/26; remind 137/26, 140/27, 241/9; *imp. refl.* reflect upon, remember 108/10, 174/28; ~ *on* 40/8. *be remembird on* remember 82/12.

remembraunce *n.* memory 20/17, 143/12; keepsake 239/6. *haue in ~* remember 101/29, 176/6.

remeve *v.* stir 6/11. **removith** *pr. 3 sg.* moves 114/9. ~ *from* take away 72/11.

renne *v. intr.* run 13/26, 208/4, 209/4; spread 57/1, 178/31; prevail, be current *168/17; *tr.* incur 222/28. ~ *owte from* forsake 13/28. ~ *to* rush headlong into 155/28; have recourse to 96/32. ~ *vpon* attack 201/23. ~ *their course vndir the tyme* pass through earthly life 136/16. **ronne** *pp.* 178/31. **rennyng** *pr. p.* flowing 92/20.

renomme *n.* report 199/15.

renoveled *pp.* renewed 102/32.

renteth *pr. 3 sg.* tears (in rage) 173/10.

reparation *n.* maintenance 148/2, 149/1.

repent *v. impers.* cause to repent 235/20 (*OED* no ex. without pron. obj.).

replicacion *n.* reply 220/34, 240/17, 244/12.

replike *n.* reply 241/15, 245/13 (*OED replique*, rare, 1549).

report(e) *v. refl.* refer for support (to), appeal (to) 244/2; *pr. 1 sg.* 65/31, 172/31, 178/34, 198/16, 199/14, 245/1; **repoort** 179/32; **rapoort** 173/31.

repre(e)f(e), repryef *n.* shame 3/26, 16/23; *pl.* 109/3, 238/25; blame 59/25, 75/30, 164/31, 244/20, 245/21; expression of censure 141/31 (*OED* 1548). **repreves** *pl.* 7/23; repro-bates 61/20 (*OED* rare; Fr. 're-prouuez').

repre(e)ue *v.* condemn 39/13, 150/5, 151/6; find fault with 30/7, 47/9; rebuke, chide 7/28, 194/18, 195/17; reject 9/5. **repre(e)uid** *pp.* 82/17, 240/24, 241/23; **reprived** 180/7.

represse *v.* curb 210/30; *pp.* re-strained from fulfilling natural func-tion 20/31 (*OED* c.1557).

repreu(e)able *adj.* reprehensible 10/23, 93/13; **reproueable** 41/27.

reprevers *n. pl.* condemners 3/15.

reprocheth *pr. 3 sg.* see 121/30 note.

repugnaunte *adj.* contradictory 114/30.

repugnynge *pr. p.* opposed 213/14 (see note).

repu(n)gnaunce *n.* opposition 29/10, 127/11.

reputest *pr. 2 sg.* think 43/29. **reputed** *pp.* held in esteem 90/26. ~ *for* regarded as 190/22, 191/22. ~ *by* attributed to 241/6 (Fr. 'imputé a'). ~ *vpon* assigned to 222/14 (*OED* omits *by, upon* as const.; Fr. 'est sur').

requere, requyre *v.* ask, request 107/12, 178/26, 241/15; entreat 123/16; demand, call for 145/3, 152/30, 153/27; seek 124/29; see 91/26 note. ~ *to* make request of 87/11. **requyrith** *pr. pl.* 114/29, 145/3; **requer** 112/27.

requerer *n.* asker 123/19; seeker 127/14.

rere *pr. subj.* collect 189/9; *pp.* levied 189/3.

reserve *v.* preserve 18/7; *pp.* kept back 42/2. ~ *for* keep in store for 197/24; sim. ~ *to* (without dir. obj.) 196/25. ~ *vnto* set apart as a responsibility of 59/6.

residwacions *n. pl.* relapses 208/24 (*OED residuation*, rare error for *recidivation*; only ex. 1534).

resyn *see* **risen**.

resist(e) *v.* offer resistance (against) 44/26; sim. (without prep.) 44/5, 152/9, 153/9 (*OED* a1547).

resolucions *n. pl.* answerings of questions 52/7 (*OED* 1548).

restablish *v.* restore 107/18; *pp.* 104/6.

rest(e)[1] *v.* (fr. Fr. *arrester*) ~ *at* (*in, vpon*) stop over, fix the attention on 62/13, 65/33, 107/8 (*OED* no uses exactly like these; see 62/13 note).

restith[2] *pr. 3 sg.* (fr. OE *ræstan*) gives rest 85/11; is vested 47/17; is based or founded 68/16. **restin** (error for *-ith*) has place, lies 24/17. **resten** *pl.* put trust, remain confident 80/18, 85/29.

restith[3] *pr. 3 sg.* (fr. Fr. *rester*) is left 9/8, 107/1, 139/3; remains, con-tinues 215/16; remains in a speci-fied state 201/22; remains to be dealt with 85/25 (*OED* 1577). **restith** *pl.* 200/22, 214/20; **rest** 143/31. *rest so* remain in that state 139/30. **restid** *pa. t.* 74/28.

restore *v.* repair, amend 110/18 (*OED* rare, 1567); *pa. t.* reestabli-shed 61/16; *pp.* reinstated 108/21.

retchith *pr. 3 sg.* cares 11/20; cf. **rekke**.

retournable *adj.* reciprocal, mutual 10/11 (*OED* meaning om.; Fr. 'reciproque'; see note).

ret(o)urne *v. tr.* reverse 119/14 (*OED* no ex. exactly like this); *pr. pl.* turn back (the face) 60/12; *intr.* turn back 79/12, 84/15; *pp.* turned round 8/30. ~ *into* change into (something else) 105/18; *pp.* 115/29; changed back into (a former state) 54/17. ~ *to himself* revive himself spiritually 99/22.

retrayeth *pr. 3 sg.* withdraws 9/16.

r(e)ule, ruele, rewle *n.* behaviour 44/33, 197/32, 245/22; principle governing conduct 196/6; *pl.* 221/20; order, discipline 142/28. *owt of* ~ in a disordered state 56/28.

r(e)ule *v. refl.* conduct oneself 101/6; *pass.* 223/18. **rueled** *pp.* exercised 113/22. **revled to** directed toward 113/20.

reule *adj.* disciplined 97/6.

reue *v.* rob 223/28.

reuenge *v.* punish 243/23; see 140/2, 141/3 note.

reuerceth *pr. 3 sg.* overturns 35/18. **reuerseth** overthrows 135/20. **revercid** *pp.* thrown down, stretched out (of the body) 6/6; **reuersid** 149/23, 165/22.

reuertid *pp.* withdrawn 77/6 (**reuersyd** J).

revile *v.* debase 112/28.

revoke *v.* see 65/33 note.

riall *adj.* royal 167/19.

ryalte *n.* magnificence 9/9.

right *n.* law 227/26; *pl.* 136/6. *of* ~ rightfully 30/14.

right *adj.* appropriate 171/9.

rynde *n.* bark of a plant 85/18.

ryotouse *adj.* unrestrained 7/21 (*OED* 1508).

risen *pa. t. pl.* ~ (*vp*) fig., gained their feet after a fall 102/1; *resyn vp* took up arms 109/21; *rose vp* 104/29. *rose on hyght* (*sg.*) was greatly elated with hope 103/1. **risen** *pp.* 182/26, 184/18.

ryvelid *adj.* wrinkled 4/31.

royalte *n.* magnificence 226/5; cf. ryalte.

roylith *pr. 3 sg.* totters, reels 142/11 (*OED* meaning om. under *roll*; Fr. 'chancelle').

rome *n.* fig., place 235/27 (*OED* 1577).

routes *n. pl.* fig., roots, causes 179/15.

rowe *n.* in *alle in oone* ~ all in one category 207/2 (*OED on a row*).

rude *adj.* common 137/20; coarse 187/5; harsh 147/16, 153/24; ignorant 57/23, 86/21. **rudest** *superl.* 215/8.

ruine *n. attrib.* disastrous 205/4 (see note).

ruynous *adj.* disastrous 204/4 (*OED* 1526).

sacred *pp.* sanctified 50/11.

sacrid *adj.* see 50/13 note.

sad *adj.* steadfast 193/3.

sadnes *n.* see 95/23 note.

say *v.* tell 105/7. **seyn** *pr. pl.* 153/1. **seid** *pp.* called 141/30. *as who seith* as they say 214/21.

saintuarye *n.* sanctuary 48/2, 131/5 (**sayntewoary** J).

saluable *adj.* saving, protecting from anything undesirable 239/27; **soluable** 225/3 (*OED* meaning om.; Fr. 'salvable'; see 238/28 note); cf. savable.

saluacion *see* savacion.

sanctification *n.* action of making believer(s) holy 50/5, 88/4 (*OED* 1526); hallowing 122/19 (*OED* 15--).

Sapience *n.* 'God' 30/28.

satify *v.* satisfy 125/10 (**satysfye** N). ~ *of* set free from doubt 126/31 (*OED* meaning 2 under *satisfy* 1596).

satisfaccion *n.* atonement 102/21.

saude *see* sowde.

saudoiers *see* souldeiours.

sauen, sawyn *see* sowen.

saughe *see* see.

saute *pr. pl.* assault 163/14; *pp.* 169/30.

savable *adj.* saving, protecting from anything undesirable 238/28 (see note).

savacion *n.* preservation from destruction, etc. 216/21, 226/2; **saluacion** 217/14, 225/24.

save onely *conj.* unless 85/26. **sauf oonly that** except that 245/19.

sauours *n. pl.* tastes 159/7.

scandalouse *adj.* grossly disgraceful *203/5 (*OED* 1611; Fr. 'scandaleuse').

schare *n.* ploughshare 168/4.

s(c)harpely *adv.* sagaciously 43/18; harshly 72/30.

schette *pp.* closed 118/22. **shete** locked 6/17.

s(c)hrewed *adj.* wicked, evil-disposed 38/17, 146/7.

s(c)laundir (-re) *n.* disgrace, evil name 41/3, 84/10; source of shame, disgraceful act, wrong 97/26, 196/7, 197/6. *make ~ in* cause the moral fall of 52/1.

sclaundre *pr. pl.* cause to lapse morally 45/34. **sclaundird** *pp.* spoken evilly of 192/33; **sclaundred** 193/33.

scomfyte *v.* vanquish 204/21. **scomfite** *pa. t. sg.* discomfited 87/23.

scomfiture *n.* defeat 103/6.

scripyl *n.* in *haue a ~ vpon* have a doubt about (*OED* phr. under *scruple*, 1719). *withowt scruples* without doubts 121/11 (*OED* phr. in sg., 1526; **scripules** N).

scripture *n.* written records 137/28; *pl.* 229/12.

seacyng *vbl. n.* in *withowt ~* constantly 21/15; cf. **sykyng**.

season *n.* in *owt of ~* inopportunely 170/14, 171/13.

seced *see* **cesse**.

secreelye *adv.* secretly 209/7.

secrees *n. pl.* mysteries 27/10.

secretaire *n.* secretary 135/8 (*OED* rare).

secrete *adj.* private, i.e. within a household group 81/16.

sedicion *n.* ? seducing people to err in belief or conduct 89/22 (see note); violent discord 203/24; *pl.* 135/29, 175/21. **seducion** 202/25; *pl.* 174/21.

seducyous *adj.* tending to lead astray 19/3 (*OED* meaning om.; see note).

seduys *ppl. adj.* led astray in belief or conduct 175/16 (*OED* as *v.* 1519–20, as *ppl. adj. seduced* 1584).

see *n.* throne 35/15.

se(e) *v.* protect 151/9; keep in view

223/8. **seen** *pr. pl.* see 9/10; **seyne** see to it 82/28 (see note). **sawe** *pa. t.* 140/7; **saughe** 144/8.

seegis *n. pl.* seats used by persons of rank 35/17, 39/21.

se(e)ke *adj.* perverse 19/11; corrupt through sin 122/15; deeply affected by strong emotion such as sorrow 20/31; ill 43/11, 215/13. **sike** 214/16.

se(e)k(e)nes(se) *n.* illness 22/9, 161/2; transf. 136/13, 137/15; moral or spiritual ailment 18/13, 241/28.

seese, sessed *see* **cesse**.

seete *see* **sett**.

seigneuries *n. pl.* lords 245/5.

seigniour *n.* ? lord; ? lordship 157/7 (Fr. 'seigneurie').

sekyng *see* **sykyng**.

semblably of ? *adj., adv.* similar to 55/22; cf. **sembleable**.

semblaunce *n.* outward aspect 20/17; form, likeness 15/17, 39/29; appearance (as opposed to reality) 87/20 (*OED* 1599). *by ~* by comparison 76/25; *see* **visage**.

semblaunt *n.* demeanour 145/11.

sembleable *n.* (one's) fellow-man 239/2; **symblable** 36/13.

sembl(e)able *adj.* similar 55/16, 76/26. *in ~ maner* similarly 195/21. *~ wyse* 182/28.

sembled *pa. t.* assembled 105/35.

semest *pr. 2 sg. tr.* think 33/6. **semith** *3 sg.* makes it appear (followed by cl. as if *v.* were impers.) 180/14; sim. **seemyng** *pr. p.* 181/12. *me semes* (*impers.*) it seems to me 57/9–10, 118/30; *me se(e)myth* 9/24, 187/9. sim. *him semes* 80/27–8. *me (them) semyd* 5/6, 76/30–1, 142/27.

sencetif *adj. ~ body* body endowed with faculty of sensation 67/3 (*OED* 1555). *spirite ~* part of soul concerned with sensation 5/20 (see note). *sensetiffe vertue* faculty of sensation 5/25 (see note). *apetite sensitif* inherent drive attributed to the mental 'faculties' 21/18.

sengelly *adv.* by themselves 236/21.

sense, sence *n.* meaning 82/8, 91/32 (*OED* 1513).

sente *pa. t. sg.* sent a message 38/2. **sende** *pp.* sent 129/26.

sentence *n.* opinion 33/21; pronouncement 80/28; judgement, determination 35/16, 134/16, 135/19; sentence of excommunication 48/23; statement 21/6; *pl.* 40/8; subject 4/9; meaning 60/29, 82/5; significance 146/15, 147/14; maxim 45/24, 226/18, 227/18; sound judgement 218/12; *pl.* laws 98/13.

serche (owt) *v.* make oneself thoroughly acquainted with 80/32, 188/26; look for 78/2, 112/6, 190/29.

serymonymously *adv.* in accordance with the Ceremonial Law 128/22 (*OED* 1596).

serteyne *n.* certain (used as synonym for **Demonstratyue**) 23/15.

seruage *n.* bondage 9/31. *vndir* ~ *in* bondage 16/21. *vndir the* ~ *of* in bondage to 61/4.

seruaunt-tailoure *n.* servant to a tailor 203/2 (*OED servant* as attrib. n. 1832).

serue *v.* assist (a workman by handing him materials) 229/20 (*OED* 1525); *pr. pl.* ? treat in a specified way; ? put in bondage (*OED* om.) 153/19 (see note); *pp.* treated 10/7. ~ *to* be a means of effecting 108/7.

sett *n.* seat 149/22; *seete* 170/6, 171/5. *royall* ~ throne 162/26, 163/24.

sette *v.* cause to be, put 95/20, 103/31, 143/24, 195/25; place (trust, belief, etc.) 98/16, 100/6; centre (on) 41/14, 100/32; arrange 147/12; appoint (a boundary) 85/13, 105/25; lay (a siege) 231/22; add 141/12; *pass.* be seated 207/19; have one's mind or will fixed (to) 126/8. *be* ~ have become, are 200/20. ~ *alofte* exalt, raise in position 198/27. ~ *apart* dismiss from consideration 171/31. ~ *forthe* express 183/15 (*OED* 1530); send out (soldiers, etc.) for service 188/27; set on the way 205/23 (*OED* 1525). ~ *in* give 54/22; establish 137/18. ~ *like* consider or value together 8/12. ~ *vp* raise in position or situation 185/18; *refl.* 199/23; exalt, raise 220/33. ~ *an ende in* end 211/4. ~ *on high* (*hight*) exalt, place in high position 8/34, 89/14. ~ *in ordre*

mention 102/25. ~ *payn* attempt, go to some trouble 195/8. ~ *litle payn* exert little effort 165/13. ~ *not by* scorn 76/33-4 (Fr. 'mesprise'); have no regard for, not value at all 14/24, 45/16, 53/18; ~ *nothing by* 4/30; *nought* ~ *by* 102/32-3; ~ *at nought* 11/17, 29/30. *the hande most be* ~ *to the deede* the deed must be set about 155/14. **sett(e)** *pr. pl.* 79/22, 199/23; **seet** 165/13; **sittith** 183/15. **sette** *pp.* 54/22, 149/6; **seet** 231/22; *see* **aventure, weye.**

seu(i)rly *adv.* with confidence and safety 12/20 (**sourly** J), 186/21. **suerly** securely 205/34.

seu(i)rte(e), surete, suertye (-tee) *n.* security, confidence 4/27, 27/3, 60/2; *pl.* 150/15; safety 3/22, 15/1, 212/7, 213/6, 224/23, 225/17; safeguard 192/3, 193/3; certainty 22/12, 69/24. *to haue a* ~ to be certain 12/19. **sewerte** confidence 208/6 (Fr. 'secrete').

s(e)ure, sevir, sevre *adj.* certain 9/29; safe 13/6; secure 107/27; confident 184/25, 185/23.

sewe *v.* follow 20/4, 234/5; take as pattern 76/24; comply with 85/33; occupy oneself with 34/11. **sewe** *pr. pl.* 44/6; **sewen** 38/16.

shadow(e) *n.* symbol, prefiguration 23/30; fig., darkness 78/2; protection from observation, pretext 200/6. *vndir* (*the*) ~ *of* under pretence of 152/24, 167/21 (*OED* 1523). *vndir our shadew* under our protection 188/23.

shadowed *pp.* screened from blame 44/12.

shakyn *pp.* caused to totter 145/16.

shame *n.* in *thinke* ~ are ashamed 46/23-4. **shames** *pl.* shameful injuries 109/2.

shamefast *n.* one who feels shame 23/10.

shamefastenesse *n.* feeling of shame 21/3.

sharpe *adj.* ? vigilant 45/32 (see note).

sheldis *n. pl.* see 196/18 note (Fr. 'sens').

shete *see* **schette.**

shewe, schewe *v.* reveal, make

evident 42/17, 62/9, 144/12, 145/11, 184/32; present 11/18; inform, teach 8/20, 107/2; describe 63/3; foretell 61/1, 73/21; *abs.* 85/10; decree 63/21, 170/8; present for a specific use 24/23; fig., place (light) where it can be seen 20/21, 21/15; prove 42/15, 185/30, 198/31, 199/27; be evident 39/19; be indication of 48/11, 99/28; seem 38/9, 202/9; *refl.* 222/4; appear to have 40/7; cause to have 87/21; manifest through behaviour 224/8; *refl.* allow oneself to be seen 62/26, 206/10; *intr.* be seen and admired 40/6; *impers.* be seen or proved 193/10. *shewed owt of* manifested in 55/18; brought forth from 7/24. **shewith** *imp.* 62/5. **shewe** *pr. pl.* 200/10; **s(c)hewith** 39/19, 126/2; **shewen** 136/9. **shewdist** *pa. t. 2 sg.* 63/3, 176/7.

shewer *n.* announcer 63/1; one who exhibits 78/22; *pl.* 53/25.

shewing *vbl. n.* outward appearance 99/28, 129/11, 198/22; outward appearance of truth 80/25; exhibition, manifestation 56/16, 113/3; *pl.* 117/21, 158/13; revelations, teachings 40/16, 66/22, 97/12.

shyne *pr. pl.* are brilliantly evident 62/11.

short(e)ly *adv.* speedily 14/23, 64/2, 174/4; briefly 132/20. *the short-lyer* the more quickly 61/29.

shortinge *vbl. n.* shortening 169/14.

shrincke away *v.* recede 80/4.

syde *n.* part 218/34. *on the (that) othir (tothir)* ~ on the other hand, also 25/32, 37/13, 124/28, 220/3, 226/28. *on this* ~ here in this world 92/29. *now on this* ~, *now on that* ~ now here, now there 64/29 (*OED* om.; Fr. 'deça, dela').

sideling to *adj.* fig., not directly concerned with 127/2 (*OED* fig. om.; non-fig. a1548; Fr. 'lateral'; see note).

syghing *ppl. adj.* accompanied by sighs 18/10.

significacion *n.* sign 70/29 (**sygnefyaunce** NJ); *pl.* 65/12.

signified *pa. t.* foreshowed 196/32.

sike *see* **seeke.**

sikernes(se) *n.* security 151/21; safety 167/10; certainty 175/29.

sykyng, sekyng *vbl. n.* in *withowt* ~ constantly 93/4, 126/25 (*OED* spellings om.; see 93/4 note); cf. **seacyng.**

symblable *see* **sembleable.**

similitude *n.* resemblance 88/22; comparison 76/26; simile 115/15, 172/6, 173/8; allegory 75/5. ~ *of* practice similar to 92/7.

symp(e)ly *adv.* indifferently 212/34; inadequately 220/32.

symple, sympyll *adj.* not composite (implying oneness of God) 119/31; humble 47/25, 48/19; foolish 184/13; feeble 5/34, 164/23; deficient, little 220/35, 247/23; lacking knowledge, easily misled 4/21, 27/16, 81/11; *superl.* 215/8; *sb.* 214/9.

simplenes(se), sympilnes(se) *n.* humility 21/6, 27/30; innocence 66/32; lack of knowledge or acuteness 236/7; ? weakness 144/2 (Fr. 'pusillanimité').

singler *adj.* particular, individual 101/16 (frequent in NJ).

singuler (-are) *adj.* remarkable 104/35; special 206/9; private, individual 81/13, 152/16, 153/15, 216/31, 217/24.

syn(ne) *adv.* ago 10/14. *agoo* ~ 3/5.

syn(ne) *prep.* since, after 53/14, 61/33; *conj.* since 28/29, 37/2, 190/1; ~ *that* 244/26.

sith *adv.* afterward 215/14.

sith(e) *prep.* for 175/30; *conj.* since 65/26, 151/22, 180/6; ~ *that* 76/14, 175/4.

sithen *prep.* after 59/5; *conj.* since 177/32, 189/13; ~ *that* 181/6.

sithin *adv.* afterward 6/7, 64/5.

sittith *pr. 3 sg. impers.* is proper 75/30. **sitting(e)** *pr. p.* fitting, proper 58/2; **settinge** 223/5.

skantly(e) *adv.* scarcely 139/3, 195/16; inadequately 231/13.

skaundre *n.* disgrace 179/29 (*OED* rare; see note).

skonche *v.* ? hide; ? blot out 229/1; extinguish 209/2; *pp.* 165/10 (*OED* om.; see 165/10 note).

slake *v.* allow to become slack 168/21, 169/24.

slaughfull *adj.* slothful 151/4 (*OED slowful*).

slee *v.* slay 159/2; *refl.* commit suicide 76/31. slewe *pa. t. sg.* 106/9; slewghe 162/4; slwe 163/4; slough 104/22. slwe *pl.* 163/3; slowghen 162/3.

slewgh *adj.* slothful 78/26 (*OED* om.; related to *slewful* and *sleuth*; slow NJ).

slewthe *n.* sloth 148/21; sleuthe 180/7; cf. slowthe.

slide *v.* slip away 179/13; fig., pass easily 237/27.

sliding *vbl. n.* pulling 147/17 (Fr. 'detrainer').

sloughth *pr. pl.* allow to slip through slothfulness 204/36 (slowth NSJ).

slow(e) *adj.* slothful 150/3; dilatory in action 192/35. sloughe unwilling 73/3.

slowthe, slouthe *n.* sloth 166/6, 196/16; as personification 69/5, 78/33.

smal(l)e *adj.* fig., fine (as opposed to coarse) 101/10; common, humble in position 39/22, 198/15; *sb.* 196/4.

smallnesse *n.* small mental capacity 237/6.

smerte *adj.* painful 213/18; smarte 223/2.

smetyn *pp.* overthrown, afflicted 50/30, 62/20; smytten 95/11.

so *adv.* such 25/2, 28/33.

so that *conj.* so long as, provided that 100/4, 111/33, 183/17.

soc *n.* ploughshare 169/6.

sode(i)nly(e), soda(i)nly *adv.* suddenly 5/3, 20/12, 142/7, 143/6, 242/15; sodeingly 142/9.

soft(e) *adj.* lazy 78/33; weak 156/3, 157/3 (*OED* 1593).

softnes *n.* gentleness 96/17.

sokeryng *vbl. n.* succouring 186/5.

solempnytes *n. pl.* ceremonies 130/21.

soluable *see* saluable.

solucion *n.* answer 221/26; explanation 116/27; *pl.* 66/22.

som(e)tyme *adv.* once, formerly 3/27, 24/12, 135/24, 138/17, 231/17; sumtyme 230/16.

som(m)e, sume *n.* summary 122/30/ 168/31. *in a* ∼ to sum up 239/29 (*OED* 1562). *pl.* sums 219/25.

somwhat *n.* something 141/11.

sondry *adj.* different 141/29, 145/20.

soole *adj.* in *oon* ∼ only one, a single 131/28; *oon soule* 237/10.

sophistyk *adj.* deceitful 79/4 (*OED* 1591). Sophistique *sb.* specious but fallible reasoning 23/16.

soteltees *see* subtilite.

so(u)ld(e)iours *n. pl.* soldiers 105/31 (sowudyours N), 160/32, 212/2, 222/25; saudoiers 161/34; sowdiours 213/2. saudeours *gen.* 223/24.

sowde *n.* wages 200/8; saude 201/9; *pl.* 221/9.

sowen *pp.* scattered 123/31, 144/22. sawyn spread 208/6; sauen 209/7.

sownde *v.* have a tendency toward (helping), have some connection with 224/9; ∼ *to* 186/23. sowned *pp.* ? declared, proclaimed 94/27 (see note).

space *n.* time 18/11. (*by*) *the* ∼ *of* for 14/2, 60/21-2, 73/13, 107/28, 152/3-4. *of long* ∼ for a long time 164/19-20. *in a shorte* ∼ quickly 63/27; *in litle* ∼ 205/19.

spackest *pa. t. 2 sg.* spoke 48/2. spa(c)ke *3 sg.* 53/10, 148/20.

spairboilled *see* sparpelith.

spar(e) *v.* shun 184/14, 185/12; *pr. 3 sg.* hoards up 170/15; *pp.* reserved 184/33, 185/31. spared *sb.* saving 203/20 (*OED* om.).

sparynge *vbl. n.* in *a* ∼ something saved 171/20. sparyngis *pl.* savings 202/21 (*OED* sg. om.; *pl.* 1628).

sparpelith *pr. 3 sg.* disperses (improperly) 170/12. sperpuled *pp.* dispersed 80/5; spairboilled 191/4.

spe(e)de *v.* further 210/11. ∼ *wele* (*pr. subj.*) fare well 240/5. *spedde of* (*pp.*) successful in obtaining 87/6.

spende *pr. pl.* waste 170/18. spendid *pp.* used up 198/35; spent 196/27; spent 197/25.

sperpuled *see* sparpelith.

spices *n. pl.* species 56/6.

spirite *n.* in *in* ∼ by purely intellectual perception 48/1-2.

spring(e) *n.* source 138/14, 139/12, 240/31, 241/29; source, in reference to God, Understanding, etc. 21/9, 25/20, 70/4; dawn 142/4; *pl.* impelling forces 115/5 (*OED* c.1616).

springith *pr. 3 sg. tr.* ~ *abrode* spreads abroad 45/30 (*OED* only intr. with *wide*). ~ (*owt*) *of* originates from 156/18; *pl.* 122/33. **spronge** *pp.* arisen 177/30.

sta(a)te *n.* existence 142/25; normal condition 166/19.

stable *v.* make stable 132/30.

stablely(e) *adv.* constantly 120/23; firmly 183/22.

stablischinge *vbl. n.* setting in office 37/27.

stablisshe *v.* ~ *to* make (oneself) stable in 99/18. **stablis(s)hid (-ischid)** *pa. t.* set in office or dignity 34/4, 134/10, 172/11; brought into settled order 102/10; founded 58/30 (*OED* 1591); strengthened, reinforced 68/29; *pp.* 41/8; ordained 33/23, 57/13; rendered stable in virtue 182/22.

staied *pa. t.* held up 149/12 (*OED* 1548).

stayes *n. pl.* fig., supports 12/27 (*OED* fig. 1542).

staunche *v.* repress 244/22; *imp.* quench 106/15.

stere *v.* move, urge 73/30, 208/12. **steren** *pr. pl.* 152/32.

sterid *pa. t. refl.* guided himself 74/1 (Fr. 's'admonnestoit').

steryng *vbl. n.* instigation 63/11.

sterne *n.* steering gear of a ship 231/9.

sterte *v.* escape 192/1.

stye *v.* ascend 51/27.

stond(e), stande *v.* be, remain 53/3, 125/11, 147/5, 218/6; last 33/28. ~ *ayeinst* resist 22/3. ~ *in* depend upon 81/5. ~ *with* side with 64/12; bear the brunt of 169/5. **stonde** *pr. pl.* 62/28; **stondin** 9/9.

stonyet *pp.* stupefied 40/15 (**stonned** S).

stoppith *pr. 3 sg.* stops up 38/26. **stop(pe)** *pl.* prevent 14/4. ~ *your erys* (*earis*) refuse to listen 158/15, 159/12.

store *n.* necessities 170/16.

stories *n. pl.* histories 177/16, 224/10, 225/8, 228/10.

straite, straitely *see* **streighte, streightly.**

straunge *adj.* foreign 13/34, 176/23, 177/23; difficult 104/1; too great 150/19, 151/24; ? unusual; ? error for *strang* = 'strong' 148/21 (see note).

straungely *adv.* ? error for *strangly* = 'strongly' 11/31 (Fr. 'fort'; see note).

straungenes *n.* discouraging attitude and actions 131/22.

straunge places *n. pl.* error for *strang places* = 'strong places', fortresses 237/18 (Fr. 'forteresces').

straung(i)er(i)s *n. pl.* foreigners 13/21, 61/5, 220/15, 221/11.

strecche *v.* extend: ~ *aftir* be adequate for 219/21. **stretchith** *pr. 3 sg.* ~ *vpon* is adequate to reach 31/30. *intr.* directs its course 72/6. *pl.* tend (towards) 68/21.

streight(e), streyte, straite *adj.* narrow 7/26, 22/19, 116/17; affording little room 59/28; severe in action 192/35; strict 93/26, 222/4, 223/4; causing hardship 159/6.

streightly, streitly, straitely *adv.* tightly 6/18; strictly 139/10, 226/19, 227/19, 234/27.

streyned *pa. t.* clasped 5/5.

streitis *n. pl.* narrow places 116/13. **streyghtes** narrow places between mountains 243/8.

strengest *see* **stronge.**

strenght *n.* strength 57/24; violence, force 237/19. **strenketh** (N) 70/21, 162/21.

strengthin *pr. 3 sg.* confirms 120/20. **strengthid** *pp.* strengthened 27/25, 74/5.

stretchith *see* **strecche.**

strikin *pp.* struck 140/21. ~ *of* cut off 227/30.

stryue *v.* ~ *ayeinst* behave mutinously against 51/24; struggle against physically 53/3. ~ *with* seek to surpass, try to compete with 31/6; ? stick obstinately to 80/33 (*OED* meaning om.; Fr. 's'aheurter'). *pr. p.* disputing 207/18.

stryving *vbl. n.* waging spiritual warfare 43/19.

stroyed *pa. t.* destroyed 102/3.

stroke *n.* act of divine chastisement 132/13; *pl.* 141/22; acts causing pain or death 232/10. ~ *of the bataile* full force of the battle 125/28. *at one* ~ at once 111/2, 205/22.

strong(e) *adj.* arduous 5/28; harsh 96/25. **strengest** *superl.* strongest physically 184/20; *see* **straunge**.

stvdye *n.* deliberate effort 65/15.

studieth *pr. 3 sg.* considers (with indir. question) 80/6. **studyen** *pl.* 53/22; **study** 65/4; endeavour 82/33.

stuff *n.* material 74/4.

subaltare *adj.* subordinate, inferior 68/21 (*OED subaltern*, 1581).

subdewed *pp.* reduced 154/29 (*OED* 1605; see note).

subg(i)et *n.* inferior 192/28, 193/28. **subiettes** *pl.* things open to some influence 120/28; subjects (to a lordship) 180/3; **subgit(t)es** 143/13, 155/1; **subiectis** 142/14, 154/1.

subiecte *adj.* ? subordinate; ? submissive 79/10 (see note).

substanciall *adj.* reliable 46/12.

substantyve *adj.* not dependent upon or subsidiary to anything else 79/28 (*OED* 1561).

substa(u)nce *n.* essence 31/15; being 120/1; foundation 67/32; meaning 91/32; goods necessary for subsistence 162/22, 163/20, 170/12, 171/11; material goods 223/16. *of no* ~ valueless 66/13.

subtil(i)te(e) *n.* sagacity 17/17, 27/16; craftiness 31/4, 238/32; *pl.* intelligent schemes 66/12, 240/3. **soteltees** treacherous acts 203/28.

subtill (-ile) *adj.* crafty, sly 81/12, 90/18, 177/19; wise 142/24, 143/21.

subtilly *adv.* ingeniously 30/2.

subtilnesse *n.* treachery 187/26.

subtraccion *n.* withdrawal 135/31.

subuersion (-cion) *n.* overthrow 33/28, 156/4, 157/4; *pl.* 136/25; ruin 138/15, 139/13.

subuerte *v.* overturn 148/32; over-

throw 35/25, 89/5, 139/23; *pr. 3 sg.* fig., casts down 134/17.

succeders *n. pl.* successors 61/29.

suche *adj.* so great 177/24; *see* **wyse**.

suertee *see* **seuirte**.

suff(e)raunce *n.* delay 43/20, 74/32 (*OED* 1523); consent 44/18; patient endurance of pain, punishment, etc. 43/8, 192/2.

suffisaunce (-siaunece, -ciaunce, -cience) *n.* ample means 47/24; contentment 212/7, 213/6; enough to supply one's needs 223/12; sufficient quantity (of) 226/13. *in* ~ sufficiently 227/13.

suffise (-ice), souffise *v.* be able 142/19, 143/18; satisfy 108/6; *imp. refl.* be satisfied 45/8; *pa. t.* was satisfied 105/34. ~ *it* let it be enough 99/15. *it* ~ *vs* it is enough for us 31/21.

suffrage *n.* help 122/26; *pl.* 100/2; prayers 122/32. ~ *of prayer(e)* prayer(s) 113/24, 125/33; *pl. phr.* help given by prayer 126/4 (*OED* only pl. phr. given).

suffre (-er, -ir, -ur) *v. tr.* permit, allow (with dir. obj.) 142/12, 143/11, 206/13, 207/11; (with cl.) 193/22; (with inf.) 28/33, 87/25, 157/12, 174/29; endure, undergo 11/8, 18/13, 174/16, 175/17, 178/1, 179/1; tolerate 154/35, 155/31; admit of 127/11 (*OED* rare); *intr.* wait patiently 52/29; leave off 247/4; endure pain, punishment, etc. patiently 193/2; allow oneself, consent 8/22, 65/8, 159/26; *refl.* 154/3, 163/30. **suffre (-ir)** *pr. pl.* 62/5, 162/33, 163/30; **suffren** 179/26, 188/20; **suffirn** 178/28; **sufferyth** 64/11.

suyled *ppl. adj.* dirty 4/33 (see note).

sume *see* **somme**.

suotte *n.* soot 5/1.

superexcellence *n.* greatest excellence 72/10 (*OED* 1652).

superflue *adj.* useless 87/10; excessive 94/23.

superfluite *n.* extravagant conduct 157/11.

suppose *v.* believe, think 30/23; *pr. 1 sg.* 220/23; *pa. t.* believed (oneself) (with inf.) 11/12, 124/13; *ppl.*

adj. thought to exist 107/18 (*OED* 1582).

suppositif *adj.* particular, subordinate 21/22 (*OED* om.; Fr. 'suppost' fr. L. 'suppositus'; see note).

supprise *v.* overcome, betray 58/4; *pp.* attacked unexpectedly 13/12; affected violently 16/4.

surmountable *adj.* conquerable 243/4 (*OED* 1611; see note).

surmounte *v.* ~ *aboue* excel 53/27. **surmountith** *pr. 3 sg.* is above the capacity of 97/33; **surmowntith** 25/17 (*OED* 1502); *pa. t.* overcame 63/8; exceeded 93/20; excelled 238/17; *pp.* 239/16.

suspec(c)ion *n.* suspicion 65/19. *by* ~ on the basis of mere supposition 198/25. *had in* ~ suspected 106/23.

suspect(e) *adj.* regarded with suspicion 14/11; deserving distrust 99/32; suspected (of) 199/21. *haue* (*holde*) ~ be suspicious of 164/32, 165/32.

suspection *n.* suspicion 6/28.

suspend *pa. t. sg.* revoked 23/14.

susteyn(e) *v.* support 28/32, 204/2, 205/3; succour, support 100/4, 172/12, 173/14; assert 223/7; preserve 46/27, 59/7; keep going 153/2, 189/9; provide for the needs of 172/4, 173/5; support (nature) with necessaries 98/31; withstand 30/26; endure 95/13, 174/16, 175/17; undergo, endure 52/25, 107/28, 168/27, 169/28; bear (burden, expense) 188/8; hold erect 114/1; hold in position 121/3; fig., hold up 79/26; *refl.* feed oneself 163/29. ~ *to endur* withstand 20/33. **susteyigne** *inf.* 74/2 (*OED* spelling om.; **susteyn** NJ).

swage *v.* mitigate 237/24; *pp.* decreased 241/3.

sware *pa. t. sg.* swore 217/21. *sworn to* (*pp.*) bound by oath (to serve) 106/21.

swellid *pp.* fig., swallowed 203/17.

swete *n.* toil 166/8, 167/7.

swetely *adv.* lovingly 162/23; **switely** 163/21.

swol(l)ow(e) *n.* pit 202/22, 224/24; fig. 218/30 (*OED* 1607).

swomme *pa. t. pl.* swam 119/6.

table *n.* stone tablet 51/19. *a peire of tables* a writing-tablet 7/5.

tachid *pp.* stained with guilt 202/17.

take *v.* feel 131/26; give (to) 51/20; consider 117/24; esteem 90/26; overtake (of sleep) 145/5; capture 37/15, 61/3; do 45/10; undertake 230/23; accept 100/19, 235/13; assume 180/6, 181/5. ~ *awaye* seize 41/26. ~ (*as*) *for* consider as 47/21, 57/2, 192/33, 242/26. ~ *to* consider as 87/30; *refl.* adopt, put on (clothes) 186/6. ~ *vpon* (one) adopt, assume 46/28, 88/18, 101/28; make bold 174/11; claim 128/2. ~ *harte* pluck up courage 214/17, 215/14. ~ *a knowlege of* know, remember 218/13. ~ *in custome* receive willingly as a custom, accustom oneself 59/23, 86/14. ~ *in* (on) *hand* undertake 163/25, 243/29. ~ *to recorde* call as witness 214/9. ~ *hede to* pay attention to 38/30, 180/10. ~ *litill hede* care little 16/28, 158/3. ~ *me* (*imp.*) consider 202/2. **take** *pp.* 9/24, 104/20, 192/18, 230/20; **taken** 64/31, 230/23, 235/13; *see* **weye.**

takers *n. pl.* undertakers 3/15.

taking *vbl. n.* capture 159/23.

tale *n.* statement 194/16; *pl.* 196/31; falsehoods 84/12.

tary vpon *v.* put trust or confidence in 100/1.

tastid of *pa. t.* experienced 127/22 (*OED* 1526).

tatche *n.* moral spot 222/28.

tellist forth *pr. 2 sg.* go on telling abroad 204/18.

tempestes *n. pl.* calamities 109/7.

tempeth (J) *pr. 3 sg.* tempts 126/20 (**tempes** N, **temptith** R).

temporalles *adj. pl.* temporal 131/15.

tendre (-ir) *adj.* weak, unable to bear hardship 5/34, 15/25, 27/17, 157/3, 197/15.

tendrely *adv.* indulgently 247/25.

terme *n.* limit in time 41/7; *pl.* 77/25.

terminacion *n.* determination, judgement 60/26 (**determinacyon** NJ).

testament *n.* covenant between man and God 48/31.

thanke *n.* in *haue* ~ be rewarded

22/6–7. *yeue* ~ *to* give credit to, honour 193/33.

thankyngis *n. pl.* merits, rewards 154/18 (Fr. 'louenge'). *yeve* ~ *to* give credit to, honour 192/32–3.

that *pron. rel.* that which 54/22, 119/27, 147/14, 167/1, 188/14, 190/30, 191/29, 211/22. *dem.* ~ *more is* what is more 13/10.

that, þat *conj.* used like Fr. 'que' in place of repeating preceding conj. 118/29, 138/36, 180/14, 193/21, 199/22, 217/15; in order that 92/12; in consequence of which 146/21, 155/19, 187/17; since 65/23. ~ *than* than 145/10.

the *pers. pron.* they 124/13, 128/10, 131/3, 183/22, 207/20, 234/11.

thenke *see* **thinke.**

þer *adv.* in this matter 129/6. **ther** *rel. adv.* where 3/5.

thereas *conj.* where 155/3, 195/20, 205/11.

therfor *adv.* for that, for it 14/14, 47/13.

therof *adv.* there 233/30.

Thymotracye *n.* timocracy 55/33; **Tymotracie** 56/9 (*OED* 1586, spellings om.; see 55/33 note).

thin(c)kith *pr. impers.* in *me* ~ it seems to me 87/5, 152/27; sim. *him* ~ 78/18. *me thinke* 244/27. *me thought* (*pa. t.*) 144/7, 145/7; sim. *him* ~ 90/23.

thing *n.* experience (here, future life) 42/12 (Fr. 'vie'); property 128/29; *pl.* matters 223/3.

thinke, thenke *v.* imagine 38/14; remember 177/14. ~ *in* expect of 65/14 (*OED in* om.; Fr. 'esperera en'). ~ (*on*) *imp.* consider, remember 32/20, 57/27, 154/15, 155/12.

this *adj. pl.* these 12/1, 184/11, 186/12; **thise** 188/30; **thais, þais** (N) 28/8, 108/6, 122/23, 152/27, 178/21, 178/33, 246/22 (*OED* spelling listed only under *those*; **thes** RSJ).

tho(o) *pron. pl.* those 163/6, 173/17; *adj.* 243/20.

thorough *prep.* in *what* ~ on account of 198/17.

thoughtfull *adj.* careful 99/5; anxious 169/6.

throwen *pp.* ~ *vndir* overcome 86/4 (*OED* phr. om.; Fr. 'sucumbé'). ~ *at large* given out without restraint 222/3 (*OED* phr. om., see ~ *open* and *at large*).

thurst downe *v.* humble 210/30 (**threst** SJ).

tyme *n.* in *in* ~ *that* when 217/12; *what* ~ *that* 124/21, 216/17. *tyll* ~ *that* until 152/6; *vnto the* ~ (*that*) 20/19, 30/22. *at the furst* ~ at first 127/20. *at some* (*sum*) ~ sometimes 8/31, 188/2. *from* ~ *to* ~ continually for a long time 52/29 (*OED* 1553). *of long* ~ for a long time 154/26–7, 168/6; *so long* ~ 155/23. *of olde* ~ in ancient times 139/15; formerly 165/27. *on a* ~ once 8/21, 91/2, 238/8–9. *withowt* ~ *of mynde* forever 84/9; *see* **lenghe, passe, renne.**

tyrauntly *adv.* tyranically 162/5; **tirauntlye** 163/5 (*OED* rare; see 162/5 note).

tissued *pp.* woven 145/20.

tyteleris *n. pl.* small birds, with overtones of 'tittlers' = 'whisperers, tell-tales' 196/30 (*OED* om.; Fr. 'mouetes'; see note).

title *n.* recognized right 193/26. *vndir* ~ *of* in the name of 51/9 (*OED* phr. om.).

to *prep.* for the purpose of 24/23, 47/23, 54/30, 77/1, 150/20, 151/26, 169/30, 180/27, 225/7; for 46/13, 57/20, 81/13, 173/11, 196/26, 200/30, 201/30; as 190/30; so as to cause 44/17, 54/35, 166/26, 167/24; with regard to 58/19, 193/5; in 99/18, 157/33; of 220/18; according to, by 28/21, 81/14, 153/19, 245/6; to the extent of 232/16; against, upon 47/23, 163/6, 191/16; toward 54/34, 245/24; joined to 209/8.

to and fro *adv.* from one thing to another 183/34.

tobroken *pp.* destroyed 41/13, 102/30.

tobruse *v.* fig., crush to pieces 148/32.

togedirs *adv.* together 229/26.

tokenyng(e) *vbl. n.* in *yeve* ~ *of* presage 62/17, 141/22 (*OED* phr.

om).). *in* ~ as evidence 144/14, 145/13.

tonelle *n.* net for catching partridges 14/26.

tonnefullis *n. pl.* as much as fills tuns 192/17 (*OED* 1562).

torne, tornyng *see* **turne.**

tossid *pp.* pitched 154/2 (*OED* 1506).

touch *n.* short form for 'touch-wood' 47/19 (*OED* 1541-2).

touch, towch *v.* attain 28/21; affect 69/32; rebuke 207/21. ~ (*to*) relate to 24/18, 140/27, 141/28, 236/6, 237/5. **towchith** *pr. pl.* 140/27; **touche** 204/27. **tuch** *subj.* 236/6.

touching *prep.* in *as* ~ as to, with respect to 115/14; *as towching* 210/15.

tough *n.* tow 40/12 (*OED* spelling om.; **towghe** NS, **towe** C).

towaile *n.* ? shroud 7/17 (*OED* meaning om.; Fr. 'suaire').

transforme *v.* change in condition 177/15 (*OED* 1556).

transitories *adj. pl.* transitory 34/28, 73/32.

translacion *n.* removal 109/14.

translatid *pp.* transferred 51/1, 82/19, 138/27, 139/26.

transmygracion *n.* removal of the Jews into captivity in Babylon 60/30, 83/15.

transmutacion *n.* change 31/10.

transportith *pr. 3 sg.* fig., transfers from one person to another 35/33.

transsumpcion *n.* transfer of terms 117/24.

trauth *see* **trouthe.**

travaile, trave(i)le *v. intr.* exert oneself, labour 31/4, 61/11, 178/8, 233/4; sim. (const. *for*) 56/30; sim. (with inf.) 103/24, 154/14; *tr.* afflict, weary 4/20, 148/12; put to work 160/10.

traueilous *adj.* hard-working 155/10.

traveling *ppl. adj.* suffering 22/12.

traversable *adj.* fig., moving to and fro, hence confused 119/7 (*OED* meaning only under *v. traverse;* Fr. 'entreuerchiez' = 'complicated, confused'; see note).

traversing *ppl. adj.* digressing 127/3 (*OED* rare, 1530; see note); Law,

contradicting formally a previous pleading; disputing 140/31 (see note).

treasour *n.* treasury 184/26, 185/24. **tresoure** fig., ? treasurer; ? treasury 98/34 (**tresoresse** NJ; see note).

trewage *n.* tribute 122/34.

tryacle *n.* medicinal compound used against venomous bites 69/30.

tributys *n. pl.* 173/13 (see 172/10-12 note).

trinall *adj.* threefold 21/8, 24/16 (*OED* 1590).

tristen *pr. pl.* trust 25/24. **trustyng** *pr. p.* having confidence 86/7 (**trastyng** J).

triumphous *adj.* celebrating victory 161/24 (*OED* rare, 1501; see 160/22-4 note).

troubelith *pr. 3 sg.* oppresses 126/20. **trowbelid** *pp.* disturbed 176/32; **troubled** 177/31; injured 38/30; *pa. t. intr.* for *pass.* ? was disturbed 141/16 (*OED* rare, only ex. 1618; Fr. 'debatuz'); *ppl. adj.* confused 118/10.

trouble *adj.* disturbed 184/9.

troublouse *adj.* unclear 84/31 (*OED* no use like this).

trouth(e), treuthe, trauth(e), troughe *n.* honesty 11/16; virtue 224/7, 225/6; steadfastness, loyalty 159/5, 180/3, 180/22, 181/3, 220/19, 221/15. *for to say* ~ indeed 87/13.

trumpe *n.* trumpet 73/25.

trussid *pp.* girdled 6/21.

trust(e) *n.* fidelity 81/21; self-confidence 31/16; hope 87/6. ~ *to* (*on*) confidence in 81/22, 100/6. *in* ~ *of* hoping for 215/20.

trustyng of *vbl. n.* hoping for 43/6.

tunne *n.* large cask 7/11.

tvnnith *pr. 3 sg.* fig., stores 85/17 (*OED* 1589; see note).

turet *n.* tower 69/22 (see note).

turne, to(u)rne *v. tr.* pervert to a different religion 96/7; ? use; ? appeal to 100/22 (see Introd., p. 17); turn upside down 210/18; *intr.* go, come 23/8, 40/2, 100/23; turn out 186/12, 187/12; defect 215/27; be driven 46/33; apply (to) some purpose 54/28; fall (on, upon) 39/5, 47/22; change 17/33; turn upside down 33/29. ~ *in* (*to*, *into*) change into, become 18/3, 51/30, 171/28. ~ *into* change so as to bring into 102/16. ~ *on* direct towards 207/23. ~ *to* tend to bring about 97/27, 115/13. *warr turnid to* defected to 214/33; *see* **influence.**

turnyng *vbl. n.* returning 230/28.
turnyng *ppl. adj.* variable 63/7.

vnarayed *adj.* in disorder 144/15 (**vnrayde** J).
vnatemprid *adj.* intemperate 53/32.
vnbinde *v.* destroy 94/21; *pr. 3 sg.* 34/28; absolves 41/15.
vnccion *n.* anointing of a king 34/5.
vnconyng *n.* ignorance 16/23.
vncouenable *adj.* unseasonable 62/20; inappropriate 64/1.
vnderlaied *pp.* made subject 165/7.
vndir *adv.* in subjection 105/15.
vndir (-er) *prep.* subject to 39/32; according to 80/21; distressed by 168/10, 169/11; *see* **fourme, maner.**
vndirmyne *v.* overthrow stealthily 30/6 (Fr. 'reprendre').
vndirstonde *v.* understand 32/21. ~ *to be* believe oneself to be 81/21. **wndirstoode** *pa. t.* 27/5. **vndirstonde** *pp.* 32/27, 158/23; **vndirstanden** recognized 221/28.
vndrest *ppl. adj.* in disorder, uncombed 159/18.
vnease *n.* discomfort 173/34.
vnexpert *adj.* untrained 86/21.
vnfeyned *ppl. adj.* sincere 85/1.
vngarnisshid (-nisched) *ppl. adj.* lacking 142/16. ~ *of* lacking in 73/15, 184/26, 185/24.
vnhabited *ppl. adj.* uninhabited 107/25, 169/3.
vnhappy *adj.* disastrous, causing misfortune 5/13, 59/32; evil, miserable 65/1, 83/22; see 35/8 note.
vnhoneste *adj.* morally offensive 44/32.
Vnitive *n.* see 21/23 note (*OED* sb. om.; adj. 1526).
vniuersall *adj.* ~ *people* all the people 128/28.

vnkemyd *ppl. adj.* uncombed 159/17.
vnkempte *ppl. adj.* uncombed 158/21 (*OED* 1742).
vnkynde *adj.* ungrateful 8/9, 176/18; wicked 112/21; devoid of natural feeling 150/29, 151/28, 151/34.
vnkynd(e)nes(se) *n.* absence of natural feeling 108/33; ingratitude 134/27, 196/10; as *pl.* unkind acts 7/6; showings of ingratitude 11/7, 174/28.
vnkyndly *adj.* lacking natural affection in family relations 17/9 (*OED* 1590; also in Malory); unnatural in relations with others 156/5.
vnknyt(t) *imp.* sever 152/31; *pp.* destroyed 62/23.
vnknowen *pp.* unacknowledged, unrecognized 59/19, 76/7; *ppl. adj.* 176/17, 177/17; unfamiliar 108/2.
vnknowyng *vbl. n.* ignorance (of) 138/33, 142/34. ~ *of* failure to know 197/16.
vnmaketh *pr. 3 sg.* deprives of rank and station 9/2 (*OED* 1554). *maketh,* ~ in ref. to God's power, makes and unmakes in the broadest sense 136/4, 137/4.
vnmanly *adj.* dishonourable 202/26, 203/25.
vnmercyable *adj.* unmerciful 32/14.
vnmeryte *n.* lack of reward 112/30 (*OED* om.).
vnmyghty *adj.* powerless 88/33.
vnnaturall *adj.* of persons, devoid of natural feeling 150/23, 151/28 (*OED* 1552); excessively cruel and wicked 110/10 (*OED* 1529).
vnneth(e) *adv.* scarcely 106/7, 138/3, 146/15.
vnpacience *n.* impatience 178/16.
vnpacient *adj.* unwilling (with inf.) 155/31 (*OED impatient* 1565). ~ *ayeinst* 156/9 (*OED* ~ *of*).
vnperfecte (-fight, -fite) *adj.* imperfect 59/32, 79/20, 118/10.
vnpossible *adj.* impossible 26/18,103/14.
vnpurse *v.* disburse 183/5.
vnrefrayned *ppl. adj.* immoderate 95/30 (*OED* c.1550).
vnreyned *ppl. adj.* immoderate 98/12 (*OED* 1609).

vnroted *pp.* torn up by the roots 147/18 (*OED* 1570).

vnstaunchable *adj.* insatiable 152/18.

vntestable *adj.* detestable 205/3 (*OED* om.; Fr. 'detestables').

vnthankfully *adv.* reluctantly, ungraciously 189/30 (*OED* meaning om. under adv., see *unthank* and *thankfully*; Fr. 'a regret').

vnto *prep.* even as far as 24/15, 65/18, 163/28; with a view to 25/26; of 42/3; ? with regard to 131/12 (see note).

vntr(e)w(e), vntr(e)ue *adj.* unjust, wrong 35/26, 182/33, 183/34, 202/33, 203/32; unfaithful, disloyal 44/12, 162/10, 163/10; false 194/25, 195/25.

vntr(e)wely, vntruely *adv.* incorrectly 38/24; guilefully 91/31; dishonestly 130/8; disloyally 194/32.

vntrough *n.* disloyalty 214/32; **vntrouth(e)** 142/14, 143/13.

vnwytty *adj.* ignorant 173/2.

vnwourthily *adv.* undeservedly 67/10.

vp(p)on *prep.* concerning 25/33, 29/33, 64/27, 142/16, 200/31, 201/33; based on 29/2; over 27/27, 34/21, 145/2, 167/4, 201/13; above 165/6; against 43/14, 134/27 (see note), 135/31, 162/16, 174/23, 175/22, 180/5, 181/4; by means of 132/21; through use of 128/29; during 159/8; of 106/33; following upon 196/34; among 206/30.

vp so down(e) *adv.* upside down 19/3, 48/27, 156/3, 166/3.

vpsterte *pa. t. sg.* sprang up 19/16.

vre *n.* fortune 79/5, 164/3.

vrous *see* **eureuse**.

vsage *n.* conduct 152/21; use 186/17, 187/16; practice, custom 153/19, 166/3, 184/25, 220/36, 221/31. *longe* ~ long-continued use 8/13. *in* ~ as a practice 86/17. *turned in* ~ became custom 87/16.

vsaunce *n.* practice 185/22.

vse *v.* practise 55/27, 181/20; do 156/16, 157/18; follow (a course of life) 86/31, 158/19, 159/15; accustom 56/27; treat 56/23; pass (period of

time) 93/9; consume 146/17; uphold 182/21 (see note); discharge the function of 54/33; make use (of) 81/12. **vse** *pr. pl.* 54/33; **usen** 181/20.

vsing *vbl. n.* engaging in 157/31; manner of use 221/31.

vsurpacions *n. pl.* usurpatory powers 56/7 (*OED* rare, 1654).

vsurpe *v. intr.* attempt arrogantly 41/33, 54/28; *tr.* claim or assume wrongly (a name) 77/35, 91/13 (*OED* 1549); seize wrongfully 48/2, 163/5. ~ *vpon* 162/5; encroach upon 35/10; appropriate 82/34 (*OED* 1531). **vsurpe** *pr. pl.* 77/35; **vsurpin** 48/2.

vtilite *n.* advantage, welfare 151/14, 227/24, 245/30.

vttirly *adv.* straightway, without extenuation 36/24; truly 240/8; altogether, fully 19/10, 79/22 (**outturly** J), 89/5, 162/8.

vttirmest *adj.* extreme 140/8; final 140/18.

vaylid *ppl. adj.* lowered 154/3 (*OED* rare, 1591).

vayn(e), veyne *adj.* lacking wisdom 5/34; worthless, fruitless, idle 16/4, 51/7, 53/36, 140/2, 141/2; **wayn** 195/24, 201/24.

valew *n.* amount 182/5.

valure *n.* in *of no* ~ of no efficacy 118/30-1.

vanischid *ppl. adj.* ? removed from sight; ? in a swoon 5/9 (*OED* meaning om.; see note).

vanyte *n.* emptiness, folly 99/16.

vauntyng *vbl. n.* boasting 212/28.

Vegetatyve *adj.* in *Party* ~ 21/17. *Power* ~ see 21/22 note.

veile *n.* sail 155/3.

vendengith *pr. 3 sg. abs.* fig., gathers (grapes for making wine) 85/17 (*OED* om.; Fr. 'vendenge'; see note).

ver(a)y, verray, verey *adj.* rightful 3/8; true, real 10/9, 19/20; veritable 79/1, 218/30, 219/28; valid 218/24; actual 167/24.

vergeus *see* **vigen**.

vertu(e) *n.* physical strength 20/31,

63/9, 164/22, 165/24; power in a divine being 24/3, 31/29; courage 156/25, 157/26; vigour 59/11. *by* ∼ *of* by the power of 6/3. *in the* ∼ *of* 96/5.

vertuous(e) *adj.* glorious 8/3; powerful 125/34; efficacious 247/10.

vertuously *adv.* powerfully 208/8 (*OED* 1588).

viage *n.* voyage, journey 99/14, 116/4; *pl.* 220/14, 221/10; warlike enterprises 232/4.

vicarye *n.* earthly representative (of God) 24/31; *pl.* 46/16.

vigen *n.* in *etteth his* ∼ *in vergeus* fig., drinks his wine as verjuice, eats his grapes before they are ripe 171/12 (Fr. 'menjut sa vigne en verjus').

vylaynye *n.* in *brought vnto* ∼ dishonoured 41/29–30.

vynours *n. pl.* vine-growers 55/9 (**vynerous** NJ).

violacion *n.* desecration 49/15 (*OED* 1546).

violent *adj.* very great (of feelings) 49/26 (*OED* 1593); forced 87/18 (*OED* 1560).

visage *n.* semblance 87/21. *vndir the semblaunce of two visagis* in a two-faced way 154/33. *with .ij. visages* 155/29.

visite *v.* look into 141/35.

vittis *see* **witte**.

vituperable *adj.* reprehensible 239/18.

viuificacion *n.* being vivified in a spiritual sense 24/20 (*OED* 1548).

void(e) *adj.* empty 6/20; unfilled (with sustenance) 99/1 (*OED* exact sense om.); vacant 21/29; lacking good qualities 17/32; futile, worthless 66/13, 240/2, 241/2; invalid 88/7 (*OED* 1526). ∼ *of* not graced by 73/5; free from 119/30; clear of (enemies) 53/15 (*OED* a1548). ? *sb.* empty place 9/8 (*OED* 1697).

voyde *pr. pl.* empty 170/14 (*OED* 1506). ∼ *away* (*pp.*) cleared away 38/9; left undone 160/5. ∼ *owt of* cast from 61/10, 156/21.

vois *n.* voice 165/25; words 197/28; **voice** 196/29; **wois** 203/31. **vois** *pl.* voices 173/23.

volage *adj.* fickle 161/7.

volucion *n.* fig., rolling or revolving movement 69/10 (*OED* 1610; Fr. 'inuolution').

voluntary will *n.* self-will, wilfulness 157/1; as personification 171/6.

volunte *n.* will, desire 137/5, 161/6, 175/27, 217/24. **volunte(e)s** *pl.* 141/10, 157/9, 183/27.

uolupte *n.* sensual pleasure 157/22. **voluptes** *pl.* 157/31.

voluptuosite *n.* voluptuousness 156/20.

waygoers *n. pl.* travellers 116/3.

wayn *see* **vayne**.

waketh *pr. 3 sg.* ∼ *vpon* keeps watch over 75/13. *waken ouir* (*pl.*) 35/24. **wake** are put in action 22/33.

wanhope *n.* erroneously used for 'vain hope' 89/12, 100/15; *see* **opinatiffe**.

warde *n.* guardianship 122/35; *pl.* places to be guarded 204/35, 205/35, 236/18, 237/17.

-ward(e) *phrasal suff.* in *to him* ∼ toward him 211/10; sim. *to hem* ∼ 149/25; *to the erthe* ∼ 149/17. *from a bataile* ∼ away from a battle 239/17.

Wardeyn *n.* guardian, 'God' 100/26.

warre *adj.* aware 69/13.

wasche *v.* ∼ *ther handis therfrom* clear themselves of blame 198/13 (see note). ∼ *clene their hondis from the spottis of* clear themselves of the guilt of 44/14.

waste *n.* destruction 146/17, 147/16 (*OED* 1560).

wastith *pr. 3 sg. intr.* is consumed 21/27 (**westyth** J). **wasten** *pl. tr.* ravage 13/23. **wastid** *pp.* 162/7, 163/7; spent wastefully 196/22; **vasted** 197/21.

watche *n.* vigilance 192/8. *make* ∼ be continually observant 22/32.

watche *v.* fig., stay awake, hence alive 17/29 (see note).

watching *vbl. n.* remaining awake for purpose of devotion 78/29.

wawes *n. pl.* waves 71/10, 154/4.

webbe *n.* fig., woven fabric 74/4 (*OED* 1576).

wedyr *n.* in *wynde and* ∼ stormy weather 155/3.

we(e)nyng *vbl. n.* thinking, hoping 186/15, 191/26.

wene *v.* expect 13/12; *pr. 1 sg.* think (followed by cl.) 195/14. **we(e)nyst** *2 sg.* 44/2; (followed by inf.) 179/13.

wey(e), way(e), veye *n.* means, course of action 194/25, 195/25; *pl.* 146/8, 147/8; voyages 11/13; roads 209/11. *by* ∼ *of* by means of 243/4. *owte of the* ∼ *of* gone astray from 148/24. *at the longe* ∼ in the long run 225/3 (*OED* om.; Fr. 'au paraller'). *in this* ∼ in this respect 219/22 (*OED* 1598). *this* ∼ *helde* followed a (certain) course of action without deviation 215/23. *holdith anothir* ∼ pursues a different course 207/13; sim. *takith anothir* ∼ 206/15. *is in the* ∼ *of* has a good chance of achieving 113/26. *put in the* ∼ *of* put in condition to achieve 233/26–7; sim. *settith in good* ∼ *of* 135/32–3. *make a* ∼ facilitate passage 106/2. *made the* ∼ *large of* facilitated easy passage to 242/21; sim. *made the large* ∼ *of* 243/19. *made opyn the* ∼ *of* led to 204/1; sim. *open the* ∼ *of* 205/1; *see* leest, mydde, opyn.

weyke *adj.* weak 175/10.

wekyrs *n. pl.* wickers 79/30.

wele-avised *ppl. adj.* prudent 5/11, 100/12. **wele-aduysid** well thought out 242/6.

wele-countenauncid *ppl. adj.* of noble bearing 20/24 (*OED* om., *countenanced* 1594).

well *adj.* satisfactory 215/4.

well, wele *adv.* by good evidence 52/30, 145/11, 165/20; much 151/13; greatly 146/13; rightly 167/19, 173/32.

well-purweyed *ppl. adj.* well-equipped 95/21.

welthe *n.* well-being 43/23, 186/22.

were *v. tr.* wear 46/22, 230/21; *pr. 3 sg. intr.* loses sharpness from use 36/14. **ware** *pa. t. sg.* 23/25, 144/16.

werke *n.* affliction 166/13. **warke** deed 104/15. **werkis** *pl.* 10/23, 194/23; ornamentations 144/20, 145/20; ? fortifications; ? error for *werkirs* 228/21.

werke *v.* act 122/8; **wirche** 77/16. **werkith** *pr. 3 sg.* effects 165/12. **wrought** *pp.* made, embroidered 144/20, 147/2; worked upon 187/6.

werkmanship *n.* labour 191/8.

werre *pr. 1 sg. intr.* make war 168/29 (see note). **werride** *pp. tr.* made war upon 169/30; **werried** 212/32; **werred** 213/29.

wevid *pp.* woven 74/4.

wex(e), wax(e) *v.* grow (old) 4/13, 151/5. **wexith** *pr. pl.* become, grow 15/8; **waxen** 105/14; **wex** 141/21. **wexith** *pa. t. sg.* 4/28. **waxen** *pp.* 20/22; **woxen** 174/9.

whan(ne) *conj.* seeing that 106/32, 151/35, 154/20. *as* ∼ when 35/10.

whannese *conj.* when 194/24.

what *pron. adj.* whatever 195/4; *adv. interj.* how 130/6, 194/23. ∼ . . . *and* some . . . others 90/7; both . . . and 90/16, 180/19–20.

whatkyns *n.* in *aftir* ∼ wherever 121/7. *suche* ∼ whatever 120/25.

whatsomeuir *pron.* no matter who 78/23; no matter what 114/3, 184/5. ∼ *that* 184/10.

whedir *conj. adv.* whither 202/22.

whennese *adv.* where 148/31.

wher(e) *adv. conj. interj.* in what situation 188/16; *rel.* in consequence of which 143/18; and there 227/28.

wher(e)as, wharas *rel. adv. conj.* where 6/7, 9/24, 188/24; to which 140/25; wherever 148/11; in the circumstances in which 42/26; in the case in which, when 25/18, 194/20, 235/26; whereupon 142/19; seeing that 51/12, 201/3; and there 93/19; while on the contrary 56/30 (*OED* 1535); although 82/17.

wherynne *see* become.

wher(e)of *adv. inter.* from what source 57/26; *rel.* of which 21/26, 145/19; from which 31/14, 165/18; about which 52/2; in which 203/3; because of which 205/4; by means of which 147/8; that by which (with ellipsis of antec.) 166/32.

whereto *rel. adv.* for which purpose 164/11 (*OED* 1535).

wherfor(e) *inter. adv.* why 17/28; in what circumstances = where 137/32 (*OED* meaning om.).

wherin *rel. adv.* in respect of which 14/21.

whethir *conj.* introducing a direct question giving two alternatives 88/32, 200/28; introducing simple direct question 61/8. ~ . . . *and* ~ if on the one hand . . . and if on the other hand 38/34. **wheder** whether 113/27, 230/27.

whethirsomeuir *conj.* whether 218/32 (*OED whethersoever*).

which(e) *pron.* what 243/24; serving merely to link two clauses together = when, and 89/9, 137/25; error for conj. 'that' 166/4 (Fr. 'que').

whider *inter. adv.* whither 13/6.

whyfor *adv.* and therefore = wherefore 188/29.

who *pron.* if anyone, whoever 99/2; ~ *that* 99/19. **ho(o)** who 183/16, 240/26.

wighty *adj.* hard to bear 212/18 (*OED weighty* 1540, spelling om.).

will(e) *n.* pleasure 156/1; carnal appetite 95/28; desire, inclination 52/26, 80/24, 200/19, 201/20; *pl.* 100/8, 155/10, 156/9; as personification, self-will 170/7; determination, good will 232/30; *pl.* 156/10. *be in* ~ intend, wish 75/24. *haue* ~ 18/7.

will(e) *v.* desire, intend (followed by inf.) 9/14, 81/23; (followed by inf. and acc.) 114/33; (followed by obj. cl.) 13/1, 50/18; (followed by dir. obj.) 119/25, 155/13; decree (followed by obj. cl.) 10/10; *abs.* 42/27. **will(e), woll** *pr. 1, 3 sg.* 13/1, 31/21. **wolte** *2 sg.* 30/32. **wolde** *pa. t. 1, 3 sg.* 51/8, 123/26. **woldest** *2 sg.* 52/33.

wil(le)fully *adv.* willingly, of one's own free will 26/32, 76/19, 158/33, 159/26.

willeth *wk. v. pr. 3 sg.* desires, decrees 170/8, 171/7.

willfull *adv.* freely, gladly 95/29 (Fr. 'voulentiers').

wynnynge *vbl. n.* gain 43/27.

wirche *see* werke.

wise *n.* way 137/24, 143/11. *in like* ~ likewise 59/32. (*in, on*) *this* ~ in this way, thus 21/6, 45/16, 81/5, 142/26, 193/25, 194/26, 195/18; *in thes* ~ 172/29. *suche* (*a*) ~ (*that*) so that, in such a way that 20/35, 56/28, 125/21. *suche* ~ *as* as if 123/10. *in suche* ~ *onely as* only as 115/2. *thus* ~ thus 106/14.

with *prep.* by 17/7, 33/27, 35/31, 136/33, 137/34; in the sight of 114/25. *what* ~ in view of 182/33. ~ *more* moreover 64/8.

withdrawe *v.* restrain 31/3; take away 73/31; divert 23/18; *refl.* draw away 101/4. **withdrowe** *pa. t. sg.* 35/1; **withdrewe** 62/2. **withdrawe** *pp.* 23/18, 61/33.

withdrawte *n.* place of retreat 50/8.

withholde *pp.* reserved 50/10; kept 100/3.

withowt(e), withoute *prep.* except 91/26; in addition to 241/7; *conj.* unless 124/8, 140/32, 189/9. ~ *that* 210/14, 211/15.

witt(e) *n.* way of thinking, judgement 6/2, 81/8, 234/5; wisdom 215/16; reason, understanding, knowledge 15/8, 25/11, 51/34, 161/9, 198/8, 199/7; *pl.* intellects 5/22, 138/36, 139/34; skills 81/3, 142/24, 160/9 (Fr. 'engins'); talents 81/3 (Fr. 'dons'). **vittis** 88/13. *owtward wittes* five senses 120/4.

witte *v.* know 53/10. **wote** *pr. 1, 3 sg.* 64/22, 79/1, 198/20, 205/33. **wottist** *2 sg.* 13/7; **wotest** 74/20. **wote** *pl.* 187/11. **wist** *pa. t. pl.* 86/23.

wittely *adv.* wisely 154/14.

witty *adj.* ingenious 210/23; *see* excercise, polecye.

wondirful *adj.* ? full of evil, ? distressing 20/5 (*OED* meanings only under *wonder*).

woode *adj.* mad 211/2; rabid 194/28, 195/29.

wo(o)dman *n.* madman 172/7; *pl.* 210/2.

wo(o)dnesse *n.* fury 96/32; extravagant folly 112/28; fit of madness 173/10.

wo(o)rd(e) *n.* statement 205/8, 218/9, 219/8.

worde *n.* world 114/19.

working *vbl. n.* doing 22/23; *pl.* deeds 28/15, 144/27.

wor(l)dely(e) *adj.* human, mortal 116/12, 195/24; worldly 142/6, 177/13.

worldy *adj.* earthly 137/17; worldly 227/7 (*OED* rare; ? scribal error).

wo(u)rs(c)hip *n.* honour 3/14, 41/33, 148/8, 159/4; valour 157/18; *pl.* positions of honour 40/16, 149/9; acts of veneration 49/22. *gatte the ∼ ouir* gained the honour of overcoming 111/4.

wo(u)rthy (-i, -ie) *adj.* deserving by wrongdoing 204/8, 205/8; deserved 221/22; worth 209/20; appropriate to 140/22.

writen *ppl. adj.* mentioned 245/14.

wronge *adj.* perverse 147/7.

ʒa *see* ye.

yate *n.* gate 22/21; *pl.* 8/18, 138/2, 139/2. **ʒate** 110/14; *pl.* 110/8.

ye *adv.* truly, even 107/34; **ʒa** 131/18.

ye(e)lde *v.* render 45/31; cause (one) to be 201/11; pay 128/16; occasion, cause 202/23, 203/22 (*OED* 1576); give 73/2; *refl.* surrender 237/19; *refl.* become 27/21, 114/21; *pass.* forced to surrender 15/30, 229/21. *∼ ageyne* give back 130/4. *∼ vnto*

cause to be (with *n.* complement) 66/23. **yelde** *pp.* 27/21, 203/22; **yolden** 15/30, 229/21.

yefte *n.* gift 71/15; *pl.* 47/3, 220/15; **yefftis** 222/10; **yiftes** 155/11. **giftes** bribes, fees 233/15; **yeftys** 232/13.

yerde *n.* fig., instrument of punishment 142/31.

yere *n.* in *this .iiij. ∼ day* for four years 233/3.

yet(te) *adv.* moreover 64/2, 76/25, 82/34, 138/19, 190/2; **yit** 191/1.

yeve, yiue, gyf *v.* give 25/14, 33/3, 137/26, 141/34; *abs.* 15/13; prompt 74/19; allow 201/31; assign 43/22; address (to) 58/26, 177/7; cause to have 173/19; surrender, give up 57/24, 185/1; sacrifice 190/13, 191/13; dedicate, devote 150/13, 151/19; *refl.* 126/3; attribute 62/6 (*OED* 1559); offer to view, impart 241/25. *∼ vp* sacrifice 44/15. *∼ a fall* bring down, i.e. into subjection 54/11. *∼ a lawe* make legal 93/32. *∼ place* yield one's place 67/27. **yeve** *pr. pl.* 44/7, 145/2; **yiue** 199/26; **yiven** 199/25; **yevith** 198/30; **gyf** 173/19. **gaf(e)** *pa. t.* 77/11, 177/7; **gave** 5/13. **yeve** *pp.* 43/22, 144/2; **yevin** 21/19, 198/31; **yiven** 205/8; **youen** 203/7, 241/25; **yovin** 150/13; **geve** 5/13; **gyven** 204/8.

ʒolke *n.* core 123/4.

A LIST OF NAMES

193/12; **Batell of the Caves** 125/5; **Bataile of Caves** 158/28, 192/13–14.

Capadoce Cappadocia 89/22.

Capitale Capitol of Rome 162/31 (**Chapitolie** N); **Capitol(l)e** 163/28, 186/2 (**Chapitole** N), 187/2.

Cappue Capua 156/22; **Capoue** 157/24.

Carie Caria 89/23.

Cartage Carthage 138/16, 139/14, 192/17, 193/16.

Castille 107/26; **Castyll** 107/20.

Catilyina Catiline 176/21; **Catilina** 177/21.

Caton Cato 17/1, 76/18.

Caves see **Cannes.**

Cesar Julius Caesar 14/32, 17/2; **Iulius** ~ 58/18, 86/1.

Champayne, Erle of Henry I, Count of Champagne, leader of a faction against Philip II of France 110/31–2.

Charlemayn(e) Charlemagne 108/18, 108/31, 126/6; **Kyng(e) Charles the Gret(t)e** 242/10, 243/10.

Charles Charles of Anjou, King of Sicily 107/17.

Charles (-ys) the Fyfte Charles V of France 53/14, 111/16; **Kyng(e)** ~ 242/12, 243/12.

Charles Regnault Charles VII of France 111/16.

Chartir, Aleyn Alain Chartier 134/4; **Alain Charietere** 135/7.

Chelderych Childeric, King of the Franks 108/11.

Cycille Sicily 107/15.

Cyrus founder of the Persian Empire 106/10.

Cysara, Duke Sisera 103/7.

Cite of God, The by Saint Augustine 88/9.

Clottorye Clotaire II, son of Chilperic, King of the Franks 126/5.

Clouis son of Childeric, King of the Franks 65/30, 108/14, 126/5.

Cocta C. Cotta 228/15, 229/15.

Codrus 224/13, 225/11.

Constantyne 47/7.

Coradyn Conrad, son of Conrad IV 107/15.

Corroȝayne ? Khurasan 90/4.

Dagonbert Dagobert, son of Clotaire II, King of the Franks 126/6.

Danyel 132/24.

Danys Danes 109/11.

Darye King Darius 152/5, 153/4; **Dayre** 238/33, 239/32.

David 74/1; **Dauid** 34/7, 37/12, 40/26, 48/1, etc.

Decius Decius Mus 225/25, 226/1.

Delbora Deborah 102/33.

Delphos 14/29, 51/12; **Yle of** ~ 124/29.

Demostenes Demosthenes 10/34.

Denys, Seint Saint Dionysius 98/9.

Detharmich corruption of 'Talmud' 84/12 (see note).

Dido 17/26.

Dioclisian Diocletian 27/28.

Divine Institucions by Lactantius 88/10.

Domycian Domitian 27/28.

Ector see **Hector.**

Effyginee Iphigenia 124/20.

Egipcians Egyptians 27/8.

Egipte 58/23, 63/3.

Empyre Holy Roman Empire 108/19, 109/4.

Eneas Aeneas 13/35.

Engestus see **Angestus.**

English(e)men 107/22, 111/9, 111/13; **Englysshmen** 107/31.

Englond(e), Inglond(e), Kyng(e) of John Lackland 110/32; Henry V 140/7, 141/7; Richard II 162/5, 163/5.

Eolus Aeolus 124/23.

Eraclius, Emperoure Byzantian emperor 89/16.

Esdras 102/25, 102/30.

Ethiope Ethiopia 105/24.

Europe 89/25.

Ezechiell Ezekiel 49/20, 83/1.

Fabius Maximus 192/10, 193/10.

Fabricius 234/26, 235/24.

Fenyce Phoenicia 89/24.

Flore Florus 103/23.

Florence, poete of Dante 47/5–6.

Florentynes 55/32.

Forgestus corruption of 'Horsa' 160/32; **Fergestus** 161/33.

Foroneus *59/4.

Fra(u)nce 48/7, 63/4, 134/4, 140/8, 142/10, 143/9, etc.

French(e)men 44/15, 50/18, 59/23, 156/3, 158/9, etc.; Frensch(e)men 53/13, 170/11, 194/5; Frens(s)h(e)men 138/30, 139/28, 172/7, 184/7.

Frigye Phrygia 89/23.

Gabaon Gibeon 125/25.

Gabriell the angel 95/6, 95/12.

Galba 17/21.

Gallo-Grecye Galatia 162/30; Gallo-Grecide 163/27.

Gaules 51/10.

Gedeon Gideon 103/7.

Genouyeue, Seint Saint Genevieve 109/23.

Germayn(e)s Germans 138/30, 139/28.

Gomer Gomorrah 84/6.

Gothis 109/11.

Grece Greece 16/25, 58/18, 162/29; Greke 163/27. Chirche of ~ Greek Orthodox Church 131/15–16.

Gre(e)kes 14/1, 14/30, 138/28, 139/26, 152/4, 153/3.

Grette Brytaigne, Kyng of Vortigern, legendary fifth century king 160/33; Kynge of Grete Brytayne 161/34.

Gudy Fr. 'Engady' 110/3.

Haniball 17/9, 104/20, 106/16, 156/21, 157/23, 192/14, 192/30, 193/13, 216/18, 217/13, 242/7, 243/8.

Hector 242/6; Ector 238/31, 239/30, 243/7.

Heliodorus 50/29.

Hely Eli 132/21.

Hercules 105/25.

Huns 109/11, 109/27.

Ilion 139/2; Yllion 138/2.

Isaie Isaiah 64/27; Ysaye 36/25, 48/34, 83/9; Ysaie 62/29, 140/19, 141/20, 211/19; Isai 210/17.

Israel(l) 27/6, 34/8, 36/27, 178/15, 179/17, 214/32, 215/26, etc.; Ysraell 103/2.

Italye 195/1; Ytaly 194/1.

Iabyn Jabin 103/3.

Iacob 24/12.

Iason 103/30.

Ieconyas Jeconiah 83/15.

Ieremye Jeremiah 60/32, 83/9.

Ierome, Seint Saint Jerome 43/17.

Ierusalem 61/1, 83/17, 216/1, 217/1.

Iewes (-ys) 61/31, 81/29, 83/10, etc.; gen. 92/5.

Ihesu Criste 92/2, 98/25, 125/30, etc.

Ioachym, Abbot Joachim of Flora 63/3.

Iohn, Kyng(e) John II of France 158/30, 159/23.

Iosephus 83/31.

Iosue Joshua 125/23.

Iuda Judah 82/19, 83/9, 216/14, 217/10; Iude 102/3.

Iugurthe Jugurtha *17/16.

Iule Ceste corruption of 'Celsus' 103/23 (see note).

Iupater the god Jupiter 86/28.

Iustyn Justin 103/23.

Iustynean Justinian 59/5.

Lacedemoyn(e) Laconia 103/33, 138/10; Lacedomone *139/8.

Lactaunce Lactantius 88/10.

Laemedon Laomedon 103/31.

Langdok Languedoc 158/29; Languedoke 159/22.

Latyn Chirche Roman Catholic Church 131/11.

Levy Levi 128/25.

Lybye Libya 89/23.

Lycie Lycia 89/23.

Lyeu, Seint Saint Lupus, Bishop of Troyes 109/26.

Ligurgus Lycurgus 59/4, 138/11, 139/10.

Loreyne Lorraine 108/11.

Lowes Louis, son of Charlemagne 108/17.

Lowys Louis, son of Philip II of France 110/28.

Lucan(e) 8/21, 103/23, 138/21, 139/19.

Lucius Quintus L. Quinctius Cincinnatus 234/26, 235/25.

Lucius Tucius C. Titius 228/18, 229/18.

Lucresse Lucrece 17/25, 76/21.

Macabeus Judas Maccabaeus 238/32.

Macedonye Macedonia 105/30.

Machabites the Maccabees 101/31; **Machabees** 214/30; **Macabees** 215/25, 239/31.

Madien, Kyng of King of Midian 103/8.

Mageste Almagest 58/22.

Mahomet(e) Mohammed 89/13, 93/26, etc.

Maynfray Manfred, King of Sicily 107/15.

Malachias Malachi 45/27.

Manasse Manasseh 103/13.

Manlius Torquatus 227/29; **Mavlius T.** 226/30.

Marche, Erle of the Hugh, Duke of La Marche 110/33.

Marcius Currius M. Curtius 224/24; **Marcus Tulius** 225/17; **Marcus Tucius** 76/19 (see note).

Marcus Staurus Marcus Aemilius Scaurus 238/6, 239/6.

Marryus Marius 104/32; **Marrious** 176/22; **Marius** 177/21.

Martyne, Seint Saint Martin, Bishop of Tours 109/25.

Mathathias Mattathias 101/30, 214/30, 215/24.

Maximian 27/28.

Medtryraine Mediterranean Sea 106/4.

Me(e)des 36/29, 51/1.

Meke Mecca 93/12.

Mesopotayne Mesopotamia 89/24.

Messias the Messiah 82/20.

Mynerue Minerva *86/31.

Mitridate Mithridates 17/2, 104/2; **Mydrydates** 58/25; **Mytrydace** 105/28.

Moyses Moses 23/29, 51/20, 62/30, 92/2, 98/2, 125/20, 178/16, 179/18.

Munycious M. Minucius Rufus 192/27; **Municius** 192/29; **Municus** 193/27.

Nabugodonosor Nebuchadnezzar 35/20.

Neemyas Nehemiah 83/19, 102/25.

Neptunis *dat.* the god Neptune 124/22.

Nero 10/30, 17/19, 27/28, 28/6.

Nestor 16/24.

Nestoryne heresie(s) heresy inspired by Nestorius 95/19, 95/21.

Nestoryus *89/19.

Nynive Nineveh 136/30; **Niniue** 137/32.

Nynus Ninus 86/10.

Noe Noah 27/2, 125/19.

Nusye corruption of 'Mysia' 89/23.

Occean Sea Atlantic Ocean, as distinct from the Mediterranean Sea 105/26.

Octauien Octavius, later Augustus 241/1.

Offny Hophni 132/21.

Ogier 242/10; **Oger** 243/11.

Olyuere Oliver 242/11, 243/11.

Omir Homer 103/22.

Orliaunce Orleans 109/19.

Orose Orosius 103/22.

Ostomyen ? Osman; ? scribal error for 'Octauien' 238/34.

Othe, Emperour Otto IV, German emperor 110/31.

Palestyne 89/24.

Panonye Pannonia 89/27.

Paphagonye Paphlagonia 89/23.

Parseantes Persians 51/1; **Perciens** 138/28, 139/26; **Perces** 36/29.

Paryes Paris 109/23.

Paule, Seint(e) 40/33; **S. Pawle** 22/8; *see* Apostle.

Pentatheuke Pentateuch 23/29.

Perce Persia 152/5; **Perse** 153/5.

Petir, Seint 24/28, 28/7.

Petre Pedro the Cruel, King of Castille 107/20.

Pharnates Pharnaces, son of Mithridates 17/7.

Philip Philip II of France 110/27; **Philippe Dyeudone** 110/20.

Philip(e) Philip of Macedon 103/35, 105/30.

Philistiens Philistines 226/3, 227/2.

Phynees Phinehas 132/21.

Plato 58/8, 98/7.

Policitatus corruption of 'Polycrates', tyrant of Samos 86/5 (see note).

Polixene Polyxena, daughter of Priam 124/26.

Pompey 50/25.

Pont 17/2, 58/25, 89/23, 104/2.

Pryam, Kyng 124/28; **Priamus** 103/32, 242/5, 243/6.

Pyraynes Pyrenees Mountains 108/16.

Pyrrus Pyrrhus, son of Achilles 124/25.

Rama3an, Moneþe of Month of Ramadan 92/33.

Reede See Red Sea 27/7.

Ryne Rhine River 108/16.

Robert, Kyng Robert II the Pious of France 126/7.

Roboam, (Kyng) Rehoboam 34/14, 170/34, 171/29.

Robusces mistranslation 90/8 (see note).

Rolland Roland 243/10; **Rowland** 242/10.

Romayn(e) n. Roman 192/10, 193/10; pl. 17/10, 37/29, 138/17, 139/16, etc.; **Romayn(e)s** gen. 176/17, 177/16, etc.; **Romayn(e)** adj. 184/16, 222/19, 223/19, etc.; **Romaynes** adj. pl. 227/30.

Ro(o)me 10/32, 17/18, 28/3, 138/20, 139/18, 158/27, 159/20, etc.

Saba, Quene of corruption of 'Queen Basina' 65/29.

Saignys 95/18 (see note).

Salomon Solomon 34/8, 43/31, 50/26, 58/10, 125/29; **Salmon** 74/27; **Salamon** 238/31, 239/30.

Sampson 226/2, 227/2, 238/32, 239/31.

Samuel 38/2.

Sara3in(e)s Saracens 92/8, 93/14, 98/33, 99/7; **Sarsines** 109/11.

Sardanapallus 156/28; **Sardana Pallus** 157/28.

Saul 34/3.

Saxons 160/32, 161/33.

Scipio(n) Affrican Scipio Africanus Major 125/4, 156/18, 216/16, 238/4; **Scipion the Affrican** 157/20; **Scipion the Aufrican** 239/3; **Scipion** 217/11.

Scytis Scythians 152/4; **Scithiens** 153/4.

Scotlonde 108/5.

Scottis Scotsmen 107/28, 107/30.

Semyramys 105/23, 158/20, 159/17.

Seneck(e) Seneca 10/29, 106/27.

Serye Syria 89/24.

Silla Sulla 176/21, 177/21.

Symeon Simeon 73/19.

Sipiouns followers of Scipio 238/3; **Scipions** 239/2.

Socrates 98/7.

Sodom 84/6.

Solacye error for 'Galatia', perhaps in confusion with 'Salacia' 89/22.

Spaygne Spain 89/26.

Spaynardis Spaniards 107/23.

Stace Statius 103/23.

Syphace, the wif of Kyng Sophonisba, wife of King Syphax 17/27.

Tarace Thrace 89/26.

Tessalye Thessaly 86/4.

Thamarys, Quene Queen Tomyris of the Massagetae 106/11.

Thebes 103/33, 138/6, 139/5.

Theorich, Kyng King Theodoric 11/3.

Theseus 103/30.

Tholome Ptolemy 11/18, 58/23.

Tyte Liue Livy 103/22; **Titus Livius** *234/23; **Titu Liuius** 235/21.

Titus 83/29.

Toures Tours 109/24.

Troiannes Trojans 104/13; **Troyans** 152/2; **Troiens** 153/2.

Troy(e) 14/1, 14/30, 103/30, 124/21, 138/1, 139/1, 152/3.

Troye Pompe Trogus, Pompeius 103/22.

Tullius Cicero 10/31.

Turkye Turkey 90/6.

Vlixes Ulysses 238/33, 239/31.

Valere Valerius Maximus 51/14, 103/23, 132/31, 140/3, 141/3, 226/18, 227/18; **Valerye** 124/5.

Vandres corruption of 'Vandals' 109/11; **Wandres(se)** 109/20, 109/21.

Varo Gaius Terentius Varro 192/13, 193/12.

Vegece Vegetius 186/1, 187/1.

Venycians Venetians 55/28.

Venus the goddess 93/13, 94/26.

Vincent Vincent of Beauvais 103/24.

Virgile 14/2, 103/22.

Virginyus Virginius Rufus 17/21.

Wandres(se) *see* **Vandres**.

Xerses Xerxes 239/32; **Ӡerces** 103/35, 105/35; **Yerces** 238/34.

Ӡedechias, Kyng Zedekiah, King of Judah 37/14.

Ӡendebus corruption of 'Mundiuch' or 'Mundzucus', father of Attila 110/3.

EARLY ENGLISH TEXT
SOCIETY

LIST OF PUBLICATIONS
1864–1979

SEPTEMBER 1979

Orders from non-members of the Society should be placed with a bookseller. Orders from booksellers for volumes in part 1 of this list should be sent to Oxford University Press, Press Road, Neasden, London NW10 0DD. Orders from book-sellers for volumes in part 2 of this list should be sent to the following addresses: orders for E.E.T.S. reprints to Oxford University Press, Press Road, Neasden, London NW10 0DD; orders for Kraus reprints from North America to Kraus Reprint Co., Route 100, Millwood, N.Y. 10546, U.S.A., from other countries to Kraus Reprint Co., FL 9491 Nendeln, Liechtenstein.

EARLY ENGLISH TEXT SOCIETY

The Early English Text Society was founded in 1864 by Frederick James Furnivall, with the help of Richard Morris, Walter Skeat and others, to bring the mass of unprinted Early English literature within the reach of students and to provide sound texts from which the New English Dictionary could quote. In 1867 an Extra Series was started of texts already printed but not in satisfactory or readily obtainable editions. In 1921 the Extra Series was discontinued and all publications were subsequently listed and numbered as part of the Original Series. In 1970 the first of a new Supplementary Series was published; unlike the Extra Series, volumes in this series will be issued only occasionally, as funds allow and as suitable texts become available.

In the first part of this list are shown the books published by the Society since 1938, Original Series 210 onwards and the Supplementary Series. A large number of the earlier books were reprinted by the Society in the period 1950 to 1970. In order to make the rest available, the Society has come to an agreement with the Kraus Reprint Co. who reprint as necessary the volumes in the Original Series 1–209 and in the Extra Series. In this way all the volumes published by the Society are once again in print.

Membership of the Society is open to libraries and to individuals interested in the study of medieval English literature. The subscription to the Society for 1979 is £7·50 (or for U.S. members $18.00, Canadian members Can. $22.00), due in advance on 1 January, and should be paid by cheque, postal order or money order made out to 'The Early English Text Society', and sent to Dr. Anne Hudson, Executive Secretary, Early English Text Society, Lady Margaret Hall, Oxford. Payment of this subscription entitles the member to receive the new book(s) in the Original Series for the year. The books in the Supplementary Series do not form part of the issue sent to members in return for the payment of their annual subscription, though they are available to members at a reduced price; a notice about each volume is sent to members in advance of publication.

Private members of the Society (but not libraries) may select in place of the annual issue past volumes from the Society's list chosen from the Original Series 210 to date or from the Supplementary Series. The value of such texts allowed against one annual subscription is £9·50, and all these transactions must be made through the Executive Secretary. Members of the Society may purchase copies of books O.S. 210 to date for their own use at a discount of 25% of the listed prices; private members (but not libraries) may purchase earlier publications at a similar discount. All such orders must be sent to the Executive Secretary.

Details of books, the cost of membership and its privileges, are revised from time to time. The prices of books are subject to alteration without notice. This list is brought up to date annually, and the current edition should be consulted.

September 1979

ORIGINAL SERIES 1938-1979

O.S. 210 **Sir Gawain and the Green Knight**, re-ed. I. Gollancz, with £2·40
introductory essays by Mabel Day and M. S. Serjeantson.
1940 *(for* 1938*), reprinted* 1966.

211 **The Dicts and Sayings of the Philosophers**: translations made £7·00
by Stephen Scrope, William Worcester and anonymous
translator, ed. C. F. Bühler. 1941 *(for* 1939*), reprinted* 1961.

212 **The Book of Margery Kempe**, Vol. I, Text *(all published)*, ed. £6·50
S. B. Meech, with notes and appendices by S. B. Meech and
H. E. Allen. 1940 *(for* 1939*), reprinted* 1961.

213 **Ælfric's De Temporibus Anni**, ed. H. Henel. 1942 *(for* 1940*),* £3·80
reprinted 1970.

214 **Forty-Six Lives translated from Boccaccio's De Claris** £4·80
Mulieribus by Henry Parker, Lord Morley, ed. H. G. Wright.
1943 *(for* 1940*), reprinted* 1970.

215, 220 **Charles of Orleans: The English Poems**, Vol. I, ed. R. £5·75
Steele (1941), Vol. II, ed. R. Steele and Mabel Day (1946 *for*
1944); *reprinted as one volume with bibliographical supplement*
1970.

216 **The Latin Text of the Ancrene Riwle**, from Merton College £4·00
MS. 44 and British Museum MS. Cotton Vitellius E. vii, ed.
C. D'Evelyn. 1944 *(for* 1941*), reprinted* 1957.

217 **The Book of Vices and Virtues**: A Fourteenth-Century English £7·00
Translation of the *Somme le Roi* of Lorens d'Orléans, ed.
W. Nelson Francis. 1942, *reprinted* 1968.

218 **The Cloud of Unknowing and The Book of Privy Counselling**; £4·50
ed. Phyllis Hodgson. 1944 *(for* 1943*), corrected reprint* 1973.

219 **The French Text of the Ancrene Riwle**, British Museum MS. £4·80
Cotton Vitellius F. vii, ed. J. A. Herbert. 1944 *(for* 1943*),*
reprinted 1967.

220 **Charles of Orleans: The English Poems**, Vol. II; *see above*
O.S. 215.

221 **The Romance of Sir Degrevant**, ed. L. F. Casson. 1949 *(for* £4·50
1944*), reprinted* 1970.

222 **The Lyfe of Syr Thomas More, by Ro. Ba.**, ed. E. V. Hitch- £5·75
cock and P. E. Hallett, with notes and appendices by A. W.
Reed. 1950 *(for* 1945*), reprinted* 1974.

223 **The Tretyse of Loue**, ed. J. H. Fisher. 1951 *(for* 1945*),* £3·80
reprinted 1970.

224 **Athelston: a Middle English Romance**, ed. A. McI. Trounce. £3·80
1951 *(for* 1946*), reprinted* 1957.

225 **The English Text of the Ancrene Riwle**, British Museum MS. £4·50
Cotton Nero A. xiv, ed. Mabel Day. 1952 *(for* 1946*), re-*
printed 1957.

226 **Respublica**: an interlude for Christmas 1553 attributed to £2·75
Nicholas Udall, re-ed. W. W. Greg. 1952 *(for* 1946*),*
reprinted 1969.

O.S. 227 **Kyng Alisaunder,** Vol. I, Text, ed. G. V. Smithers. 1952 (*for* £7·00
1947), *reprinted* 1961.

228 **The Metrical Life of St. Robert of Knaresborough,** together £3·80
with the other Middle English pieces in British Museum MS.
Egerton 3143, ed. Joyce Bazire. 1953 (*for* 1947), *reprinted*
1968.

229 **The English Text of the Ancrene Riwle,** Gonville and Caius £3·25
College MS. 234/120, ed. R. M. Wilson with an introduction
by N. R. Ker. 1954 (*for* 1948), *reprinted* 1957.

230 **The Life of St. George by Alexander Barclay,** ed. W. Nelson. £3·60
1955 (*for* 1948), *reprinted* 1960.

231 **Deonise Hid Diuinite** and other treatises related to *The Cloud* £4·50
of Unknowing, ed. Phyllis Hodgson. 1955 (*for* 1949), *reprinted*
with corrections 1958.

232 **The English Text of the Ancrene Riwle,** British Museum MS. £2·75
Royal 8 C. i, ed. A. C. Baugh. 1956 (*for* 1949), *reprinted*
1959.

233 **The Bibliotheca Historica of Diodorus Siculus** translated by £7·20
John Skelton, Vol. I, Text, ed. F. M. Salter and H. L. R.
Edwards. 1956 (*for* 1950), *reprinted* 1968.

234 **Paris and Vienne** translated from the French and printed by £3·80
William Caxton, ed. MacEdward Leach. 1957 (*for* 1951),
reprinted 1970.

235 **The South English Legendary,** Corpus Christi College £5·75
Cambridge MS. 145 and British Museum MS. Harley 2277,
with variants from Bodley MS. Ashmole 43 and British
Museum MS. Cotton Julius D. ix, ed. C. D'Evelyn and A. J.
Mill. Vol. I, Text, 1959 (*for* 1957), *reprinted* 1967.

236 **The South English Legendary,** Vol. II, Text, ed. C. D'Evelyn £5·75
and A. J. Mill. 1956 (*for* 1952), *reprinted* 1967.

237 **Kyng Alisaunder,** Vol. II, Introduction, commentary and £4·50
glossary, ed. G. V. Smithers. 1957 (*for* 1953), *reprinted with*
corrections 1969.

238 **The Phonetic Writings of Robert Robinson,** ed. E. J. Dobson. £2·75
1957 (*for* 1953), *reprinted* 1968.

239 **The Bibliotheca Historica of Diodorus Siculus** translated by £2·75
John Skelton, Vol. II, Introduction, notes and glossary, ed.
F. M. Salter and H. L. R. Edwards. 1957 (*for* 1954), *re-*
printed 1971.

240 **The French Text of the Ancrene Riwle,** Trinity College Cam- £4·80
bridge MS. R. 14. 7, with variants from Paris Bibliothèque
Nationale MS. fonds fr. 6276 and Bodley MS. 90, ed. W. H.
Trethewey. 1958 (*for* 1954), *reprinted* 1971.

241 **Þe Wohunge of Ure Lauerd** and other pieces, ed. W. Meredith £4·00
Thompson. 1958 (*for* 1955), *reprinted with corrections* 1970.

242 **The Salisbury Psalter,** ed. Celia Sisam and Kenneth Sisam. £7·75
1959 (*for* 1955–6), *reprinted* 1969.

243 **The Life and Death of Cardinal Wolsey by George Cavendish,** £4·00
ed. R. S. Sylvester. 1959 (*for* 1957), *reprinted* 1961.

244 **The South English Legendary,** Vol. III, Introduction and £2·75
glossary, ed. C. D'Evelyn. 1959 (*for* 1957), *reprinted* 1969.

ORIGINAL SERIES 1864–1938

O.S. 1 Early English Alliterative Poems . . . from MS. Cotton Nero A. x, £4·40
ed. R. Morris. 1864, *revised* 1869, *reprinted* 1965.

2 Arthur, ed. F. J. Furnivall. 1864, *reprinted* 1965. *Paper.* £1·00

3 William Lauder Ane conpendious and breue tractate concernyng ye £1·80
Office and Dewtie of Kyngis, ed. F. Hall. 1864, *reprinted* 1965.
Also available reprinted as one volume with O.S. 41 $9.00
William Lauder The Minor Poems, ed. F. J. Furnivall. 1870, *reprinted*
Kraus 1973.

4 Sir Gawayne and the Green Knight, ed. R. Morris. 1864. Superseded
by O.S. 210.

5 Alexander Hume of the Orthographie and Congruitie of the Britan £1·80
Tongue, ed. H. B. Wheatley. 1865, *reprinted* 1965. *Paper.*

6 The Romans of Lancelot of the Laik, re-ed. W. W. Skeat. 1865, *re-* £3·80
printed 1965. *Paper.*

7 The Story of Genesis and Exodus, ed. R. Morris. 1865, *reprinted* $14.00
Kraus 1973.

8 Morte Arthure [alliterative version from Thornton MS.], ed. E. Brock. £2·50
1865, *reprinted* 1967.

9 Francis Thynne Animadversions uppon Chaucer's Workes . . . 1598, £4·80
ed. G. H. Kingsley. 1865, *revised* F. J. Furnivall 1875, *reprinted* 1965.

10, 112 Merlin, ed. H. B. Wheatley, Vol. I 1865, Vol. IV with essays $33.00
by J. S. S. Glennie and W. E. Mead 1899; *reprinted as one volume*
Kraus 1973. (See O.S. 21, 36 for other parts.)

11, 19, 35, 37 The Works of Sir David Lyndesay, Vol. I 1865; Vol. II $28.00
1866 The Monarch and other Poems, ed. J. Small; Vol. III 1868 The
Historie of . . . Squyer William Meldrum etc., ed. F. Hall; Vol. IV
Ane Satyre of the Thrie Estaits and Minor Poems, ed. F. Hall.
Reprinted as one volume Kraus 1973. (See O.S. 47 for last part.)

12 Adam of Cobsam The Wright's Chaste Wife, ed. F. J. Furnivall. 1865, £1·00
reprinted 1965. (See also O.S. 84.)

13 Seinte Marherete, ed. O. Cockayne. 1866. Superseded by O.S. 193.

14 King Horn, Floriz and Blauncheflur, The Assumption of our Lady, £4·50
ed. J. R. Lumby. 1866, *revised* G. H. McKnight 1901, *reprinted* 1962.

15 Political, Religious and Love Poems, from Lambeth MS. 306 and £5·75
other sources, ed. F. J. Furnivall. 1866, *reprinted* 1962.

16 The Book of Quinte Essence . . . Sloane MS. 73 *c.* 1460–70, ed. F. J. £1·00
Furnivall. 1866, *reprinted* 1965. *Paper.*

17 William Langland Parallel Extracts from 45 MSS. of Piers Plowman, $8.00
ed. W. W. Skeat. 1866, *reprinted* Kraus 1973.

18 Hali Meidenhad, ed. O. Cockayne. 1866, *revised* F. J. Furnivall 1922 $6.00
(*for* 1920), *reprinted* Kraus 1973.

19 Sir David Lyndesay The Monarch and other Poems, Vol. II. See
above, O.S. 11.

20 Richard Rolle de Hampole English Prose Treatises, ed. G. G. Perry. $4.00
1866, *reprinted* Kraus 1973. *Paper.*

21, 36 Merlin, ed. H. B. Wheatley. Vol. II 1866, Vol. III 1869; *reprinted* $31.00
as one volume Kraus 1973.

22 The Romans of Partenay or of Lusignen, ed. W. W. Skeat. 1866, $16.00
reprinted Kraus 1973.

O.S. 23   Dan Michel Ayenbite of Inwyt, ed. R. Morris. 1866, *revised* P. Gradon,   £4·80
      reprinted 1965.

24   Hymns to the Virgin and Christ . . . and other religious poems, ed. F. J. $8.00
     Furnivall. 1867, *reprinted* Kraus 1973.

25   The Stacions of Rome, The Pilgrims Sea-Voyage etc., ed. F. J. Furni- $4.00
     vall. 1867, *reprinted* Kraus 1973. *Paper.*

26   Religious Pieces in Prose and Verse from R. Thornton's MS., ed. G. G $21.00
     Perry. 1867, *reprinted* Kraus 1973.

27   Peter Levins Manipulus Vocabulorum, ed. H. B. Wheatley. 1867, $20.00
     reprinted Kraus 1973.

28   William Langland The Vision of Piers Plowman, ed. W. W. Skeat.   £3·50
     Vol. I Text A 1867, *reprinted* 1968. (See O.S. 38, 54, 67, and 81 for
     other parts.)

29, 34   Old English Homilies of the 12th and 13th Centuries, ed. R. Morris. $18.00
     Vol. I. i 1867, Vol. I. ii 1868; *reprinted as one volume* Kraus 1973. (See
     O.S. 53 for Vol. II.)

30   Pierce the Ploughmans Crede etc., ed. W. W. Skeat. 1867, *reprinted* $5.00
     Kraus 1973. *Paper.*

31   John Myrc Instructions for Parish Priests, ed. E. Peacock. 1868, *re-* $7.00
     printed Kraus 1973.

32   Early English Meals and Manners: The Babees Book etc., ed. F. J. $26.00
     Furnivall. 1868, *reprinted* Kraus 1973.

33   The Book of the Knight of La Tour-Landry (from MS. Harley 1764), $14.00
     ed. T. Wright. 1868, *reprinted* Kraus 1973.

34   Old English Homilies of the 12th and 13th Centuries, Vol. I. ii. See
     above, O.S. 29.

35   Sir David Lyndesay The Historie of . . . Squyer William Meldrum etc.,   £1·80
     ed. F. Hall. 1868, *reprinted* 1965. *Also available reprinted as one*
     volume with O.S. 11, 19, and 37. See above, O.S. 11.

36   Merlin, Vol. III 1869. See above, O.S. 21.

37   Sir David Lyndesay Ane Satyre . . . Vol. IV. See above, O.S. 11.

38   William Langland The Vision of Piers Plowman, ed. W. W. Skeat.   £3·80
     Vol. II Text B 1869, *reprinted* 1972. (See O.S. 28, 54, 67, and 81 for
     other parts.)

39, 56   The Gest Hystoriale of the Destruction of Troy, ed. G. A. Panton   £9·50
     and D. Donaldson. Vol. I 1869, Vol. II 1874; *reprinted as one volume*
     1968.

40   English Gilds etc., ed. Toulmin Smith, L. Toulmin Smith and L.   £9·00
     Brentano. 1870, *reprinted* 1963.

41   William Lauder The Minor Poems. See above, O.S. 3.

42   Bernardus De Cura Rei Famuliaris, with some early Scottish   £1·80
     Prophecies etc., ed. J. R. Lumby. 1870, *reprinted* 1965. *Paper.*

43   Ratis Raving, and other Moral and Religious Pieces in prose and verse, $8.00
     ed. J. R. Lumby. 1870, *reprinted* Kraus 1973.

44   Joseph of Arimathie: the Romance of the Seint Graal, an alliterative $8.00
     poem, ed. W. W. Skeat. 1871, *reprinted* Kraus 1973.

45   King Alfred's West-Saxon Version of Gregory's Pastoral Care, ed. H. $17.00
     Sweet. Vol. I 1871, reprinted with corrections and an additional note
     by N. R. Ker 1958, *reprinted* Kraus 1973. (See O.S. 50 for Vol. II.)

46   Legends of the Holy Rood, Symbols of the Passion and Cross-Poems, $14.00
     ed. R. Morris. 1871, *reprinted* Kraus 1973.

47   Sir David Lyndesay The Minor Poems, ed. J. A. H. Murray. 1871, $12.00
     reprinted Kraus 1973. (See O.S. 11, 19, 35, 37 for other parts.)

48   The Times' Whistle, and other poems; by R. C., ed. J. M. Cowper. $12.00
     1871, *reprinted* Kraus 1973.

O.S. 49   **An Old English Miscellany**: a Bestiary, Kentish Sermons, Proverbs of $17.00
Alfred and Religious Poems of the 13th Century, ed. R. Morris. 1872,
reprinted Kraus 1973.

50   **King Alfred's West-Saxon Version of Gregory's Pastoral Care**, ed. H. $13.00
Sweet. Vol. II 1871, reprinted with corrections by N. R. Ker 1958,
reprinted Kraus 1973. (See O.S. 45 for Vol. I.)

51   **þe Liflade of St. Juliana**, ed. O. Cockayne and E. Brock. 1872, *re-*   £3·25
printed 1957. (See O.S. 248 for more recent edition.)

52   **Palladius On Husbandrie**, ed. B. Lodge. Vol. I 1872, *reprinted* Kraus $12.00
1973. (See O.S. 72 for Vol. II.)

53   **Old English Homilies of the 12th Century** etc., ed. R. Morris. Vol. II $16.00
1873, *reprinted* Kraus 1973. (See O.S. 29, 34 for Vol. 1.)

54   **William Langland The Vision of Piers Plowman**, ed. W. W. Skeat.   £4·80
Vol. III Text C 1873, *reprinted* 1978. (See O.S. 28, 38, 67, and 81 for
other parts.)

55, 70   **Generydes**, a romance, ed. W. A. Wright. Vol. I 1873, Vol. II $14.00
1878; *reprinted as one volume* Kraus 1973.

56   **The Gest Hystoriale of the Destruction of Troy.** Vol. II. See above,
O.S. 39.

57   **Cursor Mundi**, ed. R. Morris. Vol. I Text ll. 1–4954, 1874, *reprinted*   £3·60
1961. (See O.S. 59, 62, 66, 68, 99, and 101 for other parts.) *Paper.*

58, 63, 73   **The Blickling Homilies**, ed. R. Morris. Vol. I 1874, Vol. II   £6·50
1876, Vol. III 1880; *reprinted as one volume* 1967.

59   **Cursor Mundi**, ed. R. Morris. Vol. II ll. 4955–12558, 1875, *reprinted*   £4·50
1966. (See O.S. 57, 62, 66, 68, 99, and 101 for other parts.) *Paper.*

60   **Meditations on the Supper of our Lord,** and the Hours of the Passion, $4.00
translated by Robert Manning of Brunne, ed. J. M. Cowper. 1875,
reprinted Kraus 1973. *Paper.*

61   **The Romance and Prophecies of Thomas of Erceldoune**, ed. J. A. H. $7.00
Murray. 1875, *reprinted* Kraus 1973.

62   **Cursor Mundi**, ed. R. Morris. Vol. III ll. 12559–19300, 1876, *reprinted*   £3·60
1966. (See O.S. 57, 59, 66, 68, 99, and 101 for other parts.) *Paper.*

63   **The Blickling Homilies**, Vol. II. See above, O.S. 58.

64   **Francis Thynne's Emblemes and Epigrames**, ed. F. J. Furnivall. 1876, $7.00
reprinted Kraus 1973.

65   **Be Domes Dæge, De Die Judicii**: an Old English version of the Latin   £2·75
poem ascribed to Bede, ed. J. R. Lumby. 1876, *reprinted* 1964.

66   **Cursor Mundi**, ed. R. Morris. Vol. IV ll. 19301–23836, 1877, *reprinted*   £3·60
1966. (See O.S. 57, 59, 62, 68, 99, and 101 for other parts.) *Paper.*

67   **William Langland The Vision of Piers Plowman**, ed. W. W. Skeat. $26.00
Vol. IV. 1 Notes, 1877, *reprinted* Kraus 1973. (See O.S. 28, 38, 54,
and 81 for other parts.)

68   **Cursor Mundi**, ed. R. Morris. Vol. V ll. 23827–end, 1878, *reprinted*   £3·60
1966. (See O.S. 57, 59, 62, 66, 99, and 101 for other parts.) *Paper.*

69   **Adam Davy's 5 Dreams about Edward II** etc. from Bodleian MS. Laud $7.00
Misc. 622, ed. F. J. Furnivall. 1878, *reprinted* Kraus 1973.

70   **Generydes**, a romance, Vol. II. See above, O.S. 55.

71   **The Lay Folks Mass Book**, ed. T. F. Simmons. 1879, *reprinted* 1968.   £8·00

72   **Palladius On Husbandrie**, ed. B. Lodge and S. J. Herrtage. Vol. II   £3·80
1879. (See O.S. 52 for Vol. I.) *Paper.*
Also available reprinted as one volume with O.S. 52.

73   **The Blickling Homilies**, Vol. III. See above, O.S. 58.

74   **The English Works of Wyclif** hitherto unprinted, ed. F. D. Matthew. $32.00
1880, *reprinted* Kraus 1973.

75   **Catholicon Anglicum**, an English–Latin Wordbook 1483, ed. S. J. H. $25.00
Herrtage and H. B. Wheatley. 1881, *reprinted* Kraus 1973.

O.S. 76, 82 Ælfric's Lives of Saints, ed. W. W. Skeat. Vol. I. i 1881, Vol. I. ii   £5·60
1885; *reprinted as one volume* 1966. (See O.S. 94 and 114 for other
parts.)

77 Beowulf, autotypes of Cotton MS. Vitellius A. xv. 1882. Superseded
by O.S. 245.

78 The Fifty Earliest English Wills . . . 1387–1439, ed. F. J. Furnivall.   £4·50
1882, *reprinted* 1964.

79 King Alfred's Orosius, ed. H. Sweet. Vol. I Old English Text and Latin $15.00
Original (*all published*) 1883, *reprinted* Kraus 1974.

80 The Life of Saint Katherine, from Royal MS. 17 A. xxvii etc., ed. $14.00
E. Einenkel. 1884, *reprinted* Kraus 1973.

81 William Langland The Vision of Piers Plowman, ed. W. W. Skeat. $29.00
Vol. IV. 2 General Preface and indexes. 1884, *reprinted* Kraus 1973.
(See O.S. 28, 38, 54, and 67 for other parts.)

82 Ælfric's Lives of Saints, Vol. I. ii. See above, O.S. 76.

83 The Oldest English Texts, ed. H. Sweet. 1885, *reprinted* 1966.   £9·50

84 [Adam of Cobsam] Additional Analogs to The Wright's Chaste Wife,
ed. W. A. Clouston. 1886, *reprinted* Kraus 1973. (See also O.S. 12.)

85 The Three Kings of Cologne, ed. C. Horstmann. 1886, *reprinted* Kraus $17.00
1973.

86 The Lives of Women Saints etc., ed. C. Horstmann. 1886, *reprinted* $14.00
Kraus 1973.

87 The Early South-English Legendary, from Bodleian MS. Laud Misc. $29.00
108, ed. C. Horstmann. 1887, *reprinted* Kraus 1973.

88 Henry Bradshaw The Life of Saint Werburge of Chester, ed. C. Horst- $14.00
mann. 1887, *reprinted* Kraus 1973.

89 Vices and Virtues [from British Museum MS. Stowe 240], ed. F.   £3·60
Holthausen. Vol. I Text and translation. 1888, *reprinted* 1967. (See
O.S. 159 for Vol. II.) *Paper.*

90 The Rule of S. Benet, Latin and Anglo-Saxon interlinear version, ed. $10.00
H. Logeman. 1888, *reprinted* Kraus 1973.

91 Two Fifteenth-Century Cookery-Books, ed. T. Austin. 1888, *reprinted*   £3·80
1964.

92 Eadwine's Canterbury Psalter, ed. F. Harsley. Vol. II Text and notes $15.00
(*all published*) 1889, *reprinted* Kraus 1973.

93 Defensor's Liber Scintillarum, ed. E. W. Rhodes. 1889, *reprinted* $14.00
Kraus 1973.

94, 114 Ælfric's Lives of Saints, ed. W. W. Skeat. Vol. II. i 1890, Vol. II.   £5·50
ii 1900; *reprinted as one volume* 1966. (See O.S. 76, 82 for other parts.)

95 The Old English Version of Bede's Ecclesiastical History of the English $23.00
People, ed. T. Miller. Vol. I. i 1890, *reprinted* Kraus 1976.

96 The Old English Version of Bede's Ecclesiastical History of the English $23.00
People, ed. T. Miller. Vol. I. ii 1891, *reprinted* Kraus 1976. (See
O.S. 110, 111 for other parts.)

97 The Earliest Complete English Prose Psalter, ed. K. D. Bülbring. $12.00
Vol. I (*all published*) 1891, *reprinted* Kraus 1973.

98 The Minor Poems of the Vernon MS., ed. C. Horstmann. Vol. I 1892, $23.00
reprinted Kraus 1973. (See O.S. 117 for Vol. II.)

99 Cursor Mundi, ed. R. Morris. Vol. VI Preface etc. 1892, *reprinted*   £3·25
1962. (See O.S. 57, 59, 62, 66, 68, and 101 for other parts.)

100 John Capgrave The Life of St. Katharine of Alexandria, ed. C. Horst- $26.00
mann, forewords by F. J. Furnivall. 1893, *reprinted* Kraus 1973. *Paper.*

101 Cursor Mundi, ed. R. Morris. Vol. VII Essay on manuscripts and   £3·25
dialect by H. Hupe. 1893, *reprinted* 1962. (See O.S. 57, 59, 62, 66, 68,
and 99 for other parts.) *Paper.*

102 Lanfrank's Science of Cirurgie, ed. R. von Fleischhacker. Vol. I Text $18.00
(*all published*) 1894, *reprinted* Kraus 1973.

O.S. 131 The Brut, or the Chronicles of England . . . from Bodleian MS. Rawl. £4·80
B. 171, ed. F. W. D. Brie. Vol. I 1906, *reprinted* 1960. (See O.S. 136 for Vol. II.)

132 The Works of John Metham, ed. H. Craig. 1916 (*for* 1906), *reprinted* $12.00
Kraus 1973.

133, 144 The English Register of Oseney Abbey . . . *c*. 1460, ed. A. Clark. $16.00
Vol. I 1907, Vol. II 1913 (*for* 1912); *reprinted as one volume* Kraus
1971.

134, 135 The Coventry Leet Book, ed. M. D. Harris. Vol. I 1907, Vol. II $31.00
1908; *reprinted as one volume* Kraus 1971. (See O.S. 138, 146 for
other parts.)

136 The Brut, or the Chronicles of England, ed. F. W. D. Brie. Vol. II $17.00
1908, *reprinted* Kraus 1971. (See O.S. 131 for Vol. I.)

137 Twelfth Century Homilies in MS. Bodley 343, ed. A. O. Belfour. £2·50
Vol. I Text and translation (*all published*) 1909, *reprinted* 1962. *Paper.*

138, 146 The Coventry Leet Book, ed. M. D. Harris. Vol. III 1909, Vol. $22.00
IV 1913; *reprinted as one volume* Kraus 1971. (See O.S. 134, 135 for
other parts.)

139 John Arderne Treatises of Fistula in Ano etc., ed. D'Arcy Power. £4·00
1910, *reprinted* 1968.

140 John Capgrave's Lives of St. Augustine and St. Gilbert of Sempring- $10.00
ham and a sermon, ed. J. J. Munro. 1910, *reprinted* Kraus 1971.

141 The Middle English Poem Erthe upon Erthe, printed from 24 manu- £2·75
scripts, ed. H. M. R. Murray. 1911, *reprinted* 1964.

142 The English Register of Godstow Nunnery, Vol. III. See above, O.S.
130.

143 The Prose Life of Alexander from the Thornton MS., ed. J. S. West- $6.00
lake. 1913 (*for* 1911), *reprinted* Kraus 1971.

144 The English Register of Oseney Abbey, Vol. II. See above, O.S. 133.

145 The Northern Passion, ed. F. A. Foster. Vol. I 1913 (*for* 1912), $14.00
reprinted Kraus 1971. (See O.S. 147, 183 for other parts.)

146 The Coventry Leet Book, Vol. IV. See above, O.S. 138.

147 The Northern Passion, ed. F. A. Foster. Vol. II 1916 (*for* 1913), $12.00
reprinted Kraus 1971. (See O.S. 145, 183 for other parts.)

148 A Fifteenth-Century Courtesy Book, ed. R. W. Chambers, and Two £2·75
Fifteenth-Century Franciscan Rules, ed. W. W. Seton. 1914, *reprinted* 1963.

149 Lincoln Diocese Documents, 1450–1544, ed. A. Clark. 1914, *re-* $20.00
printed Kraus 1971.

150 The Old English Versions of the enlarged Rule of Chrodegang, the $7.00
Capitula of Theodulf and the Epitome of Benedict of Aniane, ed.
A. S. Napier. 1916 (*for* 1914), *reprinted* Kraus 1971.

151 The Lanterne of Liȝt, ed. L. M. Swinburn. 1917 (*for* 1915), *reprinted* $18.00
Kraus 1971.

152 Early English Homilies from the Twelfth-Century MS. Vespasian D. $8.00
xiv, ed. R. D.-N. Warner. 1917 (*for* 1915), *reprinted* Kraus 1971.

153 Mandeville's Travels . . . from MS. Cotton Titus C. xvi, ed. P. $13.00
Hamelius. Vol. I Text 1919 (*for* 1916), *reprinted* Kraus 1973. *Paper.*

154 Mandeville's Travels . . . from MS. Cotton Titus C. xvi, ed. P. £3·60
Hamelius. Vol. II Introduction and notes. 1923 (*for* 1916), *reprinted*
1961. *Paper.*

155 The Wheatley Manuscript : Middle English verse and prose in British $8.00
Museum MS. Additional 39574, ed. M. Day. 1921 (*for* 1917), *reprinted* Kraus 1971.

156 The Donet by Reginald Pecock, ed. E. V. Hitchcock. 1921 (*for* 1918), $16.00
reprinted Kraus 1971.

O.S. 182 Speculum Christiani, ed. G. Holmstedt. 1933 (*for* 1929), *reprinted* $25.00
         Kraus 1971.

   183 The Northern Passion (Supplement), ed. W. Heuser and F. A. Foster. $8.00
        1930, *reprinted* Kraus 1971. (See O.S. 145, 147 for other parts.)

   184 John Audelay The Poems, ed. E. K. Whiting. 1931 (*for* 1930), *re-* $16.00
        printed Kraus 1971.

   185 Henry Lovelich's Merlin, ed. E. A. Kock. Vol. III. 1932 (*for* 1930), $16.00
        reprinted Kraus 1971. (See E.S. 93 and 112 for other parts.)

   186 Nicholas Harpsfield The Life and Death of Sr. Thomas More, ed.   £9·25
        E. V. Hitchcock and R. W. Chambers. 1932 (*for* 1931), *reprinted*
        1963.

   187 John Stanbridge The Vulgaria and Robert Whittinton The Vulgaria, $10.00
        ed. B. White. 1932 (*for* 1931), *reprinted* Kraus 1971.

   188 The Siege of Jerusalem, from Bodleian MS. Laud Misc. 656, ed. E. $8.00
        Kölbing and M. Day. 1932 (*for* 1931), *reprinted* Kraus 1971.

   189 Christine de Pisan The Book of Fayttes of Armes and of Chyualrye, $16.00
        translated by William Caxton, ed. A. T. P. Byles. 1932, *reprinted*
        Kraus 1971.

   190 English Mediaeval Lapidaries, ed. J. Evans and M. S. Serjeantson.   £4·50
        1933 (*for* 1932), *reprinted* 1960.

   191 The Seven Sages of Rome (Southern Version), ed. K. Brunner. 1933 $13.00
        (*for* 1932), *reprinted* Kraus 1971.

   191A R. W. Chambers: On the Continuity of English Prose from Alfred to   £2·25
        More and his School (an extract from the introduction to O.S. 186).
        1932, *reprinted* 1966.

   192 John Lydgate The Minor Poems, ed. H. N. MacCracken. Vol. II   £6·75
        Secular Poems. 1934 (*for* 1933), *reprinted* 1961. (See E.S. 107 for
        Vol. I.)

   193 Seinte Marherete, from MS. Bodley 34 and British Museum MS.   £4·50
        Royal 17 A. xxvii, re-ed. F. M. Mack. 1934 (*for* 1933), *reprinted* 1958.

   194 The Exeter Book, ed. W. S. Mackie. Vol. II Poems IX–XXXII. 1934 $14.00
        (*for* 1933), *reprinted* Kraus 1973. (See O.S. 104 for Vol. I.)

   195 The Quatrefoil of Love, ed. I. Gollancz and M. M. Weale. 1935 (*for* $5.00
        1934), *reprinted* Kraus 1971. *Paper*.

   196 An Anonymous Short English Metrical Chronicle, ed. E. Zettl. 1935 $14.00
        (*for* 1934), *reprinted* Kraus 1971.

   197 William Roper The Lyfe of Sir Thomas Moore, knighte, ed. E. V. $19.00
        Hitchcock. 1935 (*for* 1934), *reprinted* Kraus, 1976.

   198 Firumbras and Otuel and Roland, ed. M. I. O'Sullivan. 1935 (*for* $14.00
        1934), *reprinted* Kraus 1971.

   199 Mum and the Sothsegger, ed. M. Day and R. Steele. 1936 (*for* 1934), $9.00
        reprinted Kraus 1971.

   200 Speculum Sacerdotale, ed. E. H. Weatherly. 1936 (*for* 1935), *re-* $15.00
        printed Kraus 1971.

   201 Knyghthode and Bataile, ed. R. Dyboski and Z. M. Arend. 1936 (*for* $14.00
        1935), *reprinted* Kraus 1971.

   202 John Palsgrave The Comedy of Acolastus, ed. P. L. Carver. 1937 (*for* $14.00
        1935), *reprinted* Kraus 1971.

   203 Amis and Amiloun, ed. MacEdward Leach. 1937 (*for* 1935), *reprinted*   £4·50
        1960.

   204 Valentine and Orson, translated from the French by Henry Watson, $20.00
        ed. A. Dickson. 1937 (*for* 1936), *reprinted* Kraus 1971.

   205 Early English Versions of the Tales of Guiscardo and Ghismonda and $16.00
        Titus and Gisippus from the Decameron, ed. H. G. Wright. 1937
        (*for* 1936), *reprinted* Kraus 1971.

   206 Osbern Bokenham Legendys of Hooly Wummen, ed. M. S. Serjeantson. $16.00
        1938 (*for* 1936), *reprinted* Kraus 1971.

O.S. 207 The Liber de Diversis Medicinis in the Thornton Manuscript, ed. £3·80
          M. S. Ogden. 1938 (*for* 1936), *revised reprint* 1969.

    208   The Parker Chronicle and Laws (Corpus Christi College, Cambridge £14·50
          MS. 173); a facsimile, ed. R. Flower and H. Smith. 1941 (*for* 1937),
          reprinted 1973.

    209   Middle English Sermons, from British Museum MS. Royal 18 B. £7·00
          xxiii, ed. W. O. Ross. 1940 (*for* 1938), *reprinted* 1960.

EXTRA SERIES 1867–1920

E.S. 1   The Romance of William of Palerne, ed. W. W. Skeat. 1867, *reprinted* $20.00
          Kraus 1973.

    2   On Early English Pronunciation, by A. J. Ellis. Part I. 1867, *reprinted* $12.00
        Kraus 1973. (See E.S. 7, 14, 23, and 56 for other parts.)

    3   Caxton's Book of Curtesye, with two manuscript copies of the treatise, $5.00
        ed. F. J. Furnivall. 1868, *reprinted* Kraus 1973. *Paper*.

    4   The Lay of Havelok the Dane, ed. W. W. Skeat. 1868, *reprinted* Kraus $12.00
        1973.

    5   Chaucer's Translation of Boethius's ' De Consolatione Philosophiæ', ed. £3·60
        R. Morris. 1868, *reprinted* 1969.

    6   The Romance of the Cheuelere Assigne, re-ed. H. H. Gibbs. 1868, $4.00
        reprinted Kraus 1973. *Paper*.

    7   On Early English Pronunciation, by A. J. Ellis. Part II. 1869, *reprinted* $12.00
        Kraus 1973. (See E.S. 2, 14, 23, and 56 for other parts.)

    8   Queene Elizabethes Achademy etc., ed. F. J. Furnivall, with essays on $10.00
        early Italian and German Books of Courtesy by W. M. Rossetti and
        E. Oswald. 1869, *reprinted* Kraus 1973.

    9   The Fraternitye of Vacabondes by John Awdeley, Harman's Caveat, $7.00
        Haben's Sermon etc., ed. E. Viles and F. J. Furnivall. 1869, *reprinted*
        Kraus 1973.

   10   Andrew Borde's Introduction of Knowledge and Dyetary of Helth, with $21.00
        Barnes's Defence of the Berde, ed. F. J. Furnivall. 1870, *reprinted*
        Kraus 1973.

11, 55   The Bruce by John Barbour, ed. W. W. Skeat. Vol. I 1870, Vol. IV £5·75
         1889; *reprinted as one volume* 1968. (See E.S. 21, 29, for other parts.)

12, 32   England in the Reign of King Henry VIII, Vol. I Dialogue between $22.00
         Cardinal Pole and Thomas Lupset, ed. J. M. Cowper (1871), Vol. II
         Starkey's Life and Letters, ed. S. J. Herrtage (1878); *reprinted as one
         volume* Kraus 1973.

   13   Simon Fish A Supplicacyon for the Beggers, re-ed. F. J. Furnivall, $7.00
        A Supplycacion to . . . Henry VIII, A Supplication of the Poore
        Commons and The Decaye of England by the great multitude of shepe,
        ed. J. M. Cowper. 1871, *reprinted* Kraus 1973.

   14   On Early English Pronunciation, by A. J. Ellis. Part III. 1871, *re-* $20.00
        printed Kraus 1973. (See E.S. 2, 7, 23, and 56 for other parts.)

   15   The Select Works of Robert Crowley, ed. J. M. Cowper. 1872, *re-* $12.00
        printed Kraus 1973.

   16   Geoffrey Chaucer A Treatise on the Astrolabe, ed. W. W. Skeat. 1872, £3·60
        reprinted 1968.

17, 18   The Complaynt of Scotlande, re-ed. J. A. H. Murray. Vol. I 1872, $17.00
         Vol. II 1873; *reprinted as one volume* Kraus 1973.

   19   The Myroure of oure Ladye, ed. J. H Blunt. 1873, *reprinted* Kraus $23.00
        1973.

20, 24   The History of the Holy Grail by Henry Lovelich, ed. F. J. Furnivall. $25.00
         Vol. I 1874, Vol. II 1875; *reprinted as one volume* Kraus 1973. (See
         E.S. 28, 30, and 95 for other parts.)

E.S. 21, 29   The Bruce by John Barbour, ed. W. W. Skeat. Vol. II 1874, Vol.   **£8·00**
III 1877; *reprinted as one volume* 1968. (See E.S. 11, 55 for other part.)

22   Henry Brinklow's Complaynt of Roderyck Mors, The Lamentacyon of a   **$8.00**
Christen agaynst the Cytye of London by Roderigo Mors, ed. J. M.
Cowper. 1874, *reprinted* Kraus 1973.

23   On Early English Pronunciation, by A. J. Ellis. Part IV. 1874, *re-*   **$24.00**
printed Kraus 1973. (See E.S. 2, 7, 14, and 56 for other parts.)

24   The History of the Holy Grail by Henry Lovelich, Vol. II. See above,
E.S. 20.

25, 26   The Romance of Guy of Warwick, the second or 15th-century   **£6·75**
version, ed. J. Zupitza. Vol. I 1875, Vol. II 1876; reprinted as one
volume 1966.

27   John Fisher The English Works, ed. J. E. B. Mayor. Vol. I (*all pub-*   **$24.00**
lished) 1876, *reprinted* Kraus 1973.

28, 30, 95   The History of the Holy Grail by Henry Lovelich, ed. F. J.   **$21.00**
Furnivall. Vol. III 1877; Vol. IV 1878; Vol. V The Legend of the Holy
Grail, its Sources, Character and Development by D. Kempe 1905;
reprinted as one volume Kraus 1973. (See E.S. 20, 24 for other parts.)

29   The Bruce by John Barbour, Vol. III. See above, E.S. 21.

30   The History of the Holy Grail by Henry Lovelich, Vol. IV. See above,
E.S. 28.

31   The Alliterative Romance of Alexander and Dindimus, re-ed. W. W.   **$7.00**
Skeat. 1878, *reprinted* Kraus 1973.

32   England in the Reign of King Henry VIII, Vol. II. See above, E.S. 12.

33   The Early English Versions of the Gesta Romanorum, ed. S. J. H.   **£9·00**
Herrtage. 1879, *reprinted* 1962.

34   The English Charlemagne Romances I: Sir Ferumbras, ed. S. J. H.   **£4·80**
Herrtage. 1879, *reprinted* 1966.

35   The English Charlemagne Romances II: The Sege of Melayne, The   **$12.00**
Romance of Duke Rowland and Sir Otuell of Spayne, ed. S. J. H.
Herrtage. 1880, *reprinted* Kraus 1973.

36, 37   The English Charlemagne Romances III and IV: The Lyf of   **£4·80**
Charles the Grete, translated by William Caxton, ed. S. J. H. Herrtage.
Vol. I 1880, Vol. II 1881; *reprinted as one volume* 1967.

38   The English Charlemagne Romances V: The Romance of the Sowdone   **£4·50**
of Babylone, re-ed. E. Hausknecht. 1881, *reprinted* 1969.

39   The English Charlemagne Romances VI: The Taill of Rauf Coilyear,   **£3·80**
with the fragments of Roland and Vernagu and Otuel, re-ed. S. J. H.
Herrtage. 1882, *reprinted* 1969.

40, 41   The English Charlemagne Romances VII and VIII: The Boke of   **$33.00**
Duke Huon of Burdeux translated by Lord Berners, ed. S. L. Lee. Vol. I
1882, Vol. II 1883; *reprinted as one volume* Kraus 1973. (See E.S. 43,
50 for other parts.)

42, 49, 59   The Romance of Guy of Warwick, from the Auchinleck MS.   **£9·50**
and the Caius MS., ed. J. Zupitza. Vol. I 1883, Vol. II 1887, Vol. III
1891; *reprinted as one volume* 1966.

43, 50   The English Charlemagne Romances IX and XII: The Boke of   **$14.00**
Duke Huon of Burdeux translated by Lord Berners, ed. S. L. Lee.
Vol. III 1884, Vol. IV 1887; *reprinted as one volume* Kraus 1973.

44   The English Charlemagne Romances X: The Foure Sonnes of Aymon,   **$17.00**
translated by William Caxton, ed. O. Richardson. Vol. I 1884, *re-*
printed Kraus 1973.

45   The English Charlemagne Romances XI: The Foure Sonnes of Aymon,   **$20.00**
translated by William Caxton, ed. O. Richardson. Vol. II 1885, *re-*
printed Kraus 1973.

46, 48, 65   The Romance of Sir Beues of Hamtoun, ed. E. Kölbing. Vol. I   **$25.00**
1885, Vol. II 1886, Vol. III 1894; *reprinted as one volume* Kraus 1973.

E.S. 47   **The Wars of Alexander, an Alliterative Romance**, re-ed. W. W. Skeat. $26.00
1886, *reprinted* Kraus 1973.

48   **The Romance of Sir Beues of Hamtoun**, Vol. II. See above, E.S. 46.

49   **The Romance of Guy of Warwick**, Vol. II. See above, E.S. 42.

50   The English Charlemagne Romances XII: **The Boke of Duke Huon of Burdeux**, Vol. IV. See above, E.S. 43.

51   Torrent of Portyngale, re-ed. E. Adam. 1887, *reprinted* Kraus 1973. $8.00

52   **A Dialogue against the Feuer Pestilence by William Bullein**, ed. M. W. $8.00
and A. H. Bullen. 1888, *reprinted* Kraus 1973.

53   **The Anatomie of the Bodie of Man by Thomas Vicary**, ed. F. J. and $18.00
P. Furnivall. 1888, *reprinted* Kraus 1973.

54   **The Curial made by maystere Alain Charretier**, translated by Caxton,   £1·10
ed. P. Meyer and F. J. Furnivall. 1888, *reprinted* 1965.

55   **The Bruce by John Barbour**, Vol. IV. See above, E.S. 11.

56   **On Early English Pronunciation**, by A. J. Ellis. Part V. 1889, *reprinted* $48.00
Kraus 1973. (See E.S. 2, 7, 14, and 23 for other parts.)

57   **Caxton's Eneydos**, ed. W. T. Culley and F. J. Furnivall. 1890, *reprinted*   £4·50
1962.

58   **Caxton's Blanchardyn and Eglantine**, ed. L. Kellner. 1890, *reprinted*   £5·75
1962.

59   **The Romance of Guy of Warwick**, Vol. III. See above E.S. 42.

60   **Lydgate's Temple of Glas**, ed. J. Schick. 1891, *reprinted* Kraus 1973. $16.00

61, 73   **Hoccleve's Works : The Minor Poems**, Vol. I ed. F. J. Furnivall   £5·75
(1892), Vol. II ed. I. Gollancz (1925 *for* 1897); reprinted as one volume
and revised by Jerome Mitchell and A. I. Doyle 1970.

62   **The Chester Plays**, ed. H. Deimling. Vol. I 1892, *reprinted* 1967. (See   £3·25
E.S. 115 for Part II.)

63   **The Earliest English Translations of the De Imitatione Christi**, ed. J. K. $17.00
Ingram. 1893, *reprinted* Kraus 1973.

64   **Godeffroy of Boloyne, or the Siege and Conqueste of Jerusalem** by $21.00
William, archbishop of Tyre, translated by William Caxton, ed. M. N.
Colvin. 1893, *reprinted* Kraus 1973.

65   **The Romance of Sir Beues of Hamtoun**, Vol. III. See above, E.S. 46.

66   **Lydgate and Burgh's Secrees of old Philisoffres : a version of the** $8.00
Secreta Secretaorum, ed. R. Steele. 1894, *reprinted* Kraus 1973.

67   **The Three Kings' Sons**, ed. F. J. Furnivall. Vol. I Text (*all published*) $12.00
1895, *reprinted* Kraus 1973.

68   **Melusine**, ed. A. K. Donald. Vol. I (*all published*) 1895, *reprinted* $22.00
Kraus 1973.

69   **John Lydgate The Assembly of Gods**, ed. O. L. Triggs. 1896, *reprinted* $12.00
Kraus 1976.

70   **The Digby Plays**, ed. F. J. Furnivall. 1896, *reprinted* 1967.   £2·25

71   **The Towneley Plays**, re-ed. G. England and A. W. Pollard. 1897, $20.00
reprinted Kraus 1973.

72   **Hoccleve's Works : The Regement of Princes and fourteen minor poems**, $15.00
ed. F. J. Furnivall. 1897, *reprinted* Kraus 1973.

73   **Hoccleve's Works : The Minor Poems**, Vol. II. See above, E.S. 61.

74   **Three Prose Versions of the Secreta Secretorum**, ed. R. Steele and $16.00
T. Henderson. Vol. I (*all published*) 1898, *reprinted* Kraus 1973.

75   **Speculum Gy de Warewyke**, ed. G. L. Morrill. 1898, *reprinted* Kraus $16.00
1973.

76   **George Ashby's Poems**, ed. M. Bateson. 1899, *reprinted* 1965.   £2·75

E.S. 77, 83, 92   The Pilgrimage of the Life of Man, translated by John Lydgate $43.00
from the French by Guillaume de Deguileville, Vol. I ed. F. J.
Furnivall (1899), Vol. II ed. F. J. Furnivall (1901), Vol. III introduction, notes, glossary, etc. by K. B. Locock (1904); *reprinted as one
volume* Kraus 1973.

78   Thomas Robinson The Life and Death of Mary Magdalene, ed. H. O.   £2·75
Sommer. 1899. *Paper.*

79   Dialogues in French and English by William Caxton, ed. H. Bradley. $5.00
1900, *reprinted* Kraus 1973. *Paper.*

80   Lydgate's Two Nightingale Poems, ed. O. Glauning. 1900, *reprinted* $7.00
Kraus 1973.

80A Selections from Barbour's Bruce (Books I–X), ed. W. W. Skeat, $28.00
1900, *reprinted* Kraus 1973.

81   The English Works of John Gower, ed. G. C. Macaulay. Vol. I   £5·50
Confessio Amantis Prologue–Bk. V. 1970. 1900, *reprinted* 1978.

82   The English Works of John Gower, ed. G. C. Macaulay. Vol. II   £5·50
Confessio Amantis V. 1971–VIII, *In Praise of Peace.* 1901, *reprinted*
1978.

83   The Pilgrimage of the Life of Man, Vol. II. See above, E.S. 77.

84   Lydgate's Reson and Sensuallyte, ed. E. Sieper. Vol. I Manuscripts,   £4·50
Text, and Glossary. 1901, *reprinted* 1965. (See E.S. 89 for Part II.)

85   The Poems of Alexander Scott, ed. A. K. Donald. 1902, *reprinted* $7.00
Kraus 1973.

86   The Poems of William of Shoreham, ed. M. Konrath. Vol. I (*all* $14.00
published) 1902, *reprinted* Kraus 1973.

87   Two Coventry Corpus Christi Plays, re-ed. H. Craig. 1902; *second*   £2·70
edition 1957, *reprinted* 1967.

88   Le Morte Arthur, a romance in stanzas, re-ed. J. D. Bruce. 1903, $9.00
reprinted Kraus 1973.

89   Lydgate's Reson and Sensuallyte, ed. E. Sieper. Vol. II Studies and   £3·25
Notes. 1903, *reprinted* 1965. (See E.S. 84 for Part I.)

90   English Fragments from Latin Medieval Service-Books, ed. H. Little- $3.00
hales. 1903, *reprinted* Kraus 1973. *Paper.*

91   The Macro Plays, ed. F. J. Furnivall and A. W. Pollard. 1904. Superseded by O.S. 262.

92   The Pilgrimage of the Life of Man, Vol. III. See above, E.S. 77.

93   Henry Lovelich's Merlin, ed. E. A. Kock. Vol. I 1904, *reprinted* Kraus $22.00
1973. (See E.S. 112 and O.S. 185 for other parts.)

94   Respublica, ed. L. A. Magnus. 1905. Superseded by O.S. 226.

95   The History of the Holy Grail by Henry Lovelich, Vol. V. See above,
E.S. 28.

96   Mirk's Festial, ed. T. Erbe. Vol I (*all published*) 1905, *reprinted* Kraus $20.00
1973.

97   Lydgate's Troy Book, ed. H. Bergen. Vol. I Prologue, Books I and II, $22.00
1906, *reprinted* Kraus 1973. (See E.S. 103, 106, and 126 for other
parts.)

98   John Skelton Magnyfycence, ed. R. L. Ramsay. 1908 (*for* 1906), $13.00
reprinted Kraus 1976.

99   The Romance of Emaré, ed. E. Rickert. 1908 (*for* 1906), *reprinted*   £2·70
1958.

100   The Middle English Harrowing of Hell and Gospel of Nicodemus, $14.00
ed. W. H. Hulme. 1908 (*for* 1907), *reprinted* Kraus 1976.

101   Songs, Carols and other Miscellaneous Poems from Balliol MS. 354, $14.00
Richard Hill's Commonplace-book, ed. R. Dyboski. 1908 (*for* 1907),
reprinted Kraus 1973.

E.S. 102   **The Promptorium Parvulorum**: the First English–Latin Dictionary, $29.00
ed. A. L. Mayhew. 1908, *reprinted* Kraus 1973.

103, 106   Lydgate's Troy Book, ed. H. Bergen. Vol. II, Book III, 1908; $25.00
Vol. III, Books IV and V, 1910; *reprinted as one volume* Kraus 1973.
(See E.S. 97, 126 for other parts.)

104   **The Non-Cycle Mystery Plays,** ed. O. Waterhouse. 1909. Superseded by S.S. 1.

105   **The Tale of Beryn,** with a Prologue of the Merry Adventure of the $14.00
Pardoner with a Tapster at Canterbury, ed. F. J. Furnivall and W. G.
Stone. 1909, *reprinted* Kraus 1973.

106   **Lydgate's Troy Book,** Vol. III. See above, E.S. 103.

107   **John Lydgate The Minor Poems,** ed. H. N. MacCracken. Vol. I £6·50
Religious Poems. 1911 (*for* 1910), *reprinted* 1961. (See O.S. 192 for
Vol. II.)

108   **Lydgate's Siege of Thebes,** ed. A. Erdmann. Vol. I Text. 1911. £4·25
reprinted 1960. (See E.S. 125 for Vol. II.)

109   **The Middle English Versions of Partonope of Blois,** ed. A. T. Bödtker. $25.00
1912 (*for* 1911), *reprinted* Kraus 1973.

110   **Caxton's Mirrour of the World,** ed. O. H. Prior. 1913 (*for* 1912), $18.00
reprinted Kraus 1978.

111   **Raoul Le Fevre The History of Jason,** translated by William Caxton, $12.00
ed. J. Munro. 1913 (*for* 1912), *reprinted* Kraus 1973.

112   **Henry Lovelich's Merlin,** ed. E. A. Kock. Vol. II 1913, *reprinted* £4·00
1961. (See E.S. 93 and O.S. 185 for other parts.) *Paper*.

113   **Poems by Sir John Salusbury and Robert Chester,** ed. Carleton Brown. $9.00
1914 (*for* 1913), *reprinted* Kraus 1973.

114   **The Gild of St. Mary, Lichfield**: Ordinances and other documents, $5.00
ed. F. J. Furnivall. 1920 (*for* 1914), *reprinted* Kraus 1973. *Paper*.

115   **The Chester Plays,** ed. Dr. Matthews. Vol. II 1916 (*for* 1914), *reprinted* 1967. £3·25

116   **The Pauline Epistles in MS.** Parker 32, Corpus Christi College, $20.00
Cambridge, ed. M. J. Powell. 1916 (*for* 1915), *reprinted* Kraus 1973.

117   **The Life of Fisher,** ed. R. Bayne. 1921 (*for* 1915), *reprinted* Kraus $8.00
1973.

118   **The Earliest Arithmetics in English,** ed. R. Steele. 1922 (*for* 1916), $6.00
reprinted Kraus 1973.

119   **The Owl and the Nightingale,** ed. J. H. G. Grattan and G. F. H. $7.00
Sykes. 1935 (*for* 1915), *reprinted* Kraus 1973.

120   **Ludus Coventriæ,** or The Plaie called Corpus Christi, Cotton MS. £5·50
Vespasian D. viii, ed. K. S. Block. 1922 (*for* 1917), *reprinted* 1961.

121   **Lydgate's Fall of Princes,** ed. H. Bergen. Vol. I 1924 (*for* 1918), £5·75
reprinted 1967.

122   **Lydgate's Fall of Princes,** ed. H. Bergen. Vol. II 1924 (*for* 1918), £5·75
reprinted 1967.

123   **Lydgate's Fall of Princes,** ed. H. Bergen. Vol. III 1924 (*for* 1919), £5·75
reprinted 1967.

124   **Lydgate's Fall of Princes,** ed. H. Bergen. Vol. IV 1927 (*for* 1919), £8·00
reprinted 1967.

125   **Lydgate's Siege of Thebes,** ed. A. Erdmann and E. Ekwall. Vol. II $13.00
Introduction, Notes, Glossary etc. 1930 (*for* 1920), *reprinted* Kraus
1973.

126   **Lydgate's Troy Book,** ed. H. Bergen. Vol. IV 1935 (*for* 1920), *reprinted* Kraus 1973. (See E.S. 97, 103, and 106 for other parts.) $36.00

University Press, Oxford, England